New Mexican Lives

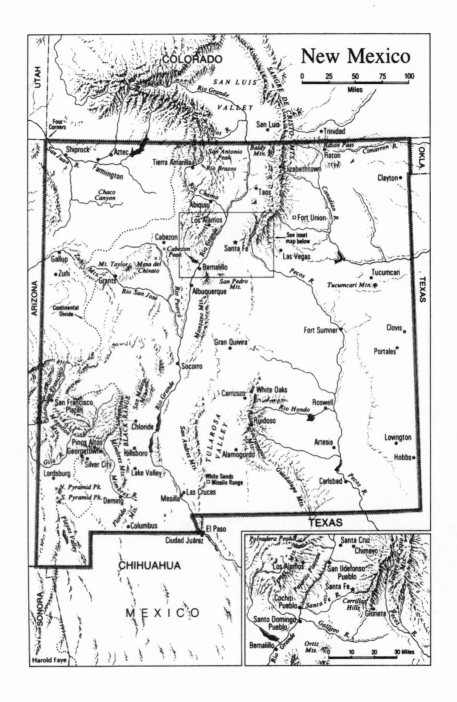

FRONTISPIECE. Map of New Mexico. From Marc Simmons, *New Mexico*
(Albuquerque: University of New Mexico Press, 1977), p. xiii.

New Mexican Lives

Profiles and Historical Stories

EDITED BY
RICHARD W. ETULAIN

Published in cooperation with the
UNM Center for the American West

UNIVERSITY OF NEW MEXICO PRESS
ALBUQUERQUE

© 2002 by the University of New Mexico Press
All rights reserved.
First edition

Library of Congress Cataloging-in-Publication Data

New Mexican lives : profiles and historical stories /
    edited by Richard W. Etulain. — 1st ed.
        p.   cm.
Includes bibliographical references and index.
    ISBN 0-8263-2432-0 (cloth) — ISBN 0-8263-2433-9 (pbk.)
    1. New Mexico—History.   2. New Mexico—Biography.
I. Etulain, Richard W.
    F796.5 .N49 2002
    978.9—dc21

                                        2001006432

JACKET AND COVER ILLUSTRATIONS:

front
    Victorio, Chihenne band leader of the Chiricahua Apache. *(page 151)*
    A reflective Hillerman in the early 1990s. *(page 297)*
    Senator Dennis Chavez in his office. *(page 244)*
    Equestrian statue of don Juan de Oñate by Sonny Rivera, Oñate Monument and
        Visitors Center, Alcalde, New Mexico. *(page 47)*

back
    William H. Bonney, alias Billy the Kid, ca. 1879. Image has been altered from original.
        (page 208)

JACKET AND COVER DESIGN: Melissa Tandysh

For four superb authorities on New Mexico history:

John Kessell
Darlis Miller
Marc Simmons
David Weber

Also by Richard W. Etulain

AUTHOR

Owen Wister

Ernest Haycox

Religion in the Twentieth-Century American West: A Bibliography

Re-imagining the Modern American West: A Century of Fiction, History, and Art

The American West—Comparative Perspectives: A Bibliography

COAUTHOR

Conversations with Wallace Stegner on History and Literature

The American West: A Twentieth-Century History

EDITOR

Jack London on the Road: The Tramp Diary and Other Hobo Writings

The American Literary West

Western Films: A Short History

Writing Western History: Essays on Major Western Historians

Basques of the Pacific Northwest: A Collection of Essays

Contemporary New Mexico 1940–1990

Myths and the American West

Does the Frontier Experience Make America Exceptional?

César Chávez: A Brief Biography with Documents

COEDITOR

Interpretive Approaches to Western American Literature

The Popular Western: Essays Toward a Definition

The Idaho Heritage

Idaho History: A Bibliography

The Frontier and the American West

Anglo-America Contributions to Basque Studies

Basque Americans

Fifty Western Writers: A Bio-Bibliographical Guide

A Bibliographical Guide to the Study of Western American Literature

Faith and Imagination: Essays on Evangelicals and Literature

The Twentieth-Century West: Historical Interpretations

Religion and Culture

The American West in the Twentieth Century: A Bibliography

Researching Western History: Topics in the Twentieth Century

Religion in Modern New Mexico

By Grit and Grace: Eleven Women Who Made the American West

Portraits of Basques in the New World

With Badges and Bullets: Lawmen and Outlaws in the Old West

The Hollywood West

Contents

INTRODUCTION   *1*

1. Prologue: Prehistoric Man and Woman in New Mexico   *5*
   RICHARD W. ETULAIN

2. Popé, the Pueblo Revolt, and Native Americans in Early New Mexico   *19*
   JOE S. SANDO

3. Juan de Oñate, Diego de Vargas,
   and Hispanic Beginnings in New Mexico   *45*
   RICK HENDRICKS

4. Juanotilla of Cochiti, *Vecina* and *Coyota:*
   Nuevomexicanas in the Eighteenth Century   *78*
   DEENA J. GONZÁLEZ

5. Padre Martínez and Mexican New Mexico   *106*
   E. A. MARES

6. Mangas Coloradas and Mid-Nineteenth-Century Conflicts   *131*
   EDWIN R. SWEENEY

7. Kit Carson and the "Americanization" of New Mexico   *163*
   BARTON H. BARBOUR

8. Billy the Kid, Susan McSween, Thomas Catron,
   and the Modernization of New Mexico   *193*
   KATHLEEN P. CHAMBERLAIN

9. Mabel Dodge Luhan and New Mexico's Anglo Arts Community   *220*
   LOIS PALKEN RUDNICK

10. Dennis Chavez and the Making of Modern New Mexico   *242*
    MARÍA E. MONTOYA

11. "The Inalienable Right to Govern Ourselves": Wendell Chino and the
    Struggle for Indian Self-Determination in Modern New Mexico   *265*
    MYLA VICENTI CARPIO AND PETER IVERSON

12. Tony Hillerman and the Turn-of-the-Century American Southwest   *285*
    FERENC M. SZASZ

13. New Mexico History: A Bibliographical Essay   *310*
    RICHARD W. ETULAIN

CONTRIBUTORS   *323*

INDEX   *326*

Introduction

Americans enjoy biography. Although changing fashions of historical writing cycle in and out, stirring life stories of leaders as well as common folk continue to intrigue our nation's readers. Through the centuries, beginning with the earliest Native American Creation Stories to our most recent histories, we have narrated and interpreted the lives of thousands of significant men and women.

This persisting interest in biography proves that, quite simply, we are drawn to tales about other humans. We look to their courageous and triumphal actions as models for our lives, and we also learn lessons from the tragedies and failures that beset other people. Century after century, the lives of historical figures, if clearly and invitingly portrayed in compelling biographies, overflow with a vicarious power that continues to draw readers.

Not surprisingly, New Mexicans follow other Americans in their strong interest in biography. Our histories, too, are alive with dramatic figures. New Mexico's historical stories, commencing with the close-range battles of prehistoric New Mexicans with their gigantic foes, moving through Native American contacts with incoming Europeans, and ending with more recent Anglo, Hispanic, and Indian activities, are replete with intriguing men and women. Since the sixteenth century, historians of New Mexico have marched thousands of human figures across their pages, like so many high-stepping performers in a never-ending parade.

This history of New Mexico builds on that long, clear interest in biography. We, too, are convinced that stories of the past speak helpfully to the present. Individual lives, as well as the memorable events and ideas in which those individuals participated, have shaped and will continue to mold the history of New Mexico. This volume, then, is a history of the state as seen through the illuminative lives of several emblematic men and women.

In planning this book, the volume editor asked contributors to accomplish two overlapping goals. They were to deal with the lives of notable New Mexicans, but they were also to demonstrate how each of these lives illustrated or broke from the main currents of the state's history. These revealing links between important New Mexicans and their times are featured ingredients of all these essays.

A few words of introduction are necessary to make explicit the connections between these subjects and their times. In the first major section of this book, following the editor's brief prologue summarizing New Mexico's prehistory, three scholars employ four men and women to illustrate important dimensions of New Mexico history from the sixteenth century through 1821. Joe S. Sando, himself of Pueblo heritage, shows in his imaginative essay how the important Native American figure Popé led Indians into and through their successful rebellion against the Spanish in the Pueblo Revolt of 1680. In the next essay Rick Hendricks, a scholar of the Borderlands, uses the lives of two leaders, Juan de Oñate and don Diego de Vargas, to illuminate Spanish experiences in New Mexico from the late sixteenth to early eighteenth centuries. Deena González, an authority on Hispanic women in early New Mexico, uses the life of the relatively unknown Juanotilla of Cochiti, a woman of mixed-race heritage, to reinterpret eighteenth-century New Mexico.

Four other scholars, in treating the long, complex history of New Mexico in the nineteenth century, select, for the most part, a well known cast of characters. Historian and novelist E. A. Mares skillfully limns the important roles controversial Padre José Antonio Martínez played in Mexican New Mexico and the years immediately following. Edwin R. Sweeney, a much published military historian and biographer, focuses on the Native American leader Mangas Coloradas to reveal several complexities of Indian-white relations at midcentury. Barton H. Barbour, an authority on frontier history, reveals similar complexities in the life and times of Kit Carson, who, the author convincingly argues, was much more than the "Indian killer" recent negative accounts have portrayed. In the fourth chapter on the nineteenth century Kathleen Chamberlain, a specialist on southwestern Indians and frontier settlers, demonstrates how Thomas

Catron, Billy the Kid, and Susan McSween, although quite different people, nonetheless taken together help illuminate New Mexico's attempts to modernize and become a state.

Three other notable New Mexicans are central figures in essays on the twentieth century. American Studies scholar Lois Palken Rudnick, in a valuable essay on the many-sided Mabel Dodge Luhan, discusses important cultural currents swirling through New Mexico in the first half of the century. Historian María Montoya, a scholar of Hispanic experiences in New Mexico of the nineteenth and twentieth centuries, undertakes the challenging task of employing Dennis Chavez to treat the political history of post-1900 New Mexico. In the third chapter of this section Peter Iverson, one of the country's best-known authorities on recent Native American history, and his student Myla Vicenti Carpio (Jicarilla Apache) show how the emblematic actions of Apache leader Wendell Chino represent the drive for Indian self-determination in the second half of the twentieth century.

In the epilogue Ferenc M. Szasz, a widely published scholar on western social and cultural topics, uses the life of New Mexico's best-known recent writer, Tony Hillerman, to discuss significant developments in the state's history since the 1960s. In the closing section the volume editor provides a brief, evaluative guide to some of the most useful books written about New Mexico. Each contributor also has appended to his or her essay helpful comments on valuable sources for that chapter.

This collection of essays is intended primarily for students and general readers. Still, the contributors were also urged to base their chapters on the best scholarship available on their subjects. We think specialists in the state's history, as well as other regional and national historians, will also find the collection appropriate for their research projects and for their classrooms.

The editor wishes to acknowledge the help of several people in the preparation of this volume. First, thanks to the contributors for their diligent work on these instructive and readable essays. Thanks also to Michael Fischer, dean of Arts and Sciences at the University of New Mexico, and Richard Robbins, chair of the UNM History Department; both strongly supported the UNM Center for the American West, through which this project was planned and completed. Cindy Tyson, David Key, Brian Freels-Stendel, and Amy Elder also helped in various ways. Later Karen Taschek saved all of us from many errors with her careful and competent copyediting. My history colleague Durwood Ball, while still at the University of New Mexico Press, helped in the initial stages of planning for this volume. Most of all, I want to express my gratitude to David Holtby, associate director and editor in chief at UNM Press. At every step in the launching and finishing of this project he provided guidance, aid, and encouragement. David is not only a superb editor but a good friend of authors.

1

Prologue

Prehistoric Man and Woman in New Mexico

RICHARD W. ETULAIN

In the mid-1920s, a rambling cowboy stumbled on a few ancient remains near the town of Folsom, New Mexico. He alerted a friend of his, an amateur paleontologist, who in turn took some of the bison bones to a staff member of the Denver Museum of Natural History. Soon thereafter that museum uncovered a rich, revealing collection of Paleo-Indian remains, a discovery that helped gain the name of Folsom Man for the dig. Within a year or two, archaeologists uncovered an equally important Paleo-Indian site in Blackwater Draw, adjacent to Clovis, New Mexico. There, ancient big-game hunters, known later as Clovis people, left behind a remarkable collection of "points," or spearheads, which they used to kill now extinct large animals.

These two notable archaeological finds in New Mexico in the 1920s provided important information for anthropologists and historians. Now, at the beginning of a new century, these remains furnish revealing evidence about the first humans in the American West and illuminate the lives of prehistoric men and women in New Mexico.

Although of major importance, these significant discoveries at Clovis and Folsom are not sufficient in themselves to answer larger questions that stir continuing controversies among scholars of ancient America. Those thorny questions remain: When did humans first set foot on the North American continent, and how did they make their way to the American Southwest? Debates surrounding those and similar conundrums still divide students of human origins. For nearly a century, and especially since the 1920s, scholars have hotly contested these questions. At this point, only a tentative story of these shadowy happenings, based on recent but not immutable evidence, is possible.

Some archaeologists trace the origins of humankind in the Southwest as far back as 30,000 B.C., but the most widely accepted evidence points to human entry into New Mexico from about 11,000 to 10,000 B.C. Even after three or four generations of diligent study, these dates are subjects of intense controversy. Nonetheless, a few generalizations can be made about these ancient men and women of New Mexico.

Most students of the earliest Americans accept that these prehistoric people migrated from Siberia across the Bering Strait to Alaska. Some speculate that as far back as seventy-five thousand years ago or as recently as fifteen thousand years ago, humans crossed over a land passage then connecting Asia and North America. These prehistoric people, whose southward route was blocked for centuries by a gigantic ice sheet covering much of present-day Canada, possibly found a western passageway through the glaciers, or they may have traveled south along the far-western coasts. At any rate, sometime later, perhaps by about 11,000 B.C., they had arrived in the Southwest.

Who were these Paleo-Indian or Pleistocene people? How much do we know about them, and why did their ways of life seem to disappear soon after 8000 B.C.? The important discoveries at Clovis and Folsom, as well as those at other, similar sites along the Rio Grande, tell us these people were primarily big-game hunters and gathers of varied kinds of plant food. Using spears with carefully fluted points, they ranged over wide territories, hunting mammoths, sloths, and other huge animals. The mammoths, even larger than modern-day elephants, served these ancient men and women much as the all-purpose bison did the Plains Indians centuries later. Quite possibly the megafauna (the big-game animals) determined the locations of base camps and kill sites of the hunters; as the quarry migrated, so did their trackers.

Most of our limited understanding of these Paleo-Indians comes from their kill sites and base camps. We know them primarily as skilled users of stone and bone implements, their tool kits. Perhaps like other late Stone Age people, they traveled in small bands of twenty-five to fifty. Spear points, bones, hearths, and other debris at excavations indicate that these Pleistocene peoples probably lived as nomadic hunters.

Spear points discovered at Clovis, Folsom, and other southwestern sites are similar to those found elsewhere in North America from the same era. These parallels suggest that early men and women of the Southwest were in contact with other humans nearby. If the big-game hunters, in search of mammoths and other quarry, traveled in circular territories of up to one hundred miles or more, they also set up base camps close to their hunting and killing areas. Often the kill sites were near rivers, other watered areas, and bogs; the hunters undoubtedly drove the megafauna into these places, where they were easier to trap and kill.

The evidence uncovered in these sites encourages a few speculations about early prehistoric lifeways. Were these hunting camps, like those of more recent hunters, occupied by a small group of men? Were the nearby base camps locations for their women and families, replicating the layout of more recent elephant hunters? And did the ancients follow a sexual division of labor, with men as hunters and protectors and women as aids in hunting, makers of clothing, and nurturers of children? If so, they were following patterns familiar to Native Americans at the point of first European contact in the fifteenth and sixteenth centuries. These speculations about the inner hums of Paleo-Indian social life seem possible, even from our limited knowledge of their daily lives.

Toward the end of the Pleistocene and the beginning of the Holocene period (about 9000 to 8000 B.C.), the big-game animals disappeared. Had the hunters overkilled their major food source? Some anthropologists think so. Others argue that dramatic climatic shifts transformed terrains, drastically reducing the food supplies for the megafauna and thus changing the lives of the hunters. As a result, fewer kill sites are evident, more contain the remains of earlier, larger bison, and settlements are now closer to water and grass, suggesting that plant gathering became more important to these ancient men and women.

So marked were these transformations that archaeologists call the centuries following 8000 B.C. the Archaic or Holocene period. Peoples of the Archaic era turned to new sources of food to survive. To replace the extinct big-game animals, they searched for smaller animals such as bison, deer, and birds. They also fished. But the largest adjustment came in their gathering habits. In the words of one scholar, Archaic men and women became "gathering gourmets," collecting numerous kinds of seeds, roots, and nuts.

Just as climatic shifts and the disappearance of the mammoths wrought changes in the food chain of these ancient people, so those transformations reshaped their material culture and lifeways. Replacing the implements of the big-game hunt were the technologies of food gatherers. These changes are particularly illustrated by the numerous stones used for grinding seeds and by the baskets constructed to gather plant foods. These processing tools show the growing reliance of the Archaic peoples on plants rather than on the meat of large animals. Snares recovered in sites in north-central New Mexico likewise reveal the growing significance of rabbit hunting to men and women of the Archaic period. Probably these seed-gathering and snaring efforts involved men and women alike, perhaps closing the divisions of sexual labor apparent in the pre-Archaic centuries.

Settlement locations also changed. The Archaic peoples, needing to find new animals and more plants to fulfill their food needs, relocated to sites with those food sources in mind. Earlier, Paleo-Indian sites were primarily linked to big-game hunting, but humans of the Archaic era frequently lived in well-watered areas, near small lakes (playas), or in canyons. These new locations brought them near varied food sources. Yet archaeological evidence suggests that the men and women of the Holocene period were less mobile, less inclined to ramble through as large a territory as the Pleistocene peoples had. Population increases, the establishment of plant-gathering patterns, and mounting stability of settlement led to less nomadism and, simultaneously, to a shrinking set of social networks. For the humans of the Archaic period, local social ties were stronger; those important ties were less likely to spread through the larger, regional networks of the big-game hunters.

Over the many centuries of the middle and later Archaic periods (6000–5000 B.C. to 300–200 B.C.), the lifeways of Archaic men and women, although undergoing change, nonetheless settled into a few recognizable patterns. Learning the rhythms of smaller animals, birds, and fish, these ancient peoples adapted to those cycles, migrating to take advantage of annual patterns. Obviously the Archaic residents were suiting their lifeways to the seasonal cycles of their food sources.

Other transitions took place over time. As Archaic peoples gained additional and more varied food supplies, their groups expanded in size and density. These developments encouraged the stronger bonds of support needed to survive in precarious times. Moreover, increased specialization took place. More complex tool kits and larger accumulations of midden (mounds of ash, bones, stone fragments, and other cultural debris) reveal this growing specialization. Some scholars even point to evidence that implies increased attention being paid to burial rituals and social class organization.

The most significant innovation of the later centuries of the Archaic period is the transition to agriculture. Perhaps as early as 1500 B.C. maize from Mexico was introduced into New Mexico. In the centuries that followed, squash and beans joined corn as the most widely cultivated crops. As we shall see, the introduction of horticulture revolutionized the lives of New Mexicans even before the Christian era. These transformations are notably illustrated in the economic and social organizations of the late Archaic period.

Although the transition to agriculture noticeably influenced ancient New Mexico, the cultivation of crops did not immediately replace all the earlier hunting and gathering systems. Cultivation began as a part-time endeavor to supplement the other food supplies of the hunters and gatherers. From about 1000 B.C. to A.D. 500 horticulture continued on a smaller scale, rather circumscribed in production, and with limited dependence on it. In fact, during this period the wildlife and southwestern landscapes resembled those the Spanish would encounter much later, in the 1500s. The late Archaic peoples were small in number and nomadic, collecting wild plants and hunting small wild animals for their food. Since the big-game animals were now extinct, deer, antelope, rabbits, birds, and rodents were targets of their hunts. Generally they were a foraging economy beginning to cultivate crops. The most recent archaeological research suggests, however, that this transition to agriculture occurred more rapidly than first thought.

By the first decades A.D., as solid evidence indicates, agriculture became increasingly important to early New Mexicans. These people became more sedentary, able to adapt to and utilize more dependable food sources. Storage pits for corn and other products became part of the later Archaic settlements. Wells were also dug, suggesting the need for additional groundwater for mushrooming populations and agricultural efforts. Other signals of the more sedentary ways were the technical advancements in pottery and basket making.

New forms of housing also show the more sedentary ways of New Mexicans in the last centuries B.C. and the first centuries A.D. Families gradually moved from campsites to pit houses and on to permanent villages. These new types of homes were clustered in small towns of aggregated family huts or pit houses. Settlements now expanded beyond the twenty-five to fifty people who inhabited the earlier, more nomadic camps.

Over time, these nascent settlements began to exhibit regional varieties.

These areas or subregions (anthropologists call them *culture areas*), through the centuries, evolved into the Hohokam, Mogollon, and Anasazi regions of the Southwest. The Hohokam area stretched to the west and south of New Mexico, the Mogollon region spread over much of southwestern New Mexico and southeastern Arizona, and the Anasazi peoples inhabited the modern-day Four Corners area, especially northwestern New Mexico and northeastern Arizona. Most archaeologists consider the Hohokam the ancestors of the Tohono O'odham Indians and the Mogollon and the Anasazi the forerunners of the modern Pueblo Indians. The Mogollon and particularly the Anasazi cultures reveal a great deal about early New Mexico from the last century B.C. until the first Spanish *entradas* in the sixteenth century.

Living to the north and east of the Hohokam and to the south of the

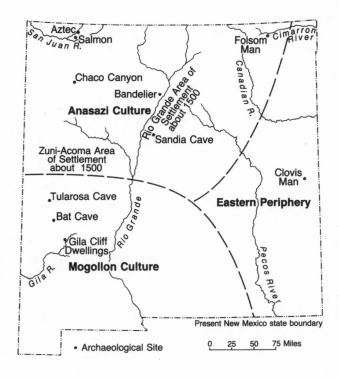

FIGURE 1.1. Early cultures in New Mexico. From Calvin A. Roberts and Susan A. Roberts, *New Mexico* (Albuquerque: University of New Mexico Press, 1988), p. 7.

Anasazi were the Mogollon people. Their name came from the east-central Arizona and west-central New Mexico areas that historians named after an early Spanish governor. As it did for the Hohokam and Anasazi, the rise of the Mogollon culture signaled the end of the Archaic period and the commencement of nascent village life in the Southwest. This transition period, from about 200 B.C. to A.D. 600–800, further illustrates the shift from a more nomadic to a sedentary life. By A.D. 600 to 800 men and women of the Southwest area were living year-round in villages.

The increased cultivation of crops was a major step toward settled life for the Mogollon people. Once maize, beans, and squash crops were under cultivation, group settlements were more possible. At first pit houses characterized these new villages. The new pit houses and the simultaneous appearance of pottery to supplement earlier baskets were other evidence of the end of the Archaic and the beginning of the village periods.

The Mogollon villages were often situated at the tips of mesas. Probably these sites allowed for greater protection since they were frequently surrounded on three sides by sharp cliffs. Nearby, usually in valleys below the villages, the Mogollon people tended their crops. At first their pit houses were constructed of wood, brush, and mud; these buildings, with either top or side entrances, were time-consuming efforts, demonstrating considerable advancement over earlier Archaic houses. Later, in the period from about A.D. 900 to 1000, joined and aboveground houses were erected, like those of the historic Pueblo cultures. These large apartment complexes were usually adjacent to a subterranean area, perhaps a large kiva, where varied ceremonies took place. The Mogollon also differed from the previous Archaic men and women in burying their dead in single graves.

Like the Hohokam, the Mogollon were farmers, but they relied less on irrigation. For other food sources, they collected wild plants, including nuts, berries, and cactus fruit, and hunted a variety of small animals. One subgroup of the Mogollon, the Mimbres, produced impressive black-on-white ceramics. But generally the Mogollon did not work as extensively with stones or shells as did their neighbors to the west.

One Mogollon village, the SU ("Shoe") in west-central New Mexico, featured nearly forty houses. It was a fairly large site and seemed to exhibit a nascent class organization among these peoples. The larger homes at this site may have been those of headmen, with a nearby extensive pit area serving as a ceremonial gathering place for such a leader. The SU layout also prefigured the later physical organization of the Anasazi in Chaco Canyon, where one larger site was surrounded by much smaller villages.

After the century stretching from A.D. 700 to 800, Mogollon culture underwent a barrage of change. Persisting immigration into the area, especially in the northern sections of the Mogollon area, continually redirected lifeways. So large and influential were these migrations and the resultant changes that some archaeologists argue that by A.D. 1100, there was no longer a separate Mogollon cultural tradition. In the north, it had been swallowed up by nearby more expansive peoples. In the south, nearer present-day Mexico, the continuities of Mogollon culture were more durable and long lasting.

The expanding peoples were the Anasazi, the most researched and widely discussed village culture of the Southwest. In the language of the Navajo, the modern-day Native Americans who inhabit much of the earlier Anasazi homelands, the word *Anasazi* means "old ones." Although like the Hohokam and Mogollon cultures, the Anasazi emerged after the Archaic period of southwestern prehistory, they eventually became the most dominant of these cultures, especially after about A.D. 1000.

The physical location of the Anasazi changed over time. In various periods they occupied parts of southern Nevada, Utah, and Colorado and even larger sections of northern Arizona and New Mexico where the modern states join. Through time, the Anasazi shifted about, gradually moving south and east into northwestern New Mexico, the northern Rio Grande valley, and areas adjacent to these regions. The Anasazi are best known for their large buildings—the cliff dwellings of Mesa Verde in Colorado and Canyon de Chelly in Arizona, the extensive buildings near Aztec, New Mexico, and the sprawling villages in Chaco Canyon, New Mexico. These monumental buildings remain impressive testaments of the strength and endurance of the Anasazi as they prepared the way for the later Pueblo peoples.

Since the 1920s, anthropologists, attempting to make chronological sense of the long period from about 200 to 100 B.C. to the A.D. 1500s, divide Anasazi history into two extensive periods. Since these men and women initially were not makers of pottery, their history from about 100 B.C. to A.D. 700 is divided into Basket Maker periods. Then, when marked changes redefined the Anasazi after A.D. 700, the followed stages have been labeled the Pueblo periods of their culture. These two names and the eras they designate help us to understand the major stages of development the Anasazi experienced in these roughly sixteen centuries. The Anasazi cultural identity solidified more slowly than cultural identities in the Hohokam and Mogollon areas. From about 100 B.C. to A.D. 200, the Anasazi were basket makers who tended to live in impermanent shelters. Moving about in bands of a dozen or so, they ate the meat of deer primarily but also that of rabbits and porcupines. In addition, they gathered plant food in the form of mustard, sunflower, and other seeds. For clothing, they utilized the skins, hair, and bones of animals and the fibers from rushes and yucca plants. Since precipitation levels at Chaco Canyon were lower than in later periods, the Anasazi were not yet residents there, instead living in more well-watered areas such as those near Mesa Verde.

Increased rainfall after A.D. 200 led to changes in the Anasazi villages. Now town builders commenced constructing pit houses as permanent buildings. These subterranean homes with smoke holes in the top sometimes included a sipapu indentation in the floor, indicating that, like the later Pueblo Indians, the Anasazi may have believed that they emerged through a hole in the ground from a subterranean otherworld to life aboveground. Present-day Pueblo Indians believe that in the distant past they too emerged from a subterranean place, suggesting a continuity of belief between the early Anasazi and the Pueblo peoples of today. During the period after A.D. 200 the Anasazi also began to produce their first decorated pottery.

Soon after A.D. 400 a more favorable climate encouraged the increasingly sedentary ways of the Anasazi. By A.D. 700 sizable numbers began to live in the Chaco Canyon area, where they commenced cultivation of a few fields and garden plots. During these centuries, pit houses were expanded, and the first large kivas, some up to twenty meters in diameter, began to appear. Dogs also became more plentiful in these Anasazi villages, evidently as hunting companions or as pets. Animal hides and plant fibers continued to be the main sources for clothing and sandals.

Although the increased precipitation led to more settled lives, life was not easy for the basket-making Anasazi. Crop failures often forced these ancient men and women to be foragers. The widespread sipapu symbols also imply that they tried to rely on supernatural help to offset the large demands on their uncertain lives. In addition, useful and sometimes expensive implements appear in graves, suggesting a belief in an afterlife and, quite possibly, the necessity of appeasing the spirits in charge of their natural world.

After A.D. 700 the Anasazi gradually transitioned from the Basket Making to the Pueblo period of their history. Perhaps the boundary between these two stages of Anasazi development is not as sharp and distinctive as once thought, but the Anasazi were moving away from their basket-making, nomadic lives toward the village-situated, more sedentary existence of later centuries. Once the Anasazi began the path toward concentrated, settled village life, they never retreated from that journey.

During the next three centuries, the Anasazi made several clear advances. Most important, they were now living in aboveground homes. Although some of the pit houses were retained as kivas, the Anasazi, like their cultural cousins the Mogollon, were now living in clustered villages of apartmentlike dwellings. These stone buildings (a bit later made of adobe) utilized several timbers to support house roofs. The clustered villages were most often situated near the best farmlands, with burgeoning numbers of residents living in fewer settlements. Kivas became increasingly stylized and perhaps were set aside as a place for men to meet in a society that otherwise often cohered around female social organizations. Clans, clan rituals, and kivas became linked as Anasazi culture took on more structure.

Problems continued to plague the Anasazi. They faced, for one, uncertain climatic conditions. Unpredictable rains were particularly troublesome. Too often precipitation failed in the winter and spring and then flooded down in summer storms. Moreover, as increased numbers of men and women and their families moved into the clustered villages, additional pressures came to bear on precarious food supplies. Even before A.D. 1000, the Anasazi were facing food shortages that would eventually help undermine their society two to three centuries later.

During the century or so following A.D. 1000, Anasazi culture flourished. Then it dramatically became something else. Up to about 1150, expansion, development, and growing power typified the Anasazi culture. Beneath these clear achievements, however, lurked underlying problems that the Anasazi were unable to solve. Eventually these unsolved dilemmas led to the end of the Anasazi.

Increased concentration in clustered towns characterized the Anasazi at the apex of their achievement. Anasazi towns dotted the Four Corners area, but most of their expansion mushroomed toward the upper Rio Grande. Their most notable settlement in New Mexico arose near Chaco Canyon in the west-central area of the state. Often these villages were constructed in D-shaped, aggregated towns (pueblos) in which a straight-backed edifice ballooned out in a circular front. These pueblos were tiered, beginning at ground level and sometimes rising to four or five stories, as in the incomparable Pueblo Bonito at Chaco. Other Anasazi villages were constructed as cliff-dwelling towns, such as those in Mesa Verde and Canyon de Chelly.

Generally rainfall was sufficient during these halcyon centuries to sustain the Anasazi towns. Crops grew in abundance, and sufficient food was available. To increase dependable food supplies, the Anasazi built flood control and irrigation systems and utilized as many springs as they could find. They also developed extensive trade and exchange systems among the Anasazi towns and even with a few people outside the culture area. Clear evidence indicates, too, that increased physical proximity led to more

FIGURE 1.2. Pueblo Bonito, Chaco Canyon. Photo courtesy Museum of New Mexico, neg. no. 36177.

complex social organization. As the Anasazi concentrated in close-limit towns, they developed a hierarchy of classes built most often on wealth, power, and tradition.

The Anasazi culture in New Mexico reached its pinnacle of achievement in Chaco Canyon. By the time of the Classic Bonito Phase (A.D. 1020–1120), the towns in the canyon area had expanded to sixteen. The four hundred or so settlements scattered up and down the canyon probably hosted as many as five thousand to six thousand inhabitants. Much of the population was centered in a few large towns on the canyon floor. The surrounding, smaller villages seem less tightly structured—physically and socially. Indeed, a truism has emerged from several studies of Anasazi towns in or near Chaco Canyon: the largest towns were the most highly structured socially, the smaller pueblos the less socially concentrated.

In several ways, Pueblo Bonito, the most spectacular of these towns, represents the major achievements of Anasazi culture in New Mexico. Built in the century and a half after A.D. 900, Pueblo Bonito eventually sprawled over more than three acres, rose to four or five stories at its back, and may have contained as many as 650 rooms, with more than three hundred on the ground floor. At its peak in about A.D. 1100, Pueblo Bonito quite possibly housed up to twelve hundred people. The pueblo also contained thirty-two kivas and two Great Kivas. As one account states, Pueblo Bonito was clearly "the largest and most important town in Chaco Canyon."

Pueblo Bonito and other Chaco towns reveal a good deal about Anasazi culture. Architecturally these multitiered edifices were major accomplishments. Using core-centered as well as veneer-covered masonry walls, Anasazi builders constructed strong buildings that endured much longer than many modern apartment complexes. The kivas were also skillfully constructed places, with ventilators, benches for seating, fireplaces, heat deflectors, and strategically placed roof supports. The Chaco towns likewise were part of a trade grid that included a well-developed road system linking the Chaco area with outlying colonies. Evidently organized labor forces were also utilized to build these roads, to construct new buildings, and to help maintain the necessary food support systems.

The less obvious aspects of social life among the Chaco Anasazi are more difficult to understand. Undoubtedly social organization was necessary to establish and keep up community obligations, but what these structures were is not clear. Probably, over time, religious and clan leaders rose to leadership in Pueblo Bonito and other towns. In fact, rich funerary objects in some graves but not in others, imply that class systems characterized these towns. Despite these unanswered questions, one must agree with two scholars who assert: "Chaco Canyon and its spheres of interaction was a bustling, thriving reality during . . . [A.D. 1020 to 1120] and well deserves its reputation as the culmination of Anasazi accomplishment."

Then in the next century Chaco Canyon and the other major Anasazi towns changed dramatically. Early on, anthropologists concluded that Athapascan peoples (ancestors of the present-day Navajo and Apache tribes) invaded the Anasazi pueblos and drove them out. But we now know that those invaders came later, after the Anasazi sites had been abandoned. Environmental disaster and natural catastrophes were not the culprits but long, sustained droughts. Major lack of rainfall from about A.D. 1130 to 1190 drove out the Anasazi. They could no longer sustain their large populations when rainfall failed year after year in Chaco Canyon and similar areas. Too many people with too little food brought an end to the Anasazi culture.

Beginning in the 1200s, the Anasazi scattered in search of new environments that could sustain them. They moved in several directions, but the largest numbers of men and women immigrated to the upper Rio Grande valley and to nearby areas. Over the next two centuries, they built new towns in these areas. There they were living when the first Spanish explorers, missionaries, and settlers marched into the far-northern frontier of New Mexico in the sixteenth century.

Essay on Sources

The romance and mystery of the prehistoric Southwest has attracted a large number of scholars and general writers. For overviews of the subject, one might begin with Dean R. Snow, *The American Indians: Their Archaeology and Prehistory* (London: Thames and Hudson, 1976); Stuart J. Fiedel, *Prehistory of the Americas,* 2d ed. (Cambridge: Cambridge University Press, 1992); Stephen Plog, *Ancient Peoples of the American Southwest* (New York: Thames and Hudson, 1997); or Brian Fagan, *Ancient North America: the Archaeology of a Continent,* 3d ed. (New York: Thames and Hudson, 2000).

Other helpful sources include Linda Cordell, *Archaeology of the Southwest,* 2d ed. (San Diego: Academic Press, 1997); David E. Stuart, et al., *Prehistoric New Mexico: Background for Survey* (Albuquerque: University of New Mexico Press, 1988); and Carroll L. Riley, *Rio del Norte: People of the Upper Rio Grande from Earliest Times to the Pueblo Revolt* (Salt Lake City: University of Utah Press, 1995).

The most recent overview of an important subject is David E. Stuart, *Anasazi America: Seventeen Centuries on the Road from Center Place* (Albuquerque: University of New Mexico Press, 2000). On a more focused subject, see Robert H. Lister and Florence C. Lister, *Chaco Canyon: Archaeology and Archaeologists* (Albuquerque: University of New Mexico Press, 1984).

Finally, for a somewhat dated but still useful listing of pertinent books and essays, see Dean R. Snow, *Native American Prehistory: A Critical Bibliography* (Bloomington: Indiana University Press, 1979).

2

Popé, the Pueblo Revolt, and Native Americans in Early New Mexico

JOE S. SANDO

On August 10, 1680, the Pueblo Indians rose up to drive their Spanish conquerors from New Mexico. Uniting against the invaders after more than eighty years of "submissive resentment," the Native Americans in the next few weeks chased the Spaniards out of the far-northern province. These events of late summer 1680 proved to be a watershed in the region's history. When the Spanish were invited to return in July 1683 if they would promise not to burn other villages, and after they came back following more than a decade in exile, they ruled the province differently, never as arbitrarily as they had earlier. More accommodation, acceptance, and assimilation characterized Spanish rule until the end of their dominance in 1821.

The leader of the dramatic Indian revolt in 1680 was the mysterious El Popé. A Tewa Indian from the San Juan Pueblo, Popé succeeded in forging ties among the Pueblos that helped them expel the Spaniards. Popé's important role as a religious leader as well as fresh memories of his ill treatment at the hands of the Spanish in the 1670s undoubtedly motivated him to unite the Indians in their revolt of 1680. Although not all the Pueblos joined the rebellion, most did, and Popé was the most important person in directing the overthrow of the Spanish.

During those tumultuous weeks in the late summer of 1680, one of the defining moments of New Mexico history took place. If the Pueblo Revolt signaled that the Spanish were never again able to subjugate the Indians as they had from 1598 onward, it also symbolized a new kind of relationship between the Pueblos and Spaniards that would gradually emerge during the next century. Equally significant, the central role of Popé in these memorable events demonstrates once again how much notable people shape the events of human history. As we shall see in this chapter, Popé and the Pueblo Revolt provide an important window from which to view Native Americans in sixteenth- and seventeenth-century New Mexico. Even though the nomadic Indian groups of New Mexico, especially the Navajos and Apaches, were not as involved as the Pueblos in the revolt of 1680, their lives were also markedly changed as a result of this historic occurrence.

The Native population the Spanish encountered in the sixteenth and seventeenth centuries lived in areas scattered throughout what later became the territory and state of New Mexico. The major groups came to be known as Pueblos, Navajos, and Apaches. Cultural, social, and linguistic differences, among others, distinguished these Indian groups from one another. Those dissimilarities, which the Spanish gradually recognized, provided a rich, varied spectrum of Native identities for newcomers to the far-northern frontier in the late 1500s.

The Pueblos, the largest of the tribal groups, experienced the most numerous contacts with the Spanish. Living along the northern Rio Grande from below modern-day Albuquerque northward to Taos and across areas east of the river and west into Arizona, the Pueblos were primarily sedentary Indians. Many of their ancestors had lived in these areas for several centuries before the first Spaniards rode north in the early to mid-decades of the sixteenth century. Primarily living along the Rio Grande or in other areas sufficiently well watered to raise crops, the Pueblos were by far the most rooted of the New Mexico Natives of the 1500s.

By the time of the initial Spanish *entradas,* the Pueblos had worked out recognizable patterns of cultural and social organization. They had become settled Indians, living in one area, as opposed to the nomadic Natives, whose lives usually consisted of hunting, gathering, and raiding. Without giving up their skills in hunting and gathering, the Pueblos had also become horticulturists, raising crops such as corn, squash, and beans. These foodstuffs, harvested and stored against years when an undependable climate militated against sufficient crops, often meant the difference between adequate and starving times. Located near the pueblos and water sources and tilled by men and women alike, these fields and crops greatly aided the Pueblos in attaining a stable and even expanding society. By the first Spanish settlements in the late 1500s, the Pueblos numbered, it is thought, between thirty thousand and fifty thousand people.

The Pueblos were community-minded Natives. Rather than emphasize individual deeds, as the Navajos and Apaches were more inclined to do, the Pueblos celebrated accomplishments that aided and buttressed the group. Living in an area of open space and seemingly endless time, the

Early Tribal Locations

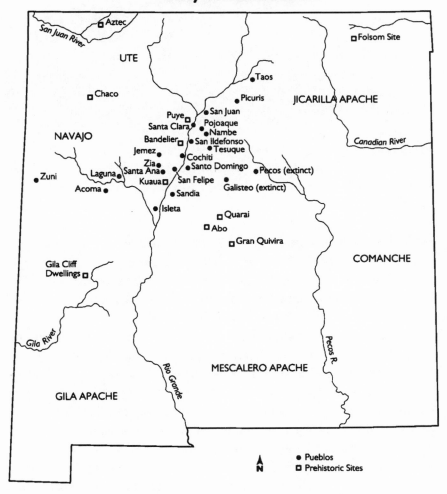

FIGURE 2.1. Early tribal locations. From Marc Simmons, *New Mexico*
(Albuquerque: University of New Mexico Press, 1977), p. 50.

FIGURE 2.2. *First Meeting of Spanish and Indians at Hawikuh,* Coronado Mural, Center Panel. Painting by Gerald Cassidy, 1921. Photo courtesy Museum of New Mexico, neg. no. 20205.

Pueblos were people who carefully considered changes before implementing them. They were not an impetuous culture.

The Pueblos spoke a variety of languages. Some conversed in the Tiwa dialect, others in the Tewa, and some in the Towa, all parts of a common Tanoan language group. Still other Pueblos communicated in Zunian and Keres languages. The westernmost Hopi, for the most part, spoke one language (with varied dialects) that belonged to the Uto-Aztecan family.

Religious beliefs, as well as rites and rituals associated with these beliefs, served as unifying elements of Pueblo culture. The creation story of Indians living at the Acoma Pueblo illustrates some of these unities. For Acomans, this story began at Sipapu, a mysterious underground location. There Tsichtinako (Thought Woman) nursed the sisters Nautsiti and Iatiku and helped prepare them to live in a new world above. With the aid of Badger and Locust, the sisters climbed through a hole in the ground and at once created the mountains, lakes, and canyons of Pueblo country. Although Snake and Magpie brought discord and disappointment and

Nautsiti departed, Iatiku remained and gave birth to many children. With the help of other spirits and kachinas, Iatiku taught the Acoma people how to erect homes, construct a village, and build a kiva. Extending into the ground, the kiva reminded Pueblos of their entrance into this world from the sacred Sipapu. Over time, the people of Acoma believed their pueblo, joining earth and sky, was the center of their world.

Living in other parts of the New Mexico area were two other Native groups, the Navajo and the Apache. At first, the Pueblos—and later the Spanish—referred to all these peoples as "Apaches," which to the Natives meant "enemies." After early contacts, the Spanish often called these Indians, as well as the nearby Utes and Comanches, *los Indios bárbaros*. Actually, the Navajo and Apache had something of a common heritage: both were Athapaskan speakers who, over the centuries, had migrated from western Canada to the Southwest. They probably arrived two hundred years or so before the initial Spanish contacts and moved into former Pueblo settlements when drought and other pressures drove many of those peoples into the Rio Grande valley.

The Navajos became the larger of the two groups. For the most part, they settled and remained in the present-day Four Corners area. Calling themselves the Diné, or The People, the Navajo were nomads, more often hunters than gatherers. Once they settled on the land, they built hogans, round or hexagonal structures usually of mud and wood, rather than the adobe-tiered apartments of the Pueblos. Even though the Navajos eventually raised corn, they never became as thoroughly agricultural as the Pueblos. By the time the Spanish came, the Navajos had learned well how to adapt to their new southwestern homelands.

More roving and less sedentary than the Pueblos, the Navajos also arranged themselves differently from their neighbors to the south and east. Early on, the Navajos lived in loosely organized gatherings of hogans. Small groups of extended families, or kinfolks, clustered into "outfits" that provided needed protection and sustenance for their members. Sometimes these clusters of hogans developed into clans, with headmen as leaders. The idea of the Navajo as one large tribe, or well-organized political unit, came much later. The outfits or clans elected war leaders, but each of the units could decide separately from the others.

The Navajos' religious beliefs seem to have been more open-ended than those of the Pueblos. Perhaps they seem less structured because we know less of them. Like the Pueblos, however, they believed in nature gods and chanted and recited hundreds of songs and prayers. Later the Navajo exhibited much less interest in Christianity than did the Pueblos.

Lifeways changed dramatically when the Navajos obtained horses. Already experienced traders and raiders, the Navajos greatly expanded their capacities for transportation of trade and stolen goods once they became horsemen. Stories of Navajo success in running off Spanish and Pueblo livestock became more numerous in the chaotic years of weakened Spanish control in the early 1600s. The Navajo, once on horseback and in possession of sheep and goats purloined from the Spanish and sedentary Natives, became much stronger economically and militarily throughout the seventeenth and well into the next century.

Meanwhile the Navajos' linguistic cousins, the Apaches, resided in scattered areas of the Southwest. The Apaches not only roamed the northern canyons and forested areas between the Navajos of the northwest New Mexico and the northern Pueblos but also lived in the southeastern and southwestern areas of the region. Like the Navajo, they too were first hunters and gatherers and then began to raise a few crops. The Apaches were most likely to inhabit brush shelters but also frequently moved about from place to place.

Over time the Apaches gained reputations as incredible fighters. Revenge, it is said, was often the driving force that motivated these skillful warriors. As remarkably healthy people, they could and did exist on almost anything. Early observers also were astounded at how the Apaches could live nearly naked in freezing temperatures.

Although the scattered Apache groups followed varying social patterns, they were much less sedentary than the Pueblos or the Navajos. As mountain people often moving from ridge to ridge, they rarely stayed long periods in one place. Instead they traveled often, taking advantage of the cycles of food and forage in several locations. Their tipi-style brush houses, sometimes called wickiups, were easily and quickly erected. As their patterns of existence clearly indicated, the Apaches became masters at adapting to the demanding southwestern environments in which they lived. They frequently traveled in small groups, were often matrilineal in organization, and placed more importance on individuals and their deeds than did the community-minded Pueblos.

Revealingly, the earliest Spanish explorers said little about the Apaches. Over time, however, the Europeans encountered the Apache *rancherías,* the loosely organized clusters of huts of these hunting and fighting peoples. Because the early Apaches were a roaming society and hunted much more than they farmed, their contacts were less numerous with the Spaniards than those of the Pueblos and even of the Navajos. Once they gained horses, however, the Apaches became superb horsemen. It was one of the great ironies of early New Mexico history that the Spaniards inadvertently revolutionized early Native societies in the region by supplying the horses that the Apache and other Indian raiders used so successfully in devastating the livestock herds of the Spanish and the Pueblo Indians.

Before long, the Pueblo Indians learned how much the Spanish invaders would demand of them. First, during Coronado's brief journey of exploration into New Mexico in 1540–42 and later, especially in Juan de Oñate's governorship from 1598 to 1607, the Europeans made clear their large expectations. In economic, cultural, and military arenas, they would lay heavy obligations on the Pueblos. Over time, in the decades stretching from Oñate's founding colony in 1598 until the lid flew off in New Mexico in 1680, the Spaniards' excessive demands festered in the minds and hearts of the Indians. Although on a few occasions the Spanish visited their large claims on the Navajos and Apaches, it was the Pueblos, saddled with most of these requirements, who finally rose up in rebellion.

One of the major problems leading up to the revolt was the *encomienda* system of the Spanish. This arrangement forced the Pueblos to donate annually a part of their crops to support Spanish missions, military forces, and civil institutions. Something like the later American system of tithing, encomienda went even further in forcing Natives to contribute amounts well above what they could afford. To the Spanish, Indian tribute in this form was considered necessary to support the institutions of a privileged ruling class. Although encomienda supposedly promised Natives military protection and religious instruction in exchange for their contributions, these pledges were often broken, and even some of the promises were not welcomed among all Pueblos.

Repartimiento was somewhat similar. Here, instead of contributions in the form of commandeered crops, Pueblos were forced to work in Spanish fields and households. Again the Indians had no choice. They were required to perform a given amount of labor annually, and the amount was not small. Encomienda and repartimiento had their origins in much earlier feudal practices. In these agreements, the Spanish crown had temporarily granted Spanish knights manorial rights over peasants who inhabited lands the Spanish took from the Moors. During the centuries of this Reconquista, which ended in the expulsion of the Moors in 1492, the very year of the Columbian discovery, the Spanish had worked out the details of the encomienda and repartimiento. Now they were put to work in the New World.

Harsh and humiliating as were these systems of forced payment and work, religious persecution from 1598 to 1680 may have been even more galling to the Pueblos. The assaults on Native beliefs evoked more resistance. Franciscan priests were convinced, as were most other Spaniards and European Catholics, that Natives must give up their "heathen" beliefs, convert, and be baptized as Catholics. The new converts must then take religious instruction, attend mass, and hearken to the teachings of the Franciscans. Despite relentless pressures from the conquerors, the Pueblos held tenaciously to many of their traditional beliefs. They might participate in some Catholic rites and rituals, but they also retained their own sacred convictions. After all, their religion had served them well from time immemorial; it continued to link them with their Creator and deities. It gave them faith to survive the vicissitudes of nature and life.

Other Spanish actions also alienated the Pueblos. As early as Coronado, then under Oñate, and particularly during the seventeenth century, the Europeans often dealt harshly with Pueblo discontents. If the Natives failed to provide demanded food stores and blankets, refused to follow Catholic teachings, or showed rebellious spirits, as the pueblo of Acoma did in December 1598, the Spaniards frequently reacted with a vengeance. Nor did the Pueblos cheerfully agree to demands the Spanish made on them militarily. True, the Pueblos realized that attacks were necessary on the Navajo and Apache to keep these nomads from continually raiding the Pueblo and Spanish settlements. But on some occasions, the Spanish calls for Indian soldiers seemed to benefit the Europeans much more than their reluctant Pueblo allies.

These Spanish actions severely disrupted Pueblo economic, social, and tribal mores. On occasion, the Pueblos stoutly refused to accede to Spanish demands. More often they resisted without openly rebelling. All the while, discontent was gradually coming to a boil as the seventeenth century wore on. Just the right circumstances—and the right person—were needed for the discontent to boil over.

The story is one familiar to all Americans. A group of frontier farmers, traders, and hunters living on the edge of wilderness were oppressed by an autocratic foreign government. This alien kingdom, which ruled by decree, taxed them unjustly, gave them no voice in governmental decision making, and denied them freedom to worship as they chose. It was a system to which they had been subjected for years. During this time uncorrected grievances and hostile, even cruel treatment at the hands of the representatives of a monarchy housed in luxurious palaces across the Atlantic had forced them to a point of no return. They had to drive the Europeans out of their country even though they lacked the armed power of the empire. So the men gathered clandestinely in their villages to plot their uprising and to choose their best men as leaders. It was done in great secrecy, mindful of the possibility of a leak to the enemy; some of the family members of the revolutionaries were in the camp of the foreigners, officeholders, and sympathizers with the ruling order.

Finally the time came, and messengers sped to notify the people that the insurrection had begun. All men and boys capable of making war were needed. Underarmed, considered inferior by the bureaucrats and royally appointed officials, the frontiersmen nevertheless prevailed and won their freedom to live and worship as they pleased and to govern themselves.

But these were not the farmers and villagers of Concord and Lexington fame. These were the Pueblo Indians of New Mexico, who in 1680, nearly a century before the more celebrated American Revolution of 1776, staged the first successful American revolution against a foreign colonial power. Their leader was not a patrician planter. He was a man of the people, an Indian about fifty years old. His world was bounded largely by the pueblos up and down the Rio Grande and a few others distant from the river. That world was also connected to the south by the Camino Real (Royal Road), the avenue by which supplies came north and Native products were taken south and east to the seats of empire.

Into this combined Pueblo and Spanish world was born Popé, in about 1630, in the village of Oke Owinge (the pueblo of San Juan). Early in life, he was probably given the name of Po-pay or Po-pyn ("ripe cultigen," meaning he was of the Summer clan). Later the Spaniards called him Popé and often referred to him as El Popé. His early years in Oke Owinge seem not to have set him apart from his companions; that difference came afterward, in his maturity.

In fact, Popé undoubtedly grew up like any other Pueblo boy of his time. Probably he followed the rules and rhythms of the community, in which religion was woven into the patterns of Pueblo life. Even during the periods of intensive physical labor—when hoeing, irrigating, harvesting, and drying and storing food and medicinal herbs for later uses—religious observances were not neglected. When ceremonies demanded, other members of the extended families took care of seasonal business while men were in the kiva or on retreat praying for rain.

This was the early life Popé would have known. But, as the Pueblos say, his future was already decided at the place of his origin—heaven, as the non-Indians called it. Following tradition, Popé as a young man would have gone to the river on ordained mornings to take a ceremonial bath, making him physically and mentally strong. Each morning he cast corn pollen to the east to the rising sun, toward Cikumu (Chakomo Peak) and Sipofenae (Sipapu), and asked the deities for a good life and blessings for his people. For Popé's Pueblos, the ideal life was in harmony with all creation.

As Popé matured, he would have begun to participate in tribal ceremonies. That meant taking part in cloud and turtle dances as well as in the animal dances of the winter months. As the years progressed, he evidently began to serve as an assistant to the war captain to help supervise the dances the tribe held to entertain the people.

The next step for Popé was appointment by the village leaders to the post of war captain. In this position he would have become increasingly aware of the pressures the Spanish government, missionaries, and nomadic tribes were exerting on the Pueblos. Like other leaders, he would have realized how Spanish governmental and religious leaders were coercing the Pueblos to abandon their own traditions and to take up the practices of the Europeans. The Indians especially resisted, even without overt conflict, the Spanish imposition of Roman Catholic practices. Like other Pueblo people, Popé undoubtedly questioned abandoning a religion that was a daily system, interwoven into every part of their lives. Calling for much fasting and sacrifice on behalf of the world and the peoples they knew, these religious beliefs formed the Pueblo worldview and engendered their peaceful attitudes and outlooks. Even though the entire year of the Pueblos was crowded with meaningful religious activities, the Spaniards were asking them to give up all this for new beliefs they did not understand.

Part of Popé's education would have been the hard lesson of how much the Spanish demanded. Giving little in return, the Spanish men came to Tewa families, taking food and wood, as part of the encomienda system that the European governor in Santa Fe enforced. Beyond these large, arduous requirements, Tewa men and women were forced to work for Spanish settlers while the Spaniards were away as citizen soldiers. Sometimes they and the professional soldiers explored the Llano Estacado or the other plains to the east; sometimes they fought against the raiding nomadic tribes to the east and north.

As a leader, Popé would also have experienced how much the Spanish harassed war chiefs and captains as well as religious leaders. On occasion the invaders filled a Tewa *estufa* (kiva) with sand so that nightly dances were impossible. Although these acts were sacrilege to the Indians, the Spaniards viewed the destruction of estufas as a mandate from God, meaning that these desecrations were not only legitimate but praiseworthy. These conclusions resulted from previous European debates about whether Indians were humans, whether they had immortal souls like the Europeans. Concluding that the Indians did have souls, the Spaniards thought it their duty, as did other European Christians, to bring the faith to the "heathen" of the New World.

Against the backdrop of these upsetting events, Popé and other Tewa war captains began meeting to talk about what might be done. The unities and harmonies of the Indians' lives were being threatened, sometimes even undermined. When their indigenous religion was disrupted or forbidden, the natural order of life was threatened. The suppression of their religion meant that links between their natural and spiritual worlds were being upset, including their own places in this great chain of meanings. Simultaneously, when a severe drought occurred in the 1670s, Indians took it as a signal of the disruption of the natural order, caused by Spanish hostility toward their Native religion.

The Pueblo tribes near Santa Fe came to another conclusion. They observed the ongoing struggles between Spanish governmental officials and Franciscan padres. The Natives realized that these clashes were over ultimate authority: who would collect tribute and labor from the Indians—while there was still something to collect. To the onlookers, it seemed that the balance of power favored the Franciscans.

During the 1670s, Popé and other Tewa leaders met from time to time. Always coming to fore at these gatherings were the galling problems of oppression that the inconsistent yet self-serving Spanish civil and ecclesiastical rulers imposed on the Indians. How long would they have to put up with the persecutions and exploitations they suffered? Something needed to be done, but what? The situation seemed to have worsened. Their religious freedoms were increasingly impinged on, their rights of conscience seriously threatened, their personal and economic security endangered under the coercive encomienda system. Life itself was obviously in danger.

These sporadic meetings discussing the misfortunes of the Pueblos drew a variety of leaders. Spokesmen of the northern Pueblos invited leaders from the south, including those from Galisteo, San Cristóbal, Pecos, and San Lazaro. In addition, representatives from San Marcos and La Cienega de Cochiti were invited, even though they were not Tanoan speakers. Not among the invitees, however, were Pueblo leaders known as *governadores*. These men were avoided because they owed their offices to the Spanish governmental system set up in villages in about 1620. Popé and his

FIGURE 2.3. Taos Pueblo, North Building, 1880. From this site Popé helped
          orchestrate the Pueblo Revolt. Photo by John K. Hillers. Courtesy
          Museum of New Mexico, neg. no. 16096.

colleagues suspected the loyalty of these officials since they owed their authority to the Spanish.

After a few meetings, Popé clearly stood out as the most outspoken and the most knowledgeable of the Pueblo leaders. More and more his voice carried the most weight. One leader might say to another person, although not in the presence of Popé, that the man from Oke Owinge had "the cunning of the fox and the heart of the bear." Yet according to tradition, Popé was not arrogant but always willing to learn, to listen to and consider suggestions and advice, and to explain his decisions. In view of an uncertain future, the Pueblo men wanted an overall leader who would evidence calmness and wisdom, be reliable, and exert a leadership to be respected, even admired. They were beginning to see these important strengths in Popé.

At first, the Pueblo leaders explored how to approach the Spaniards. They wanted to deliver a reasonable ultimatum on how the Spaniards should change their system to provide more respect for Indian customs and traditions. But as time went on, Popé and the other leaders came to a major decision: the Spaniards must go. For the Pueblos, it became clear that the Europeans had to be evicted before the Indians could be safe in their homes and religion.

Oral tradition is the source of information for the Indian side of these meetings and their involvement in the Pueblo Revolt of 1680. Unfortunately, these traditions contain few details about specific happenings at the planning meetings. Yet these oral traditions, combined with other information about ancient Pueblo council procedures, allow one to imagine scenes and conversations that took place prior to the momentous rebellion.

Picture a large meeting room lit only by the glow of a dying ember in a log burning in the fireplace behind the door. A small round opening is barely visible on the wall next to the fireplace, but the mica in it permits only the sunlight in; no one—inside or outside—can see through it. Against another wall next to the entry door are a pair of three-pronged juniper posts planted in the dirt floor. Each holds an olla (clay jar) of water, and from each post hangs a gourd ladle for drinking. Seated along the wall under the mica opening are members of the host council. Drawing on the warmth of the fireplace, the men also utilize the pile of corn husks and tobacco placed nearby. In the fireplace, their ends glowing, are three sunflower stems, which will be circulated to light corn husk cigarettes. The faces of the delegates are obscured by the gloom, but out from it comes the quiet talk of several delegates.

Then a figure makes his way to the front of the fireplace. Drawing on well-known traditions and oral stories, we can surmise what the speaker might have said. He undoubtedly would have begun by reminding his listeners of how much the Indians had suffered since the Spaniards came. The Europeans had attacked Indian customs and sometimes even them personally. Another man might arise to speak angrily of how the Spanish had attacked the nearby Apache and ruined friendly relationships with these nomads. Other speakers, equally angry, denounced the violent Spanish mistreatment of Pueblo political and religious leaders.

The last of these speakers might urge Popé to tell of his abuse at the hands of the Spanish in the mid-1670s. He had been among the Pueblo leaders captured and tortured by the Spaniards. If Popé then spoke, he might have risen to his feet, gathered his robes around him, and said the following to those gathered:

> Yes, as most of you know, a few years ago forty-seven of us from different villages were rounded up and arrested. We were taken to Santa Fe for trial. Four were condemned to die and to be hanged by the Spaniards. They were taken to their own villages and hanged in front of their people as an example. Forty-three of us were condemned to lashings and imprisonments. I was one of those humiliated by being whipped publicly, and I shall never forget that. But while we were in prison, as you all know, our leaders got together and went to Santa Fe in a group to confront Governor Treviño. Our people came prepared to fight if the governor did not release us. That saved us. Having seen the numbers of our warriors, some Spaniards interceded for us. The governor relented. Not only were we released, but the governor gave our people some woolen blankets. As a result of this and all the other things we have heard our brothers discuss, I am telling the Spaniards to leave our country or suffer the consequences.

After his speech, Popé probably quietly took his seat. These were strong words, but ones that reflected the feelings of most of the men present. The men assigned to monitor the night skies would then call out that morning approached—it was time for the council to end. No action had been planned; there was much to consider before they met again. Popé called for the next meeting to be held at Tet-sugeh (Tesuque), the date to be determined by pressures of the time.

The frictions with the Spanish persisted—in fact became more oppressive. So the Pueblo leaders continued to communicate. Messengers were sent out by the Tewa leaders while the other villagers worked as usual in their cornfields. One evening the delegates began arriving secretly at the meeting place in Tet-sugeh. After the host *opi,* or war leader, offered a short prayer, the work of the meeting began. One of the messengers opened the formal gathering by reporting that the people of the southern Tiwa village of Tuei (Isleta) had returned to the law of the Spanish God and were pledging obedience to the Spanish king. These actions raised serious doubts about inviting these Tiwas to join the planned revolt.

Gradually reports from the varied messengers pushed the Pueblos toward one conclusion: they had no other choice than to make a show of force. Before the discussion went further, however, one messenger called upon those gathered to select a leader. They had to have a man who could inspire them, to unite them against the Spanish, and lead them through the dangerous times that lay ahead. Then a Tewa man took the floor. Undoubtedly, his statement would have been something like the following: "As you know by now, we Tewas have been involved for some time. In our meetings we have all agreed without acting on it that our brother Popé, from Oke, will be the leader that we are looking for." Next the host opi might have added: "As my brother has indicated, we have studied our brother Popé and agree that he will be an excellent choice. Since we have many more things to discuss, why don't we make this choice of a leader short by agreeing on Popé?" After moments of consultation, a spokesman for each group assembled agreed with what had been said. All looked toward Popé.

Most likely Popé, the newly chosen leader, would have risen slowly and solemnly moved to the middle of the assembly room. He would have thanked the delegates for choosing him and then asked for a roll call of the villages to assess the forces that might be mounted against the Spanish. After discussing these pueblos and leaders who could not be counted on, the members moved on to the momentous decision of when to attack and drive out the Spanish.

Perhaps Popé offered a suggestion. The supply caravan of the Kwan-Ku (Spanish) from Chihuahua was scheduled to arrive in September 1680. Why not strike before the Kwan-Ku got more powder, swords, and shields? After additional discussions, it was agreed that the revolt would start in early August. Then one delegate asked, how would they be able to inform those not attending of the exact date of the outbreak? Another delegate provided an ingenious answer. Why not use narrow strips of tanned deer hide tied into a number of knots; these knotted ropes could be carried to each of the conspiring villages. The number of knots would correspond to the number of days remaining before the start of the uprising. The day the last knot was untied would be the day of action. Agreement came quickly on this excellent idea, and the host opi offered to send two of his aides as messengers with the knotted strips to the villages.

Possibly Popé spoke to the delegates before they left, just as the false dawn was starting to light the eastern sky. "This is not the way of our people," he might have begun. "But," he continued:

> we have been forced to the blinded path, and we can find no alternative. Our people do not approve of wars. Nevertheless, when such times do come upon us, the war chiefs can call us to defend our lands. Our people also exercise unlimited obedience to these leaders who

FIGURE 2.4. Kiva, Plaza of San Ildefonso Pueblo, ca. 1935. Spanish violation of Pueblo kivas helped lead to the Pueblo Revolt. Photo by T. Harmon Parkhurst. Courtesy Museum of New Mexico, neg. no. 3693.

act under the religious leaders. It is considered the great duty of the people to abide by the decisions of these leaders. I can see no other possibility of escaping from the hand of the oppressor, and the deities know we have tried. I am fearful that the way we have just chosen will have to be the only way. In conclusion, I say to you brothers, go to your Owinges and await further word. *Singe de ho* [good-bye].

With these words, Popé sat down. Then the war chief might have said a few prayers, calling upon the deities, especially the twin war gods, to guide the people and warriors along the chosen path until the conflict was over.

If we could penetrate the past to understand exactly what happened, we probably would have seen delegates leaving this meeting with heavy hearts. They now knew that war was inevitable. Yet they undoubtedly were infused with a determination from this meeting, the most important gathering the Pueblos had convened since the arrival of the first Spanish settlers in the 1590s. War would come.

The plans made at Tet-sugeh were put into action on the morning of August 9, 1680. The two young men designated as messengers left for Tanogeh. They made their first contact at Pecos, but unfortunately Christian Indians spotted them and hurried to their pastor to inform him that two visiting Tewas had gone to the home of the cacique (town official). The informers thought the men might have come to announce a general uprising of all Pueblos that had been rumored for weeks. Realizing the urgency of the situation, the priest scribbled a note of alarm and sent the message to Governor Antonio de Otermín in Santa Fe.

Then the two Tewa messengers hurriedly left Pecos and quickly went to Galisteo, San Cristóbal, and San Marcos to spread the call for revolt. But at Galisteo the pair were again recognized, and word of their appearance was sent immediately to the governor. When Otermín received these alarming reports, he sent a company of men to arrest the two messengers. The Spanish soldiers found the Tewa runners south of Santa Fe and took the two youths for interrogation to the governor, who placed them under house arrest at the capital. The carefully developed Pueblo plan at Tet-sugeh was threatening to fall apart.

On the evening of August 9, word spread rapidly through Tewa country. Tempers flared, tension heightened. In one incident, angry Natives arose to kill a Spaniard. Since the uprising had now been exposed, what would be the next step?

When the Tet-sugeh padre, Fray Juan Pío, returned from spending the night in safety in Santa Fe, he discovered his village deserted. Father Pío found the villagers in the nearby hills. They were armed with bows and arrows, lances and shields, their faces painted red. Going to them, he asked why they were thus gathered. He urged them to return to their village, where he would say mass for them.

Pedro Hidalgo, a Spanish soldier who accompanied Padre Pío back to Tet-sugeh, later related what he witnessed. After the priest descended into a ravine where the villagers were gathered, Hidalgo saw the war chief of the village walking out of the ravine with a shield the soldier recognized as Pío's. A bit later, the village interpreter also emerged from the ravine, bespattered with blood. Then, when a group of the Natives came at Pedro and threatened to take his horse and sword, the soldier, fearing death, jammed his spurs into his horse's flanks and broke free to escape. Narrowly avoiding the volley of arrows the villagers sent after him, the Spaniard raced to Santa Fe to report the fearful happenings he had seen. As it turned out, Pedro Hidalgo fatefully announced the outbreak of the dramatic Pueblo Revolt of 1680.

As arranged, the uprising began the instant Padre Pío was killed, although that occurrence came ahead of schedule. Now there was no holding back. Messengers went north, west, and south, carrying word of the rebellion. From each of the various villages, once they got the signal, other messengers were sped on their way to inform neighboring pueblos. When the message bearers arrived at the home of each war chief, that official climbed to the highest rooftop in the village to give the dreaded war cry. No other expressions were necessary. Everyone knew that fearful sound. They had heard the cry before when raiding tribes had come sweeping in from the plains, hills, and mountains. As on other occasions, the men and older boys quickly collected their weapons and reported to their war society leaders. Each Pueblo tribe differed slightly in this regard, but most had war societies headed by a war chief or bow chief.

In each case, one group of warriors went to the padre's residence. Others hurried to the homes of the *alcalde mayor* (district leader) and other Spanish officials stationed in the villages. The Europeans were ordered to leave. Some of the most dedicated priests who had hoped to remain to save souls refused to leave. The war cry sounded again, and they were martyred. When other Spaniards tried to defend themselves and to save their ranchos, they met the same fate as the padres. The Indian numbers were overwhelming, and the tribes were enraged.

In all, twenty-one of the thirty-three Franciscan friars in the Pueblo country were killed, as were some four hundred of the more stubborn Spaniards. The Pueblos were on a mission: to persuade the Spaniards to leave or be killed. The Spanish churches and other centers of religious activity were, of course, targets for the rebellious Indians, who had seen their own holy places desecrated, a chief reason for the revolt.

For all their fury, the Pueblos refrained from rape and mutilation. According to the rules of the war societies, such outrages were prohibited. That war gods frowned on sexual misbehavior is highlighted in an oral story passed down through generations. It seems that a certain young soldier, overcome by the sight of a Spanish woman, fondled her breast. A few days later, a burro kicked the hand that touched the woman. True, taking a scalp from a Navajo or an Apache could be done ceremonially as part of the initiation of a war chief, but the Pueblos did not take scalps routinely. Besides, this uprising was a different kind of war, a struggle to rid their country of the outsiders.

In three or four days, the Pueblos had ousted the Spaniards and destroyed their houses of worship in an ironic turnabout. By Tuesday, August 13, the tribes closest to Santa Fe had invaded the capital. They were from Pecos, the Tanos from Tanogeh (including Galisteo, San Cristóbal, and San Lazaro), and warriors from the Keresan villages of San Marcos and La Cienega de Cochiti. Numbering about five hundred, they were led by Juan El Tano, who, having worked around Santa Fe, was fluent in Spanish. On the day the revolt began, Juan had been sent by his Spanish overseers to his home village of Galisteo to deliver a letter to alcalde mayor José Nieto. Now Juan returned to the capital as the leader of the Native emancipators.

In the meantime, two other Indians, servants of Spaniards, took another letter to Nieto. On their way, they saw the advancing warriors, their faces painted for war, moving on Santa Fe. The servants rushed back to the capital, breathlessly reporting what they had seen. Alarmed, the authorities sent out a reconnaissance patrol that reported seeing Juan, on horseback, leading a column of warriors. The soldiers said that Juan was armed like a Spaniard with harquebus, sword, and dagger and wearing a leather jacket and a sash of red taffeta that they recognized as from the missal of the convent of Galisteo.

When Juan entered the capital city, he was persuaded to come to the plaza to parley with Governor Otermín. Rather than being intimated before the Spanish official, Juan presented the governor with an ultimatum—

get out or perish. The Indian leader told Otermín he had been elected captain of his force and that the Pueblos were bringing two crosses: one white, for peace; the other red, for war. If the Spaniards chose the white cross, Juan said, their lives would be spared; they could depart peacefully from Pueblo territory. Choose red and they would die. Then Otermín reminded Juan that the governor and the other Spaniards were Christians. He asked Juan how the Indians expected to live without the Christian religion. Juan laughed in his face and left.

Shortly afterward, following a talk with his followers, Juan returned to the plaza to meet again with the governor. Juan delivered the demand from his people that all the Apache men and women whom the Spaniards had captured in war be turned over to the Pueblos. He also ordered that his wife and children, whom Juan had left in Santa Fe, be given to him. If these things were not done, Juan warned, the Indians would declare war immediately and would not leave. Otermín temporized, saying there were no Apaches in Santa Fe because that tribe was at war with Spaniards as well as with the Pueblos. Juan countered by telling the governor that time was running out, that more Pueblo warriors would be arriving soon, and that together they would destroy the Spaniards.

Meanwhile across the Agua Fria River, Juan's followers had begun to pillage the abandoned houses of Mexican Indians and had set fire to the Chapel of San Miguel. Otermín pleaded with Juan to stop his men, but when Juan approached them, he was met with peals of bells, blaring trumpets, and loud war cries. The Indians began streaming across the river.

Otermín called on his soldiers to attack. So pressed were the soldiers in their efforts that the governor himself joined in the engagement with the Indians. The battle raged for most of the day. At one juncture, the Spanish thought they had overcome the rebels, but then Tewa warriors from the north joined the fray. The fighting wore down at nightfall, with the Indians withdrawing to the eastern hills. The next day, the warriors returned to the villa, but the day passed without further combat. On August 15, there were several light skirmishes, mainly efforts by the Spaniards to prevent the burning and sacking of houses distant from the center of the villa.

By Friday, August 16, many more Pueblo fighting men had arrived from Tootho, Welai, and Walatowa. They were joined by Keresans from Rio Abajo. According to Otermín's later report, twenty-five hundred warriors laid siege to Santa Fe. The Pueblos entrenched themselves in houses and blocked entrances to all streets. They also cut off the water that came down the arroyo as well as that in the irrigation canal in front of the *casa reales* (royal palace). Although the Spanish soldiers diligently fought to keep control of their valuable water supply, they were unable to do so. Next Indian warriors burned the church and set fire to the doors of the fortified towers of the royal palace. As the siege settled in, the Spanish realized the peril they faced without water for themselves and their livestock.

By this time, the opposing forces were within talking distance. At one point, a group of Indian warriors met Spanish soldiers on horseback. When the Spanish officer in charge, whom the Indians knew, tried to speak to them, they shouted him down. "This man talks a great deal," one Indian cried. "You know he needs a whole day in which to talk. Leave it off. It is already too late."

After a bit, the officer managed to tone down the taunting and clamoring and, with the help of his chaplain, attempted to make peace. The Spaniards spotted the Keresan leader, Alonzo Catiti, and focused on him since his brother, Captain Pedro Márquez, also a mixed-blood *coyote*, was a Christian fighting for His Spanish Majesty in New Mexico. Catiti was told that he was condemned and that his sins were many. To these assertions he answered: "If what you are telling me is true, will you pardon me before God and Santa María and in the name of the king?" The officer replied, "Before the Virgin and her precious Son and in the name of the King, our Lord, I pardon you and all the rest if you will come down and submit." Mistrustful, Catiti was unwilling to move. Instead he replied, "I am fearful and do not believe you; they have told me here that they must take me to Spain to be severely punished." The talk was interrupted by the clamor of warriors advancing to fight. The Spaniards then left. Other encounters that day between groups of Spaniards and Indians allowed discussions of possible peace, but they amounted to little.

As Saturday morning dawned, the Indians pressed harder. They fired harquebuses, shot arrows, and hurled stones at the besieged Europeans. By this time, according to Spanish accounts, the colonists were highly fatigued and, worst of all, very thirsty. Their animals were dying from hunger and lack of water. In this desperate circumstance, the Spaniards had little choice. It was fight to the death or make an all-out try to win.

At first, they chose the latter option. With a few mounted men and infantrymen armed with harquebuses, plus Indian allies with bows and arrows and still in the service of the Spaniards, the Castilians made an audacious charge that caught the Pueblos off guard. The Indians fought bravely against the first wave but were put to flight in subsequent attacks. Some of the Natives fortified themselves in houses, but when the Spanish started burning these buildings, the Indians fled to the hills. Later accounts indicate that in this encounter and others more than one hundred warriors died. Many were trampled under the hooves of Spanish horses. Forty-seven warriors were also captured.

Although the Spaniards claimed a minimum number of losses, theirs was a Pyrrhic victory. Santa Fe was laid to waste and nearby fields stripped. There was no food and but a trickle of water. No more of either would be forthcoming from the Pueblos. The future of the Spanish in Santa Fe was dim indeed. Faced with this scenario, Otermín decided to abandon Santa Fe and to leave the Pueblo territory.

Thus on Wednesday, August 21, after the governor had interrogated and executed the Pueblo prisoners, he distributed provisions from his own stores to his people for the long journey south. Later Otermín would write that the Spaniards left Santa Fe without a crust of bread or a grain of wheat or corn and with no other provisions for a convoy of a thousand refugees. In fact, the Spanish caravan left Santa Fe with four hundred animals—horses, cows, sheep, and goats—and with two loaded carts belonging to a private individual.

The Pueblo warriors watched from the hills as the hated Spaniards retreated south. There was no more need to attack. The former overlords had heeded the grim Native ultimatum. As Malacate, a Keresan leader, had cautioned them earlier, no further bloodshed was necessary.

After the Spanish retreated down the Rio Grande, the exultant warriors gathered in the plaza. They listened to their leaders give victorious addresses on the return to a free world and the old ways. Each speaker thanked the Great Spirit and, of course, the twin war gods, Maseway and Oyoyewey. The deities had rescued the people, as the old men had said they would.

If Popé spoke at this time, he probably addressed his followers in words like these:

Within and around the world, within and around the hills and mountains, within and around the valleys, your authority returns to you. Therefore return to your people and travel the corn pollen trail again. A trail with no pebbles, no boulders, and no obstructions. Go home and enjoy your families, the birds, the clouds, the mist, the rain, the lightning, the wind, the rivers, the mountains, the trees, and the sky. Remember the words of our leaders—upon arriving home, go to the rivers and cleanse yourselves of the recent past. Lastly, don't you forget, each morning before our father, the sun, makes his appearance, to take feathers in one hand and corn pollen in the other hand and offer them to the deities in the mountains, in the clouds, in the valleys, to the north, to the west, to the south, to the east, to Sipofenae and to Waynema [a lake in Arizona where the rain gods reside]. Singe de ho.

After these words, each warrior would have taken his corn pollen pouch from his belt and offered a prayer to the twin war gods for their assistance. Then, after casting the pollen into the winds, they would have brushed themselves with their hands to expunge any ill effects from their experiences.

It was over. The tyrants with the sword had been driven from the lands of the Pueblo people. The first American revolution had succeeded.

Even before the Spaniards fled from New Mexico into Mexico in early fall 1680, they were planning a reconquest. But the earliest efforts at reentry came to nothing. The Pueblos were not willing to reaccept the Spanish and their harsh, demanding ways. On their part, the Spanish were unable to mount a strong effort to retake New Mexico until the 1690s. Even then, with a larger, more powerful force under the leadership of don Diego de Vargas in 1692–93, the reconquest was not easy. Other, partial uprisings in 1694 and 1696 indicated that there were still unsettled questions for the Spanish in New Mexico.

Meanwhile changes in Pueblo leadership and attitudes helped open the doors for Spanish reentry into the far-northern frontier. When droughts, disappointing harvests, and plagues devastated the Pueblos after the Spanish exit, dissension and conflict split Popé's followers. In addition, not all Pueblos followed Popé's determined leadership. Indeed, even before the rebellion of 1680, it was rumored that he had killed his son-in-law Bua, who had remained friendly to the Spaniards. Popé urged the Pueblos to destroy all vestiges of Spanish contact and control—not only the symbols of European political, religious, and cultural domination but also horses, other livestock, and Spanish implements. That was too much for some Pueblos. When clashes over these and other issues broke out among the varied pueblos, Popé's strength was further eroded, leading to his disposal and replacement. Additional bad crops and mounting attacks by nomadic Indians, including those by Utes, made some Pueblos more willing to reaccept the Spaniards.

After the Spanish reassumed control of New Mexico, they gradually demonstrated a willingness to ease up on some of their earlier excessive requirements. The hated encomienda system ended, and religious leaders seemed amenable to a syncretic belief system that combined Spanish and Native rites and rituals. And as raids from roaming Indians mounted in the seventeenth century, the Spanish, more diplomatically than before, worked with the Pueblos to erect a joint defense against the raiders. Now rather than primarily a conflictive relationship, the Pueblos and the Spanish were beginning to converse more often across their two cultures.

Clearly, then, the Pueblo Revolt of 1680 was a watershed event in New Mexico history. When the Pueblos rose up to drive out their Spanish conquerors, they indicated that a new, less onerous relationship had to be fashioned. No one did more to engineer this historic revolt than the Pueblo leader Popé. His able, energetic leadership before and during this dramatic event earns him a central place on the stage of early New Mexican history.

ESSAY ON SOURCES

Readers who wish to pursue further the subject of Popé and the Pueblo Indians in early New Mexico history could begin with the author's other works on these subjects. This essay draws on Joe S. Sando, *Pueblo Nations: Eight Centuries of Pueblo Indian History,* rev. first ed. (Santa Fe: Clear Light Publishers, 1998). Also see Joe S. Sando, *The Pueblo Indians* (San Francisco: Indian Historian Press, 1989), Sando, *Pueblo Profiles: Cultural Identity through Centuries of Change* (Santa Fe: Clear Light Publishers, 1998), and Sando, *Nee Hemish: A History of Jemez Pueblo* (Albuquerque: University of New Mexico Press, 1982). For the views of another Pueblo authority, see Alfonso Ortiz, "Popay's Leadership: A Pueblo Perspective," *El Palacio* 86 (winter 1980–81): 18–22, and Ortiz, *The Tewa World: Space, Time, Being, and Becoming in a Pueblo Society* (Chicago: University of Chicago Press, 1969).

Several scholars have prepared overviews of Pueblo Indians and other Native American groups of the Southwest. For example, consult ethnologist Bertha P. Dutton's *American Indians of the Southwest* (Albuquerque:

University of New Mexico Press, 1983), Edward P. Dozier's *The Pueblo Indians of North America* (New York: Holt, Rinehart and Winston, 1970), Carroll L. Riley's *Rio del Norte: People of the Upper Rio Grande from the Earliest Times to the Pueblo Revolt* (Salt Lake City: University of Utah Press, 1995), and John L. Kessell's *Kiva, Cross, and Crown: The Pecos Indians and New Mexico, 1540–1840*, 2d ed. (Albuquerque: University of New Mexico Press, 1987).

Other scholars have focused on the contacts between Native Americans and non-Indians in the Southwest. An exceptionally good study of this kind is Edward H. Spicer, *Cycles of Conquest: The Impact of Spain, Mexico, and the United States on the Indians of the Southwest, 1533–1960* (Tucson: University of Arizona Press, 1970). Similar strong works are Elizabeth A. H. John, *Storms Brewed in Other Men's Worlds: The Confrontation of Indian, Spanish, and French in the Southwest*, 2d ed. (Norman: University of Oklahoma Press, 1996), and Oakah L. Jones, *Pueblo Warriors and Spanish Conquest* (Norman: University of Oklahoma Press, 1966, 1980).

For those who wish to study the dramatic, complex events of the Pueblo Revolt of 1680, several book-length examinations are available. Robert Silverberg, *The Pueblo Revolt* (Lincoln: University of Nebraska Press, 1994), Andrew L. Knaut, *The Pueblo Revolt of 1680: Conquest and Resistance in Seventeenth-Century New Mexico* (Norman: University of Oklahoma Press, 1995), and Franklin Folsom, *Indian Uprising on the Rio Grande: The Pueblo Revolt of 1680* (Albuquerque: University of New Mexico Press, 1996), are readable, narrative accounts. For a brief but deft summary, see Marc Simmons, "The Pueblo Revolt: Why Did It Happen?," *El Palacio* 86 (winter 1980–81): 11–15. More recently, David J. Weber has gathered several notable selections and provided a helpful introduction and useful bibliographical listings in his edited collection, *What Caused the Pueblo Revolt of 1680?* (Boston: Bedford/St. Martin's, 1999).

For two scholarly but conflicting interpretations of Popé, one can consult Fray Angélico Chávez, "Pohé-Yemo's Representative and the Pueblo Revolt," *New Mexico Historical Review* 42 (April 1967): 85–126, which downplays Popé's role in the revolt of 1680. A challenge to Chávez's interpretation is presented in Stefanie Beninato, "Popé, Pose-yemu, and Naranjo: A New Look at Leadership in the Pueblo Revolt of 1680," *New Mexico Historical Review* 65 (October 1990): 417–35.

Still other researchers have focused on later periods of Spanish-Pueblo conflict. For a pioneering study of the 1690s, see J. Manuel Espinosa,

Crusaders of the Rio Grande: The Story of Don Diego de Vargas and the Reconquest and Refounding of New Mexico (Chicago: Institute of Jesuit History Publications, 1942). The fullest story of this earlier period, as well as other eras of Spanish influence in the Borderlands, is David J. Weber's magisterial *The Spanish Frontier in North America* (New Haven, Conn.: Yale University Press, 1992).

Finally, those wishing to sample the original documents for Popé's life, the details of the Pueblo Revolt, and Spanish contact with Indians of the Southwest have several hefty volumes of original sources available to them. Among the best of these books is Charles W. Hackett, ed., and Charmion C. Shelby, trans., *Revolt of the Pueblo Indians of New Mexico and Otermín's Attempted Reconquest, 1680–1692*, 2 vols. (Albuquerque: University of New Mexico Press, 1942, 1970). See also J. Manuel Espinosa's collection of documents and helpful editorial comment in his *Pueblo Revolt of 1696 and the Franciscan Missions in New Mexico* (Norman: University of Oklahoma Press, 1988). Finally, one should also consult the multivolume don Diego de Vargas Papers, under the general editorship of John L. Kessell and published by the University of New Mexico Press.

𝒮3

Juan de Oñate, Diego de Vargas, and Hispanic Beginnings in New Mexico

RICK HENDRICKS

INTRODUCTION

𝓘n April 1598, after a trip of five months, an expedition of European settlers and soldiers arrived at the south bank of the Rio Grande. Most of the last four hundred miles of their journey had been over harsh desert, and the travelers arrived at the river tired and thirsty. Within a few days, advance scouts located a suitable ford upriver. When they reported to their leader, don Juan de Oñate, he immediately called a halt. It was April 30, 1598, the Day of the Ascension. The time had come to take possession of New Mexico, the land where the colonists were to make their new homes. On these occasions, Spanish law and tradition required elaborate ceremonies, religious and civil. To that end, the journeyers constructed a bower to be used as a chapel, where the Franciscans accompanying the expedition celebrated mass and delivered a stirring sermon with everyone in attendance. Later in the day, Oñate read the official act of possession, claiming New Mexico for King Phillip II of Spain, signing the document before a royal notary. There followed a joyous celebration of thanksgiving and the performance of a play one of the expedition members had written. After resting for several days, the caravan crossed the Rio Grande on May 4, 1598, at a place that would become known as El Paso, the pass.

The leader of the expedition, don Juan de Oñate, served as governor of New Mexico for a dozen years. His tenure was tumultuous, often violent, and Oñate became a very controversial figure. He had recruited colonists largely with the knowledge that he would be granting Pueblo Indians in *encomienda,* a potentially valuable source of labor and tribute, and with the hope of discovering rich silver mines. It was soon apparent, however, that New Mexico held no such mineral wealth. This realization occasioned great disappointment. Oñate had also been instructed to explore outside of New Mexico, so he traveled to the plains of Kansas in search of Quivira and rumored riches and to the Gulf of California to discover the South Sea. These journeys meant that the governor was absent from the colony for long periods. For the settlers who remained, life was difficult. They struggled to survive shortages of food and bitter winter cold. More and more the colonists came to rely on the Pueblo Indians to supply their needs. Opposition to Oñate grew, and he and his followers brutally repressed it. Some Pueblo Indians also openly challenged Oñate and Spanish rule. Acoma Pueblo revolted, slaying a number of Spaniards, with Oñate dispatching troops that successfully put down the revolt.

Despite all the difficulties, Oñate and the settlers he recruited and led to New Mexico ushered in the long period of permanent Hispanic presence in the American Southwest. Fundamental Spanish institutions arrived with Oñate and his colonists. They brought towns and Spanish ideas of governance, the first building block of Spanish civilization in the New World. Members of the Franciscan order who accompanied the settlers also brought their organized religion, Roman Catholicism, to the region and established missions, the second building block. The initial stay in New Mexico lasted for eighty-two years, until the Pueblo Revolt of 1680 drove the Spanish out of the colony. They became refugees in El Paso for a dozen years. For the next several generations the colony endured. The adaptations of Hispanic people of diverse origins to the land and to the indigenous peoples of New Mexico produced cultural traditions that survived the years of exile and continue to the present.

Toward the end of the seventeenth century, Spaniards made several unsuccessful attempts to reconquer New Mexico. Then in early 1691, a new governor of the colony-in-exile of New Mexico, Diego de Vargas, took office. For more than a year, he was engaged in military campaigns in neighboring provinces to the south and in making general preparations for the reconquest of New Mexico. On August 10, 1692, St. Lawrence's Day, Vargas had the campaign proclaimed in all the communities of the El Paso area. He had chosen that day because it was the twelfth anniversary of the Pueblo Revolt, an event that the former New Mexicans living in El Paso

FIGURE 3.1. Equestrian statue of don Juan de Oñate by Sonny Rivera, Oñate
            Monument and Visitors Center, Alcalde, New Mexico. Photograph
            by Rick Hendricks.

vengefully recalled every year. One week later, Governor Vargas and his
troops crossed the Rio Grande and began the initial phase of the reconquest, a ritual repossession and armed reconnaissance of the pueblos.
By the middle of December 1692, Vargas and his men were back in El Paso.
From there, he launched the recolonizing expedition in October of
the following year. In sharp contrast to the largely ceremonial tour of the

pueblos of 1692, the recolonizing expedition of 1693 was marked by bitter warfare between the advancing Spaniards and the Pueblo Indians. By bringing colonists the Spaniards were obviously coming to stay, and the Pueblos resisted the Spaniards' advance.

The reconqueror and recolonizer of New Mexico, Diego de Vargas, served one term as governor of the province of New Mexico, from 1691 to 1697. Much of this first term in office was taken up with fighting. For most of 1693 and 1694, the Spaniards fought a series of pitched battles against various pueblos, literally struggling militarily for the colony's survival. Then in June 1696, a second revolt erupted and threatened the Spanish presence in New Mexico. Only after another series of sieges and battles, lasting until winter weather halted operations, did the Spaniards put down the rebellion.

In the interval between terms, Vargas was embroiled in an acrimonious dispute with the *cabildo* (the municipal council) of Santa Fe and his successor, Pedro Rodríguez Cubero. Life in New Mexico had proven to be harsh, and hundreds of the colonists over the years had built up a deep resentment against Governor Vargas. The cabildo pressed a suit against him, alleging malfeasance and bad government, and the legal battle waged by agents before authorities in the viceregal capital of Mexico City dragged on for years. Vargas was eventually exonerated of all charges and reappointed to the governorship of New Mexico. He began his second term in 1703 but died before completing it.

The Vargas era was the beginning of the ongoing presence of Hispanics in New Mexico. Improved defense of the colonists against hostile Indians helped stabilize the growing Hispanic population. The third building block of Spanish frontier civilization, the *presidio* (a term describing a military garrison and the walled fort where the troops were stationed), made this increased protection possible. Presidios took hold in New Mexico during the Vargas area. Over time, presidios evolved into towns and cities in many places on New Spain's northern frontier, although in New Mexico

FIGURE 3.2. Diego de Vargas, the only known portrait, Capilla de San Isidro, Madrid, Estudio Portillo, Madrid. Courtesy J. Manuel Espinosa. From John L. Kessell and Rick Hendricks, eds., *By Force of Arms: The Journals of don Diego de Vargas, New Mexico, 1691–93* (Albuquerque: University of New Mexico Press, 1992), p. 29.

they were situated to provide protection for the existing communities of Santa Fe and El Paso.

Most of the families of settlers who accompanied Vargas have descendants still living in New Mexico, an amazing continuity of people and place. Never again after Vargas would the colony be threatened as it had been during the period before his arrival and during his years of service. The years of violence between Spaniard and Pueblo ended, and a more pragmatic, mutual accommodation began to emerge as the two groups learned to live more peaceably together.

THE NEW MEXICO OF JUAN DE OÑATE

In 1583, King Phillip II issued a decree that directed the viceroy of New Spain to find a wealthy individual who was willing and able to lead an expedition to settle New Mexico. By that time, almost everyone had forgotten the major disappointment that followed on the heels of Francisco Vásquez de Coronado's disastrous expedition in the early 1540s. Two more recent if unsuccessful attempts at colonization of New Mexico, one led by fray Agustín Rodríguez and Francisco Sánchez Chamuscado in 1581 and another by Antonio de Espejo in 1583, had reignited the imaginations of rich individuals and poor opportunists alike. They eagerly listened to reports of Indians living in multistoried adobe houses and favorable prospects of finding mineral wealth. The Franciscans too were excited by the challenge of converting thousands of Indians to the faith, thereby saving their souls.

A number of rich and powerful men vied with Juan de Oñate for the contract to settle New Mexico, but by the late summer of 1595, he had signed an agreement with the viceroy of New Spain to carry out the expedition. That fall, the outgoing viceroy issued instructions to Oñate to guide his actions. From the crown's view, Oñate's first responsibility was to facilitate the Franciscans' conversion of the heathen Indians, but Spain was also pursuing serious geopolitical goals with the settlement of New Mexico. The New Mexican enterprise would serve to protect Spain's interests in western North America against her European rivals, particularly England, by firmly establishing a bastion deep in the interior of North America. Oñate was also instructed to locate the west coast of the continent and suitable sites for ports. The coast was vital because it was believed to hold the western opening of the Northwest Passage, what the

Spanish referred to as the Strait of Anián. Oñate agreed with these aims and anticipated the glory that would cover him upon their attainment, but he and the colonists were nonetheless primarily seeking silver or gold. Another powerful incentive to the settlers was the promise of *hidalgo* status to every head of household who remained in the colony for five years. Even though hidalgos ranked at the bottom of the Spanish nobility, they received such minor privileges as the right to use the honorific *don* before their names and exemption from certain taxes. In status-conscious Spanish society, even such minor honors were highly sought after.

Oñate had agreed to recruit two hundred men to settle New Mexico. As excitement about the impending expedition grew, he enlisted nearly five hundred men in a few weeks; the total may have eventually climbed to a thousand. But the arrival of a new viceroy, financial difficulties, and behind-the-scenes maneuvering by rivals led to numerous delays, and many of the recruits drifted away. Finally, in the winter of 1597, the expedition departed from Santa Bárbara, which Oñate had chosen as a staging area, four hundred miles north of Zacatecas.

We do not know how many people formed this initial colonizing expedition. Estimates for this first wave of colonists for New Mexico range from more than five hundred to over eight hundred men, women, and children. We do know that 129 soldiers passed muster in January of 1598. Other musters make it possible to identify several hundred people who accompanied Oñate or subsequently made their way to New Mexico in the early sixteenth century. Of those individuals who can be identified, most considered themselves Spaniards, a surprisingly elastic term at the time, encompassing rather remarkable ethnic and cultural diversity. Most of the male colonists came from Spain or from its New World possessions, principally the provinces of New Spain and Nueva Galicia. Other men came from European countries such as Portugal, Belgium, Italy, and Greece. Finally, there were doubtless many Indians and people of mixed blood— mestizos and mulattos—as well as a few African slaves who accompanied Oñate, only a few of whom can be identified. A second wave of colonists came to New Mexico in 1600, a group consisting of about sixty-five Spaniards and their twenty-five servants.

Traveling in the vanguard of his expedition, Oñate arrived at the large Tewa pueblo of Okhe on the west bank of the Rio Grande on July 11, 1598. The Tewas received Oñate in a friendly way, and he established his headquarters and provincial capital there, calling it San Juan de los Caballeros.

He soon set fifteen hundred Indians to work under Spanish overseers on the construction of irrigation ditches for a new town to be called San Francisco. But that town was never built. Within a few days of the arrival of the main body of colonists, Oñate faced a revolt, with one-third of his force plotting to abandon the enterprise and return to New Spain. Acting quickly, Oñate arrested the leaders of the mutiny and quelled the revolt. Trying to bring harmony to the disputatious colonists, he ordered the construction of a chapel for the Indians of San Juan, the first church in New Mexico. The discontent continued, however, and several soldiers deserted, stealing horses as they fled south. Two were captured and executed, and two escaped. In early December of 1598, word reached Oñate that the Indians of Acoma Pueblo had revolted, killing his nephew, Juan de Zaldívar, and ten Spanish soldiers. The specter of a general rebellion that would drive the Spaniards out of New Mexico led Oñate to respond by sending a force that subdued the rebels. After a trial, Oñate pronounced harsh sentences on the Acoma prisoners, the most notorious being the mutilation of males over age twenty-five: they were to have one foot cut off and were condemned to twenty years of servitude. As a result of what even his contemporaries considered excesses, Juan de Oñate was eventually banned from New Mexico for life.

Early in 1599, Oñate relocated his headquarters and capital across the river to the smaller Tewa pueblo of Yúngé, which the Spaniards called San Gabriel. According to all accounts, the Tewa inhabitants willingly gave up their homes, some four hundred dwellings around a central plaza, to the Spaniards and relocated elsewhere, most to San Juan.

In June 1601, Oñate departed in search of Quivira, rumored to be an Indian land rich in gold, silver, and fabrics and located far to the east of New Mexico. While Oñate was away from San Gabriel, resentment grew against the governor. Although many of the colonists had risked everything they had on the New Mexico adventure, it was now clear they would not get rich quickly in New Mexico. The colonists had made no mining strikes, and they were competing with the Indians for the meager resources the land had to offer. Surprisingly, the Franciscans joined the faction calling for abandoning the province. They could no longer gain converts because of the abuses the Spaniards were committing against the Pueblos. By early October, nearly four hundred settlers left San Gabriel for New Spain. Perhaps one or two hundred colonists remained, counting those Oñate loyalists in San Gabriel and others who lived elsewhere in the colony.

When an exhausted Oñate returned to San Gabriel in late November 1601, having found no city of gold at Quivira, he encountered the few loyal supporters who had awaited his return. Oñate moved swiftly to try to convict the traitors who had abandoned the New Mexico enterprise. He sentenced the leaders to death by beheading and sent Vicente de Zaldívar in pursuit. When Zaldívar arrived at Santa Bárbara, he learned that the mutineers were safely under the protection of royal officials. Zaldívar then decided to travel to Mexico City and Madrid, if necessary, to set matters right. The viceroy, the Conde de Monterrey, did not know which side to believe, the pro- or the anti-Oñate faction. In fine bureaucratic tradition, the viceroy decided the accusations against Oñate merited further investigation by the *audiencia,* the high court in Mexico City. Zaldívar appeared before the viceroy and the audiencia in May 1602 to present his uncle's side. Since Zaldívar had announced his intention to present the case to the king in Spain, the viceroy deferred judgment. In Spain, the king and the Council of the Indies sent the matter back to the viceroy, directing him to order an investigation and make a ruling. Vicente sailed for New Spain in 1603.

Back in New Mexico, Oñate was busy with his difficult colony. Taos Pueblo rose against the Spaniards sometime in 1603, and Oñate led a campaign to punish the rebels. In the course of putting down the revolt, Oñate was said to have killed a Taos leader. This act came back to haunt him years later when it was added to the list of abuses he was alleged to have committed in New Mexico. In fulfillment of his original instructions, Juan de Oñate traveled to the Gulf of California in search of the South Sea in October 1604. He returned from his trip in the spring of the following year. In the meantime, his supposed excesses and alleged crimes were under investigation in Spain and Mexico City. The desertion of most of his colonists greatly weakened his position. King Phillip III ordered him recalled in June 1606, but before Oñate received word of that decision, he tendered his resignation.

JUAN DE OÑATE

Although some despise him and others admire him, Juan de Oñate towers over the early history of New Mexico. No one knows when or where Juan de Oñate and his twin brother, Cristóbal, were born to Cristóbal de Oñate and Catalina de Salazar. Probably they were born in 1552, either in Zacatecas or in the family residence at Pánico (later Pánuco) about five miles north of the city. By that time, Juan de Oñate's father, Cristóbal, was a wealthy and influential man, but it had not always been so. Cristóbal and his brother, also named Juan, grew up in poor conditions in his birthplace, Vitoria, in the Basque province of Álaba in northern Spain. In 1524, Cristóbal got a job as a clerk for a newly appointed royal accountant, leaving Spain for Mexico City.

Cristóbal served with Beltrán Nuño de Guzmán, who butchered Indian peoples in what is today western and northwestern Mexico. Although Cristóbal was not noted for indulging in excesses, his brother, Juan, the uncle of the future governor of New Mexico, participated in the slaughter of Indians and eventually fled to Peru to escape prosecution. Cristóbal served as governor of Nueva Galicia several times. During the years from 1540 to 1542, Cristóbal was busy with the Mixtón War. In addition to his military activities, Cristóbal acquired encomiendas and began serious prospecting. He first located a number of mines near Guadalajara. Then in 1546, Cristóbal formed a partnership with Juan de Tolosa, Miguel de Ibarra, and Diego de Ibarra, all Basques, who discovered a silver bonanza in Zacatecas.

Juan's mother, Catalina de Salazar, was a native of Granada in southern Spain. She and his father had five sons and two daughters. Although Juan was born in the New World to an Andalusian mother, undoubtedly he grew up surrounded by Basque people and their culture. The Basques are one of Europe's oldest peoples. One of the touchstones of their culture is Euskera, a unique, difficult language of which they have always been proud. We do not know that Oñate spoke Euskera, but his father's associates may have communicated in it frequently. Surely Oñate could have and probably would have told his listeners that his name meant "at the base of the mountain pass." The business partners of Juan's father and his cousins, other relatives, and neighbors were all Basques. They formed Juan's close circle in Zacatecas, and some accompanied him to New Mexico. Pride in family meant that although relatively few Basques left their homeland, Euskadi, for the Indies, when they did, their families often joined them after they were established. Even in Spain, Basques in general did not become proficient speakers of Spanish until the seventeenth century. Especially when far from home in the New World, Basques were known for gathering and speaking their native tongue. For Juan de Oñate, language would have served as a reminder that he thought himself noble by birth and, in the Basque view, better than most people.

As a Basque, Juan would have been conscious of his people's separate history even though the Basque provinces had been incorporated into the kingdom of Castile before the sixteenth century. He may have boasted that they had never been conquered and enjoyed noble status based on ancient rights and privileges. Basques think of themselves as characterized by long-suffering fortitude. Spaniards think of them as insufferably stubborn and arrogant.

Although being Basque made Juan de Oñate different, much also made him similar to other Spaniards born in the New World. By all accounts Juan de Oñate was brought up in a strict home and raised a devout Catholic. He also took fierce pride in his loyalty to the king of Spain. From the time he was a young man, at least as early as his teens and perhaps earlier, Juan accompanied his father into battle against the fierce Chichimecas. By his early twenties he was leading such campaigns. He was a natural soldier and leader of men.

Even though by 1550 Zacatecas was the second-largest city in New Spain, it exhibited the typically rough life of a mining camp. The city lacked the formal organization typical of Spanish town planning since its development had followed the mines. As a result, the city hosted a large transient population and often crime and violence. Juan de Oñate spent much of his time ranging over the countryside, particularly to the north of Zacatecas, where he prospected for silver deposits. He made a number of finds; one of note was at Charcas. He also gradually assumed control of the family operations at Pánuco. By age thirty Juan de Oñate was a wealthy man, ready to take a wife. His choice was Isabel de Tolosa Cortés Moctezuma, the daughter of Juan de Tolosa and Leonor Cortés Moctezuma. Leonor was the granddaughter of the conquistador Hernán Cortés and his mistress, Isabel Moctezuma, the daughter of the Aztec emperor. Juan and Isabel had two children, a boy, Cristóbal, and a girl, María.

In 1592, Viceroy Luis de Velasco II tapped Juan to be the official founder of San Luis Potosí because the real founder, Miguel Caldera, had no social standing. Oñate served as *alcalde mayor* for a year, organizing the civil administration efficiently. When Phillip II called for the viceroy to find someone suitable to colonize New Mexico, Velasco may have recalled Oñate's success at San Luis Potosí. Certainly the viceroy knew of Oñate's family and wealth. He had campaigned with the Oñates against the Chichimecas. Oñate himself may have suggested the nomination, seeing an opportunity for glory and another silver strike, or a well-placed family friend and confidant may have recommended Juan de Oñate for the colonizing job.

The New Mexico enterprise, begun with much hope and the promise of riches, ended in personal disaster for many of Oñate's backers and the colonists he recruited. Oñate's career, however, did not end after a dozen trying years in New Mexico. His only son died in 1612, an emotional blow that devastated Juan de Oñate. By 1613, he was back in Zacatecas, tending to his mining and other financial interests. The following year, the new viceroy, the Marqués of Guadalcázar, tried Oñate on thirty charges for acts he was alleged to have committed as governor of New Mexico. Some of the charges were relatively minor, but others were grave. Oñate gained acquittal on eighteen charges but was found guilty on the other twelve, including application of excessive force in quelling the rebellion at Acoma, illegally putting to death two Spanish captains and two Indians, ordering the deaths of two deserters, and living openly in an adulterous relationship. As a result of the trial, Oñate was exiled from New Mexico for life, exiled from Mexico City for four years, and fined. Oñate struggled for the rest of his life to have his record expunged. In 1619 or 1620, he suffered another major loss when his wife died. After her death, Oñate decided to travel to the Spanish capital in Madrid to press his case in person. Eventually he was repaid the six thousand pesos levied on him as a fine, but his exile was not revoked. His efforts to improve his mines at Pánuco enabled Oñate to recover from his financial reverses in New Mexico. In 1624, he was named mining inspector for Spain, a prestigious position but one that earned him no salary. About June 3, 1626, Juan de Oñate died while conducting an inspection of a flooded mine in Guadalcanal.

One senses contradictions in the character of Juan de Oñate. He grew to manhood in the rough-and-tumble mining center of Zacatecas and from an early age knew firsthand the realities of Indian warfare. Yet Juan de Oñate also knew the splendor of the viceregal capital, Mexico City, and his father was the epitome of the redoubtable Basque explorer and entrepreneur as well as a good Christian man. Even as a youth, Juan gave evidence of wanting to emulate his father's successes. Apparently he had a good head for business. Oñate saw in the New Mexico enterprise an opportunity to obtain personal glory and wealth as well as a harvest of souls for the Catholic Church. He was ambitious, prideful, and persuasive, traits that enabled him to gather the financial backing and recruit the settlers needed for the colonization effort. He may also have had a hard personality, which might explain his decision to take to New Mexico his eight-year-old son, leaving his pregnant wife behind. Oñate was not given to compromise and often had recourse to violence. When a disaffected colony in New Mexico challenged his authority, he reacted harshly, condemning the deserters to death. When his nephew, Juan de Zaldívar, died at the hands of the Indians of Acoma, Oñate's grief took the form of an order for a punishment that even his contemporaries considered cruel. Perhaps more than anything else, however, Juan de Oñate was stubbornly determined. Events in New Mexico would have broken a lesser man, but he forged ahead. Although he never obtained the full exoneration he sought, he recovered financially and secured another post in the royal service.

SEVENTEENTH-CENTURY NEW MEXICO
BEFORE THE PUEBLO REVOLT

In the years after Juan de Oñate's departure, a rancorous conflict between the Franciscans and the Spanish royal governors, which pushed the province to the brink of civil war, characterized New Mexico. A fundamental change took place in 1609 when the crown decided to provide direct financial and administrative control, making the formerly proprietary colony into a royal one. Given the apparent lack of any real source of wealth in New Mexico, this decision reflected the desire to foster the Franciscans' evangelization effort and provided a measure of stability in that the crown, rather than an individual entrepreneur, was footing the bill for the support of the colony.

Pedro de Peralta, the first royal governor, arrived in New Mexico in 1609 and officially established a new administrative capital in Santa Fe in 1610. The Franciscans maintained their headquarters at Santo Domingo Pueblo. The Franciscan commissary, fray Isidro Ordóñez, arrived in New Mexico in 1612 and almost immediately began to interfere with Governor Peralta's performance of his duty. In 1613, Ordóñez excommunicated the governor, who took a shot at the priest and missed. When Peralta tried to travel to Mexico City to resolve the conflict, Ordóñez arrested him on the authority of the Inquisition. What Peralta and Ordóñez and their successors were fighting over was access to and control of the Pueblo Indians. While the church-state conflict raged, the period from 1610 to the eve of the 1680 revolt was also notable for the great expansion of the Franciscan missionization effort. Led by the efforts of fray Juan de Benavides, who headed up the Franciscans in the province from 1621 to 1629, missions were founded in most of the pueblos in northern New Mexico. In 1659, a mission was established in El Paso at the southern gateway to the colony.

Although it is very difficult to measure accurately the effectiveness of the mission program, by the middle of the seventeenth century, the Franciscans had baptized and were ministering to as many as twenty thousand Pueblo Indians.

The Franciscans' conversion effort, however, was incompatible with the governors' desire for the labor supply the Pueblos represented. In addition, the Franciscans occupied many Indian laborers in nonreligious activities, such as tending their growing livestock herds, working in mission industries, and laboring in their fields. This created competition for a limited source of labor. Beyond their own needs as frontier entrepreneurs, the governors acted in the economic best interests of the Spanish colonists, who also wanted access to Indian labor.

Pre-Revolt New Mexico was overwhelmingly rural, and its limited wealth derived from working the land. The only urban concentration was at the capital, Santa Fe. A few prominent individuals owned *estancias,* large estates of irrigated farmland and open pasture along the Rio Grande and its tributaries. Many of the estancia owners were also *encomenderos,* individuals who had been granted the right to collect tribute from a given pueblo or part of a pueblo in exchange for providing, at least theoretically, military protection and religious instruction of the Indians. Although the encomenderos were not entitled to Indian land or labor, they did need access to Indians to hire to work on their holdings. Some governors and missions operated *obrajes,* or textile-making operations, in Santa Fe, in which Indians provided the labor. Other economic activities produced animals and animal products, such as leather, tallow, and jerky as well as coarse woven goods for export to the south. Workers also gathered piñon nuts and salt for trading. Some provincial governors dominated traffic in one of the more lucrative trade items in this period—Apache, Ute, and Pawnee slaves. The competition for Indian laborers between the Franciscans and the governors and colonists led to bitter, internecine fighting within the Hispanic community. The resulting displays of ill temper and exchanges of epithets between priests and governors and the enslavement of other Indians were very bad examples of un-Christian behavior for the Pueblo Indians to observe.

New Mexico was beginning to fall apart. As the situation of the colony deteriorated rapidly from one of stability to collapse, a series of men served short terms as governor of New Mexico. Almost nothing is known of most of the early royal governors until the term of Luis de Rosas, and he is known because of the catastrophe that befell him. An epidemic struck

New Mexico in 1640, killing as many as 10 percent of the Indian population. The province was on the verge of civil war, pitting the Franciscans and their supporters against the backers of Governor Rosas. The governor had charged the Franciscans with running a successful business operation in New Mexico out of their missions and on the backs of the Pueblo Indians. He added that they had fathered bastard children of Indian women and cheated the royal treasury by accepting funds for vacant missions. To the Franciscans, Rosas was a vile tyrant and oppressor of Indians. He was replaced in the spring of 1641 but remained in Santa Fe, only to be assassinated later in the year. The following year, authorities in Mexico City sent Governor Alonso Pacheco y Heredia to investigate and punish the guilty. Squabbling between priests and government officials in a poor, distant colony was one thing, murdering an ex-governor was quite another. After a secret investigation, Governor Pacheco arrested and executed eight individuals implicated in the plot to kill Rosas.

The desperation of epidemic and the demonstration effect of seeing colonists killing each other in the Rosas affair may have emboldened some Pueblos to strike at the Spaniards. In 1645, during the administration of Governor Fernando de Argüello, Jemez Pueblo rose, joining the Apaches in revolt. In the aftermath of the unsuccessful rebellion, Governor Argüello had twenty-nine Indians hanged in Jemez Pueblo. In 1650, a wider plot hatched, reportedly involving Jemez, Keres, Tiwas, and Apaches. The allies planned to attack the Spaniards on the night of Holy Thursday, when they would be gathered together, but the would-be victims got wind of the scheme. The Spaniards hanged nine leaders and sold many more into slavery for ten years.

The church-state conflict paused from 1656 to 1659, when Juan Manso occupied the governorship. Manso was the half brother of fray Tomás Manso, one of the leading churchmen in seventeenth-century New Mexico and a future bishop of Nicaragua. The problems returned with a vengeance with Manso's successor, Bernardo López de Mendizábal. Governor López and the Franciscan custodian, fray Juan Ramírez, began their quarrel before they departed Mexico City to take up their respective posts in New Mexico. The jurisdictional battle between López and the Franciscans for control of the colony eventually proved fatal to the former governor. He died in the secret jail of the Inquisition in Mexico City (having earlier been found guilty of malfeasance by the audiencia), accused of Judaism, among many other grave crimes.

The governorship of Fernando de Villanueva, from 1665 to 1668, was a time of drought in New Mexico. Hungry Apaches stepped up their raiding on Pueblos and Spaniards alike. The Piro pueblos of the Salinas Basin were particularly hard hit, and some rebelled. Governor Villanueva hanged six Piros and sold others into slavery. An Indian governor from the Salinas pueblos named Esteban Clemente plotted a revolt that had adherents throughout New Mexico. Just as had occurred in 1650, Clemente planned to strike the Spaniards on the night of Holy Thursday. The Spanish authorities discovered the intrigue and hanged Clemente.

Severe famine followed drought in the 1670s, and the trouble with marauding Apaches became serious. In 1675, Governor Juan Francisco Treviño rounded up forty-seven Indians suspected of practicing witchcraft. Governor Treviño found the Indians guilty and, to serve as a warning, had three hanged, one each in Jemez, Nambe, and San Felipe. Among those not executed but flogged was an Indian from San Juan (later Taos), Popé. The following year, Apaches destroyed farms and churches all over New Mexico and raided the pueblos. Piled on these hardships, the encomienda tribute demanded every year in May and October made the Pueblos more resentful than ever.

The struggle for survival increased tensions among the Spaniards as well and may explain the Franciscans' apparent loss of tolerance for Native religion and their crackdown on Pueblo ceremonials. The military expedient of hanging plotters and rebels was also given the cover of religion by concluding that the insurrectionists were in league with the devil. Meanwhile intensification of Apache raiding and continued squabbles between ecclesiastical and civil-military authorities demonstrated the weakness of disunity among the Hispanic population. Trying to avert disaster, fray Francisco de Ayeta traveled to Mexico City to obtain support for the colony. When he urged the establishment of a fifty-man presidio in Santa Fe, authorities sent his petition to Madrid. Ayeta loaded up the wagons with mission supplies and set out for El Paso. Before he arrived, the long-feared disaster struck.

The trouble had been brewing for a long time, and a number of factors came together to precipitate the Pueblo Revolt of 1680. The Spanish colonists were cognizant of resentment over the suppression of indigenous religion, famine, disease, and increased labor demands, all of which were elements of the Pueblos' decision to drive their oppressors out of New Mexico. Only later did the Spaniards learn of the presence of an

effective, charismatic leader in the person of Popé and of the careful plotting begun soon after Governor Treviño freed him in 1675.

In testimony taken after the uprising, the Spaniards pieced together the
story of the revolt. From his base of operations in Taos, Popé of San Juan,
Luis Tupatú of Picuris, and Jaca of Taos planned a revolt in which all of the
Pueblos except the Piros, as well as Apaches, Navajos, and Utes, were to
participate. Timing the date of the uprising, August 13, 1680, was accomplished through the use of a knotted cord, with one knot representing the
days remaining before the coordinated attack on the entire Spanish population. Relays of runners carried the cord to each pueblo. The surprise
was spoiled, however, when Indians revealed the plot in multiple locations. Popé reacted immediately and struck the Spaniards. Taos, Picuris,
and the Tewa pueblos attacked missions and farms at dawn on August 10.
Other pueblos followed within a few days as they learned of the revolt.

With an estimated population of sixteen thousand Pueblos and about
twenty-eight hundred Spaniards, the numerical odds were much in favor
of the attackers, as were the suddenness and fury of the assault. Governor
Antonio de Otermín estimated that 380 settlers died in the uprising,
including seventy-three adult males. Twenty-one Franciscan priests also
perished. The survivors gathered in Santa Fe and at Isleta Pueblo. Three
days after the beginning of hostilities, some Indians approached Santa Fe
with red and white crosses. They said that God and the Virgin Mary were
dead and the time had come for the King of Spain to surrender too.
Otermín was to choose. A red cross meant war, and a white cross indicated
that the Spaniards would abandon New Mexico. The governor responded
by attacking, driving the rebels back. The arrival of reinforcements forced
the Spaniards to retreat into the city. The Indians laid siege to Santa Fe for
five days, at which point Otermín counterattacked. In the vicious fighting,
the Spaniards claimed to have killed three hundred rebels and captured
another forty-seven, whom they promptly executed.

On August 21, Otermín decided to abandon Santa Fe. An estimated one
thousand people departed under the watchful eyes of the Pueblos, who
were content to allow the Spaniards to leave. As the refugees traveled
south, they passed by homes, pueblos, and churches, witnessing signs of
death and destruction all along the way. They arrived at Isleta six days
later, finding it empty. Alonso García had led fifteen hundred survivors
south to Fray Cristóbal after hearing that everyone upriver was dead. At
Alamillo, Otermín tried García for abandoning his post, but he was able

to sway the governor and save his life. There, too, Pedro de Leyba arrived with thirty men in the vanguard of Father Ayeta's supply caravan. By the end of September, the refugees were established in El Paso.

Meanwhile in New Mexico, Popé directed the destruction of all vestiges of Spanish civilization. He ordered the burning of crosses and church furnishings and forbade the use of the names Jesús and María. Men who had married in the church were to leave their wives and take others. Those who had been baptized were to ritually cleanse themselves by bathing in the river and scrubbing with soapweed. Likewise, they were to drop their baptismal names. Popé also commanded the wrecking of churches and the reopening and cleaning of kivas. Indians were not to speak Spanish or cultivate non-Indian crops. Finally, he executed those who failed to carry out his directives. In proclaiming God dead, Popé seemed to want to take his place. His rule quickly became oppressive, and Pueblo unity splintered. Old animosities between Pueblos returned, and once again the Apaches began to raid their neighbors, as did the Utes.

Back in El Paso, Otermín was smarting from his defeat. In November 1681 he led an army to attempt the reconquest of the lost province. The troops found that the Piros had abandoned the southern pueblos. The evidence suggested that churches had been ruined and kivas opened and then destroyed, perhaps at the hands of the Apaches. On December 6, Otermín captured Isleta after token resistance, and the Tiwas renewed their allegiance to the Spanish crown. The governor sent Juan Domínguez de Mendoza on north. He found unoccupied pueblos that were full of stores of maize, indicating that the inhabitants had only recently fled the approaching Spaniards. At Cochiti, Domínguez met a force of warriors. A tearful Alonso Catiti of Santo Domingo Pueblo asked for forgiveness and promised to return in peace the following day. When the rebel leader did not return, Domínguez hurried back to meet Otermín. The army remained for a week at Sandia Pueblo while Otermín conducted investigations into conditions in New Mexico. The Spaniards then withdrew to Isleta. Some Isletans fled to join the enemy, and in January 1682 Otermín decided to return to El Paso with the remaining Tiwas.

Succeeding governors made several unsuccessful attempts at reconquering New Mexico. In 1687, Pedro Reneros de Posada went as far north as Santa Ana, which he burned before returning to El Paso. Then in 1689, Domingo Jironza Petrís de Cruzate traveled to Zia. In a bloody daylong battle, the Spaniards killed more than six hundred of the defenders, many of whom died in their burning pueblo, and took about seventy prisoners. These assaults accomplished nothing more than to prove to the Spaniards that the Pueblos did not want them to return and to demonstrate to the Pueblos how determined the Spaniards were to reconquer them. Until that was possible, the New Mexico refugees clung to a precarious existence in El Paso.

THE NEW MEXICO OF DIEGO DE VARGAS

Although the exile in El Paso proved to be a long one, lasting a dozen years, the importance of restoring New Mexico to the Spanish crown was recognized soon after the Pueblos' successful rebellion. In a remarkable coincidence, one century after King Phillip II had issued a decree calling for the settlement of New Mexico in 1583, King Carlos II decreed in 1683 that the colony had to be restored. This time, however, there was no real expectation of finding wealth in the far north, even though rumors persisted of a mountain of silver located somewhere in New Mexico. As before, the Franciscan order was eager to work in the mission field among the Pueblos. As it had in the sixteenth century, imperial defense against European rivals was the prime reason given to recolonize New Mexico in the seventeenth century. For one, English and French pirates were stepping up their raiding on the Atlantic and Pacific coasts of New Spain in the 1680s. Authorities in New Spain perceived this activity as a threat to the mines of the north. In addition, French colonists under the command of René Robert Cavelier, Sieur de la Salle, established a short-lived colony on the Gulf coast, posing an even greater risk to Spain's New World possessions. To the traditional European foes were added such rebellious Native American peoples as the Tarahumaras, who had apparently followed the lead of the Pueblos in seeking to drive the Spanish from their lands.

Several individuals submitted proposals for the reconquest of New Mexico. Even though the sitting governor in 1689, Domingo Jironza Petrís de Cruzate, scored an impressive victory at Zia Pueblo, the job nonetheless went to Diego de Vargas, who took office in El Paso in February 1691. After completing a rapid military tour of the rebellious pueblos in 1692, Vargas set about resettling New Mexico in earnest in October 1693. The backbone of this recolonizing effort was those families who remained from the group that the Pueblos had forced out of New Mexico in 1680. These individuals constituted some seventy families. Joining them were an additional fifty-one people whom Vargas had recruited in the provinces of

Nueva Galicia and Nueva Vizcaya earlier in 1693. In all, Vargas's recolo-nizing expedition numbered around eight hundred. In the freezing cold of December, the colonists arrived in Santa Fe, which determined Pueblo Indians had occupied and fortified. When negotiations failed, Vargas led his men in a bloody, two-day battle and defeated the rebels. As an object lesson for all would-be enemies, Vargas had seventy of the Indian defend-ers executed and distributed four hundred men, women, and children among the colonists as servants, an act remarkably similar to Oñate's con-troversial sentence against the rebel Acomas in 1599.

The lesson was lost on the Pueblos. Within a matter of weeks after the battle of Santa Fe, New Mexico was a zone of open war. For the next nine months, Vargas fought a series of battles aimed at overcoming the Pueblos, most of whom had withdrawn onto defensible mesa tops, and forced them to return to their pueblos. At the same time, Vargas was waging a different sort of war in a very different arena. Having fashioned a toehold in New Mexico, Vargas repeatedly and insistently pressed his demands on author-ities in Mexico City for more colonists and more financial support for the newly established province.

Although he never got the five hundred families he thought necessary to safeguard New Mexico, Vargas did receive two sizable contingents of additional colonists. When news of the 1692 reconquest of New Mexico arrived in the viceregal capital, it facilitated the recruitment of the first group of colonists under the watchful eyes of the viceroy. Word of Vargas's triumph in New Mexico arrived in Mexico City at a time of crisis. Crop failure in the region the previous year had led to food shortages and high prices. A dry spring in 1692 made matters worse. Finally, in June of that year food riots erupted in the viceregal capital and spread to neighboring Puebla. Still, the joyous news of victory in New Mexico and the recruit-ment of colonists that began in 1693 offered hope of new beginnings. By September, sixty-six families and one unmarried man, a total of 232 people, had come forward to become New Mexico colonists. The fifteen-hundred-mile journey to Santa Fe in wagons was arduous and lasted until April 1694. The makeup of the group changed somewhat over the course of the trip: some fled the expedition, some died, others were born, and a few others joined. In all, 217 new settlers arrived in Santa Fe. Many of these colonists practiced trades, including blacksmiths, brick masons, carpenters, cartwrights, coppersmiths, cutlers, millers, painters, stone ma-sons, tailors, and weavers. There were also a miner, a musician, and a filigree maker. Most of these individuals were considered Spaniards, were married, and were of established character.

The final large group of colonists recruited in the Vargas era enlisted in Zacatecas in 1695. This recruitment was the subject of a scheme whereby Vargas's agent paid people to form fictitious family groups to defraud royal treasury officials. According to the recruiting documents, forty-six families consisting of 146 individuals signed up to become colonists. In fact, only twenty-five families and an additional twenty-one unmarried people departed Zacatecas for New Mexico. This group of ninety-eight colonists came from varied ethnic backgrounds, including Spaniards, mestizos, mulattos, and blacks. To house the growing population of New Mexico, Vargas engaged in frontier-style urban planning. When the colonists arrived from Mexico City, he accommodated them in the capital, Santa Fe, where he had earlier displaced the occupying Tano and Tewa rebels. Then in early 1695, with news that the group from Zacatecas was on the way, he decided to found a new town, three hours by horse north of Santa Fe. This new town, called the Villa Nueva de Santa Cruz, was only the third such *villa,* or chartered municipality, in New Mexico, after Santa Fe and El Paso. The families from Mexico City were relocated to the site of the Santa Cruz, forcing the Tano and Tewa Indians to move again.

Although in practical terms the designation meant little, the status of villa conferred certain rights and privileges on those communities. After 1692, New Mexico was decidedly more urban than pre-Revolt New Mexico, although individual residences in towns tended to be widely separated. The economy also underwent fundamental changes, particularly those related to landholding. The encomienda was not reinstituted after the revolt, and the estancia system was not revived. In its place, many of the new colonists became small farmers and stock raisers. Others, especially those recruited in Mexico City and Puebla, were of the artisan class, some even masters of their trades.

The winter of 1695–96 was a trying time for these new arrivals and for those with deep roots in the colony of New Mexico as well. Food was in such short supply that starvation threatened Spaniard and Pueblo. An epidemic of an unspecified illness also racked the community, with a number of colonists dying. More worrying still were persistent rumors of another revolt by the Pueblos. That rumor became a reality on June 4, 1696, when most of the Pueblos rose in an attempt to drive the Spaniards from New Mexico. In the initial burst of fury, five Franciscans and twenty-one settlers died at

Indian hands. Of note, the Towa pueblo of Pecos, the three Keresan pueblos of San Felipe, Santa Ana, and Zia, and the Tewa pueblo of Tesuque did not join in the revolt. The warfare lasted five months, until the harsh weather of November put a stop to campaigning. As had happened in 1694, Vargas's army fought a series of battles and sieges against the rebellious Pueblos, who again sought refuge on their mesa tops. As the war progressed, so too did the level of violence in the encounters; the Spaniards seemed determined to put down the revolt once and for all. Vargas spent most of the campaign in the field at the head of his forces, and when the war was over, overt Pueblo resistance was at an end. Pueblos who remained defiant departed the Rio Grande Basin and went to live among the Navajos or the Apaches.

Even though final defeat of the Pueblos brought a measure of peace to New Mexico, the society soon entered another period of fractious, internecine struggle. In July 1697, Pedro Rodríguez Cubero arrived in New Mexico to serve a term as governor. Given Diego de Vargas's contributions to the crown, especially the successful reconquest and recolonization of New Mexico, he was not inclined to hand over his post to his successor. After the incoming governor conducted the traditional review of his predecessor's term, which resulted in no charges against Vargas, Rodríguez Cubero was informed of a criminal complaint lodged against Vargas by the Santa Fe cabildo. There ensued a protracted series of legal maneuvers carried out in Santa Fe and before viceregal authorities in Mexico City. In the proceedings, the lawyers and agents of the former and sitting governor, as well as the cabildo, waged a paper war. In the course of the suits, more than three hundred New Mexico colonists testified against Vargas, accusing him of bad government, including misappropriation of royal monies and causing Indian unrest. Accusers also alleged that he and his cronies were living in sin with women in the governor's headquarters. The legal actions dragged on until early 1703, when Vargas was fully exonerated of all charges. In fact, it was determined that the crown owed him a balance of eighteen thousand pesos. Meanwhile in 1699, Vargas had received his reappointment as governor of New Mexico and by November was back in Santa Fe. Then, in late March 1704, he fell ill while campaigning and died in early April.

Diego de Vargas

No other figure dominates the historical landscape of Spanish colonial New Mexico in the way that its reconqueror and recolonizer, Diego de

Vargas, does. He began life in the Spanish capital, far from New Mexico. On November 8, 1643, in the church of San Luis in Madrid, Spain, María Margarita Contreras y Arraíz presented her son for baptism. He was given the name Diego José de Vargas Zapata Luján Ponce de León y Contreras. Evidently his father, Alonso de Vargas, was away from the Spanish capital on campaign. At the time of his birth, Diego de Vargas had an older brother, Lorenzo, and soon would have a baby sister, Antonia. When he was five, his mother died at age twenty-six. Unfortunately, Vargas was destined to grow up without either parent, for in 1650 his father secured royal appointment as alcalde mayor of Chiapa in the jurisdiction of Guatemala. Vargas's great-grandmother, Juana Venegas Ponce de León, accepted the responsibility of raising the children while their father sought his fortune in the New World. Brother Lorenzo died, probably in 1660, and within a couple of years Vargas's aged great-grandmother was also dead. At that time he was living with his father's cousins. The Madrid that Diego de Vargas knew as a boy in the 1650s was the capital of a great empire but was also judged the dirtiest capital in Europe. Along with the magnificent houses of the wealthy and the palaces of royalty, Madrid was home to crowded tenements lining filthy streets. Because it was one of the most important cities in Europe, its thoroughfares were filled with people from all over the continent and from all walks of life. Doubtless it was an exciting and dangerous place for a young boy.

The Vargas family owned a country place some thirty miles north of Madrid at Torrelaguna. There they escaped the oppressive summer heat of the capital. There too on May 5, 1664, Diego de Vargas wed Beatriz Pimentel de Prado Vélez de Olazábal. The union produced five children in six years, beginning in 1665, with the family spending most of their time at the country residence. In the meantime, Alonso de Vargas had remarried in the New World, taking as his bride a member of a prominent family in Guatemala. When Alonso died in 1666, Diego inherited his father's heavily encumbered properties in Spain and part of his substantial estate in Guatemala. Like so many Spaniards of his day, Diego de Vargas was land rich and money poor.

When he left Spain for the Indies in 1672, it was to settle his father's affairs and get his share of the sizable inheritance. Vargas obtained leave from the unit of the palace guard in which he was serving and an appointment as a royal courier to the viceroy of New Spain. Once in Mexico City, Vargas secured the post of *justicia mayor* of Teutila in the mountains of the

present-day Mexican state of Oaxaca. While serving in Teutila, Vargas received word that his wife had died suddenly in July 1674 in Spain. Her death may have influenced his decision to remain in New Spain and seek other posts in the royal service. Vargas held office in Teutila for two terms, until 1679, when he received an appointment as alcalde mayor of Tlalpujahua, a major mining district in highland Michoacán that produced gold and silver. Even while filling these posts, Vargas maintained a home in Mexico City. Within five years of the death of his wife in Spain, Diego de Vargas had begun a New World family with a woman he never married. Her identity remains a mystery, although the evidence suggests that she was Nicolasa Rincón. In addition, he was supporting his two half brothers born to his father and his second wife in Guatemala. Vargas established his siblings in Mexico City, sending one to the university there while he remained at his post in the mountains. By all accounts, Vargas was an able administrator in Tlalpujahua. During his five years in office, crown revenue from the mines tripled, and this success came to the attention of royal authorities. Still, Vargas was out of work in 1687, seeking higher office through his agent in Madrid.

In June 1688, for a payment of twenty-five hundred pesos, Diego de Vargas received title as political and military governor of New Mexico for a term of five years beginning the day he acceded to office. As governor of New Mexico, Vargas distinguished himself through his military daring and bureaucratic persistence, succeeding in his first term against remarkable odds. He thought that his achievements merited a lifetime appointment as governor of New Mexico, but the Spanish crown had no intention of making such a grant. Even when Pedro Rodríguez Cubero was named his successor, Vargas tried every legal ploy to prevent him from taking office. For Vargas, it was a matter of honor and pride that he should not be replaced. When his successor arrived in Santa Fe in July 1697, Vargas grew more obstinate. He was certain that his reappointment would arrive any day. In September the cabildo filed its complaint against Vargas, and in October,

FIGURE 3.3. Diego de Vargas to Isabel María de Vargas Pimentel, Santa Fe, September 30, 1698. Archivo del Marqués de la Nava de Barcinas, Madrid. From John L. Kessell, ed., *Remote Beyond Compare: Letters of don Diego de Vargas to His Family from New Spain and New Mexico, 1675–1706* (Albuquerque: University of New Mexico Press, 1989), p. 402.

Governor Rodríguez Cubero confined the former governor to his quarters. He remained under house arrest until July 1700, when he departed Santa Fe for Mexico City, where he personally took up his defense. In Mexico City, Vargas met his beloved son, Juan Manuel. Against his father's orders, Juan Manuel de Vargas had traveled from Spain to visit Diego. After an extended stay, Juan Manuel sailed for home in May 1702. His father provided for him so that on his return to Spain he traveled in high style, befitting a Spanish grandee. But Vargas's plans for the future of the house of Vargas came to nothing when he received word that his son had died of plague aboard ship in the passage from Veracruz to Havana. The loss devastated Vargas. It may have contributed to his decision to return to New Mexico.

Vargas's dogged insistence on holding on to the New Mexico governorship is puzzling when weighed against opinions he expressed about New Mexico. Writing to his family in Spain, Vargas described his service in New Mexico as exile in a kingdom "at the ends of the earth and remote beyond compare." Indeed, immediately after concluding the ceremonial reconquest in 1692, he had applied for posts in Guatemala, the Philippines, Chile, or the River Plate (present-day Argentina, Uruguay, and Paraguay)—in short, anywhere but New Mexico. Late in life, Vargas also expressed a desire to return to Spain and marry someone of his station.

These contradictions in Vargas's character were never resolved. He was strongly drawn to his homeland—very much a Spaniard in the New World—but also duty and honor bound to New Mexico. Perhaps after the loss of his son, this sense of duty was all he had left. Only such motives would explain why he chose to accept reappointment as governor of New Mexico. He had won his case in court and was to be repaid eighteen thousand pesos. In addition, the crown had approved an encomienda that would provide four thousand pesos in annual income. Yet at age sixty Vargas mounted his horse for the fifteen-hundred-mile trip back to New Mexico. He arrived in Santa Fe in November 1703. In late March of the following year, he led a campaign against the Apaches in the Sandia and Manzano Mountains. After Vargas spent several days in the field, a sudden illness struck him. Although he was taken to Bernalillo and put to bed, he did not respond to medication, dying on April 8, 1704. If his last wishes were followed, he was carried to Santa Fe and buried in the church in the main chapel under the platform where the priests stood.

Fortunately for historians, Diego de Vargas left a large body of personal correspondence. It is possible to gain insight into his character through his own words. Although he grew up without either parent, Vargas lived a sheltered life, dressing well, learning to dance, and attending bullfights. He obtained some formal education, about which he boasted, but not a university degree. Vargas's letters from New Spain to his family in Spain reveal him to have been a warm and loving father and a doting grandfather. His despair over the loss of his beloved son even led Vargas to consider taking his own life. Still, his deeds in New Mexico also reveal other facets of his character. He was a bold campaigner during the Pueblo-Spanish war in New Mexico, with a keen military mind. In war he was harsh, executing seventy of the enemy after the battle of Santa Fe and escalating the violence against the Pueblos as the armed struggle dragged on. But when he made peace with the rebellious Pueblos and offered them a pardon, he kept his word. Vargas was also prideful and arrogant. He credited his success to Our Lady of the Remedies, to whom he had a special devotion, but he brazenly claimed that his exploits in New Mexico merited a lifetime appointment as governor of the province, a suggestion that authorities in Mexico City scoffed at. When his successor arrived in Santa Fe, Vargas simply refused to leave office. He so infuriated the populace of the colony that many turned against him, begging for a replacement. When his perseverance won his reappointment as governor of New Mexico, his enemies feared retaliation. There is no indication, however, that he exacted vengeance, and his death was mourned in New Mexico. Only a few years after he died, an annual celebration in his honor began in Santa Fe that continues to this day.

CONCLUSION

Even though no annual festival honors Juan de Oñate, an impressive equestrian statue depicting him stands in Alcalde, an honor given to few Spaniards in New Mexico. His biographer, in heroic fashion, refers to Oñate as the last conquistador, and the expedition of 1598 was a conquest of sorts. In the period between 1598 and 1609 the Pueblos were militarily defeated and forced to accept Spanish rule. Yet as a financial operation, with Oñate arranging the funding with the expectation of a handsome return on his investment, the proprietary colony was a dismal failure. Oñate's prospecting failed to locate ore deposits, and no one got rich from the indigenous population, even though the Spaniards extracted labor, often on demand, and tribute from the Indians through the encomienda.

After Oñate, and with crown support, the Franciscans dedicated themselves to a spiritual conquest of the Pueblos. The Spanish civil-military authorities were at odds with the Franciscan authorities throughout much of the seventeenth century. The basis for this struggle was the desire of both sides to control the Pueblos. The Franciscans demanded their right to limit access to the Pueblos in order to convert them to Christianity. At the same time, the Spanish governors realized that access to the Indians as a source of labor was one of the few potential sources of wealth in New Mexico. This constant squabbling set a very bad example for the Pueblos of the benefits of Spanish culture, as did the practice of enslaving nomadic Indians. As midcentury neared, it appeared that civil war was about to erupt in the colony. Added to this turmoil, epidemic disease and drought assailed the colony. Perhaps as a result of the increasingly fierce struggle for survival, the Franciscans took an increasingly less tolerant view of Pueblo religion.

One of the Pueblo responses to civil unrest in the Spanish colony was to revolt. Beginning in the 1640s, there were several small revolts, involving different Pueblo peoples. The reaction of the Spaniards to these uprisings was harsh. Rebels were put to death, enslaved, or publicly beaten. Popé was one Pueblo leader who received such a flogging. When he united the Pueblos to drive out the Spaniards in 1680, they went to great lengths to erase every vestige of Spanish civilization. The Pueblos desecrated and destroyed churches, took ritual baths to undo baptism, slaughtered nonnative livestock, burned books and documents, and razed farms and ranches. Try as they might to rid themselves of the culture, however, the Pueblos had lived for several generations side by side with Spaniards, and many of the adaptations they had made to one another were enduring.

That such an accommodation had occurred became readily apparent when Diego de Vargas returned the Spaniards to New Mexico in 1693. Vargas first moved to reimpose military superiority over the Pueblos in a series of pitched battles and sieges, but it is doubtful that he could have done so without the help of Pueblo allies. Pueblo unity, one of the hallmarks of the dramatic events of 1680, had not survived long into the post-Revolt period. Simply put, some Pueblos preferred to cast their lot with the Spaniards when the invaders returned.

Revealingly, Vargas also relied heavily on the services of negotiators during his governorship. These individuals indicated how intertwined Pueblo and Spanish cultures had become before 1680; a number of

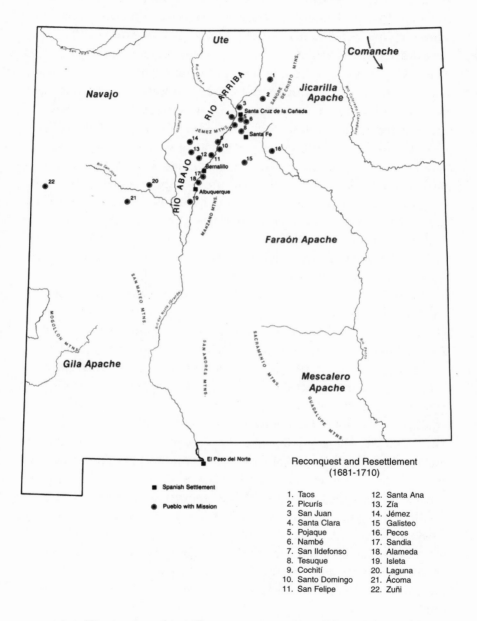

FIGURE 3.4. Reconquest and resettlement, 1681–1710. From Jerry Williams, *New Mexico in Maps* (Albuquerque: University of New Mexico Press, 1986), p. 99.

Spaniards spoke one or more Indian languages in addition to their native Spanish. Many Pueblos spoke Spanish as well as several Indian languages. Such facility with languages clearly indicated that the two peoples were intermingling socially and culturally. Moreover, both groups still remembered each other. Many of the returning colonists had friends among the Pueblos before the revolt. Some families had united in marriage across the cultural divide. In many other cases, they had learned each other's languages and lifeways. They exchanged such items as ceramics, food, furnishings, tools, and clothing. They also traded folkways and folk medicine. Likewise, Indians were often servants in Spanish homes and laborers on Spanish farms. Spaniard and Indian also traded the meager products of the land. Increasingly as time wore on, the two agricultural peoples fought together to defend their land and crops against raiding nomads, such as the Apaches, Navajos, Comanches, and Utes.

Clearly, then, the Pueblo Revolt of 1680 rent the fabric of Spanish New Mexico that Oñate and his colonists wove in the late sixteenth and early seventeenth centuries, but some of the shreds survived the dozen years of exile in El Paso. Most of the lasting threads were the families who returned to New Mexico with Vargas in 1693. They, in turn, were strengthened by subsequent waves of colonists who traveled north to New Mexico in the late seventeenth century and in later years. Here were the origins of much of the Hispanic population of New Mexico and Colorado and of Hispanic families in many other parts of the United States and northern Mexico. A truly remarkable number of the family names of settlers who came with Oñate or Vargas are still found among families who trace their lineages to these early colonists. No less noteworthy is that the culture they first brought with them to the region more than four hundred years ago is as alive and vibrant as it was when Juan de Oñate splashed across the Rio Grande in 1598 and when Diego de Vargas followed nearly a century later in 1692.

Almost a century separated the careers in New Mexico of Juan de Oñate and Diego de Vargas, yet their experiences were similar in many ways. Oñate came to New Mexico in search of riches, glory, and a bounty of souls for his religion. He was a man of the past, a conquistador when the time for such individuals had passed. After his sojourn in the colony resulted in his exile, Oñate doggedly sought to restore his honor. He was not entirely successful and remains a figure of controversy in New Mexico. He has his bronze statue, but it had a foot lopped off (since replaced) in memory of the Acoma victims. Juan de Oñate and the colonists who came with him had a spirit of adventure. In the succeeding years, a small elite of encomenderos dominated a sparsely populated colony. Those who remained after his departure also possessed a measure of determination difficult to imagine. In the face of civil unrest, disease, famine, and Indian revolts, the Spanish colonists persevered for more than ninety years. In that time, their religion, society, and culture took root deep in the New Mexican soil. But as Spanish civilization spread, Pueblo resentment grew. It finally exploded in the 1680 Pueblo Revolt, violently eradicating most vestiges of the invaders' presence.

Diego de Vargas was also a man of the past. The possibility of finding a silver mountain, as well as renown as reconqueror of the lost province, drew him to New Mexico. So too did the promise of thousands of Pueblo converts to his religion. Interestingly, Vargas proudly carried Oñate's original royal standard to New Mexico, a prized possession of the refugees of 1680. Vargas fared better in New Mexico than Oñate. His fame as reconqueror reached such heights that he was rewarded with a title of Spanish nobility. Even though the Pueblos today revile him for his actions in the Pueblo-Spanish war in the 1690s, and he has no bronze statue, he is not the subject of widespread controversy. Vargas tried to recruit colonists who would build a stable colony. Those who enrolled in Mexico City came largely from the artisan class. The settlers drawn from the mining areas around Zacatecas were primarily laborers and farmers. In post-Revolt New Mexico, these individuals initiated cottage industries based on their crafts and became small farmers. Since the conclusion of the war in 1696, Pueblos and Spaniards have been at peace. Over time the former foes came to rely on each other for mutual defense against marauding Apaches and Comanches and began to move toward a pragmatic adaptation to each other's ways.

Essay on Sources

The most approachable work on Juan de Oñate is Marc Simmons's *The Last Conquistador: Juan de Oñate and the Settling of the Far Southwest* (Norman: University of Oklahoma Press, 1991). This popular biography by one of the foremost historians of the Spanish Southwest draws from published sources, primary and secondary. Simmons's bibliographic essay is a good place to begin a search for additional material on Oñate. In addition, the basic texts for students of Oñate remain George P. Hammond and Agapito Rey's two-volume *Don Juan de Oñate: Colonizer of New Mexico, 1595–1628*

(Albuquerque: University of New Mexico Press, 1953). Hammond and Rey gathered, translated, and edited documents related to Oñate and the years he served in New Mexico.

The history of Oñate's New Mexico through the eyes of a participant and poet is available in *Historia de la Nueva México, 1610/Gaspar Pérez de Villagrá: A Critical and Annotated Spanish/English Edition*. This important original source has been translated and edited by Miguel Encinias, Alfred Rodríguez, and Joseph P. Sánchez (Albuquerque: University of New Mexico Press, 1992).

Recently there has been renewed interest in studying the names and backgrounds of the individuals who came to New Mexico with Oñate. This burgeoning research is an outgrowth of the explosion of interest in Hispanic genealogy in the United States. Two works in this vein are worthy of mention. Archaeologist David H. Snow has published a compilation of every individual—some 560—he has been able to identify among the colonists who accompanied Oñate and those who joined him in New Mexico in the early seventeenth century. This work, *New Mexico's First Colonists: The 1597–1600 Enlistments for New Mexico under Juan de Oñate, Adelante* [sic] *and Gobernador* (Albuquerque: Hispanic Genealogical Research Center of New Mexico, 1998), is the product of painstaking combing of the published record. Genealogist José Antonio Esquibel's "The People of the Camino Real: A Genealogical Appendix" in *The Royal Road: The Camino Real from Mexico City to Santa Fe*, with photographs by Christine Preston, text by Douglas Preston and José Antonio Esquibel (Albuquerque: University of New Mexico Press, 1998), is a useful study of the families who peopled New Mexico in the colonial period, including Oñate's and Vargas's colonists. This listing goes beyond genealogy to suggest new directions for social historians interested in such issues as marriage and the family.

Two pioneering works by France V. Scholes, *Church and State in New Mexico, 1610–1650* (Albuquerque: University of New Mexico Press, 1937), and *Troublous Times in New Mexico, 1659–1670* (Albuquerque: University of New Mexico Press, 1942), remain essential to the study of pre-Revolt New Mexico. Carroll L. Riley's *Rio del Norte: People of the Upper Rio Grande from the Earliest Times to the Pueblo Revolt* (Salt Lake City: University of Utah Press, 1995) traces the history of the Pueblos up to the 1680 Pueblo Revolt. John L. Kessell's *Kiva, Cross, and Crown: The Pecos Indians and New Mexico, 1540–1840* (Albuquerque: University of New Mexico Press, 1987), and Ramón A. Gutiérrez's *When Jesus Came, the Corn Mothers Went Away: Marriage, Sexuality, and Power in New Mexico, 1500–1846* (Stanford, Calif.: Stanford

University Press, 1991), cover the entire Spanish colonial and Mexican periods in New Mexico and are especially useful on the early seventeenth century.

The basic text of the Pueblo Revolt is Charles W. Hackett's *Revolt of the Pueblo Indians of New Mexico and Otermin's Attempted Reconquest, 1680–1682,* trans. Charmion C. Shelby (Albuquerque: University of New Mexico Press, 1942). A very readable account of the revolt is Andrew L. Knaut's *The Pueblo Revolt of 1680: Conquest and Resistance in Seventeenth-Century New Mexico* (Norman: University of Oklahoma Press, 1995). *What Caused the Pueblo Revolt of 1680?* (Boston: Bedford/St. Martin's, 1999) is a book of readings selected and introduced by David J. Weber, in which five historians offer different views of the Pueblo Revolt.

The fundamental work on Diego de Vargas and his era in New Mexico is the multivolume, documentary edition *The Journals of don Diego de Vargas,* published by the University of New Mexico Press. These volumes of translated and heavily annotated documents are the work of John L. Kessell and his colleagues at the Vargas Project. To date, five of six volumes have been completed: *Remote Beyond Compare* (1989), *By Force of Arms* (1992), *To the Royal Crown Restored (1995), Blood on the Boulders (1998),* and *That Disturbances Cease* (2000). The only narrative of the Vargas period remains J. Manuel Espinosa's *Crusaders of the Rio Grande: The Story of Don Diego de Vargas and the Reconquest and Refounding of New Mexico* (1942; Salisbury, N.C.: Documentary Publications, 1977). More recently, Espinosa has published a collection of documents about the events of 1696, *The Pueblo Revolt of 1696 and the Franciscan Missions in New Mexico: Letters of the Missionaries and Related Documents* (Norman: University of Oklahoma Press, 1988). A new synthesis of the Spanish period is Carroll L. Riley's *The Kachina and the Cross: Indians and Spaniards in the Early Southwest* (Salt Lake City: University of Utah Press, 1999).

The recruiting of colonists for New Mexico in the Vargas era has been the subject of two recent books: John B. Colligan, *The Juan Páez Hurtado Expedition of 1695: Fraud in Recruiting Colonists for New Mexico* (Albuquerque: University of New Mexico Press, 1995), and José Antonio Esquibel and John B. Colligan, *The Spanish Recolonization of New Mexico: An Account of the Families Recruited at Mexico City in 1693* (Albuquerque: Hispanic Genealogical Research Center of New Mexico, 1999). These two studies, particularly the latter, are primarily of interest to genealogists, but both contain significant information on the human dimension of the history of Spanish colonial New Mexico.

4

Juanotilla of Cochiti, *Vecina* and *Coyota*
Nuevomexicanas in the Eighteenth Century

DEENA J. GONZÁLEZ

*P*retend to peer, as if out toward a horizon, across landscapes. Imagine history like a play moving along in time, coming alive, even among places or people dating back three or four hundred years. Coming into focus, as if through binoculars, is the fascinating world of the far-northern empire of New Spain, today's upper New Mexico river valleys. About thirty thousand people made their home there in the late 1700s, occupying an area a few hundred miles wide. Along a stretch of today's Rio Grande, then known as El Río Bravo de el (del) Norte, people built towns and villages. In the spring and summer, with the snow thawing high above the Sangre de Cristo Mountains, the river would run full. In the winter, it tended to dry and cake, allowing shepherds and horsemen to cross it easily, uniting people rather than separating them. Crops, hides, and tallow (for candles) were loaded onto burros and horses to trade along ancient routes established by the first residents of the area, the indigenous people who had created ways of life as diverse as their cultures.

If a contemporary camera were to examine this era and region, it should begin with firsthand documents. More than any other sources, the documents of the time reveal people's thoughts, ideas, and values. In the Rio Grande towns and villages, these would be kept at the local church or in a dusty room close to the government's offices. Thousands of pieces of paper containing announcements, statements, or land deeds survive from this period. Sometimes the documents would be taken out of storage to be

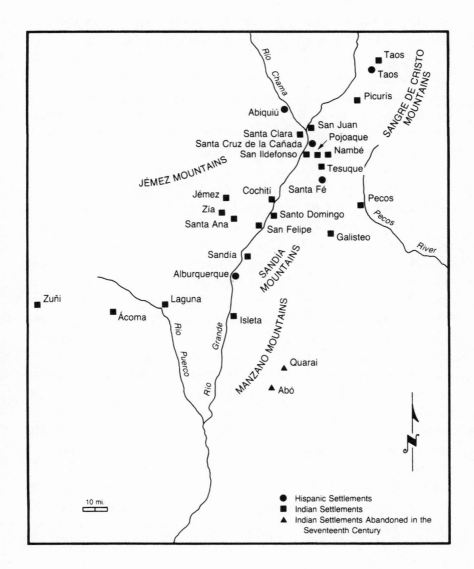

FIGURE 4.1. Principal Indian and Hispanic Settlements of the Eighteenth Century. From Charles Cutter, *Protector de Indios* (Albuquerque: University of New Mexico Press, 1986), p. 59.

read in the presence of witnesses or before other authorities, as was the case with wills or testaments.

To imagine the meaning attached to the written record is not difficult, given how well preserved these records remain even today. The story in this chapter focuses on the will of one woman from an indigenous or Indian pueblo. Cochiti, her community, was situated south of Santa Fe. The person who actually filed the will or testament of five pages was a military officer, Joachin Codallos y Rabal. He played a major role in political matters during the 1740s because he was a "captain-general" and in some documents of the era is identified as the governor. The woman, Juanotilla, was not well known. Such persons would usually not appear in history books. It is precisely the ordinary details of this will or document, and of her life, however, that make her story worth telling.

In the document that Sr. Codallos y Rabal (known as don Joachin and not Joaquín) certified in Santa Fe on August 5, 1747, Juanotilla is identified as "Juanotilla *coyota*," that is, a mixed-race person of Spanish and Indian or indigenous heritage. The word was not acceptable to everyone; that explains why it appears here in quotation marks or in italics. Although some would not use the term themselves, Juanotilla's mixed ethnicity or ancestry was nevertheless common, as it is today among many New Mexicans. Such issues make Juanotilla's story interesting because she and others were identified in the eighteenth century by ethnicity and race. It might also be assumed that as a coyota, she was probably poor. Or was she?

The long, complex colonial period (1598–1821) of New Mexican history can be depicted through the typical economic and racial hierarchies imposed under the Spanish system of governance. But royalty and the wealthy governors or officials were usually not of mixed-race origin. The poor often were of indigenous or African ancestry or combinations of the same. Altogether, more than fifty-four racial categories ranked people, from pure-blooded Spaniards (called *limpios,* a rare occurrence) to African-appearing Indians (or *zambos*). This was as true in the cities as it was on the frontiers of New Spain. Clearly a person's racial, economic, and social status helped determine how that person was treated or lived in the 1700s. Other factors were equally critical.

Historians usually stress the elite men who ruled the province—men like Codallos y Rabal, whose name appears prominently in court and church records. Men's roles can be overemphasized, however, and that of women ignored. One of don Joachin's duties, as captain-general, was to ensure that

Juanotilla's wishes were settled as the crown or court demanded. After all, this was her last will and testament, and she intended to leave her children their proper inheritance, even if they were Pueblo Indians from Cochiti or of mixed heritage as she was. In traditional history, don Joachin's important role would be emphasized, but Juanotilla's might have been depicted as less significant because of her race and gender. Both parties, the officer and the mixed-race person, however, played critical roles in the society of their time. It is also useful to remember that in the eighteenth century and since, women were a majority of the population.

Living within rather rigid rules regarding the social order, people resided in segregated communities. Organized into separate towns that the Spanish had called "pueblos," Native residents often clustered along waterways where they governed themselves. They were also governed by tradition. They retained their own names for their towns: for example, Tesuque and Pojoaque. Other locations the Spanish governors insisted on renaming with Catholic saints' names, such as San Juan, San Ildefonso, or St. John and St. Alphonse. In fact, respect for change became one of the hallmarks of the Pueblo peoples. Without changes, they and later the Hispano-Indio-blended descendants would never have survived.

Many sources detail vividly this organized New Mexican world of the 1700s. Here a woman's testament illustrates how much can be extracted from one source and why documents are important to New Mexico's past. Making one source the primary focus of discussion for this period inverts the traditional method of historical writing. Local history becomes rich and sublimates the more powerful governmental interests that generally gain central attention. Careful investigation of each detail in Juanotilla's testament, whether told from an officer's perspective or from the will maker's, reveals a different aspect of history.

Juanotilla's testament is one of the least contentious in the archives; no controversy surrounded her will. As other examples from the 1700s indicate, the records of the Catholic Church, the local courts, and private family papers plotted the social interactions of the time, including difficult and treacherous relations. Many topics—family feuds, Catholics versus non-Catholics, fighting and plotting, Indians versus Spanish—fill the court dockets and provide historians with a steady supply of interesting stories of what wrongs were committed, of what values people then upheld.

Spanish-speaking Catholics had begun arriving in the Pueblo world with Juan de Oñate's first colonization in 1598. Later Nuevo Mejico, under the Bourbon kings of Spain, who dominated the eighteenth century, was organized as a province or a department. The Spanish thought they were destined to assume control over the indigenous peoples who had lived in New Mexico for many previous centuries. In this outpost of the Spanish empire, military governance played a major role in affairs of state but also in church matters and in local politics. The military officials, including Codallos y Rabal, served by appointment of the king and queen. The governing Bourbons approved military and church rulers alike, sending them where they were most needed or helped solidify the interests of the crown. For New Mexico, this task included subduing Indians who refused to obey royal edicts or the Spanish military and legal systems.

One royal appointee, José de Gálvez, paid an official visit in the 1760s to assess the northern frontier areas and determine their governance. Although dignitaries representing the crown appeared infrequently on the scene, de Gálvez's visit was loaded with meaning. It determined the course of people's lives when he recommended more military officers and different priests. He moved on toward Tucson, making recommendations that also removed the Jesuits entirely from the northern provinces. Such extraordinary power was a direct result of de Gálvez's close relationship with the king, Charles III. Ordinarily captains and generals, lieutenants and enlistees, as much as priests and a few nuns, viewed their assignments to the far-northern frontier areas as punishments rather than as arenas for any real power. Few ever thought to remain permanently in remote parts of the world. Unlike de Gálvez, however, whose visit was officially mandated and driven by observances that the king wanted confirmed, the majority of officers and appointed minor officials never left New Mexico. De Gálvez's actions resulted in the expulsion of the Jesuit priests. In regions such as New Mexico, where priestly authority was slowly being curtailed, de Gálvez's report furthered the agendas of the crown at the expense of the Catholic Church.

The lack of interest in taking up residency by other appointees did not mean the government was lax or not serious about collecting information. A permanent, written record was a necessity in legal as in religious matters. In his report to the king and to the officials in Mexico, de Gálvez noted local conditions, remarked on the weather, and commented on the people. Respect for de Gálvez's report, as for all written material, remained a high priority in political decisions. This esteem trickled down from the highest echelons to local offices.

The court case examined here, a document bearing the final wishes of the mixed-race Pueblo/Spanish-named woman Juanotilla, demanded the utmost regard and attention. Its importance is evident in the five carefully worded pages that remain from her 1747 testament and detail her life. She lived outside the pueblo of Cochiti, a word "Hispanicized" from the indigenous name in the Keresan language, Ko-fe-te. The Spanish could not pronounce Keresan properly and changed the word to "Cochiti." Juanotilla died leaving several heirs, sons and daughters, nieces and nephews, who would inherit her property. She was a wealthy woman with large herds of animals and several pieces of land or property. Animals and pasturelands like Juanotilla's were possibly the clearest measure of any person's worth in eighteenth-century New Mexico, but so was the name a person was given. Names such as *lobo,* coyote, or mestizo signaled a rank in the ethnic hierarchy, from low to high.

Other features play equally significant roles in the story of Juanotilla, whose life we piece together from an ordinary document. Testaments or wills in northern New Mexico emphasized how geography served to unite people and anchored destinies. Mountains and rivers were critical to survival, but for a specific reason. The mountains provided fresh game and also were the chief source for water, for crops raised in the valleys in the summer months. Pasture lands like Juanotilla's were fed by the main artery, the river, and sustained communities but could also be used in the busy trade market that developed around the pueblos. Cow hides were traded for buffalo or bear skins, beef for blankets or rugs. A person's livestock and pastures played a major role in the colonial New Mexican economy. Women's as well as men's wealth was measured by how many animals and how much land was owned. Both counted, and in Juanotilla's case, her numerous cows and other herds afforded her a status higher than that of other people.

A single phrase from the testament of Juanotilla, *"de calidad coyota,"* or of coyote status, obscures all of the complexity involved in her ethnicity. It also masks Juanotilla's class or economic rank. Only by reading carefully her specific wishes and detailing her property can historians rank her economic worth as higher than that of many. Finally, the will does not reveal whether she was Spanish dominant or spoke mainly Keresan. Bilingualism would also cause her status to rise. Each of these details is significant to unraveling the social history of the period.

Another important point regarding language and the names given to land, space, or communities is that gender has always been part of this story.

FIGURE 4.2. Pintura de castas, *De indio y mestizo produce coyote,* by José de Páez, oil on canvas, circa 1780.

Gender meant male and female, maleness and femaleness, masculinity and femininity, and more; under the Pueblo systems, and that of many other indigenous groups, third-sex or two-spirited people were also allowed. Such persons adhered not to one or the other of the two sexes, but to a combination of both. They too are mentioned in the documents of the period.

Gender, like race or class status, balanced Juanotilla's life. Critical to discussions about women or men was an underlying fact that sex was the biological extension of gender, but not everyone fell neatly into organized camps of maleness or femaleness. Colonial New Mexico court decisions reported improper sexual conduct, and warring families often accused women or men of not fulfilling their correct roles as wives, husbands, or parents. Just as historians need to seek out more details to understand the life of one woman, Juanotilla, or one status, coyota, students of history need to complicate their understandings of male and female in the social order because without complexity, the images remain skewed or unrealistic.

Gender was very much a social construction. What made someone male or female came together in biologically and socially determined spheres, in what society said was suitable for men or women. Adultery was considered inappropriate, as was wife abuse. The court and church cited many instances and punishments for both. The reports, however, also serve as reminders of who had access to the legal system. Juanotilla was able to render her final will. Under eighteenth-century Spanish laws and codes, she was entitled to construct such a document and file it in court. Under the same customs, and despite the lower-ranking status coyota implies, she and all women generally maintained a standing in the legal structure.

In eighteenth-century, colonial New Mexico, the sex-gender system of political and legal governance considered it fitting for women to file wills and record many types of complaints in courts. Adultery as well as beatings, threats, or other forms of violence was duly noted and recorded. Such rights were granted throughout the Spanish Empire but were uncommon in the English-speaking world. There, the sex-gender system dictated that women leave legal affairs to men. Women could not sue or be sued in a court of law, unlike the Spanish system, where these actions were perfectly acceptable. Juanotilla's will and her act of filing her testament are not to be taken as odd; the document was proper for her era.

In the case of an eighteenth-century New Mexican's world, gender organized more than testaments, however. Then as today gender identities evoked land and space; maleness and femaleness were inherently part of the economic as well as social processes at work in this world of Native and Hispanic. Some Pueblo peoples were matriarchal, and ancestry was traced through the female line. In some communities, living and housing arrangements were also matrilocal, organized by women.

Social and economic power could be measured both in symbolic terms and concretely, in material worth or value. The river into which streams poured, for example, which anchored the social and political livelihoods of many, was known as "El Río Bravo del Norte," a masculine-sounding name. *El* Río Bravo was termed a "he," perhaps even an "it"; this big or brave river stood in sharp contrast to the more feminized regional place naming of the territory. People referred to New Mexico as part of the Spanish Empire, which they called *el reyno,* masculine for, in English, a neutral-sounding phrase, "the reign," or empire. It was the center of all governance and of state functions. By contrast, the land or territory north of that center, in this case, New Mexico, was feminized as *la provincia.*

Similarly *la Nueva México,* or "she, the province of New Mexico," was rendered feminine. He, a river, and she, the land, organized life for Spanish-speaking and indigenous people who viewed this area with healthy political respect for balance.

Northern New Spain assumed the feminine construction in official reports written in Spanish. After 1848, when Euro-Americans arrived, gender-neutral New Mexico, not male or female, sufficed. Anglicized, the territory kept the older terminology while adapting to the new.

Revealingly, colonial politics was shaped as much by gender as by ethnicity and by both men and women like Codallos y Rabal and Juanotilla. Women, once afforded a stake in legal codes and court systems, were considered important, even if they could not vote or be appointed to official positions. Moreover, ethnic, racial, gender, and class status anchored life because they revealed hierarchies in the social order, some of which lasted centuries. Many years after Juanotilla's story, the Euro-American migrants to the Borderlands area, although imposing their own Anglicized vocabulary, relied on Spanish for words such as *pueblo* for "town," *río* for river, or *pueblo* for a specific type of Indian community. They changed the *nuevo* to "New" while retaining "Mexico" (without the accent) in their name for the region they conquered. They dropped the rest of the name the Spanish had given Cochiti (San Buenaventura de Cochiti) but kept the Hispanicized term for Juanotilla's village and culture.

Just as words or names changed, concepts about women's rights and positions were altered to suit shifting political agendas whereas other words or names reflected unchanging hierarchies or social codes. After 1848, when the United States conquered New Mexico, women could no longer use the courts in the same way and were expressly forbidden to do so by the federal and territorial court system transplanted to New Mexico. Another way to look at this, however, is to understand that for more than two centuries, Spanish-speaking and indigenous women, like Juanotilla, had accessed legal codes and the local courts. The authority and power deriving from such societal and political regard cannot be underestimated: they make Juanotilla's case, along with the cases of at least two hundred other women who filed papers or documents in court in the same decades, valuable. Even one document, a will or a complaint, can serve as a window into this eighteenth-century New Mexican world, where women shaped their own lives.

Repeating "Juanotilla, la coyota," over and over, as was the custom with names in Spanish, produced a certain cadence or rhythm. The will does not mention her Keresan name. Whether of English or Spanish origin, indigenous or not, the terms mattered because they indicate the political shifts across the centuries and influenced frontierspeople who inhabited these lands of the north. By the eighteenth century, the Spanish language dominated. As we will see, a person like Juanotilla was more than her name. The Bourbons of Spain ruled to unify a crumbling empire even when this meant subduing Pueblo interests. They were, after all, creating an empire designed to withstand attacks from enemy nations, including the many Indian groups hostile to the crown. That Juanotilla was mixed blood advanced the interests of the crown because the military officials could presume that unlike the mobile, "unsettled" Apaches or Navajos, people like Juanotilla would not join raids on settlements. And the officers attempted to convince the authorities of the need for cooperation from everyone in this critical task. Even the role of the rather independent Catholic Church, according to royal governance, was subsumed to help settle military issues. Thus the last will and testament of women like Juanotilla became relevant to local governing officers, as it reinforced royal concerns voiced by the highest authorities.

Women are always present in histories, albeit not always center stage; nevertheless, they are important in telling a more complete story. In the event that unfolded in this part of New Spain on August 5, 1747, the filing date of Juanotilla's last will, the male witnesses and officials could not escape that Juanotilla was both a woman and a mixed-blood Indian. She embodied her name, her ethnicity, *and* her class.

In this document, we are introduced initially to the male figure, a man who seems imposing, larger than life. Consider his name and title. He was governor and captain-general, his title and name pompous and official sounding: Governador y Capt.-Gen. don Joachin Codallos y Rabal. We can imagine him entering the court or, rather, what then would have passed as a courtroom. Most likely, it was a small room with an aging table, a rough-looking chair, a small window or door, a compacted, dirt floor. Despite its antiquity, the room became the site for depositing official-sounding documents with a man in uniform whose entitlements were as long as his name. In this case, the paper he carried was an inventory and a testimony. It listed to the letter of the law one ordinary woman's final wishes— Juanotilla, a coyota, officially emphasizing her mixed ancestry, as she was labeled in this testament carrying the following title page:

Imbentario y diligencias sobre la distribucion de los vienes que quedaron por fin y muerte de Juanotilla coyota, vecina del Pueblo de San Buena Bentura de Cochiti, en la forma que adentro se expresa, VSA

(Inventory and listing of the distribution of the property that remained after the death of Juanotilla, coyota, resident of the Pueblo of [Saint] San Bonaventure of Cochiti, in the form expressed herein, VSA ["Inc."])

Care was taken in the document following the above introductory page, to which the governor attached his signature. It indicated dates, witnesses, and specific requests on the first two, precious sheets of paper, followed by two others regarding the satisfactory execution of Juanotilla's final wishes. Fortunately, people cared for documents and did not take lightly writing on good paper or using ink superfluously. Both were hard to come by and in great demand in a society that required people to put their complaints on paper or witness all official documents with signatures and statements, seals and testimonies.

Juanotilla's inventory and testament, as an official court document, and the presence of a man and a woman, form the ingredients necessary for this interesting human drama. These are illuminating sources for re-creating the social history of northern New Mexico in the mid-eighteenth century. Although the documents are but a few pages with a few details and most people could not read or write Spanish, the wills and testaments of women overflow with poetry, rhythm, and revelation.

The writer, Juan Vigil, dispersed Juanotilla's worldly possessions. He said that, in the language of his era, "said deceased" person named as her proper heirs four legitimate children, "conceived in holy matrimony," including "one male, the others female." After taking care of the requests made, Juan Vigil ambled along in the document about the "named deceased Juanotilla." First he stated that "alms for her soul" had been proffered. Next Vigil began describing the will's inventory, listing many types of animals and implements as well as relatives.

Not quite two decades after Juanotilla's will was filed, in 1762, another will maker, Juana Lujan, mimicked a pattern found in testaments even more common than Juanotilla's. Lujan dictated her wishes and used spiritual terms and prayer to begin her request: "In the Name of God, Amen. Hear ye, this, my final words and testament, voluntarily given, I, Juana

Lujan Diego, who believe in the Mystery of the Holy Trinity, Father, Son, and Holy Spirit, three distinct persons, whose son became man in the pure and holy womb of the Virgin Mother . . . and under whose faith I profess I wish to live and die." Catholic devotion rises in this will and dominates the remainder of the text as well. Attention to format, to style, and to grace is evident. "Knowing that death comes to all creatures, and finding myself as I do, in my sickbed, because of an accident God has willed and sent to me, . . . but of sound mind," Juana Lujan continued. The lyrical quality of the Spanish words mark the document as an important event, one performed in the presence of many people, including the scribe, the witnesses, and several others. In Lujan's case, much was at stake because she was an extremely wealthy woman. Whether the will maker was rich or poor, the same features prevailed—faith, orderliness, and *then* the declarations of property.

Men's interests were also duly recorded in the records of the time and were particularly prominent when the will maker was deceased. The contrast between the opening paragraph of Lujan's will with Juanotilla's is striking: "Chief Officer and Leading Authority, Mr. Joachin Codallos y Rabal, Governor and Captain-General of Santa Fe, sovereignty of New Mexico, Spaniard and overseer of military operations and forts for New Mexico, as I have been notified that at the Pueblo of St. Bonaventure of Cochiti a woman has died, of coyote status [*calidad*] known by the name of Juanotilla, of whom four children remain as her proper heirs, and no others."

The document, written by the officer charged to gather the oral testimony, then details specific and final wishes. Following Codallos y Rabal's signature at the bottom of the report were those of two others, Joseph Romo de Sena and Miguel de Alarid, who like the captain-general signed off with a flourish, creating something like a seal after their names.

Literacy played a significant role in eighteenth-century New Mexico, but there were ways to compensate for illiteracy, as Juanotilla's testament amply demonstrates. Even people who could not read or write left records. Her testament stated that Juanotilla had four children described as her "true heirs." Her final wishes served to document her life through details whose sum go even further. Although historians might not be able to describe Juanotilla's physical appearance, relationships, and the property, this document humanized Juanotilla. Thus the label *coyota* begins to sound too animalistic and inappropriate to the task of determining how or why her will is significant.

Another purpose is served in examining closely her will because it allows us to see Juanotilla more completely beyond what can be conveyed by one word. Ethnic labeling and classification in eighteenth-century New Mexico helped order social relations, but the categories also obscured how communities were organized. To call someone common, poor, or of mixed racial ancestry could not begin to convey a person's value to her village or family.

Juanotilla's last will and testament did not become a cause célèbre. It did not involve murder or assault—of which there were many at this time. Yet the few pages detailing Juanotilla's life provide an interesting glimpse of life in the 1700s. Here a colonial official filed a report at court in which he stated that he was about to take action because [he] had "been notified that in the Pueblo of San Buenaventura de Cochiti a resident, of coyota status and known by the name, Juanotilla, has expired." With flourish, gusto, and a pen in hand, the literate governor signed his two-page report. He was laying to rest this woman's final wishes as her testament required. Duty, obedience, and authority—his toward her wishes—were bound up in an individual's actions.

At center stage, then, is a woman of mixed status and race. She comes into the record through her first name only and a will but also through a final act, death. She resides in that record as a contrast, especially to the governor known through various titles. He occupies several positions, political and military. Many officials of this era were political appointees and military officers. His surname also displays both sides of his lineage, Codallos y [and] Rabal, his mother's and father's. But she is known simply as Juanotilla.

Juanotilla's village signifies and replicates another mantra then familiar to people about name and status, place and space: the governor-captain and a coyota. Male and female. An official and a resident. Even the renamed village of Cochiti was labeled "el Pueblo," following Spanish preferences that lent communities masculine or feminine identity.

One needs to ask at this point: Does the labeling make Juanotilla, without a surname, a simple woman, less important than the celebrated officials of the court? Hardly, as other facts embedded in the document reveal. First, she lived near a pueblo, and in New Mexico that meant an indigenous community to which she was probably linked through her mother or father's family. Because she was mixed race, she lived some distance from her relatives, not *inside* the pueblo's walls, but just outside. She was not ostracized, that we know. It was common for mixed-race people to settle around the cluster of Pueblo Indian communities, whereas those who belonged to the clans and the central political families lived within pueblo walls.

Many people of mixed inheritance lived in proximity to their families of origin. Others worked for wages outside the pueblo among the elite Spanish-speaking families, for example, in Santa Fe. Those who intramarried (marriage within their group or sphere) tended to live in the pueblos. Those who intermarried (between a Native or an Indian and a Spanish-speaking resident) lived close by but were not necessarily residents of a pueblo. Their partners were considered outsiders, and the pueblo was constructed to protect identity, not confuse it.

The governor called Juanotilla a *vecina,* or resident. The special designations, racial and ethnic, political and social, about who was a "real" pueblo resident or who was a nonresident concerned eighteenth-century New Mexicans. Masculinity and femininity also mattered. Codallos y Rabal was not just saying that Juanotilla lived near her pueblo. He was not just saying that she was a mixed-race person. He was determining a legal status for her, based on her residency and her ethnicity.

These titles or categories emanated from the crown, the government, and even the Catholic Church. Throughout Spain and its empire, the rules were understood under different terms, such as *Las Leyes de las Castas,* or the Laws of the Castes. *Coyote* was a castelike term: it designated racial and ethnic origin. It supposedly defined where people were situated economically as well as socially. There were exceptions, as Juanotilla proved. In addition, the Pueblos also had their classification schemes. For them, membership in the community was determined by the ancient laws of ancestry, of clanship, of skills and talents. Unfortunately, Spanish ignorance of the Indian classifications was neglectful or disrespectful, so few of the indigenous terms surface in the archives.

Juanotilla and few others of this era escaped the hierarchies based on race or ethnicity. Although life's exigencies, such as intermarriage across ethnic lines, shaped the designations, the language on official documents suggests rigid classification schemes. The terms were organized like pyramids, with the vast majority of common and poor people at the bottom, including Indians, mestizos, and other mixed-race populations. Moving up the pyramid, the Spanish Catholics of varied classes constituted ever smaller layers. At the top of the pyramid were those officials and dignitaries like our upper-class governor/captain-general. The authorities referred to Juanotilla by just her first name or her racial or ethnic status.

What her name was in Cochiti's language we are left to wonder. Yet the name of Juanotilla obviously derived from the Catholic Juan/John. Was she a Catholic? The testament suggests that she was. She owned saints and bequeathed them to her heirs, a strong hint about her religious affiliation. Religious persuasion was important in eighteenth-century New Mexico because it determined a person's rights and privileges. Catholics could file wills, for example, in court and in the church. This practice made their final wishes more secure or provided checks and balances to authorities who might bend the documents in their favor.

Witnesses to Juanotilla's specific requests in the will also reveal much about the official status a person held. The assistants, Andres Montoi[y]a and Gregorío Garduño, were designated *"españoles de mi asistencia,"* or "Spaniards [Hispanos] of my assistance," in other words, observers. Their role was critical to the presentation and preservation of this testimony.

Traditional practices of reciting the names of attestants remained important on a number of other levels. The point was not merely proprietary or about displaying good manners. Designation and labeling were significant to the Spanish government. Census forms inquired about race and attempted to categorize people racially or ethnically. To historians of colonial New Mexico, the old practice of insisting on documenting a person by race or ethnicity suggests that racializing a person or group was an important task, but its meaning, as seen in Juanotilla's case, extends beyond the court officer's original purposes.

In Juanotilla's lifetime, racial status held symbolic and political meanings. For the illustrious governor/captain-general and others like him, she was of lower rank, of lower social status to his more elevated, "respected," and Spanish-derived status. Her ranking was not simply a marker of "low" or "high," however, because both persons needed each other. To be of higher rank, don Joachin needed Juanotilla.

On the other hand, did Juanotilla really need don Joachin? It is not clear how many others like her within Cochiti Pueblo were also termed *coyota,* how many others were of mixed-race origin or had married outside their pueblo. Censuses then did inquire and track ethnicity, as they do today. But these documents were often incomplete, overlooking sections of entire communities, and thus must be interpreted cautiously. In addition, the friars or priests frequently listed more Indians to bolster the argument for more resources. The government officials inflated the numbers about marauding Indians for a similar purpose. It is important to know how many Pueblos married outside their communities to be able to determine if Juanotilla's situation was common or not.

In the eighteenth century, other categories became equally important in deciphering the question of what being Pueblo or Hispanic signified. Residential status, ethnicity, religion, and language were critical to social organization. As we shall see, the categories determined how people lived, acted, and treated one another. A will or an inventory specifying how a person's property was to be dispersed after her death illustrates the key social issues of the time. These demarcations are important because they explain what people valued, how people mattered to each other.

The courtroom scene where an official deposited a will or testament is not as obviously dramatic as others described later in this chapter, which involve violence or murder. Still, scrutinizing the information contained in a few, simple pages enlarges the meaning of Juanotilla's life. This single-named woman, in a period when some names were even longer than the governor's, lived close to other relatives. Her holdings were many. Her inventory lists cows, houses, pasturelands, and tools or implements, all of which indicate that she was not poor. Although Juanotilla appears in a solitary document, its component parts suggest much about her life and times. Such background details historians label "context."

A will leaves a trail of incomplete information. Other documents give information about those who created wills or about the authorities who determined the dispensing of property based on the testimonies they heard from the sick or dying. The age, for example, the wealth or class, even the health of the will makers are indeterminate. On the other hand, the household goods people owned or the crops they raised are listed. Juanotilla's will bequeathed an ax, a shotgun, stirrups, and a chisel. In some ways, just glancing at the statements or the inventories of personal property and household items reminds us about what was important to people in the eighteenth century.

Animals were among the more significant items in Juanotilla's will. These "highest-value" possessions were critical to the colonial economy. In Juanotilla's document, the list included cows, bulls, burros, mares, and horses. Tools used on the animals were also passed on to heirs, including saddles and other tack items. Micaela, Juanotilla's daughter, for example, received two axes, a hoe, a candle, and a casserole. Other bequests included a favorite saint or a cupboard made by a relative, a ladle for serving chocolate, or a pot for making the confection; these were among the more prized

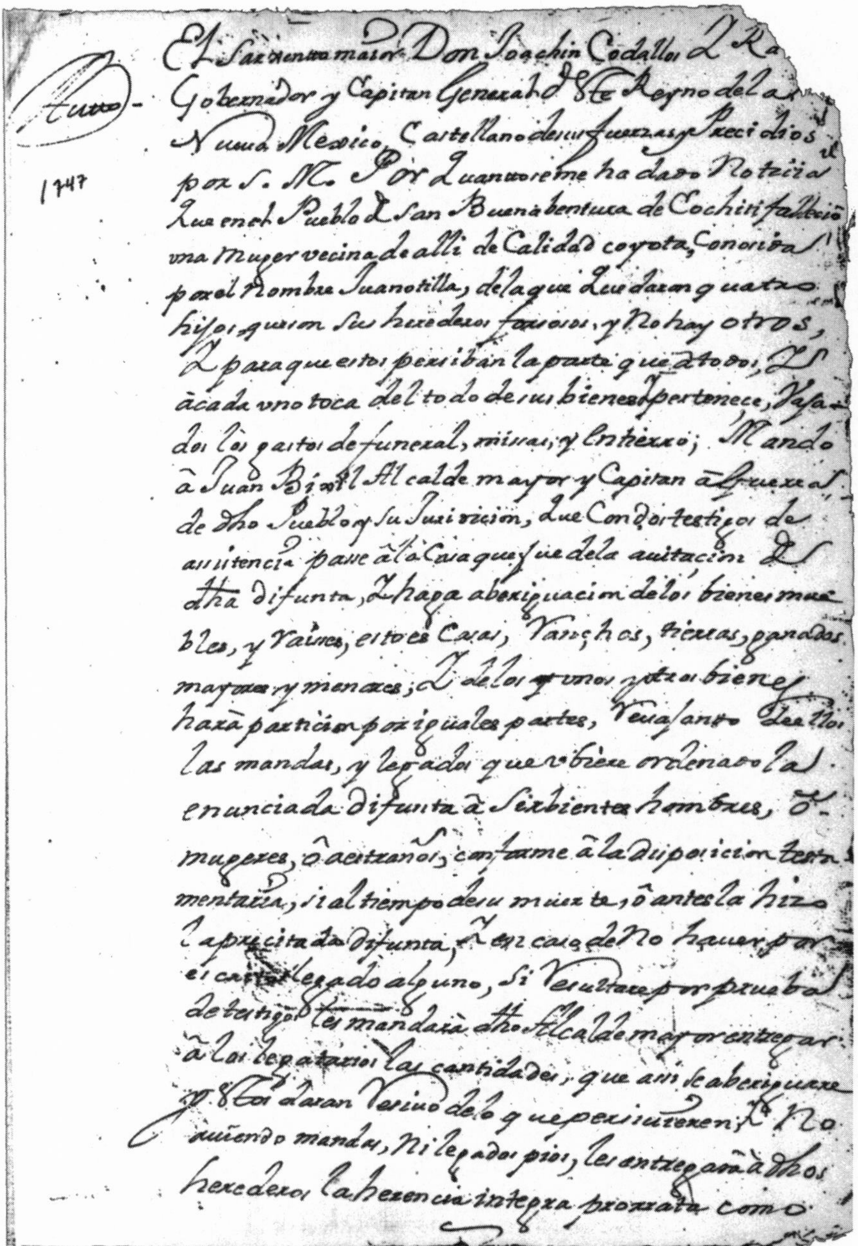

FIGURE 4.3 (two parts). Testament of Juanotilla, SANM, NMSRC, manuscript, 1747;
testament of Juana Romero, SANM, NMSRC, manuscript, 1762.

#776
SANM I
N° 817
Juana
Romero
1762

1762

En el nombre de Dios todo poderoso y de la siempre
Virgen María conpçebida sin mancha Xpo ca[s]o
original se a notorio q[ue] man[i]f[i]esto a los que la presen-
te bieren como yo Juana romero hi[j]a legitima
de Ant[oni]o romero y de nicolasa del castillo origi-
narios de este Reino de la nueba mexico becina de
la b[b]ene guilla estando en cam[m]a enferma de la en
fermedad que Dios Nuestro señor a sido serbido
serbido darme creiendo comofirme mente creo
en el misterio de la santisima trenidad padre hijo
espiri tu santo tres personas distintas y un solo
Dios berdadero y a todos los demas misterios que
tiene cree confiesa y enseña nuestra santa ma
dre iglesia catolica Romana y recibiendo por es
pe[s]ial patrona y abogada A la siempre Virgen
Maria santo angel de mi guarda santo de mi
nom bre y de mas santos de mi debosion inter
sedan con mi señor Jesu christo ponga mi al
ma en la mas segura Carrera de salbasion de
bavo de cuja intersesion orden y este mi testa
mento en la forma y manera siguiente
primeramente encomiendo mi alma a Dios
Nuestro señor que la crio y la Redimio con s[u]

FIGURE 4.4. Pintura de castas, *De español y mestiza, castiza,* by Miguel Cabrera, oil on canvas, 1763.

possessions listed. The writer of Juanotilla's inventory noted that most of the property she owned was to be evenly divided among her children, Diego, Sebastian, and Micaela. In a sentence following the one declaring these children as heirs, the scribe noted that a daughter, Ysabel, had died, but that her surviving children, Ysabel and Regina, because they "assisted her and accompanied her [Juanotilla]," were also to be considered Juanotilla's legitimate heirs.

Slowly, then, pieces of Juanotilla's life come together to fill in parts of a puzzle. They consist of children, possessions, property, and economic worth. Which mattered most, people or property, is unclear. Still, the inventory—not written in her own hand but by others who were appointed to take on the task—invites readers into the world of eighteenth-century women.

Each of her daughters received five cattle, four milking cows, an ox, seven bulls, ten goats, and six sheep, plus a portion of a home and land "as their deceased mother assigned them." This portion of the inventory concludes with "and each remained happy and satisfied." Next the document outlines what the son, Diego [Zanachi], was assigned: a hoe, an ax, a pick, a shovel, hides, four horses, one mare, five milk cows, two cattle, two burros, seven bulls, ten goats, and five sheep, plus "that portion of the house and pastures that his deceased mother had assigned him."

On page two of the inventory prepared by the witnesses and the executor, more people in Juanotilla's life appear. Of the aforementioned granddaughters, Regina is named an heir because her own mother, Ysabel, was deceased. All of this detail was included in the will because evidently it was important to the will maker. The items passed on to the granddaughter included three axes, a candle, a shovel, a sieve, three leather hides, three horses, a mare, six milk cows, four cattle, a donkey, an ox, and seven bulls. The same paragraph notes that the granddaughter shared some of these things with two nephews, Miguel and Ygnacio—the children of a deceased sister. As before, the document states that "all were happy and satisfied."

These final wishes are illustrative. First, the added details about Juanotilla: she was a mother, and some of her children preceded her in death. The executor of her estate calls her "the expressed Juanotilla," meaning that she has stipulated that the following be accomplished. Juanotilla can now be viewed as far more than what her ethnic status would denote: she is a property owner who has enumerated her desires for its dispensation. In another place, she is called a grandmother. Critically, she thought of her relatives. The document embodied relational as well as economic or cultural values.

Multiple meanings can be assigned to this document as can several characteristics of the eighteenth century. For example, death courses through the will's paragraphs, Juanotilla's own, that of at least one child, and her sister's. Her wishes might have been specified on her deathbed, but Juanotilla's life and the lives of her surviving children are equally important. Worldly possessions are meted out according to her wishes, and, as the executor states in an official capacity, satisfaction reigns among them. A mother had provided for her children.

Stating each person's relationship to the will maker illustrates family relations and family organization in this era. An interesting detail, appearing on the last page of Juanotilla's inventory, reveals that two other persons were important in her life: two *criados,* either servants or adoptees, named Xpoual (married) and Joachín (single), were given livestock and furniture for "having cared for their mother [?] until she died."

In colonial New Mexico, extended family arrangements were not extraordinary. Many households were composed of extended relatives as well as of parents and children. Extended relations were normal, meaning that several generations of family clustered together in a village or neighborhood. In Juanotilla's case, two heirs were not her biological children but evidently played a significant role and received property from her. In another situation, described in a 1762 will, Juana Romero explains how her relatives should care for her children when she died: "I pass on to my brother Juan Antonio Baca, my Antonia; to my brother, Miguel Romero, I assign Joseph Maria, and to my brother Domingo goes Ana Maria, all of whom I leave to my brothers who shall raise them and accept them like their adopted children, watching over them in God's grace, and for all that transpires, they carry parental rights."

As Juanotilla's will reveals, a single document can overflow with important social information. From her will, we learn that Juanotilla is mother, grandmother, will maker, and adoptive parent. Judging from the livestock and houses her heirs received, she was also relatively well-off. At a minimum, she was someone with substantial herds of animals and pasturelands. Altogether, more than eight people divided up her possessions or property. How common her large inventory was in comparison to the possessions of other women contemporary to her time is speculative, but clearly, hers was a world where women owned animals, managed households, and raised families, with or without men. Juanotilla demonstrates women's multiple roles within their families and communities of origin, roles not to be overlooked or minimized.

In the world outlined by this inventory, the rich texture of Juanotilla's wishes come alive. All her various concerns are enumerated, and many people close to her are included in her final document. Although we do not know if she had a husband, his name, or the surnames of her children, we know that she and her estate were sufficiently significant to receive the attention of local officials.

The life stories of other individuals of the same time period can be equally challenging to decipher. Putting the bits of information together resembles solving a mystery, with several pieces of information leading to conclusions or at least to more complete pictures of the eighteenth century and of women's roles during it. Another will maker, Juana Romero, composed her testament in 1762 and provides an interesting contrast to Juanotilla.

Romero, in her will, said that she was "ill with something our Lord who is served has seen fit to visit upon me." Romero meant that she was enduring ill health, and then she went on to stipulate how she wanted her few pieces of property dispersed. Owner of seventeen livestock, some young, others old, a bull, an ox, plus a two-roomed home, clothes, bedding, a coverlet, a cast-iron skillet, and a saintly image surrounded by glass, Romero wanted her material possessions to go to her children.

In Romero's will, as in other, similar documents, religious prayers and economic concerns are joined, revealing much about eighteenth-century women of New Mexico. In Romero's document, prayers predominate initially, as she says, "believing as I do in the Mystery of the Holy Trinity, Father, Son, and the Holy Ghost, three distinct persons and one True God, and all the other Mysteries in which it is professed, confessed, and instructed by our [Lady] Saintly Mother Church, Catholic, Roman, and receiving as special patron and adviser the Almighty Virgin Mother." Obviously possession mattered to Romero. She owned less than Juanotilla, but she wanted to ensure that her illness did not ruin her children's future. Hence she provided for their inheritance, even if it was small and she could do no more than specify funeral arrangements.

Wealthy women, including the previously mentioned Juana Lujan, and another, Manuela Rael de Aguilar, also filed their final wishes to ensure that their families remained economically secure. This was another purpose of the wills women prepared: to retain economic status and preserve within families inheritances such as livestock or pasturelands. In her will, Rael de Aguilar specified not only her lands, but also her debts, and ordered that they be paid.

Several other features of the eighteenth century come to light in women's testaments. Traditionally, it was thought that such women were illiterate. This was not always the case. Besides, the words in the testaments suggest that literacy can be measured in different ways. Words created for a will could be seen or even performed. An official scribe, appointed by the courts, took down a testator's words. Standard phrases such as "I believe in Almighty God" guided the person giving her testament.

Although men's wills contain elements of religiosity or devotion, they are rarely as extensive as women's. The women's prayers, recitations, and statements served more than one purpose. Juanotilla, Lujan, Romero, and Rael de Aguilar were not just performers but were creative speakers who injected unique ideas into their last wills and testaments. The structures of the prayers, albeit formulaic, were also punctuated with tone and rhythms, depending on the testator's level of devotion, how close to death she felt, or the types of witnesses present.

Like good storytellers, these women established themselves in the historical record through final words. Their prayers, viewed in this manner, meant far more than faith or devotion, although establishing their Catholicism was clearly one purpose of the enunciations. A second purpose resided in the act itself. Several people from a community knew what a person was leaving behind and to whom items were being left.

In a manner of speaking, will making was like a drama or play. The act carried value beyond its specific task. Sometimes the wills were wish lists. Lujan asked that her body be covered in the shroud of Saint Francis, which signified that she believed in that saint's power or mystery. Other times the desires a will conveyed were those that the will maker had not been able to make through any other avenue. Lujan recommended that more masses for her soul be paid after she was gone and that her favorite saints be cared for by her daughter and others by a friend.

One hundred years later, the communal practices included in the art form of will making began to erode slowly. Up until 1800, however, the small villages, towns, or villas surrounding Santa Fe were tightly woven places where few secrets existed, including those of a dying or departed person. In the case of a woman's final wishes, the matter of privacy was rarely considered because witnesses were brought in to listen to a testament. Not all witnesses were relatives, although it is apparent that some were. This meant that soon after a will was composed, others also knew what inheritance an ill or dying person was leaving behind. For communities suffering intense economic shortages—as many were by the late 1700s—the fact proved decisive. Younger persons or recently married couples could count on an inheritance to stabilize the difficulties created by an empire that was slowly eroding in power and stature, as was the case with Spain by 1800.

Juan Vigil, writing about Juanotilla's final dispersal of goods, stated that he and the witnesses assisting him were satisfied that all the terms of her will were met. Having no notary public (*escribano publico*) who could authenticate his procedure as the law required, the scribe ended by saying that as "he was authorized to do [by Mr. Sergeant Master Joachin Codallos y Rabal]," he thereby certified that he had completed his duties.

The social practice of making a will a performance within view of several parties inevitably caused clashes over specific possessions. When the witnesses testified in Juanotilla's will that her heirs were "happy and satisfied," they did not simply mean that her children were pleased. Rather, the witnesses were declaring in legal language that the heirs were not contesting specific points in a legal document. It was important for them to say so because a will was not considered finished until each of its terms had been met. When Captain-General Codallos y Rabal placed his signature on the dispensation of Juanotilla's property, he closed an important chapter for her and her heirs, one to which they had agreed.

Not all cases ended as easily as Juanotilla's. The court records of this period provide numerous contrasting pictures of division, ill feelings, and outward hostilities among heirs. In the contested wills, petitions, conveyances of land, and disputes over boundaries dominate. Regularly brothers and sisters sued one another over land or other property. In 1772, for example, María Joachina Mestas brought suit to settle claims presented by her husband's siblings. That same year, Rosa Montoya sued Nicolasa del Castillo over property rights. A decade later, another litigant, Theodora Ortiz, disputed the will of her deceased husband against the interests of his relatives.

The sociocultural climate of eighteenth-century New Mexico was electrifying in the matter of countersuits, too. Court dockets offer descriptions of cases where siblings united against others to dispute the division of property, especially concerning land. The constant and steady stream of such petitions and suits suggests that people were perpetually arguing about what belonged to whom. These suits can be viewed differently, from other standpoints, however. Factionalism might be seen as evidence of a vibrant, complex world. Among insiders, fights or arguments were noisy and contentious. But when the disputes ended and the dust settled, life continued.

Besides wills, other issues call into question the fantasy that northern New Mexico towns were placid. In 1741, for example, María Magdalena Baca had been found strangled in her bed. Her death followed a long series of complaints filed by her, some on behalf of her husband and others by her against her husband, Juan Márquez. Some charges included infidelity (a serious infraction because marriage vows were considered sacred, even though many people broke them); others included charges of violent behavior. In a separate, previous matter against her husband, Baca actually came to his rescue. Theirs was a complex relationship, to be sure.

The testimony of Baca's twelve-year-old son sealed Juan Márquez's fate in the case involving his wife's death by strangulation. The son claimed to have witnessed Márquez suffocating his mother. Other witnesses also confirmed that Márquez was a violent man. Still, because a minor was the only witness to the crime, Márquez was simply banished from the territory, with his accomplice also asked to leave the town. All in all, the survivors of this story each suffered for a crime that remained largely unresolved. The murder case attests to how erroneous it is to imagine New Mexico in the eighteenth century as quiet.

Still, other offenses proved damaging for litigants. These offenses were for different reasons but carried as well the punishment of banishment. One Juana Martín sued her husband on behalf of herself and her children because he kept a mistress for "over fifteen years." When it appeared that both the mistress and the husband were to be sent away, Martín pleaded for tolerance with the authorities, including the governor who was to decide the case. Apparently Martín's husband returned to her.

Clearly murders, infidelity, divorce or separation, and physical assaults existed in this period, as in any other. Men and women took these matters to court, appearing before varied magistrates appointed to handle the overflow of cases and depending on the charges. Some complaints went to the highest authorities; others remained local. Many legal cases included relatives or servants as witnesses. Like the filing of a will, the charge of a crime or complaint also became a public matter, a public performance. The entire town soon knew who was contesting against someone and why. Litigation became an important method for resolving disputes about murder, theft, divorce, or battery.

The cases involving these charges prove that northern New Mexico in the eighteenth century exhibited cultural vibrancy. The courtroom proved that people in their communities differed, argued, and fought. Tension and disputes were considered a part of life, but so was their resolution. Local conflicts between or among individuals and families also meant that wars, the death of kings, and other catastrophes might have shaped international politics and the local economy, but so did social conflicts. It mattered whether someone was on friendly terms with others. It is now clear that witnesses, judges, or scribes played a far more important role than we would have thought previously in a world stitched together by ethnicity, race, social status, and culture as well as by gender.

From a perspective three centuries later, it becomes necessary to know something about such a world composed of "great" and "small-scale" events. We include in histories men with long names and titles but also women known by only one name. Juanotilla was more than a coyota; she was a vecina, a resident, a mother and grandmother, a landowner, and a will maker. These titles are as significant as those of any official's. Juanotilla's status also carried certain entitlements. Understanding the labels and their meanings assigns different meanings to the lives of eighteenth-century *nuevomexicanas*.

ESSAY ON SOURCES

Specific works related to political, religious, and military affairs for eighteenth-century New Mexico include David J. Weber, ed., *New Spain's Far Northern Frontier: Essays on Spain in the American West, 1540–1821* (Albuquerque: University of New Mexico Press, 1979), and John Kessell, *Kiva, Cross, and Crown: The Pecos Indians and New Mexico, 1540–1840* (Washington, D.C.: National Park Service, 1979). On military policies and the treatment of Indians by the Spanish crown, see Max L. Moorhead, *The Presidio: Bastion of the Spanish Borderlands* (Norman: University of Oklahoma Press, 1975).

Several articles deal specifically with women in eighteenth-century New

Mexico. The essays by Richard Eighme Ahlborn, "The Will of a Woman in 1762," *New Mexico Historical Review* 65 (July 1990): 319–54; Rosalind Z. Rock, "'Pido y Suplico': Women and the Law in Spanish New Mexico, 1697–1763," *New Mexico Historical Review* 55 (April 1999): 145–59; and Salomé Hernández, "Nueva Mexicanas as Refugees and Reconquest Settlers, 1680–1696," in Joan Jensen and Darlis A. Miller, eds., *New Mexico Women: Intercultural Perspectives* (Albuquerque: University of New Mexico Press, 1986), are extremely helpful. Asunción Lavrin and Edith Coutourier wrote "Dowries and Wills: A View of Women's Socioeconomic Role in Colonial Guadalajara and Puebla, 1640–1790," *Hispanic American Historical Review* 59 (May 1979): 280–304, an essay that continues to inspire historical research on wills and testimonies. Earlier in this century, Louis H. Warner wrote "Wills and Hijuelas," *New Mexico Historical Review* 7 (January 1932): 75–89, and "Conveyance of Property, the Spanish and Mexican Way," *New Mexico Historical Review* 6 (October 1931): 334–59; both essays are still useful as guides to the vocabulary, itemizations, and intent such documents convey.

Different aspects of religion, politics, and culture are surveyed adequately by many other books. Readers might begin, for this period, with Ramón A. Gutiérrez, *When Jesus Came, the Corn Mothers Went Away: Marriage, Sexuality, and Power in New Mexico, 1500–1846* (Stanford, Calif.: Stanford University Press, 1991). For indigenous reviews of this work, see Ted Jojola, ed., Special Issue, *American Indian Culture and Research Journal* (fall 1992). A Pueblo historical perspective is also contained in such varied books as Paula Gunn Allen, *The Sacred Hoop: Recovering the Feminine in American Indian Traditions* (Boston: Beacon Press, 1986), and Alfonso Ortiz, *The Tewa World: Space, Time, Being, and Becoming in Pueblo Society* (Chicago: University of Chicago Press, 1969).

Women in colonial Borderlands history are the topic of numerous essays by Antonia Castañeda. They include "Gender, Race, and Culture: Spanish-Mexican Women in the Historiography of Frontier California," *Frontiers: A Journal of Women's Studies* 11 (1990): 8–20; "Women of Color and the Rewriting of Western History: The Discourse, Politics, and Decolonization of History," *Pacific Historical Review* 61 (November 1992): 501–33. Other essays in the *New Mexico Historical Review* provide information about the period covered here and survey judiciously the primary or archival record. See the indexes to this journal for articles by Myra Ellen Jenkins, Marc Simmons, Darlis Miller, and Janet Lecompte, to name just a few.

At the New Mexico Records Center in Santa Fe (the official archives for the state of New Mexico), the calendared material pertaining to women's roles and interests is organized by period. Begin with the older, *Calendar to the Microfilm Edition of the Land Records of New Mexico,* by J. Richard Salazar, ed. and comp. (1987), and follow with the *Calendar of the Microfilm Edition of the Spanish Archives of New Mexico, 1621–1821* (n.d.). In these calendars, each document is dated and given a number as it appears on the microfilm version. There is another, coexisting numbering system, the Twitchell system, with brief descriptions attached to each entry. Women's wills are indexed in this way, as are deeds, conveyances, and complaints. For later years, the Probate Court Journals, also located at the State Records Center, contain more than fifty wills by women, which I have transcribed, translated, and analyzed in a volume currently in progress, *Chicanas Bequeath.*

✐5

Padre Martínez and
Mexican New Mexico

E. A. MARES

𝒯he photographer might have been Sigmund Seligman, who advertised as Sigismundo Seligman for the large Spanish-speaking population in Santa Fe. Or it might have been James Sabine, also a Santa Fe daguerreotypist. Whoever he was, the photographer stared at the priest whose image he was about to capture. The year was probably 1848, and the *americanos* were now in possession of this Mexican far-northern frontier. In fact, it was no longer a Mexican Department but rather a Territory in what was now being referred to as the American Southwest. The sun was bright. That was what was needed for a daguerreotype to reveal its subject in vivid detail. The photographer knew he ran the risk of overexposure on the priest's torso, but he was determined to focus on that face, a countenance unlike any he had ever seen.

The priest had long, dark, receding hair, turning white and parted on the left side. He wore a dark robe or cape that emphasized, as if it needed any emphasizing, his large forehead. His jaw was pronounced and stubborn. And the slightly down turned lips were heavy, firm, and calm. This was not a handsome face, but it was strong willed, dignified, and impossible to forget. The sun's glare was harsh, so the photographer asked the priest to look away from the camera lens and to hold his pose for at least twenty seconds. The photographer may have taken more than one shot, but no one knows whether he did or not. This daguerreotype, however, the only photograph of its subject to survive, captured the image of the priest from Taos, Padre Antonio José Martínez.

Padre Martínez of Taos was a remarkable man. Hero to some, villain to others, he has become an ever more fascinating figure. In 1793 he was born in New Mexico, a colonial outpost of a Spanish empire nearing its end in the Americas. As a young man, Antonio José witnessed the transformation of this province into the far-northern frontier of the Mexican nation. And he saw the growing threat posed for Mexico by the United States in its ever increasing trade and commerce on the Santa Fe Trail. From the Mexican viewpoint, the Santa Fe Trail was the northern extension of the older Camino Real. For the United States, however, the Santa Fe Trail offered an attractive avenue for penetration of Mexico's northern frontier. As it turned out, the real end of the Santa Fe Trail was the Mexican-American War. Mexico lost about half its national territory when it signed the Treaty of Guadalupe Hidalgo in 1848, thus ending the war.

Antonio José Martínez endured these transformations. In the process he married, became a young widower, and then became a priest. He was also the first person to make significant use of the printing press in New Mexico; he published the first books, of an educational and religious nature, and he opened the first coeducational school in New Mexico.

Soon after the American occupation, a young French priest, Jean Baptiste Lamy, arrived in Santa Fe. He became the first bishop, later archbishop, of the newly created Archdiocese of Santa Fe. No doubt, Padre Martínez and Bishop Lamy are best known to contemporary readers as the brilliantly delineated figures in Willa Cather's heavily fictionalized docudrama, *Death Comes for the Archbishop*. Martínez is the dark, enigmatic, and deeply flawed priest Cather vilifies, whereas Lamy, thinly disguised as Bishop Latour, is the saintly bringer of civilization to the western frontier.

Although a contemporary of Kit Carson, Padre Martínez did not condone the mistreatment of Native Americans that Carson and others engaged in as agents enforcing the policies of the U.S. government. As an example, the great Apache chief and warrior Mangas Coloradas would have fared better with Padre Martínez than he did at the hands of the U.S. cavalry who killed him in 1862.

In life as well as in literature, Martínez clashed with the bishop of his church, but he had a range of interests far greater than a dispute with his bishop. He left a deep impression on his times that has endured to this day. More than a century after his death, he has become a symbol to Chicanos trying to find significant links to their heritage.

When Antonio José Martínez was a child, it took about eighteen months to make a round trip on the Camino Real by *carreta,* a heavy wooden-wheeled cart pulled by mules or oxen, from Mexico City to Santa Fe and back. The Indo-Hispanic settlers, a mixture of Spanish immigrants and a variety of indigenous persons with whom they had married, or Mexican Hispanic settlers, as they are often called, maintained more or less cooperative but precarious relationships with the Pueblo Indians while at the same time living in constant tension and fear of attack from nomadic tribes of Apaches to the south and west, Comanches to the east, and Navajos and Utes to the north and west, who viewed the Hispanic presence as an intrusion in their ancient homelands.

By the time the Spanish Empire in America was drawing to a close toward the last years of the eighteenth century and in the opening decade of the nineteenth century, conditions in the north were difficult for all who lived or traveled there. In 1812, as Spain found itself embroiled in the Napoleonic wars and its grip on the Americas loosened, a prominent New Mexican, Pedro Bautista Pino, traveled to Spain to inform that imperial mother country of New Mexico's needs. According to Pino, New Mexico was extremely isolated. There were only twenty-two missionaries in the province and two secular parish priests, one in El Paso and the other in Santa Fe. No bishop had visited the province in more than fifty years. With such a dire lack of priests, there was a consequent erosion of religious practices by the faithful. In fact, as early as 1778 a visiting Franciscan missionary, Fray Juan Agustín de Morfi, had noted quite similar problems in New Mexico.

Apparently nothing had changed from Fray Morfi's time to that of Pedro Pino. In his *exposición* to the Spanish government, Pino lamented the frontier dangers the Indians posed and New Mexico's general lack of agricultural, industrial, and commercial development. He pointed out that only one surgeon lived in the entire province, and indeed there was a great scarcity of persons with any professional training or education whatsoever.

New Mexico, in the early nineteenth century, was at first a rough, rural outpost of the Spanish Empire. Then it became the neglected and tumultuous frontier of the emergent Mexican nation. Spanish Catholicism, no doubt, had a civilizing effect on this frontier society. Nevertheless, modern fascination with the art of the *santeros,* particularly the nineteenth-century and early-twentieth-century carvers of sacred icons in northern New Mexico, casts an unduly holy glow back on the eighteenth-century pages of New Mexican history. The reality was a harsh and difficult Indo-Hispanic frontier surrounded by understandably hostile Indians.

After Mexican independence, struggles continued over the form of government Mexico was to adopt. There was even a short-lived Mexican Empire. In 1824 the Mexican Constitution organized the country into a federal republic made up of nineteen states and four territories. New Mexico, formerly an internal province of the Spanish Empire, now became a territory of the Mexican nation. With a government structure based on European Enlightenment thought and on the United States Constitution, the Mexican state, with its typical separation of power into executive, judicial, and legislative branches, had the appearance on paper of a young republic.

At a deeper level, however, the Mexican leadership was split between centralists and federalists. In general, the centralists were made up of the clergy, the army, and the owners of the great haciendas. This was a powerful conservative force that tended to be fixated on its narrow, regional interests. The federalists were supported by doctrinaire liberal *criollos* (descendants of Spanish ancestors but born in the New World) and *mestizos* (persons of mixed Spanish and Mexican Indian descent) who saw themselves as heirs to Enlightenment thought.

And at an even deeper level of social analysis, throughout Mexico and its northern frontier, there were the large indigenous populations present in the Americas long before the arrival of any Europeans. These indigenous people had their own village and tribal structures, their own languages and ethical systems. Despite notable exceptions in such individuals as Benito Juárez and Porfirio Díaz during the mid- and late-nineteenth century, it was rare for any member of this population to rise to power or even have significant influence on the political structures of the Hispanicized and Europeanized Mexican leading families.

The politically restricted nature of the interests represented in the Mexican governments after 1821, and their ideological disassociation from the underlying Indian populations, coupled with the vast distances of Mexican geography, led to the deterioration of internal conditions. There were bitter factional alignments, an attempted military coup, and a Spanish invasion that failed to reestablish Spanish rule. All of this chaos helped fasten upon the Mexican nation by 1833 the leadership of a brilliant political opportunist, General Antonio López de Santa Anna.

Revealingly, the change in government from Spanish to Mexican administration had very little impact on New Mexico. Royal appointees were replaced by civil appointees from the various governments that came to power in Mexico. There were, nevertheless, serious concerns with which the Mexican government had to deal on its northern frontier.

One of the most serious was the state of neglect of the frontier defenses. The most heavily populated area of the north was made up of the thin line of settlements that stretched from El Paso del Norte up the Rio Grande to Santa Fe and the mountain valleys to the north. About thirty thousand Indo-Hispanos and another ten thousand Pueblo Indians lived in this region. Although exact populations are uncertain, the Indo-Hispano population of northern New Mexico during Padre Martínez's youth probably numbered under forty thousand. This small agrarian Indo-Hispanic population, Spanish speaking and Roman Catholic, lived in close proximity to the Pueblos and spread out over an area the size of Tennessee. It was also an isolated population surrounded by threatening tribes.

It is difficult to estimate the numbers of nomadic Navajos, Apaches, Utes, Kiowas, and Comanches, to mention only some of the major nomadic divisions. They must have numbered at least a few thousand collectively. Donaciano Vigil, a prominent New Mexican at the time, complained that because of the nomadic raids, all of New Mexico was an exposed frontier.

The Mexican government, distracted by its own problems, dealt with New Mexico in a desultory fashion. The first Mexican governor, Facundo Melgares (1818–22), was a royalist who only reluctantly supported Mexican independence. New Mexico, however, had the advantage of a large enough population base to allow the frontier province to have a *diputado*, a representative in the lower house of the Mexican Congress. Some of these diputados later became governors of the Mexican territory. This was true of Santiago Abreú (governor from 1832 to 1833) and José Antonio Cháves (governor from 1829 to 1832). Often, because of the nomadic threats, the New Mexico governors held the offices of political head (*jefe político*) and military leader (*jefe militar*) simultaneously.

Moreover, New Mexico had functioning *ayuntamientos,* or local town governments, in the major towns and in many of the Indian pueblos by the 1820s. This tradition of local rule stood in strong contrast to other parts of the Mexican northern frontier, where far more restrictive policies prevailed.

The need for mutual defense had led to an alliance between the Indo-Hispanos and the Pueblos in the eighteenth century that functioned quite well. Even into the early years of the nineteenth century, Pueblos fought side by side with their Indo-Hispano allies against the nomadic Indians. All of this changed, however, after 1821. When Mexico declared its independence, it adopted the Plan de Iguala, which guaranteed that all individuals would be treated equally in the new nation. Written with the best of liberal intentions, this document nevertheless was a threat to Pueblo sovereignty and control of their own lands because, by placing individuals on an equal footing, the communal nature of the Pueblos, long recognized by the Spaniards, was undermined. Provincial political corruption led to the loss of Pueblo lands. However, the difficulties the Pueblos experienced with the Mexican government were minor compared to what they would experience with the United States.

Yet the early 1800s were relatively peaceful in New Mexico. The caravans that plied the Camino Real were still heavily fortified, and raids could occur anywhere at any time, but the shaky peace established by Governor Juan Bautista de Anza with the Comanches in 1786 held. Raiding gave way to trading as New Mexicans, supported by funding from the viceroyalty in Mexico City, purchased livestock, clothing, tools, and other goods to give to Indian allies to maintain their loyalty and preserve peace. In addition, economic expansion to the south of New Mexico, particularly the opening of silver mines in Chihuahua, Parral, Guanajuato, and Durango, led to favorable conditions for population expansion along the northern frontier. Nomadic Indians came to the Taos trade fair every autumn with horses, buffalo hides, and leather goods to exchange for food and Spanish manufactured products. The *nuevomexicano* traders, in turn, took some of these goods south to sell and trade in Chihuahua in the spring.

Genízaro outposts, such as Abiquiu, lost their military significance as the Indo-Hispano population grew. Although *genízaro,* meaning "janissary," refers to a type of frontier guard employed by the Ottoman Turks along the Austrian frontier, in northern New Mexico the Spaniards thought of the genízaros as Christianized, detribalized Indians who could form a defensive perimeter to shield Spanish imperial centers of power, such as at Santa Fe. After 1800 the genízaros tended to be identified more as the poorer elements of New Mexican Indo-Hispano agrarian society.

Antonio José Martínez, the firstborn male child of a family that included six children, found himself caught up in the social changes of the early 1800s. For some years prior to 1804, while the Pueblo population remained stagnant or declined, the Indo-Hispanic nuevomexicano population increased. The relative prosperity and concomitant population expansion to the north may have led the Martínez family to leave Abiquiu in that year and relocate in Taos, where they could put to good use the abundant grazing lands there. Still, there was danger from nomadic attacks, and the Martínez home, referred to in the contemporary world as the Martínez Hacienda, looks like what it was supposed to be—a fortress, with thick exterior walls without windows, an internal patio where there was once a well (a protected source of water), and a protected corral for animals during times of Indian assault.

The Martínez family prospered in Taos. Antonio José helped his father, Severino, administer the family's extensive farming and livestock interests. He married in 1811. Within a year, his wife died in childbirth. The child survived and was named María de la Luz in honor of her mother. Antonio José was only nineteen when fate left him a widower. After a few years of reflection on the matter and after some correspondence with the Bishop of Durango, Juan Francisco Castañiza, Martínez left Taos in 1817 and traveled to Durango to study for the priesthood.

According to Mexican historian José Ignacio Gallegos, the period in which Martínez studied at the Durango seminary was an educational "golden age," as the seminary "could rival the best [seminary] in the Republic of Mexico." Along with his ecclesiastical education, Martínez also absorbed the political ideas of classic nineteenth-century liberalism from Mexican politicians and educators, whose words he could not have failed to notice and reflect upon. Martínez, by all accounts, was an outstanding student. He was ordained a priest in 1823 and returned to New Mexico, where he eventually became the parish priest of Taos.

The six-year absence from Taos of Padre Martínez, as Antonio José would henceforth be known, coincided with a key transition period for New Mexico. During that time, Mexico gained its independence from Spain and opened the Santa Fe Trail for commerce with the United States.

Trade along the trail grew dramatically, and this continuously expanding commerce had a far greater economic impact on New Mexico than the Indo-Hispanic population growth. With the encouragement of the Mexican government, an ever growing wave of adventurers, fur trappers, explorers, and businessmen, traders in all kinds of goods, crossed the Arkansas River and entered New Mexico. Most, but not all, Mexicans ignored the drive for conquest that animated U.S. foreign policy in regard to Mexico at that time. Long before it was named "Manifest Destiny," in 1845, the belief that the United States had the God-given right to occupy and "civilize" at least all of the North American landmass, including

FIGURE 5.1. Padre Martínez and the Taos Church. Courtesy The Albuquerque Museum, Albuquerque, New Mexico, Casa San Ysidro Collection. Photo illustration by Alexandria King.

Mexico, became an ever more powerful force motivating American expansion. As early as 1826, New Mexico governor Antonio Narbona was concerned about the growing U.S. presence in the Taos valley.

Mexican concern was understandable. There was no denying the allure of American goods. New Mexicans were fascinated by the finished products that came down the Santa Fe Trail. The United States was already developing the economic infrastructure for what would in less than a century become the major industrial power in the world. As noted New Mexico author Erna Fergusson comments, "To New Mexicans this trade meant better goods at lower prices and the excitement of dealing with gringos with their harsh speech and free ways." Excitement, however, may well have given way to disillusionment as nuevomexicanos encountered the negative racial attitudes of many Americans who came to New Mexico.

The military occupation of Mexico's northern frontier by forces from the United States was a footnote to the economic conquest that Mexico had unwittingly invited by opening the Santa Fe Trail in 1821.

In keeping with the rapid changes happening in New Mexico, Padre Martínez's own life became charged with dramatic events and activities. Around 1824 or 1825, Martínez's daughter, María de la Luz, died. There is no historical evidence as to the impact of this tragedy on the padre. However, between 1825 and 1846, Padre Martínez became an extremely busy man who played many roles—priest, educator, publisher, rancher, farmer, and, to some extent, politician. It is possible that the loss of his daughter propelled him into a routine deliberately designed to keep him occupied, to keep his mind off what otherwise might have become a paralyzing trauma. It may also be the case that although Martínez took his priestly duties seriously, these duties certainly did not exhaust his curiosity about or his engagement with the world. He had a private life as well as a public persona. He was a husband before he was a priest. He was a father of flesh and blood before he was a spiritual father. He had farming and ranching interests and com-mercial interests before he became a priest. He continued some of these interests after he became a priest.

Padre Martínez observed the centrifugal forces that tore Mexico apart and reverberated in New Mexico. He must have been appalled by the chaos and anarchy that characterized Mexican political history from 1833 to 1855, well beyond the period of Mexican rule in New Mexico.

Once Santa Anna was firmly in power, he reversed his former liberal stance, set up a conservative centralist government, and abandoned the earlier liberal constitution for the centrist constitution of 1836. Under this new dispensation, the former Mexican states and territories were trans-formed into military departments, with officials appointed by the gov-ernment in Mexico City. Intent on a rigid centralization of power, the Mexican government had no time for idealistic civilizing schemes.

Not surprisingly, this government turned a deaf ear in 1843 to Padre Martínez's plea on behalf of nomadic Indians. In typical nineteenth-century liberal fashion, he argued in his *exposición* addressed to President Santa Anna that the Indians should be encouraged to ranch, farm, and engage in mining so that they could survive the imminent extinction of the buffalo.

The consequences of Santa Anna's centralization policy were severe. Rebellions against the federal authorities occurred throughout Mexico.

Eventually these revolts led to the loss of Texas in 1836, when Anglo-American rebels there succeeded in establishing an independent state. And it was this general weakening of the Mexican nation that contributed to its defeat at the hands of the United States in the Mexican-American War, from 1846 to 1848.

New Mexico reacted swiftly to the policies of the centralist government in Mexico City when that government tried to impose the equal collection of taxes in all departments. This policy was extremely offensive to nuevomexicanos, long accustomed to freedom from such taxes. It is not at all clear that the newly appointed Mexican governor, Albino Pérez, ever intended to impose the new taxes despite the federal decree. Nevertheless, by the spring of 1837 rumors spread that exorbitant taxes were about to be imposed on New Mexico.

Padre Martínez was politically quite active throughout the 1830s. In 1832, Martínez was invited to sing a high mass and to deliver a panegyric in honor of another priest, Padre Miguel Hidalgo, for a celebration of the Sixteenth of September, the day in 1810 when Hidalgo, the pastor of the town of Dolores, Guanajuato, sparked the movement for Mexican independence. Padre Hidalgo chose *el dieciséis de septiembre* because this was also the feast day of Our Lady of Sorrows (Nuestra Señora de los Dolores). His "*grito de* Dolores," or call for liberty, inaugurated eleven years of Mexican struggle to gain independence from Spain. Martínez was a young contemporary of Hidalgo. His own political philosophy, as seen in his religious and secular activities, reflected the Mexican liberalism of Hidalgo. In all likelihood, then, delivering the panegyric was an enjoyable task for Martínez.

Martínez exalted the idea of liberty in his oration. By doing so, he may have contributed to a climate of opinion that could easily be swayed to rebel against perceived threats to liberty. Since el dieciséis de septiembre was unlikely the only time or the last time that he spoke and preached about Padre Hidalgo, Martínez may have underestimated the impact of his preaching.

Matters came to a head in 1837, when the farmers and ranchers of Chimayo rose in rebellion against the Mexican government. The reasons for the rebellion are not entirely clear, but fear of unwanted taxation and resentment against the Santa Fe officials, particularly Albino Pérez, who knew little about northern New Mexico, were strong motivating factors. In this regard, Donaciano Vigil, who was to become a Mexican collaborator with the occupying American forces, complained bitterly about the low quality of some of the Mexican governors that the centralists sent to New Mexico. Vigil thought Albino Pérez (1835–37) was well intentioned but tragically lacked understanding of the department. He likewise considered Governor Mariano Martínez (1844–45) to be grossly ignorant of New Mexico.

At first the Chimayo rebels were successful. Augmented by Indian supporters from the pueblos, they marched on Santa Fe, captured and executed Governor Pérez, and installed one of their own leaders, José Gonzales, a former Taoseño, as the new governor. Once in power, the rebels were split by factionalism, and they were never able to agree on their goals or on their relationship to the Mexican government. Since American merchants and traders, by then plentiful in Santa Fe and in Albuquerque, were uneasy about the new government, they helped finance a small army commanded by a former Mexican governor, Manuel Armijo of Albuquerque, to reinstall the old Mexican government. By the fall of 1837, Armijo was firmly in control of Santa Fe. After some further skirmishing and political maneuvering, the rebellion collapsed in January 1838, and the rebel leader was executed in Santa Cruz.

Padre Martínez was present at the execution. According to Pedro Sánchez, who knew Martínez, Manuel Armijo turned to the padre and said to him, "Padre Martínez, hear this genízaro's confession so that he may be shot by a firing squad." Rightly or wrongly, after the failure of the Chimayo rebellion, Martínez was widely blamed for the affair. His *relación* of 1838 briefly notes that he helped pay for troops to suppress the uprising, that he himself had been persecuted, and that Manuel Armijo had welcomed his services as chaplain. Although Martínez defended the poor against ecclesiastical and civil abuse, he was not a political populist. The War of the Chimayosos may have been inspired by the remembered words of Hidalgo and by classic nineteenth-century liberal beliefs, but it had class overtones as it developed. The wealthy Martínez family almost certainly would have been the object of popular wrath, particularly as exemplified in its most public figure, the padre himself.

The *guerra de los chimayosos* was not the end of difficult political circumstances for nuevomexicanos. Within a few years, in 1841, the new Republic of Texas sent an expedition into New Mexico. This probe, or invasion, made up of soldiers and traders, had economic and political intentions. Texas, always eager for commercial opportunities, probably hoped to take part in the lucrative trade on the Santa Fe Trail. At the same time, given the weakened condition of the Mexican nation and the

FIGURE 5.2. General Manuel Armijo, from original chalk and pastel drawing. Photo courtesy Museum of New Mexico, neg. no. 50809.

internal struggles in New Mexico, this may have seemed an opportune moment for the Texans to seize New Mexico and incorporate it into Texas. In any case, the invasion came to naught. The Texans became lost on the Llano Estacado (the Staked Plains), and they broke into small parties still trying to reach New Mexico. Divided and suffering from Indian assaults and also from the elements, they were easy pickings for Manuel Armijo and his soldiers. The Texans were marched to Mexico City for their efforts and imprisoned.

By the 1840s the Martínez family, headed by the padre, had become the leading dynasty of Taos. Being a leading dynasty carried its burdens. One of them was the growing enmity toward the Martínez family by a number of shrewd and skillful businessmen, merchants, and land speculators who had moved rapidly to take advantage of the Mexican government's liberal land grant policy in its northern frontier territories and departments.

Land grants, in theory, were originally granted only by the king of Spain. Since the Spanish colonies in the Americas were divided into four viceroyalties, including the viceroyalty of Mexico, the viceroy, acting on behalf of the king, assumed he possessed the power to grant lands. In practice, over time, the power of the Spanish kings declined. But the great distances involved, from Spain to Mexico and then to New Mexico, the lengthy time required for correspondence to occur, and shifting political considerations in the viceroyalty itself led to many difficulties and uncertainties in regard to land grant titles.

Again, in theory, land was supposed to be distributed to discoverers and old settlers and their descendants and to the "best qualified" among them. Mexico, after gaining its independence, modified the land grant practices. Mexico provided two kinds of land grants, one for promoters or businessmen, called *impresario* grants. The other, in doctrinaire liberal fashion, was to be for individuals. These grants were to be made by the town councils, or ayuntamientos, as they were called. However, the land grant policy was not consistent between 1821 and 1846. There were many legal and political pitfalls, and there is no doubt that Hispanic *personalismo,* personal ties of family, friendship, and politics, all played a role in the granting of land. Also, for legal or political reasons, a land grant could be undone.

After the loss of Texas, Mexico expanded the land grants by transferring public lands to the private domain. Especially between 1837 and 1846, Manuel Armijo, governor at various times (1827–29, 1837–44, 1845–46), approved more than half of *all* grants made by viceregal and Mexican governments. These grants amounted to at least 16 million acres of land.

Manuel Armijo is a much maligned figure in New Mexican history. He was a businessman from Albuquerque with extensive interests and partnerships in the Santa Fe trade. He came from a wealthy family, and as a man involved with commerce on the Santa Fe Trail and the Camino Real down to Chihuahua, he was keenly aware of American wealth and power. He may or may not have been bribed to allow the Yankee troops to enter Santa Fe peacefully in 1846, but he obviously made a mistake by not organizing a more politically significant token resistance to the advancing American troops. This failure has been the source of much criticism of Armijo. Nevertheless, he considered himself a Mexican patriot; he had warned Mexico of the danger posed by the United States to its sovereignty, and after the Mexican-American War he was cleared by a Mexican court of all wrongdoing. He continued to have a prosperous career after the American occupation.

When Armijo's land grants are examined, it appears that he was desperate to use them as buffer zones against encroaching Indians, Texans, and Americans. One of the many land grants made by Armijo went to his secretary, Guadalupe Miranda, and to Canadian-born Carlos Beaubien. Two years later, in 1843, Armijo made several large grants to other Mexican and Canadian-born partners, including Cerán St. Vrain. A year later, Carlos Beaubien's daughter, Luz Beaubien, married Lucien B. Maxwell. Slowly but surely, because of many circumstances, Lucien Maxwell acquired the Beaubien-Miranda grant. To this day it is known as the Maxwell Land Grant. At one time the grant embraced 2 million acres of land in northeastern New Mexico and southeastern Colorado and eventually became the subject of almost endless litigation.

Men like Beaubien, St. Vrain, and Charles Bent, the trader and founder of Bent's Fort on the Arkansas River, saw great land speculation opportunities for themselves in the environs of Taos. These frontiersmen were accustomed to having their way. Padre Martínez and his brothers challenged their interests and stood squarely in the path of their ambitions in Taos. As a Mexican patriot, Martínez was much opposed to the cavalier fashion in which the Mexican government issued these latter-day land grants. He saw these grants as strengthening the presence of a potentially hostile power, the United States. Martínez's attitude inspired the hatred of opportunistic americanos. The irrationality of Bent's hatred is obvious in a letter he wrote that has survived from that time. In it the semiliterate Bent says, among other things about Padre Martínez, that "his greate name deserves to be written in letters of gold in all high places that this gaping and ignorant multitude might fall down and worship it, that he has and done condisend to remain amongst and instrkut such a people." After the American occupation, the enmity toward the Martínez family continued. Only now the padre and his brothers and their families were even more vulnerable in a milieu where all the rules had suddenly and drastically changed.

For Padre Martínez, the most serious change of all would be the change in church jurisdiction. Although Martínez had received a liberal political education based on his experiences in Mexico, Lamy was from southern, rural, conservative France. He was unhappy with the politically revolutionary changes occurring in France in the late 1840s, and he had a deep vocation for missionary work. Even though Martínez was a priest, his experience was much more worldly than that of Lamy. Lamy had never married. He had never had to manage secular estates, and his contact with the scruffy world of the New Mexican frontier was concerned primarily with church affairs. Although these two men should not have been fated to come into conflict, unforeseen events led to that end.

Prior to the American occupation and the advent of the Lamy years, Padre Martínez was active on many fronts. On three separate occasions under Mexican rule, in 1830, 1831, and 1836, he served as a deputy in the Departmental Assembly of the Territory of New Mexico. By 1835 Martínez had acquired a small press and begun publishing books of a religious and didactic nature. Among the titles, in addition to an arithmetic book, was a primer and a Spanish speller. Although various writers have claimed that Padre Martínez published the first newspaper in New Mexico, no solid historical data indicates this. It is true, however, that the spelling book of 1835, *Cuaderno de Ortografía,* was the first book published in New Mexico. Fray Angélico Chávez, a restrained admirer of Martínez, believed the priest greatly enriched his homeland with these publishing efforts.

An account of the padre's activities in the 1830s would be incomplete if it left out two of the most heatedly debated elements of his life and times. One was his involvement with the Holy Brotherhood of Our Lord Jesus Christ, or the Penitentes, as they are popularly called. The other was his alleged involvements with women.

Penitential rituals date to at least the early Middle Ages in Christendom. Regardless of the exact route or historical agency that brought such practices to New Mexico, they arrived as early as don Juan de Oñate's colonizing expedition of 1598, when his soldiers whipped themselves before crossing the Río Grande. As several scholars have argued, the Brotherhood developed from about 1790 to 1810.

Many factors contributed to the rise of the Penitentes. The Spanish government added to the problem of the shortage of priests by ousting the Franciscans. Later, the Mexican government ousted the Spanish priests. And with the arrival of the Americans in what was to become "the American Southwest," that is, Mexico's former northern frontier, the flight of Mexican priests added to the criticality of the shortage.

Another factor was the lack of sacred images on the frontier. In Europe and in the large urban centers of the Hispanic world, numerous cathedrals, churches, statues, and paintings reminded the faithful of their beliefs. Nuevomexicanos had to carve their own *bultos* and *retablos* to remind them of their devotions and to display the fervor of their beliefs. The Penitentes used bultos of Jesús Nazareno (Jesus the Nazarene) for their Lenten acts of devotion. And they may have been influenced by popular passion plays in a milieu where public drama was a rare and powerful event. Penitente devotions culminated in the mythic re-creation of the crucifixion of Christ on Good Friday.

Whatever their origins, the Penitentes were and are a unique and continuing manifestation of folk Catholicism in New Mexico. Padre Martínez, it is fairly certain, assumed a position of spiritual leadership for the Penitentes when he was authorized, in 1832, by the last of the Franciscan regional superiors to supervise whatever "Penitentes were to be found in the country north of Santa Fe."

Padre Martínez's personal life has attracted more than its fair share of attention from many writers and commentators. They have had an obsessive fascination with the priest's alleged fathering of children other than his legitimate daughter. At one extreme are the novelistic fancies of Willa Cather, who has the padre fathering children all over northern New Mexico. A more temperate view is that of Fray Angélico Chávez, who infers from strong circumstantial evidence, particularly curious baptismal entries by Martínez, that the priest fathered as many as five children. All the documentary evidence is inferential and indirect. Hard evidence, that is, direct statements in surviving documents or other kinds of incontrovertible primary source or material evidence, has yet to be discovered. At this late date it is unlikely that such evidence will be found.

If the War of the Chimayosos in 1837 and the Texas intrusion of 1841 were the harbingers of major changes in New Mexico, those transformations came with the American invasion of 1846. It was no surprise to nuevomexicano leaders, but it was a somber event for them. As the American invasion was in progress, Governor Manuel Armijo sent a poignant message to Pascual Martínez and a number of prominent *norteños,* including the padre. The message lamented the American invasion and called the recipients to meet to see what, if anything, could be done for the mother country, Mexico, in this sad hour.

Always the pragmatist, Martínez had witnessed the ever growing American presence in Taos. He was aware of the enmity some of these americanos had for him, and he must have noticed the racist attitudes of many of them toward Mexicans and Indians. Still, he knew military resistance was utterly futile against the more numerous and better-armed invading armies of the United States. Early on, he had advised his students to study law because, as he put it, "the American nation is a donkey ridden by lawyers."

Within a year of the invasion, residents of Taos rebelled against the American occupation. Charles Bent, who had been appointed the first American governor of New Mexico, was killed in the action. Detractors have claimed that Padre Martínez instigated the rebellion. No historical evidence supports this claim. Clear, however, is the compassion Martínez felt for the defeated rebels. He wrote a letter, dated April 12, 1847, to Manuel Alvarez, a merchant in Santa Fe, concerning a project to build a road from La Cieneguilla to Embudo that he was supporting. After discussing the road, the padre's letter suddenly jumps to the issue that was obviously foremost in Martínez's mind: the execution of the Taos rebels by the American army. Martínez states with great hyperbole that the executions would hinder the road project because there would be no one left to work on it. This comment is obviously a thinly veiled message about the excessive American reprisals. Martínez also mentions in this letter that he has written to Colonel Sterling W. Price, officer in charge of Union garrison forces in New Mexico, discussing these matters. That letter to Price reveals much about Padre Martínez's character. He admonishes the American that a frightful proceeding is taking place in Taos, and he warns that it could lead to a new uprising. He reminds Colonel Price of the deep injustice of a legal process conducted entirely in English when the defendants speak and understand only Spanish.

These are not the words of a man who is afraid to speak his mind or who is trying to keep a low profile after a failed rebellion. It is inconceivable that American authorities would have allowed Martínez to protest in this manner had there been any evidence of his involvement in the Taos uprising. It is equally inconceivable that they would have allowed him to serve, as he did, on several occasions in the New Mexico Territorial Assembly after 1846.

From his northern perch in Taos, as it were, Martínez observed the changes occurring in New Mexico. He adjusted to these changes as best he could, and he was proactive in many of them. Furthermore, he seemed not to be personally threatened by them.

He saw military rule reestablished in New Mexico after the assassination of Governor Bent indicated the territory's uncertain political status. That questionable status was emphasized by the Compromise of 1850, which allowed California to be admitted as a state but maintained New Mexico as a territory. That territorial status would not change until New Mexico was granted statehood in 1912, long after the passing of Martínez's era.

By 1855 a string of forts was built, Fort Union, Fort Stanton, and Fort Burgwin among others, to protect American interests. Martínez would have been aware of all of this and also of the disputes concerning the southern border of New Mexico when it was discovered that the Disturnell map used to establish the treaty boundary between Mexico and the United States was inaccurate. The disputes were settled in 1853, when James Gadsden negotiated an agreement with Mexico, known as the Gadsden Purchase, that enlarged the southern border of New Mexico and the United States. Railroad construction could now link California to the rest of the nation.

At the very heart of all the new activity related to the coming of the Americans was the city of Santa Fe. By 1850, 80 percent of the nearly five thousand inhabitants were Indo-Hispanic. Yet the Anglo minority held the key positions in the professions, commerce, and the political structure and controlled most of the wealth.

Socially, Santa Fe was a bustling small urban center transformed by commerce. It had an active nightlife with cantinas and gambling halls such as the one operated by Gertrudis Barceló, who became quite wealthy off the gambling and drinking and amorous habits of her patrons. The sight of women like Barceló smoking cigarettes attracted the negative attention of Anglo observers like Susan Shelby Magoffin and many others. The more relaxed lifestyles of nuevomexicanos, including their dress and social behavior, excited the curiosity and, no doubt, the passions of the Americans, especially after the arduous journey down the Santa Fe Trail from Independence, Missouri.

Meanwhile Padre Martínez went about his activities as priest of Taos, ministering to his parishioners and participating in the rich social life of the extended Martínez family. He was on good terms with the Americans, including the Protestants, who were so numerous among them. Generally speaking, Martínez had adjusted well to the political takeover of the Southwest by the United States.

A far more dangerous turn of events for Padre Martínez occurred, however, when Jean Baptiste Lamy arrived in Santa Fe as vicar apostolic in early August 1851. Born in Lempdes, a village in southern France, in 1814, Lamy was almost a generation younger than Martínez. Unlike Martínez, Lamy desired to become a priest from his early childhood. In the seminary as a young man, he met a slightly older seminarian, Joseph Projectus Machebeuf. They were to remain friends and collaborators in religious undertakings for the rest of their lives. Before coming to New Mexico, Lamy and Machebeuf served as missionary priests in Mount Vernon and Sandusky, in the diocese of Cincinnati, Ohio. While Lamy was cerebral and reserved, Machebeuf was a friendly, practical, down-to-earth person. They shared the same missionary zeal, and they worked well together.

Unlike Martínez, with his deep roots in the Mexican northern frontier, Lamy was a known quantity to the American bishops. He reflected the strong religious and moral conservatism of the Catholic Church in the United States at that time. At first the new bishop was greeted with some suspicion by the native New Mexican priests, but that soon passed.

What Lamy saw in New Mexico paralleled what Father Juan Agustín de Morfí noted as early as 1778 in his travels in the territory. That is, New Mexico was a frontier where life could be coarse and disorderly by European or even by American standards of the more settled areas of the East and the Midwest. Women had more freedoms here, but less formality also surrounded day-to-day activities of nuevomexicanos. Although a deeply religious fervor characterized some New Mexicans by the early nineteenth century, as manifested in the rituals of the Penitentes, they had little, if any, of the puritanical spirit that affected even the American Catholic Church by then.

Despite the cultural gaps between Lamy and Martínez, no serious problems arose at first between them. Soon, however, problems did surface. Machebeuf, possibly unaware of the tightly knit family structures and communities of northern New Mexico, made comments that some parishioners interpreted as violations of the seal of confession—a very serious charge in the Catholic religion. The charges against Machebeuf were brought to the attention of Martínez, who wrote letters to Lamy complaining about Machebeuf.

FIGURE 5.3. Gertrudis Barceló, La Doña Tules, 1854. Photo courtesy Museum of New Mexico, neg. no. 50815.

Other conflicts ensued between Machebeuf and the Hispanic clergy. In effect, a cultural clash poorly understood by all parties developed in New Mexico between the zealous bishop Lamy and the nuevomexicano clergy long accustomed to little, if any, outside interference in their lives. Under Mexican rule, the bishop had been far away in Durango. Now the bishop was in the very midst of New Mexico, and his ways were different.

Nuevomexicanos had good reason to be wary of Lamy. The bishop was patronizing to his primarily Spanish-speaking faithful. On one occasion, Lamy wrote a very self-damaging letter in which he said that Mexicans faced a sad future because they didn't have the intellectual liveliness of Americans and their morals were primitive. The nuevomexicano priests and their parishioners were no fools. They undoubtedly noticed and felt the disdain and contempt so implicit in Lamy's words, even if he didn't address them directly in the letter.

Other problems developed. As Protestant missionaries entered New Mexico in substantial numbers after 1848, Padre Martínez greeted them in an ecumenical spirit far ahead of his times. This openhanded approach must have aggravated Bishop Lamy. There were other disagreements: disputes over tithing, interpretations of church law, and the rights of lay parishioners under U.S. law.

By early 1856 relations between Lamy and the nuevomexicano clergy had deteriorated even further. Padre José Manuel Gallegos, another recalcitrant priest and a former student of Padre Martínez, was then an elected territorial deputy to Washington. He and other nuevomexicano priests wrote a letter to the Pope directly attacking Lamy. Although Martínez was not involved with this letter, his health was in decline, and he became far less active. He nevertheless continued to write broadsides to the *Santa Fe Gazette* that no doubt irritated Lamy.

Then in April 1856 Martínez offered to resign if he could name and train his successor. This offer was not as arrogant as it may seem, considering Martínez's great knowledge of northern New Mexico. Cleverly Lamy accepted the resignation but sent his own priest to replace Martínez. Further disputes with Martínez ensued, and a frustrated Lamy finally excommunicated him and Padre Mariano de Jesús Lucero, a follower of Martínez, in the spring of 1858. Martínez, for his part, never acknowledged the validity of the excommunications.

In later years, to his credit and despite the toll that age took on his mental powers, Padre Martínez continued to show flashes of insight and eloquence in his writings. In September 1859, at age sixty-six, he published a broadside titled simply "Religión." In it he developed his all-inclusive vision of religion and Christianity. He argued the justice of small honorariums for the religious work of priests, given the excessive demands made on them in New Mexico. He also pointed out the injustice of denying the sacraments to anyone for mere financial reasons. Again, however, he confused the secular with the religious by taking the whip to the New Mexico Territorial Legislature for not taxing these unjust tithes and reinvesting them in good works for the Territory!

In this same broadside, Martínez denounced the Inquisition and all its inhumane excesses and excommunications. This attack was probably a not-so-veiled jab at Bishop Lamy for the 1858 excommunications and for the bishop's general intolerance of Protestants. All in all, the writing in "Religión" is enlightened, ecumenical, and deeply humane. It is also highly imaginative and inventive, even if it confuses the spiritual and secular domains under American rule. Martínez signed the broadside on a touching and defiant note: "He who signs his name here professes the Roman Catholic and Apostolic Faith. He proclaims that he lives and will die in this faith."

Padre Martínez died on July 27, 1867. The Penitentes gave him a burial service that would have honored a king.

There are three particularly significant aspects of Padre Martínez's legacy. First, he belonged to an older Mexican agrarian tradition. His ideological axis and his personal, social, political, and economic beliefs ran north to south, from the Mexican northern frontier to Mexico City and to the Spanish-speaking world beyond. He embodied Indo-Hispanic values less regarded in nineteenth- and twentieth-century America. Specifically, without being a provincial, he exemplified a sense of belonging, a communal sense of rootedness in a time and place, in contrast to the individualistic rootlessness of much of contemporary industrial and postindustrial America. In addition, Padre Martínez embraced a cultural and ethnic identification, call it Mexican or Mexican American, that only recently has experienced a revival, for example, in the Chicano movement. He embodied a cultural and intellectual heritage that owed much more to the Hispanic world than to the Anglo-American tradition.

Second, Padre Martínez was the single most important intellectual link of nuevomexicanos to the literary and cultural riches of the Hispanic world. His own education and experience of the world were almost entirely contexted within the Indo-Hispanic tradition. His coed school conducted in Spanish, his publishing of religious and educational books in Spanish, his liberal political activism, and his defense of nuevomexicano rights left a legacy only recently rediscovered by Chicano scholars and activists.

Third, within New Mexico itself, the religious and personal conflict between Martínez and Bishop Lamy helped lead to the rise of Protestantism, particularly Presbyterianism, in northern New Mexico. In the wake of the two men's dispute, the Catholic unity of northern New Mexico was shattered. For better or worse it has never been restored. On his part, Martínez was headstrong and proud in this conflict. In his dotage, his grasp of his own ecclesiastical situation may very well have slipped away from him. Bishop Lamy, on the other hand, was insensitive in the extreme to his faithful parishioners, with documentary evidence revealing the deep contempt he had for Mexicans in comparison with Americans. If peace, harmony, and cultural diversity are important human values, these values were set back for at least a century by the bitterness that still lingers after the dispute between the two priests.

With hindsight and the passage of time, the Mexican period of New Mexican history (1821–46) stands out as the most significant formative period in the life of Padre Martínez. Leaving childhood and early young-adult experiences aside and granting their importance, it was nevertheless during the Mexican period that Martínez completed his formal education in the Durango seminary and became a priest, experienced the loss of his daughter, and entered into the swirl of personal, political, social, religious, educational, and publishing activities that mark him as a distinct historical personality. The Mexican period, then, was the deep structural formative time without which the events after 1846, in reference to Padre Antonio José Martínez, lose their resonance.

Essay on Sources

For this essay, primary source materials were used whenever possible. Among the most valuable sources were the Reed Collection, New Mexico State Records Center and Archives, Santa Fe, New Mexico; the Pascual Martínez Papers, Center for Southwest Research, Zimmerman Library, University of New Mexico, Albuquerque; Historical Archives of the Archdiocese of Durango, available on microfilm from the Rio Grande

Historical Collection/Hobson-Huntsinger University Archives, New Mexico State University, Las Cruces; the personal collections of Vicente Martínez in the Padre Martínez Study Center, Vicente Martínez Home, Taos. Also consulted were the Martínez primary source holdings of the Huntington Library, San Marino, California, and the Bancroft Library, University of California, Berkeley. A published book that is also a primary source in reference to its writer is Pedro Sánchez, *Memorias del Padre Antonio Jose Martinez* (Santa Fe: Compania Impresora del Nuevo Mexicano, 1903), a first edition of which is in the possession of the author.

The following books are widely available and of interest to the general reader: Ray John de Aragon's *Padre Martinez and Bishop Lamy* (Las Vegas, N.Mex.: Pan-American Press, 1978) illustrates the love and high esteem of many nuevomexicanos for Padre Martínez. The book also contains the best reproduction this author has seen of the sole daguerreotype photograph of Padre Martínez. Lynn Bridgers has crafted a beautifully written biography of Joseph P. Machebeuf in *Death's Deceiver: The Life of Joseph P. Machebeuf* (Albuquerque: University of New Mexico Press, 1997). Machebeuf is a key figure in the Padre Martínez story. Bridgers's views on Machebeuf stand in sharp contrast with those expressed by Fray Angélico Chávez in *But Time and Chance* (Santa Fe: Sunstone Press, 1981). This book, despite its personal preoccupations and idiosyncrasies, remains the best biography to date of Padre Martínez.

Willa Cather produced a forerunner of the docudrama with her novelistic account *Death Comes for the Archbishop* (New York: Knopf, 1927). Her book remains the first introduction for many Americans to the Southwest, New Mexico, and the fictionalized versions of Bishop Lamy and Padre Martínez. Cather's book is a brilliant mix of literature and fictionalized history. As such, it should be read with caution for historical research and understanding. On Jean Baptiste Lamy, one should read Paul Horgan's significant, although not definitive, biography of Jean Baptiste Lamy in *Lamy of Santa Fe* (New York: Farrar, Strauss, Giroux, 1975).

Several other volumes are of general use. Janet Lecompte's *Rebellion in Río Arriba—1837* (Albuquerque: University of New Mexico Press, 1985) is an invaluable source of information on the guerra de los chimayosos. E. A. Mares offers a dramatization of Padre Martínez, *I Returned and Saw Under the Sun* (Albuquerque: University of New Mexico Press, 1989). Another book he edited, *Padre Martínez: New Perspectives from Taos* (Taos: Millicent Rogers Museum, 1988), is a collection of essays that present a broad spectrum of historical and literary research and opinions on the priest. Michael C. Meyer and William L. Sherman's *The Course of Mexican History,* 3d ed. (New York: Oxford University Press, 1987), provides an excellent general overview of Mexican history. Meanwhile Richard L. Nostrand presents a readable and detailed social geography of northern New Mexico, *The Hispano Homeland* (Norman: University of Oklahoma Press, 1992). Thomas J. Steele, S.J., *Folk and Church* (Colorado Springs, Colo.: Hulbert Center for Southwest Studies, Colorado College, 1993), is a collection of occasional papers written with exacting scholarship and keen humor dealing with Padre Martínez and northern New Mexico materials. David Weber's *On the Edge of Empire* (Santa Fe: Museum of New Mexico Press, 1996) is a clear and detailed history focused on the Taos hacienda of the Martínez family. The author also wishes to acknowledge here the helpful comments and insights in conversations with Tomás Atencio, Father Luis Jaramillo, Ward Alan Minge, Richard Rudisill, Father Thomas Steele, S.J., Vicente Martínez, and David Weber.

6

Mangas Coloradas and Mid-Nineteenth-Century Conflicts

EDWIN R. SWEENEY

*S*hortly before dusk, on October 18, 1846, two miles west of Santa Rita del Cobre in the heart of Chiricahua Apache country, a dramatic meeting took place between the leaders of two very different cultures. As the American force passed the walls of the once prosperous mining center, deserted because of Apache hostilities, they must have sympathized with the residents who had had the courage to live in this isolated settlement. Leading the Americans was Brigadier General Stephen Watts Kearny, a veteran officer of the American West noted for his strict discipline and energetic temperament. He had recently occupied New Mexico in response to the declaration of war between the United States and Mexico. Soon after the command bivouacked, the news that three mounted Apaches were approaching from the west stirred the camp. The Indians, as it turned out, were led by Mangas Coloradas, the powerfully built tribal leader of the Chiricahua Apaches, who had directed his people in a fierce and uncompromising war against northern Mexico for much of the previous fifteen years.

Kearny had just occupied New Mexico with his "Army of the West." Leaving the bulk of his command in northern New Mexico, he had decided to take a small detachment of troops to California. His march through southern New Mexico placed him in the domain of Mangas Coloradas. Although Mangas Coloradas had never heard of Kearny, it is safe to assume that the American general knew of him. For Mangas Coloradas was the most celebrated yet most misunderstood Indian leader of the Southwest. The two men quickly discovered that they shared one important interest: they had a common enemy in Mexico. This sentiment alone was enough for Mangas Coloradas to warmly welcome Kearny's force and to pledge "good faith and friendship to all Americans."

The face-to-face meeting with the tribal leader of the Chiricahua Apaches went far better than Kearny could have expected. He encountered a race that its enemies described as sinister and savage—a reputation earned during their centuries of resistance against Spanish and Mexican forces. But their foes had painted them with a very broad and partisan brush without any understanding of or consideration for the Apache culture. As far as most whites were concerned, Apaches were cruel and merciless, warlike and incorrigible. These characterizations were certainly apt when describing their mode of warfare and their methods of dealing with their enemies.

Yet what most Anglos and Mexicans failed to understand was that these Apaches, members of the Southern Athapaskan linguistic family, were not warlike by nature. On the other hand, Mangas Coloradas, because Americans had not done anything to merit that designation, did not consider them his enemy. That evolution from friend to foe was earned by systematic abuses of the relationship or by egregious acts of treachery that took Apache lives. Only when Americans betrayed that trust did Mangas finally go to war. For now, the greatest Apache leader of his time, who had earned his reputation fighting the forces of Sonora and Chihuahua, saw Americans as potential allies in his just war against Mexicans—a war that had come about because of a steady pattern of mistreatment by Mexicans of Apaches. One Apache chief (perhaps it was Mangas Coloradas himself) declared to Kearny, "You have taken New Mexico and will soon take California, go then and take Chihuahua, Durango, and Sonora. We will help you. . . . The Mexicans are rascals; we hate and kill all of them."

When Kearny occupied New Mexico, he told residents that he had come to liberate them from Mexican rule. He promised that his army would pay for everything it required and pledged to protect citizens from the incursions of hostile Indians. Kearny had brought a force of 1,658 men, of whom three hundred were regular U.S. troops of the First Regiment of Dragoons.

FIGURE 6.1. Mangas Coloradas's home range in Arizona and New Mexico, 1790–1863. From Edwin R. Sweeney, *Mangas Coloradas: Chief of the Chiricahua Apache* (Norman: University of Oklahoma Press, 1998), p. 6.

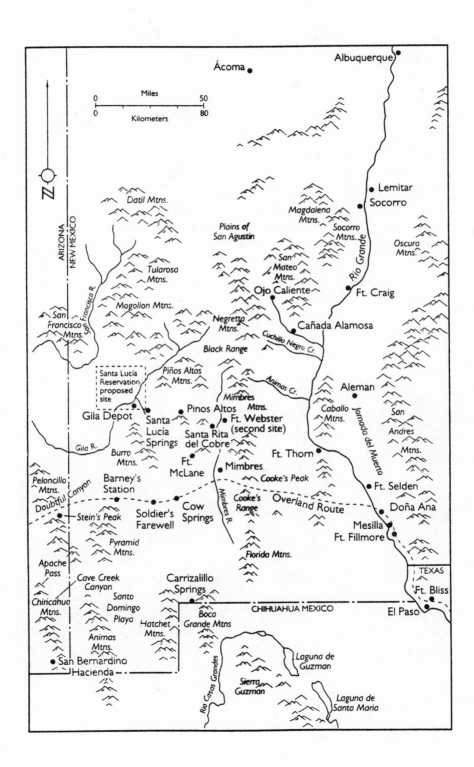

The balance was composed of Missouri Volunteers, most of them mounted, whose stay in New Mexico was destined to be short. Colonel Alexander William Doniphan took most of the Missouri Volunteers and invaded Mexico, where he fought several battles and eventually occupied Chihuahua City. To replace Doniphan's command, Colonel Sterling Price led another force of twelve hundred volunteers from Missouri and Illinois, thus providing a much needed military presence in northern New Mexico for the duration of the war. In August 1848, with the Mexican War over, most of the Volunteers were discharged from service.

These Volunteers were replaced by the regular army, whose primary mission was to provide protection to New Mexican settlers and peaceful Indians (such as the Pueblos) from the incursions of hostile Indians. The army's sphere of influence, however, extended far beyond its military role. It would also affect the fabric of New Mexico's cultural, economic, and political systems. For these newcomers from eastern states brought their Anglo values to the region. Hispanics and Indians were suddenly con-

FIGURE 6.2. Santa Lucía Springs, New Mexico. Near today's Mangas Springs, this location was the favorite camping site of Mangas Coloradas. Photo by Kathi Plauster.

fronted with different political, economic, and religious philosophies. With Anglo rule came a civic structure founded on democratic ideals, an economy ruled by the free market that was based on cash instead of barter, and a religious freedom to worship (many of the American newcomers were Protestants, whereas most of New Mexico's citizens were Catholic). These developments gradually forced changes in the traditional ways of life of Hispanics and Indians that some historians have termed the Americanization of the region.

In October 1848 Major John Macrae Washington, Third Artillery, fresh from service in Mexico, arrived in New Mexico and became the military governor of the territory. He had but five hundred troops at his disposal and could not expect any reinforcements until the following summer. As for his principal mandate, controlling the Indians, he faced an impossible task. By the terms of the Treaty of Guadalupe Hidalgo, which ended the Mexican War, Mexico formally ceded New Mexico to the United States. One article of the treaty obligated the United States to prevent hostile Indians from entering Mexico to commit depredations. Of course, Major Washington could do nothing to enforce this condition. His force was so limited, he could station only 150 men at Socorro and Doña Ana on the Rio Grande in the middle of Mescalero and Chiricahua country. Both tribes considered themselves at war with Mexico, despite the Treaty of Guadalupe Hidalgo. The commander also had little support from his superiors in Washington, who had neither formulated an official policy nor allocated any funds for the Indians of New Mexico.

The American presence would alter the balance of power, though it is questionable whether the Indians of New Mexico realized it then. The military and civil authorities had arrived with preconceived notions of Indians, believing they were just another obstacle in the path of destiny and progress. To most whites, Indians were subhuman and their way of life deficient and uncivilized. It remained the responsibility of the civilized society to elevate these savages from their lower order into a culture with morals and ideals. Initially military officials made little attempt to understand these Indians, and their goal was to preserve peace as long as the natives stayed in line. They would respond to hostilities, no matter who was at fault, swiftly and harshly. And each time such an incident occurred, the military rattled its saber, and the Indians they subdued ended up weaker than before.

It would be several years before the new regime formulated a coherent

Indian policy. Unlike the Spanish, and to a lesser extent the Mexicans, who felt some empathy for Indians who tried to live in peace, the new conquerors of New Mexico shared none of those feelings. The military failed to understand that during the first half of the nineteenth century, the tribes inhabiting northern New Mexico, the Jicarilla Apaches of the eastern and central areas of the northern part of the state and the Navajos in the northwestern region, had striven to maintain a peaceful coexistence with their Hispanic and Pueblo neighbors—one based on trade. Even the tribes living in the southern part of the territory, the Mescalero Apaches in the southeastern area and the Bedonkohe and Chihenne bands of the Chiricahua Apaches in the southwestern area, enjoyed peaceful trading relations with the settlements situated along the Rio Grande, especially at Socorro and Doña Ana, New Mexico. Yet the Chiricahuas and Mescaleros considered themselves at war with Sonora and Chihuahua, which formed the American perception that they were incorrigible and warlike by nature. Although these four tribes were separated by geography and their philosophies differed because of various experiences, they shared one common thread: they were of the Athapaskan linguistic family.

These Athapaskans were late arrivals to the Southwest, probably reaching their historic homelands by the sixteenth century. Besides a common language, these Southern Athapaskans, frequently called Apaches, shared several cultural traits. They lived in small, mobile bands or groups, usually in mountainous areas. They were hunters and gatherers and were quick to adopt new technology from the people with whom they came into contact. A spiritual people, they believed that both animate and inanimate objects possessed power that could be handed over to tribal members. By nature they were peaceful and usually went to war to protect their territory or their families or to exact vengeance upon enemies who had abused them. That they sustained some warfare for prolonged periods, as in the Chiricahuas' warfare against the Spanish and later the Mexicans and Americans, was a function of a self-perpetuating cycle of violence that became a way of life from one generation to another.

The Athapaskans in northern New Mexico, the Jicarillas and Navajos, had learned how to coexist under Spanish and Mexican rule. The Athapaskans in southern New Mexico, the Mescalero and Chiricahuas, were initially unaffected by the American presence, continuing to wage war against northern Mexico. Discord between citizens and Apaches was bound to break out, and the military (and most Americans of that time), ever disdainful of the Indian point of view, tended to support the local citizenry. Moreover, peace and war factions divided the tribes (particularly the Jicarillas, Mescaleros, and Chiricahuas), and it was customary for Apaches to seek vengeance against those who wronged them. This equation would lead to war.

The Navajos were the first to feel the wrath of American punitive expeditions. Unlike their Apache relatives, who were organized into distinct bands, the Navajos lived in clans scattered over a large territory in northwestern New Mexico and northeastern Arizona. They were easily the most numerous of the Southern Athapaskans, perhaps numbering ten to twelve thousand persons. They were hunters and gatherers, but they also had learned the benefits of raising crops and livestock and had accumulated great herds of sheep and horses. This self-sufficiency made them the envy of their Indian neighbors. Although the Apaches were reputed to be fierce raiders and fighters, the Navajos were equally accomplished in their day and just as formidable.

In response to a few Navajo raids in the late summer of 1849, Major Washington organized an expedition into their country. His forces included regular troops and New Mexico Volunteers, primarily Pueblo Indians. They penetrated deep into Navajo country. In the Chuska Mountains, which straddle today's Arizona–New Mexico line, the two sides met in council. When the Indians refused to return a horse stolen from a settlement, Washington's army attacked them and even fired several rounds of artillery. At the end of this unfortunate affair, one chief, Narbona, lay dead, riddled with wounds. One Volunteer rushed forward and scalped the peace chief. Several days later Washington's army made a treaty with a few Navajo headmen, whose sole purpose in acquiescing was to rid their country of the American invaders. Instead of securing a worthwhile peace, Washington's senseless assault prompted a typical Athapaskan response: the Navajos retaliated and killed several Americans, Zunis, and Pueblo Indians. All told, the incident served only to create additional distrust of Americans.

The army also abused the Jicarilla Apaches. Longtime allies of the Utes, the Jicarillas numbered about a thousand souls and were divided into two bands: the Olleros (Mountain Valley people) and the Llaneros (Plains people). The Olleros band, which consisted of six smaller units, called local groups, lived in the mountainous country south and west of Taos; the Llaneros were divided into eight local groups and claimed the Cimarron country north of Mora and Las Vegas. Although the Jicarillas retained much of their Athapaskan culture, they did embrace other cultural traits of the Plains Indians, such as the tipi and travois. In addition, they adopted agricultural practices of the Pueblo Indians of the upper Rio Grande. The Llaneros band ventured into the Texas Panhandle and Llano Estacado, usually with the Utes, to hunt buffalo. At these times they had to be particularly vigilant because the Southern Plains tribes, the Kiowas, southern bands of Cheyennes and Arapahos, and especially the Comanches were inveterate enemies. In contrast to the Llaneros, the Olleros remained closer to their mountain homes and specialized in making pottery and baskets that they traded in the local Hispanic villages. As a tribe, they preferred peace to war, though small raiding parties, with the Utes, had reportedly committed raids against isolated New Mexican settlements during the first few years of Anglo rule.

Hostilities erupted unexpectedly when a group of forty Jicarillas of the Llaneros band made a customary visit to Las Vegas to trade in August 1849. Lieutenant Henry Bethel Judd, Third Artillery, who had no understanding of the political organization of Apaches, believed they had been raiding. Instead of talking to get the Indians' point of view, he decided, in a pattern that would be repeated countless times in the Southwest, to initiate military action. As the Jicarillas were leaving town, he ordered his soldiers to attack them for their alleged depredations. A skirmish followed, and at the end of the day this uncalled-for assault had succeeded in killing fourteen and capturing six Jicarillas, including the daughter of Lobo Blanco, a prominent band leader. The survivors fled panic-stricken to their camps with cries of foul play and treachery.

Two months later the Jicarillas avenged this wanton assault in an attack that drew national attention. In extreme northeastern New Mexico, near Point of Rocks, an important landmark along the Santa Fe Trail, a band of Jicarillas and Utes approached a party of Americans led by noted Santa Fe merchant James M. White. White, his wife and daughter, and an African American servant girl with four other men had decided to travel ahead of the main wagon train when Indians confronted them on October 28, 1849. According to the Jicarillas, they had approached White's party as friends, but the Americans opened fire on them. The Indians responded in kind, eventually overwhelming the small group, killing White and his four companions and capturing his wife, daughter, and servant. Once the officials at Taos and Las Vegas heard the news, they dispatched troops to punish the Jicarillas and to recover White's family. The command from Las Vegas, which brought the daughter of Lobo Blanco along as guide, failed to find the Indians. The soldiers were forced to kill the girl after she grabbed a knife, slit the throat of one mule, and tried to stab two soldiers. Lobo Blanco would later avenge his daughter's death, holding the military accountable. The other command, guided by Kit Carson, discovered the Indian village in which the Jicarillas were holding Mrs. White. Tragically, before they could negotiate for her release, the Indians fired upon the soldiers and abandoned their village, but not before killing Mrs. White and probably her daughter and servant, both of whom were never heard of again.

About this time the army sent reinforcements to New Mexico in the form of ten companies of the Third Infantry, two companies of the Second Artillery, and one company of the Second Dragoons. Indian agent James C. Calhoun also reached Santa Fe and assumed jurisdiction over the Indians, and Major John Munroe replaced Washington as the military commander and governor. Yet these steps failed to deter the Jicarillas, who continued hostilities into 1850. They surprised a mail party at Wagon Mound, about forty miles northeast of Las Vegas, in which the Indians wiped out the entire party of eleven men. Naturally the military launched expeditions that eventually took a toll on the Jicarillas. Finally on April 2, 1851, Chacon, principal chief of the Olleros band, and Lobo Blanco signed a treaty at Santa Fe with Indian agent and governor James C. Calhoun, thus ending the first phase of hostilities between Jicarillas and Americans.

Calhoun, originally appointed Indian agent and soon after governor, was a sincere man who recognized that the Indians, in order to survive, required reservations remote from settlements as well as government assistance. Otherwise the Natives faced the prospects of the whites swallowing up their tribal territory and punitive military campaigns. In 1852 Congress finally acted on his recommendations and allocated funds for four Indian agents. Meanwhile in Washington the War Department had reviewed its policies concerning New Mexico and decided that the government was squandering assets by locating garrisons near the major towns along the Rio Grande. Consequently New Mexico's new military commander, Lieutenant Colonel Edwin Vose Sumner, was sent to replace Major John Munroe. Sumner shared one common sentiment with Munroe. Each despised New Mexico and thought the federal government was wasting valuable resources there. Both advocated that the government abandon the territory and thus allow the Indians and New Mexicans to fight each other for control of the state.

Sumner reached his new assignment with the mandate of the secretary of war etched in his mind: "Both economy and the efficiency of the service would be promoted by removing the troops out of the towns where they are now stationed and placing them more towards the frontier and nearer to the Indians." Sumner decided to relocate the garrisons from the settlements to the frontier, where they could better control the Indians and, in the south, better protect the Mexican border from Chiricahua and Mescalero incursions to comply with the Treaty of Guadalupe Hidalgo. On July 26, 1851, he established Fort Union, in the heart of the Llaneros band of Jicarilla country, twenty-four miles northeast of Las Vegas on the west side of Wolf Creek. In September 1851 he placed two posts near the Rio Grande, smack on the eastern border of Chiricahua country and the western range of the Mescaleros. Fort Conrad, twenty-five miles south of Socorro, and Fort Fillmore, six miles below Mesilla, were designed to control Apache raiding. Later that month his soldiers set up Fort Defiance, in the heart of Navajo country. And in early 1852 a new post was situated at the abandoned Santa Rita del Cobre, some twenty miles east of Silver City in the middle of Chihenne country. Despite Sumner's arrogance, his autocratic rule, his intolerance, and his disdain for Washington-appointed Indian agents and civilian officials (including Governors Calhoun and William Carr Lane), his actions and network of forts became the basic system of defense on the Indian frontier.

Sumner's policies were to have a profound impact on the Mescaleros east of the Rio Grande and the Chiricahua bands to the west. The Mescaleros, who numbered between twelve hundred and fifteen hundred individuals, were organized into two tribal divisions: those who lived east of the mountains (People of the Plains) and those who lived in the mountains (Rock-Crevice people). Each division was further split into local groups. They were hunters and gatherers, harvesting the agave or mescal plant in the spring and organizing buffalo hunts into Texas in the fall. Local groups lived in the White, Sacramento, and Guadalupe Mountains in southeastern New Mexico, while other groups lived in southwestern Texas in the Big Bend and Davis Mountain country. These groups, under the bellicose leader Gómez, frequently attacked parties traveling through this country, especially along the San Antonio to El Paso road.

In July 1852 the leaders of several Mescalero groups living in the White and Sacramento Mountains signed a treaty at Santa Fe with Americans. They did not represent the entire tribe, however. Other Mescaleros continued raiding, most conspicuously Gómez, who led an assault on a wagon train that killed several Americans and absconded with their property. In response, the military dispatched troops into Mescalero country, but the Indians promptly detected their presence and easily eluded the slow-moving soldiers. When isolated raids continued throughout 1854 and early 1855, Colonel John Garland, who had replaced Sumner as the department commander, decided to snap the whip at the hostile Mescaleros. Two columns, totaling some 180 men, converged on Mescalero country—one from the north (Albuquerque) and the other from the southwest (Fort Fillmore). With the Mescaleros in winter camps, the command under Captain Richard Stoddert Ewell, affectionately known to his men for obvious reasons as Old Baldy, engaged the Indians in several skirmishes and one major fight. The soldiers killed several Mescaleros and uprooted the remainder from the comforts of their winter homes at a cost of three dead, including Captain Henry Whiting Stanton, who showed much courage and bravery in the fight, according to later Apache accounts. When a few months later Colonel Garland ordered that a post be constructed in Mescalero country, he named it Fort Stanton after the brave officer who fell in the line of duty. By this time most of the Mescaleros living in southeastern New Mexico had decided they wanted peace.

Meanwhile the Mescaleros' neighbors to the west, the Chiricahuas, had remained pretty much untouched by the American presence, that is, until the establishment (in January 1852) of a post at Santa Rita del Cobre, named Fort Webster. The Chiricahuas at this time numbered about twenty-two hundred souls and comprised four bands. The Chihennes lived in the country between today's Silver City and the Rio Grande, and the Bedonkohes from Silver City west toward the Arizona border. The other two Chiricahua bands, the Chokonens, led by the celebrated Cochise, inhabited southeastern Arizona, and the fourth band, the Nednhis, called northern Mexico their home. Although the Chiricahuas had tried to remain at peace with Americans, they had fought occasional skirmishes between Kearny's arrival in 1846 and 1851. When American troops garrisoned Fort Webster on a cold and raw January day, the Apaches viewed it as an unwelcome intrusion into their ancestral country.

To this point neither forts nor settlements had been placed in their country. When they approached the fort to talk, their two leaders, Ponce and Delgadito, normally peacefully inclined men, were contemptuously received by the American commander, who was itching for a fight. Ignoring that he was trespassing on Apache land, he imperiously ordered the Indians to leave or risk an attack by his soldiers, who, he threatened, "would send them to the happy hunting grounds." Bewildered at this reception, the Chiricahuas procrastinated; the American captain interpreted the delay as an act of hostility and opened fire, first with muskets and then with his cannon, killing several Indians. A few days later the Chiricahuas, seeking vengeance, returned with a larger force and decoyed the soldiers away from the fort and killed three men.

Yet in the 1850s, hostilities between the Chiricahuas and Americans proved to be the exception rather than the rule. The Indians signed treaties with Americans in the summer of 1852, the spring of 1853, and the summer of 1855. Each pact contained terms designed to change the Indians' lifestyle, confine their movements, and make them more dependent on the government for food. Even worse, Washington officials either ignored or vetoed commitments made to the Indians by American representatives. Yet these justifications were never based on compassionate or humane reasons. Indians had no conception that federal policy was subject to the whims of each administration. Furthermore, Congress refused to allocate adequate funding to honor commitments made by agents, nor would it pay Indians for ancestral ground because it refused to recognize Indian ownership of land in New Mexico that Mexico had already ceded to the United States. Instead Indians grew more suspicious of local representatives and distrustful of the federal government in Washington.

Caught in the middle between the threat of military force or trusting American civil officials to live up to their agreements, New Mexico's Indians found these times perplexing. In the spring of 1855 President Franklin Pierce appointed Governor David Meriwether as special commissioner to make treaties with the Indians of New Mexico. Meriwether, who had assumed the governorship in the summer of 1853, had struggled for a practicable Indian policy. He concluded that he faced two options: feed them or wipe them out. Meriwether gave the latter course some consideration, but he eventually adopted the pacific course of issuing rations to the Indians while assigning them reservations away from settlements. In the spring and summer of 1855 he consummated treaties with the Navajos, Mescaleros, Chiricahuas, Utes, and Jicarillas.

For the Jicarillas, the treaty was a welcome end to another war—a war that had begun after American mistreatment of the Olleros band and the killing of one of its leaders. During eighteen months of hostilities, the

Jicarillas and their Ute allies fought several pitched battles, including an incredible fight in which they stormed out like angry hornets and killed or wounded forty-five out of a detachment of sixty men (the most American casualties in any encounter with the southwestern Athapaskans) after these troops had attacked their village. But in the end, the Americans' war of attrition, which cost the Jicarillas dearly in loss of life and supplies, inevitably forced the Indians to sue for peace.

Meriwether's treaty with the Jicarillas placed them on a reservation northeast of Abiquiu. And even though the Senate failed to ratify any of Meriwether's treaties, they did provide the framework for a workable Indian policy. Clearly, rather than extermination through military might, the Indians could expect life on a reservation sustained by minimal government support. By the late 1850s the government did begin to provide rations and annual annuities for the three tribes of Apaches, as well as the Navajos and Utes who occasionally roamed from southern Colorado into northern New Mexico.

Thus the last few years of the 1850s brought more stability between whites and Indians. Yet conflicts were still bound to occur, especially when Indians were involved with local citizens in their country. The Mesilla Guard, a militia unit organized to fight the Mescaleros and Chiricahuas who dared appear in the region around Mesilla, twice launched wanton attacks against peaceful Mescaleros at Fort Thorn and at Doña Ana along the Rio Grande. The Bedonkohe band of Chiricahuas occasionally raided ranches and settlements along the Rio Grande. In the spring of 1857 the military organized an expedition, later known as the Bonneville campaign, to punish these sorties. Although the results were not all that were hoped for, the campaign succeeded in routing a Western Apache band in Arizona and in destroying a Chiricahua camp in the Black Range, during which attack the famous chief Cuchillo Negro was mortally wounded. In another conflict, the Navajos went to war in 1860, audaciously attacking Fort Defiance in April of that year, but the military promptly quelled the uprising and accomplished yet another treaty.

Meanwhile in the spring of 1861, New Mexico's federal and civil officials were forced to redirect their military focus from Athapaskans to repel an invasion by an army from Texas. Two thousand miles to the east the Civil War had begun on April 12, 1861, with the battle at Fort Sumter, South Carolina. Soon many officers serving in New Mexico were resigning their command and joining the Confederacy, which cast its eyes on the territory of New Mexico and California. Confederate leaders dreamed of establishing a corridor to southern California, hoping to acquire Pacific ports, mineral wealth, and the military stores and equipment of the federal forces.

New Mexico's department commander, Colonel Edward Richard Sprigg Canby, assumed command of an army in shambles in May 1861. Fearing a Rebel invasion, he decided to concentrate troops in southern New Mexico at Forts Fillmore, Craig, and Stanton. In late July, Lieutenant Colonel John Robert Baylor led a Confederate force that occupied Mesilla. After a brief skirmish with Baylor's command, the Union commander, Major Isaac Lynde, evacuated Fort Fillmore and marched his entire army toward Fort Stanton. En route, Lynde's army was overtaken by Baylor's command and captured without firing a shot.

The news stunned Canby. But he soon had other concerns: former Union officer Henry Hopkins Sibley, who had resigned his commission, had gone to Richmond to seek approval of President Jefferson Davis to recruit a force of Texans to invade New Mexico. Sibley had a visionary strategy that began with the conquest of New Mexico, Colorado, and finally California. Davis approved the plan and commissioned Sibley brigadier general. He returned to San Antonio and raised a mounted force of three thousand men, many of whom were veterans of the Mexican War and experienced Indian fighters. Sibley reached Mesilla in late 1861 and readied his army for an assault at Fort Craig, where Canby had concentrated his forces.

Canby decided to make his stand at Fort Craig, which was strategically situated on a mesa on the west bank of the Rio Grande about four miles below San Marcial. First he shored up the fort's defenses, strengthening walls and bringing in reinforcements. He also called up volunteer and militia units and moved supplies and ammunition from Albuquerque and Fort Union. The first significant contest between Union and Confederate troops in New Mexico took place at Valverde, near Fort Craig, on February 21, 1862. Although Canby's force outnumbered Sibley's army, the ferocious fighting spirit of the Confederates, who boldly charged their enemy with double-barrel shotguns blazing, won the day. Sibley demanded that Canby surrender the fort; when he defiantly refused, the Rebel commander decided to bypass Fort Craig and continue his march north along the Rio Grande, as his army had already stripped the lower Rio Grande settlements of provisions. He easily captured Santa Fe and Albuquerque, facing little opposition as the Union forces had retreated east to Fort Union. The fort's vast quantities of military stores were enticing to Sibley, and he made plans to capture it. Sibley, however, was unaware that a large body of Colorado Volunteers, rugged miners itching for a fight, had reinforced Fort Union.

Colonel John P. Slough, who commanded the Colorado troops, was in no mood to wait for the Rebels. He determined to strike first. At the head of thirteen hundred fighting men, he headed for Santa Fe. On March 26 an advance detachment, under Major John M. Chivington, a Denver clergyman, skirmished with and defeated a small Rebel force at the Battle of Apache Canyon. Two days later, in a battle that would be later called the "Gettysburg of the West," the enemies met at Glorieta Pass, twenty miles southeast of Santa Fe. Despite the absence of Canby and Sibley, the fight would prove to be the turning point of the war in New Mexico. It was a bloody and hotly contested affair. About a thousand Confederate troops under Colonel William R. Scurry battled Slough's force in a dramatic six-hour fight in which musket fire and artillery dominated. By the end of the day, each side had sustained a loss of some 130 killed, wounded, and captured. With the federal force in retreat, Colonel Scurry believed his brave men had stopped the offensive in its tracks.

Yet unknown to Scurry, the Union force had an ace in the hole. Before the battle commenced, Colonel Slough had sent Major Chivington with four hundred men, guided by Lieutenant Colonel Manuel Chávez, First New Mexico Volunteers, on a grueling five-hour march through narrow defiles and over rocky ledges, hoping to get behind the Confederate force. Instead Chivington unexpectedly stumbled upon the Rebels' supply train. At once he decided to lead a charge against the encampment. After a short struggle, his men captured the whole train of eighty wagons, its supply of provisions, and the horse herd, some five hundred in all. They burned the train and with heavy hearts killed the horses by slitting their throats. The report shocked Scurry, who believed his men had won the battle. His soldiers were forced to retreat to Santa Fe, and the Confederate invasion of New Mexico was in essence over. Sibley had lost about one-third of his force. His army, lacking supplies, marched back to Texas in disgrace.

Shortly after the ouster of Sibley's army, a Union force reached New Mexico from California. With no Confederates to fight, this army restored federal rule to New Mexico during the Civil War. The twenty-three hundred men were commanded by Brigadier General James Henry Carleton. An experienced and able officer whom some called a martinet, Carleton had replaced Canby, who had been transferred east. Without Confederates to fight, Carleton turned his attention to the Indians, especially the Navajos, Mescaleros, and Chiricahuas. Carleton had little respect for Indians and viewed them as the main obstacle to stability in New Mexico. He perceived Indians as savages who deserved death if they refused to surrender unconditionally.

The Navajos and Mescaleros chiefly incurred his wrath. These two tribes he uprooted from their traditional homes, forcing them onto Bosque Redondo, a reservation in east-central New Mexico that he had opened up. He vigorously urged the same of the Chiricahua band of Victorio, but the Indian leader objected, declaring he would rather die fighting than relocate. Bosque Redondo proved to be a disaster for the Indians: crops failed, livestock died, government supplies were insufficient. Finally in 1865 the Mescaleros fled and returned to their traditional land near the White Mountains. The government assigned them an agent in the late 1860s and in 1873 finally established a reservation for them near Fort Stanton. In 1868 the military allowed the Navajos to return to their homes in the Four Corners region, and eventually a permanent reservation for them was likewise set aside.

The Chihenne and Bedonkohe bands of the Chiricahuas were without permanent reservations until 1869, when the government finally assigned an agent to oversee them. The celebrated Victorio and several of Mangas Coloradas's sons led these bands into the 1870s. In 1872 they were removed from a temporary reservation at Ojo Caliente, near today's Monticello, to Tularosa, situated in the upper Mogollon Mountains of west-central New Mexico. This location, however, did not suit them, and in 1874 Washington officials permitted them to return to Ojo Caliente. If they had been allowed to stay here, many of the difficulties with the Chiricahua Apaches from the late 1870s through the mid-1880s would not have occurred. Unfortunately, three years later this reservation was abolished and Victorio's people sent to the San Carlos Apache Reservation in Arizona.

Victorio remained only a few months, then took his followers back to New Mexico, vowing to die rather than return to Arizona. Fate eventually honored his feelings. After several major battles with American and Mexican troops during 1879 and 1880, the heroic Chiricahua patriot was killed by Mexican soldiers while defending his people. Scattered hostilities continued into the 1880s. Victorio's successor, a seventy-year-old chief named Nana, led a legendary raid into New Mexico in the summer of 1881. In 1883, 1885, and 1886 Chiricahuas, under Chato, Geronimo, Ulzana, and Mangas (a son of Mangas Coloradas), directed lightning-quick forays into New Mexico before disappearing into the Sierra Madre Mountains in Mexico. Not until the fall of 1886 (with Geronimo surrendering in September and Mangas the following month) was the entire Chiricahua tribe removed to Florida, and the Apache war in the Southwest ended.

Mangas Coloradas

New Mexico's most celebrated Indian leader of the nineteenth century was Mangas Coloradas, tribal leader of the Chiricahua Apaches. Born about 1790, probably in the mountains northwest of Silver City, Mangas was a complex man who combined wisdom and strength with pragmatism and intellect to lead his group of Chiricahua Apaches for almost fifty years. During his life Mangas fought Spaniards, then Mexicans, and finally, though reluctantly, the Americans, with whom he had usually lived in peace.

As previously mentioned, the Chiricahua Apaches consisted of four bands. Although the band was considered more important than the tribe, relationships among members existed in many ways: they usually lived in peace with one another, visited frequently, and often assembled for social dances, puberty rites, and marriages. Occasionally they united for military action or to avenge great wrongs inflicted on them by their enemies.

Within each band were three to five separate units, called local groups, which contained between ten and thirty extended families. One Chiricahua described an extended family "as a group of homes occupied by relatives. At the very least an extended family is a father and mother, their unmarried children, and the families of their married daughters." Local groups were led by men who had achieved prominence because of certain leadership qualities, such as superior intellect, exceptional fighting skills, and generosity to the less fortunate members of their group. The famous Chiricahua leaders, Cochise, Victorio, and Mangas Coloradas, were local group leaders first and band leaders second. Mangas Coloradas's favorite camping site was Santa Lucía Springs, situated in a beautiful valley along the northeastern face of the Burros Mountains, a few miles below the Gila River.

The birth of Mangas Coloradas came at a time of dramatic changes to the Chiricahua world: the Spanish and Apaches had finally resolved their long-standing conflict, and peace reigned in Apachería. Perhaps his parents could have predicted from the beginning that their son would develop into a man of enormous size and strength. The Chiricahuas believed that if the baby did not cry at birth, that child would grow up to be strong and hardy. His early Apache name is not known, but as he matured, his parents bestowed upon him his Indian name, which likely referred in some manner to his size or strength. The distinguished anthropologist Morris Opler points out that most Chiricahua names tended "to follow some physical or behavioral peculiarity of the individual bearing it, or it [referred] to a well known event in which he was involved." Later in life he received his Apache name, Kan-da-zis-tlishishen, meaning Red or Pink Sleeves, which the Mexicans translated to Mangas Coloradas. But for the first forty-five years of Mangas's life the Mexicans called him Fuerte, Spanish for "manly, strong, or stout."

As a youth Mangas learned about Chiricahua tradition and religion, which focused on the supernatural and emphasized the virtues of humility and gratitude. His father trained him to be self-sufficient, taught him how to hunt, instructed him in the art of warfare, and educated him in the history of his people. His mother taught him about Usen, the Apache supreme being, and installed in him a reverence for the natural world and powers unseen. She also ensured that the lad learned about such cultural heroes as the Mountain People, who protected the tribe and were sources for supernatural power. The Chiricahuas educated their youths for one reason: to prepare them for the responsibilities of adulthood.

By the time the boy reached puberty, he was ready to begin formal training as a warrior. He became a *dikohe,* a novice or apprentice warrior. A boy volunteered for the training when he felt old and mature enough. His family always cautioned him that portentous times lay ahead, filled with challenges, dangers, and hardships. Mangas was assigned to the care of a shaman who knew about the perils of war. The training steadily grew more vigorous; physical activities, such as wrestling, slingshot fights, bow-and-arrow contests, and footraces dominated. Status and recognition resulted from success in these contests. The maturing youth who became known as Mangas Coloradas must have been the most conspicuous of his peers.

During the first four raids the warriors called a dikohe Child of the Water. He wore a ceremonial hat for protection and learned special words that the shaman had taught him for the occasion. After the fourth raid, unless the warriors disapproved of his performance, the young man joined their ranks. Mangas's first experiences at war occurred in the early 1800s and possibly came against other Indian enemies such as the Navajos north of him or the Pimas and Papagos southwest of him. Or perhaps his group raided Sonora or the new mining center established in his country, Santa Rita del Cobre. In any event, Mangas's novice period was undoubtedly quite successful. He had grown into a large and able-bodied young man, much taller and stronger than the average Apache youth. Because Mangas Coloradas was probably the son of a leader, he undoubtedly had received excellent training. This dynamic combination of thorough training, a naturally aggressive nature, and extraordinary physical skills catapulted him very early into a leadership position among the young men of his local group.

According to Chiricahua Apache sources, Mangas Coloradas became a chief at an unusually young age. About 1810 he left his Bedonkohe band and married into a prominent family of a mixed Chihenne-Bedonkohe group that resided at Santa Lucía Springs. Following Apache tradition, he joined his wife's family, and his responsibilities and obligations bound him to his new extended family. He quickly made a name for himself. One story suggests that one of Mangas's earliest raids in which he gained notoriety and emerged as a successful war leader was against Sonora, probably about 1812. Another legend has it that just glory came to him when he killed several Navajos in a brutal hand-to-hand encounter. In any event, by 1814 he had become a group leader, and Spanish documents between 1814 and 1820 frequently were including mention of Fuerte, Mangas's early name. Chiricahua sources reveal one other important detail: that Mangas Coloradas became chief of the Bedonkohe band about 1820, after the death of their beloved leader Mahko.

By then Mangas Coloradas had clearly exhibited the qualities of character so essential to effective leadership among the Apaches. Even if the young man was naturally equipped with the necessary instincts and wisdom, he had consciously to develop superior fighting skills and an assertive personality, and he had to put together an impressive record of achievement. In this way only could he earn the respect necessary to attract and retain loyal followers. Perhaps it was courage that counted for most among the Apaches. And with Mangas Coloradas, since so many of his battles were against Mexicans, who left behind few accounts of his individual exploits, this quality is much more difficult to measure in him than in those of the later Chiricahua leaders Cochise, Victorio, and Geronimo. But certainly it was impressively present. Without great courage he could never have attracted so many followers, especially outside his band, to his cause. And we do have some testimony. We know, for example, that Mangas Coloradas rode at the head of his warriors during a skirmish with Americans in Sonora in 1849. We know that he led attacks on Mexican presidios against Janos and Fronteras in 1856 and 1858, respectively. And we know that in 1862, when Mangas was in his early seventies, an American trooper shot him from his horse as he led an assault against the defense of Apache Pass in Arizona. There can be no question that Mangas Coloradas did not lack for courage. We can assume, without hesitation, that he was for his warriors an inspiring figure.

Mangas Coloradas also exhibited another important quality: supernatural power. It was thought that most Chiricahua men enjoyed some form of supernatural power, a kind of "guardian spirit" that came in the form of healing ability, clairvoyant powers, superior skills in hunting and raiding for horses, or the expertise necessary to make war. We do not know what form of power came to reside in Mangas Coloradas, for with an Apache, this is an extremely personal matter, the kind a man is disinclined to discuss. Easier to assess and conspicuous in Mangas are the leadership qualities of generosity, wisdom, and superior oratorical skills that enabled one to speak eloquently and forcefully at public gatherings. He shared food and possessions and encouraged his followers to look out for the less fortunate. As a man of vision and foresight, as Chiricahua chief, Mangas Coloradas pointed the way and showed how to get there.

Events in the early 1820s signaled just how precarious was the peace between Chiricahuas and Mexico. In the early 1790s the Spanish had established a policy of issuing rations to Apaches who remained peaceful. But in the years following Mexico's independence from Spain in 1821, the new government in Mexico City gradually curtailed this practice. Mangas had grown accustomed to living most of his time away from Mexican contact, residing securely in his native lands in southwestern New Mexico. In August 1826, Mangas Coloradas met American adventurer Sylvester Pattie at Santa Rita del Cobre. Even then, this early, Mangas Coloradas revealed thoughts that would guide his conduct for the rest of his life. He recognized that Americans never "showed any disposition to kill, except in battle," in sharp contrast to Mexicans, who were willing to use unscrupulous methods against the Indians. Finally, in the spring of 1831, every Apache band at peace went to war with Mexico. He became increasingly aloof from Mexico and developed an unequivocal and passionate hatred of Sonora, a feeling that would persist for the rest of his life.

For Mangas Coloradas, now about forty years of age and still known as Fuerte, the coming decade would be replete with challenges. Throughout

FIGURE 6.3. Victorio, Chihenne band leader of the Chiricahua Apache.
Photo courtesy National Archives.

the 1830s Mexico responded to the Chiricahuas' aggression by sending out large campaigns. These served only to spawn a mutual distrust and resentment between the two races. Inevitably, both sides spilled blood, which of course always demanded retaliation, and thus followed a cycle of action and reaction that proved virtually impossible to halt. This staccato warfare resulted naturally in philosophical differences concerning the courses to be pursued by each race. Two of the Mexican states followed varying policies. Sonora opted for a vigorous and hawkish approach against the Apaches, going so far in 1835 as to pay bounties for Apache scalps. Chihuahua favored a more peaceful approach, calling out the soldiers to snap the whip against the hostiles only if necessary. The Chiricahuas were likewise fragmented. Mangas Coloradas and an important tribal leader named Pisago Cabezón led the faction that favored war.

In May 1832 Pisago Cabezón and Mangas Coloradas led the Chiricahuas against Chihuahua troops in one of the hardest-fought battles between the two races. This fight, which took place near the Gila River north of Santa Lucía Springs, had all the drama and heroics that a truly pitched fight would entail: hand-to-hand fighting, desperate charges, awesome displays of bravery on both sides, and heavy casualties. The Chihuahuan force drove the Chiricahuas from the field, killing a reported twenty-two warriors and wounding another fifty. The Mexicans suffered a loss of three dead and twelve wounded. Three months later the Chiricahuas, including Mangas Coloradas, humbled after their defeat, agreed to a treaty with Chihuahua at Santa Rita del Cobre. But the armistice proved brittle, and by the spring of 1833 the Chiricahuas renewed their raiding into Mexico. Mangas became even further incensed at Sonora when in the fall of 1834 it launched an expedition into his country that succeeded in capturing and then executing Tutije, the Bedonkohe's war leader.

Even worse was an incident that occurred on April 22, 1837, in the Animas Mountains of extreme southwestern New Mexico. John Johnson, an Anglo living in Sonora, posing as a trader, opened fire on a large group of Chiricahuas, killing at least a score, including two wives of Mangas Coloradas. This event naturally intensified the Indian leader's hatred of Sonora. Before this incident he had been aloof and reserved, governed by the feeling that as long as Mexicans left him alone, he would do the same to them. After this time he became more bellicose, hungry for revenge against Sonora.

Mangas Coloradas and Pisago Cabezón dominated Mexico's northern frontier in the late 1830s. In the spring of 1838 Mangas Coloradas and Pisago

Cabezón captured a supply train carrying provisions to Santa Rita del Cobre. Within months citizens and soldiers deserted the bastion that had for so long symbolized Spanish power in Apachería. Recognizing that its troops were no match for the mobile Apaches, Chihuahua opted for a novel approach to its Apache problem: it hired scalp hunters. The leader of this private army was James Kirker, a longtime veteran of the frontier who knew many of the Apaches. In 1840 he had some success against the Chiricahuas, including an attack on Pisago Cabezón's camp that killed fifteen and netted him twenty prisoners, including a son of Pisago Cabezón. For the next eighteen months Pisago negotiated with Chihuahua to get his people back, success coming only after he agreed to a formal armistice at Janos in July 1842. Mangas, however, refused to consider a truce. Rage, a deep, fuming anger, inspired by Mexican treachery and mistreatment of his people, continued to drive him.

By the early 1840s Mangas Coloradas had become undisputed war leader of each of the four Chiricahua bands. The Chihennes had often deferred to him, but his bond with the Chokonens was strengthened dramatically when one of his daughters married Cochise, their young war leader. In early 1843 Chihuahua's governor, José Mariano Monterde, sent a peace emissary to Mangas Coloradas. After a decade of war, Mangas decided to venture into Janos and discuss terms with the governor. The two men developed a friendship, and Monterde's overtures instilled confidence in Mangas. Unfortunately, within two months of the armistice, Mexican troops at Fronteras, Sonora, turned their weapons on seven Chiricahuas who had accompanied them in pursuit of a band of Western Apaches who had raided the presidio. Only one escaped to tell the story, which spread like wildfire to the Apache camps in New Mexico and Chihuahua and laid the foundation for war. The Apaches would avenge their losses!

Beginning in the summer of 1843 the Chiricahuas launched several incursions against Sonora (many under Mangas Coloradas). These forays increased in severity almost monthly through early 1845. In 1844 alone Mangas led three war parties—including one that obliterated a twenty-nine-man force from Santa Cruz, Sonora, in late July 1844. After this, Sonora's commanding general, Colonel José María Elías González, marched into Chihuahua and attacked two Chiricahua camps near Janos, killing more than one hundred, most of them women and children. The following summer Chihuahua brought back James Kirker, and in July 1846 he assaulted a peaceful Chiricahua camp near Galeana, massacring and scalping 148 Chokonens and Nednhis. Was it any wonder that three months later Mangas

Coloradas would warmly greet American general Stephen Watts Kearny, who had come to make war on Mexico?

In the late 1840s and early 1850s the Chiricahua Apaches continued to dominate Sonora's northern frontier as they assaulted presidios and forced residents to evacuate several towns along the northern frontier. Perhaps the climax to their undisputed reign occurred in January 1851, when two Chiricahua war parties invaded Sonora, leaving widespread terror in their wake. Mangas's group penetrated as far south as Hermosillo before it eventually turned back for its homeward march. Captain Ignacio Pesqueira, who would one day be governor of Sonora, gathered a force of one hundred soldiers and rode to Pozo Hediondo, concealing his force to ambush the Chiricahuas as they retired north. The Indians rode into the trap, but it was only a small vanguard; Mangas and most of the men were a few miles behind. Pesqueira's troops attacked, and the Apaches retreated with the Mexican force in pursuit. Unfortunately for the Sonorans, they ran into the main body of Indians, with Mangas Coloradas at the head. A pitched battle ensued, with the two sides so close that the Chiricahuas could use their deadly lances and accurate bows. After several hours of fighting, a second Apache force arrived at the scene. They drove the Mexicans from one hill to another. As dark approached, a lull came to the fighting. In all, the victorious Chiricahuas had killed or wounded seventy-two of the one hundred men, including every officer. Never had the Chiricahuas fought so spectacularly in battle; this was a testament to Mangas's leadership abilities.

From this time forward Mangas Coloradas would deal with Americans, who were just beginning to establish a military and civil presence in his country. On several occasions he had demonstrated his desire to have good relations with Americans. In the summer of 1849 he led a band that inadvertently attacked a group of Americans in northern Sonora who were en route to California. Once he discovered they were Americans, he raised a white flag to parley. He explained that he was a friend of Americans. Then he asked to talk with a brave thirteen-year-old boy who, during the skirmish, had defiantly emptied his six-shooter at Mangas Coloradas. Meeting the boy, Mangas said in Spanish, "*Muy malo muchacho*," not making it clear whether he was gently scolding the boy or complimenting him on his courage. The following summer, in mid-August 1850, he held his first official council with the American military since meeting Kearny four years before. Mangas met Captain Enoch Steen at Santa Rita del Cobre and assured him that although he wanted peace with Americans, with Mexico, "it was war to the knife."

Mangas's first important relationship with Americans occurred in the summer of 1851. Returning from a raid in Sonora, he visited John Russell Bartlett's Boundary Commission, which had set up headquarters at Santa Rita del Cobre. Mangas impressed Bartlett, who described him as a man of "strong common sense and discriminating judgement." About a year later Mangas traveled to the pueblo of Acoma and met Lieutenant Colonel Sumner and signed a peace treaty—the only one he ever signed with the United States. Mangas boasted to Sumner that his "will and word are law

FIGURE 6.4. General Stephen Watts Kearny, who met Mangas Coloradas on October 18, 1846, at Santa Rita del Cobre. Photo courtesy Museum of New Mexico, neg. no. 7605.

to [my] people." The treaty contained eleven articles. Mangas agreed to each condition, until the Americans addressed and further explained the one relating to raiding into Mexico.

All at once the great chief's eyes wakened and his expression changed. He had come to Acoma to make peace with Americans, not Mexicans. He reasoned: "Are we to stand by with our arms folded while our women and children are being murdered in cold blood as they were the other day in Sonora? Are we to be the victims of such treachery and not be avenged? Are we not to have the privilege of protecting ourselves?" At this outburst Sumner, who had no sympathy for Mexicans or Indians, took Mangas aside and gave him tacit permission to continue his incursions into Mexico, at least according to what the chief later told an American officer. Mangas would consent to other compacts with Americans in 1853 and 1855. Each committed the American government to issue rations and other assistance to the Chiricahuas. Instead, when the promised annuities were not delivered, the Indians became bitter, not understanding that some nebulous institution in Washington, Congress, had refused to ratify the last two agreements.

In the fall of 1854 Governor Meriwether appointed Michael Steck as agent for Mangas's people. He and Mangas Coloradas quickly developed a mutual respect that would endure until 1860. As Steck gained the confidence of the Apaches, he discovered that many were receptive to the idea of farming. Among these, surprisingly, Steck could include Mangas. By the mid-1850s the chief's lifestyle began to change. For the first time in years, and maybe decades, illness and perhaps advancing age prohibited him from making forays into Sonora. Instead he was content with the monthly rations of corn and occasionally beef that the government provided.

Yet ominous signs were on the horizon. By the late 1850s Americans and Mexicans were arriving in his country in record numbers: farmers and ranchers settling along the Mimbres River, hardy frontiersmen working for the Butterfield Overland Mail Company, which had constructed stage stations in intervals throughout Apachería, and soldiers who established a temporary post in the Burro Mountains. Although Mangas did not endorse each infringement into his country, he tolerated them as part of the changing times. In contrast, he had a difficult time accepting an invasion of miners, first at Santa Rita del Cobre and later at Pinos Altos, when Americans discovered gold there, thus triggering a gold rush to the area. With whites steadily swallowing up his country and the loss of two sons killed in a fight with Sonoran troops in 1858, Mangas confronted challenges that, as an elder statesman, he would have preferred to avoid. Usually when a leader approached the age of sixty, his position by then had evolved into one of a patriarchal leader, or, as the Chiricahuas put it, "he who commands for the home." Mangas would not enjoy this luxury. The last thing he wanted was to go to war with Americans. But in early 1861 he was compelled, as he put it, "to arm myself in self-defence [sic]" after Americans had "attacked and killed many of my people."

Mangas was referring to two incidents. The first took place in December 1860 when a group of American miners attacked a Chihenne camp on the Mimbres River, killing several men and capturing thirteen women and children. The second was the infamous Bascom Affair at Apache Pass, Arizona, in February 1861, which resulted in the deaths of at least ten Chiricahuas when Mangas's son-in-law, Cochise, was wrongfully accused for a raid committed by Western Apaches. For the next eighteen months the two greatest Chiricahua leaders of the mid-nineteenth century, emboldened by the withdrawal of the Butterfield Overland Mail Company and the evacuation of American troops from their country because of the Civil War, joined forces to drive the remaining Americans from their domain. Together they fought several engagements with Americans in 1861–62. Mangas Coloradas's last fight probably took place against the California Volunteers at the Battle of Apache Pass in July 1862; in this skirmish he was seriously wounded by an American cavalryman.

Two months later he sent a message to American authorities that he wanted peace and wished to return to his former home at Santa Lucía. Brigadier General Carleton dismissed these solicitations, writing, "I have no faith in him [Mangas Coloradas]." Carleton was obviously unaware that before the outbreak of hostilities, Mangas had always favored peace and diplomacy with Americans. Mangas Coloradas was clearly a victim of his own reputation—one, however, earned from his warlike activities below the border. Yet in New Mexico he had had a record of peaceful coexistence with Anglos since 1846. Carleton failed to comprehend this history.

Instead he ordered his subordinate, Brigadier General Joseph Rodman West, to organize a campaign against "Mangas Coloradas's band of Apaches." They clearly believed that if they could capture or kill Mangas Coloradas, they would destroy the will and backbone of the Chiricahuas. Shortly before noon on January 17, 1863, the great chief approached Pinos Altos with a few of his men, hoping to make a treaty. The citizens captured him and turned him over to the military. The next day a military guard escorted Mangas to Fort McLane, where Brigadier General West and a large force had encamped. West accused him of countless depredations, and Mangas responded that he had fought only in self-defense. But West had already ordained himself judge and jury. That evening he told the sentries that he did not want Mangas alive in the morning. Shortly after midnight Mangas's guards tried to provoke him by "heating their fixed bayonets in the fire and putting them to his feet and naked legs." Finally, after undergoing this sadistic torture for about an hour, Mangas lifted himself on his elbow and, in Spanish, told the sentinels "he was not a child to be played with." These were his last words. His two guards promptly shot him through the body. Then a sergeant rushed in and shot him execution style through the back of the head. General West reported to Carleton that Mangas was shot while trying to escape—a frontier euphemism for murder. To make matters even worse, the Americans mutilated the corpse and severed the head.

To the Chiricahuas the execution of their tribal chief and the subsequent defacement of his corpse were the "greatest of wrongs." Mangas had been the one leader who had trusted the integrity and honor of Americans. The Indians now understood that this misplaced faith not only cost him his life but also affected his spirit in the hereafter because it must go "through eternity in the mutilated condition." Instead of breaking the will of the Apaches, the callous murder had the opposite effect: it actually mobilized the Chiricahua bands. Cochise, Victorio, and Geronimo (a member of Mangas's Bedonkohe band) continued to fight Americans. That Chiricahua warfare against Americans would continue, off and on, for another twenty-three years can be attributed, in large measure, to the distrust engendered in the betrayal and murder of Mangas Coloradas. The outbreaks from the Arizona reservation in 1881 (under Geronimo) and in 1885 (led by Geronimo and Mangas, a son of Mangas Coloradas) were made because the Apaches feared Americans would seize them as they had Mangas Coloradas.

CONCLUSION

During the first half of the nineteenth century, Hispanics in New Mexico had learned to coexist with the Indians living at peace in their territory. They believed that if they treated Indians kindly and managed them judiciously, the Native Americans would respond in kind. Conversely, in the early days of Anglo occupation of New Mexico, a coherent American Indian policy did not exist. The new conquerors of the Southwest had to go through a period of trial and error, groping toward a workable Indian policy. In 1849 James Calhoun, the first Indian agent for New Mexico, formulated a policy, hoping to use force only when necessary. His successors adopted and expanded on his policies. Still, these progressive practices (treaties, reservations, and annuities) cost money, and Congress failed to ratify treaties or to allocate sufficient funds to implement their plans. Therefore promises and agreements made to the Indians often went unfulfilled. With justification Indians wondered when they could rely on the word and promises of American officials.

Just as important, the U.S. military had come to New Mexico with preconceived notions about Indians. Military contact usually occurred in response to hostilities, when the army would mount punitive expeditions. Officials had no comprehension of Indian culture and were quick to retaliate before hearing the Indians' side of the story. This pattern of action and reaction inevitably led to a breakdown in relations—especially because each tribe contained peace and war factions. Often war erupted because of senseless misunderstanding; often it resulted because of greed on the part of whites for Indian land and the mineral deposits on it.

Both races misunderstood the other. American officials had a simplistic view of Indians: they were either hostile or peaceful and in the back of their minds always savages capable of committing horrible atrocities. And the loose political structure of the Indians they confronted, mostly that of Southern Athapaskans, where leadership was vested at the local group level instead of at a tribal basis, confounded American officials, who could relate only to their own political structure. A chief could speak for his own followers or local group. But Americans, ignorant of Athapaskan culture, wanted to deal with one tribal leader and hold him accountable for the actions of his people. Likewise, the Athapaskans had little conception of American political structure—that the official government policies toward Indians were subject to change every time a new administration assumed power in Washington. Although Mangas Coloradas could not possibly have realized it then, the Indians' ultimate destiny was determined when Brigadier General Stephen Watts Kearny first set foot in New Mexico. How dramatically and abruptly their world would change could not have been foreseen by the most sagacious. In the end they shared the inevitable fate of all American Indians.

Mangas Coloradas was truly the most celebrated Indian leader of nineteenth-century New Mexico. He held a lifelong enmity of Mexicans, especially those in Sonora, because of the many injustices carried out against his people. For the last thirty years of his life Mangas fought the Mexicans with all his strength and actually halted Mexico's expansion into Apache territory. Apaches typically made war as an act of revenge. That his war against the residents of Sonora was merciless and cruel was a function of how his people practiced war. When at war, he gave no quarter and expected none in return. Mexico's methods and practices were just as harsh toward Apaches and far more unscrupulous.

He was not an ordinary man by any standards. He was brave in battle but also admired courage when it appeared in his enemies. His demeanor was serious and grave when he appeared in official councils to represent his people. But he was also a gregarious man with a lively sense of humor who liked to bask in the prominence of public life. Among his people, and with Americans, he was self-confident, sometimes ostentatious, trusting, and open. Ironically, this trust would lead to his death, murdered shamefully and premeditatedly by American soldiers after he had come in under a flag of truce to make peace. What had he done to deserve this treatment? As far as Mangas Coloradas was concerned, the Americans had driven him to war. He had retaliated with a vengeance but eventually realized that continued hostilities meant certain destruction of his people. Brigadier General West's treatment of Mangas Coloradas reflected a cavalier disdain for the culture of Indians, who, in the minds of most Americans, stood in the way of progress. In the end the military's betrayal and subsequent murder of their tribal leader served only to prolong the conflict with the Chiricahuas, laying down as it did a foundation of distrust on which was sustained the Chiricahua resistance through the Geronimo Wars of the 1880s.

ESSAY ON SOURCES

The most comprehensive source concerning the Indians of the Southwest remains the *Handbook of North American Indians,* vol. 10, Alfonso Ortiz, ed. (Washington, D.C.: Smithsonian Institution, 1983). It contains numerous chapters that examine the history and culture of the Jicarillas, Navajos, Chiricahuas, and Mescaleros. Veronica E. Velarde Tiller, *The Jicarilla Apache Tribe: A History,* rev. ed. (Lincoln: University of Nebraska Press, 1983), has written a thorough account of Jicarilla Apache history beginning with

Anglo occupation in 1846 through the twentieth century. The best single source on the Mescalero Apaches remains C. L. Sonnichsen, *The Mescalero Apaches* (Norman: University of Oklahoma Press, 1958). As for the Chiricahuas, the standard ethnological work remains Morris Opler's *An Apache Life-Way: The Economic, Social and Religious Institutions of the Chiricahua Indians* (Chicago: University of Chicago Press, 1941). For biographical treatments, see my own work, *Mangas Coloradas: Chief of the Chiricahua Apaches* (Norman: University of Oklahoma Press, 1998), and Dan L. Thrapp's superb account of the Chiricahua patriot, *Victorio and the Mimbres Apaches* (Norman: University of Oklahoma Press, 1974). For the Chiricahua point of view, see Eve Ball's two important books, *In the Days of Victorio: Recollections of a Warm Springs Apache* (Tucson: University of Arizona Press, 1970) and *Indeh: An Apache Odyssey* (Provo, Utah: Brigham Young University Press, 1980). For the Navajos, perhaps the most comprehensive account of their conflict is Frank McNitt's *Navajo Wars: Military Campaigns, Slave Raids, and Reprisals* (Albuquerque: University of New Mexico Press, 1972).

Stephen Watts Kearny's occupation of New Mexico is well covered in Dwight L. Clarke, ed., *The Original Journals of Henry Smith Turner With Stephen Watts Kearny to New Mexico and California, 1846* (Norman: University of Oklahoma Press, 1966), and Ross Calvin, ed., *Lieutenant Emory Reports: Notes of a Military Reconnoissance* (Albuquerque: University of New Mexico Press, 1951). One of the most revealing accounts of life in New Mexico in the late 1840s and early 1850s was edited by Annie Heloise Abel, *The Official Correspondence of James C. Calhoun While Indian Agent at Santa Fe and Superintendent of Indian Affairs in New Mexico* (Washington, D.C.: Government Printing Office, 1916). The best accounts concerning the role of the military from 1846 to 1861 remain Robert W. Frazer's *Forts and Supplies: The Role of the Army in the Economy of the Southwest, 1846–1861* (Albuquerque: University of New Mexico Press, 1983), and Robert M. Utley's *Frontiersmen in Blue: The United States Army and the Indian, 1848–1865* (Lincoln: University of Nebraska Press, 1981) and *The Indian Frontier of the American West* (Albuquerque: University of New Mexico Press, 1984). For an honest and realistic account of military life from an enlisted man's point of view, see James A. Bennett, *Forts and Forays: A Dragoon in New Mexico, 1850–1856* (Albuquerque: University of New Mexico Press, 1948).

For the story of the fighting between Union and Confederate forces, see the following: Ray C. Colton, *The Civil War in the Western Territories*

(Norman: University of Oklahoma Press, 1959); Robert Lee Kerby, *The Confederate Invasion of New Mexico and Arizona, 1861–1862*, 2d printing (Tucson: Westernlore Press, 1981); and Martin Hardwick Hall, *The Confederate Army of New Mexico* (Austin: Presidial Press, 1978). The significance of the California Volunteers' arrival in New Mexico during the Civil War, and the contributions they made to New Mexico politics and industry after the war, is told by Darlis A. Miller, *The California Column in New Mexico* (Albuquerque: University of New Mexico Press, 1982). Finally, for a biography of one of New Mexico's most controversial men, James H. Carleton, see Aurora Hunt's book, *Major-General James Henry Carleton, 1814–1873: Western Frontier Dragoon* (Glendale, Calif.: Arthur H. Clark Company, 1958).

7

Kit Carson and the "Americanization" of New Mexico

BARTON H. BARBOUR

DATELINE: FORT LYON, COLORADO TERRITORY, MAY 1868

*K*it Carson, the mountain man, "Indian scout," soldier, guide, and Freemason, lay dying at the age of fifty-nine. He reclined on a simple bed made of a blanket and a buffalo robe spread on the floor of his doctor's quarters at the Fort Lyon hospital, close by the banks of the Arkansas River near the mouth of the Purgatory River. Ever since 1860, when his horse lost its footing on a steep slope and dragged him for some distance, Carson had suffered discomfort from an aneurysm—a damaged blood vessel above his heart. Over time the swollen aneurysm became a painful obstruction in his upper chest that caused frequent coughing and made breathing difficult.

A recent visit to the "states" for medical consultation convinced Carson that his condition was irremediable, and he returned home by stagecoach to Boggsville, Colorado Territory, in early April. At Dr. Henry R. Tilton's behest, Carson moved from his home to the army hospital on May 14. Warm spring weather and snowmelt had flooded the Purgatory, and Carson could no longer ford the dangerous torrent to visit his doctor. Only by staying at the fort would he be assured the best available care.

Gasping for breath, Kit chatted with the doctor or other visitors when he was not in a chloroform-induced sleep. A few days slipped by as he reminisced over past deeds and old friends, and prepared to die. On May 23, in midafternoon, he requested buffalo meat and coffee, a favorite meal of the mountain men. He ate, lit a clay pipe, and began to speak with his friend Aloys Scheurich and Dr. Tilton. Suddenly Carson choked and cried out, "Doctor, *Campadre,* ADIOS!" Tilton rushed to Kit's side as blood poured from the ruptured artery, then cradled the old scout's head "while death speedily closed the scene."

Kit's wife of twenty-five years, María Josefa Jaramillo, had died about a month earlier, ten days after delivering their eighth child, a girl named Josefita. Carson dictated a letter on May 5 to Scheurich, requesting his wife, Teresina, to care for the Carson-Jaramillo children after Kit died. Teresina was Carson's niece, the daughter of Charles Bent and María Ignacia Jaramillo, Carson's sister-in-law. On May 15, Kit dictated his will. Much of his $9,000 estate was tied up in money owed him by Lucien B. Maxwell and in land at Taos that had been in his wife's name. Carson was buried next to Josefa (his beloved "Chipita") at Boggsville, but a year later their coffins were taken to Taos, New Mexico, home to Kit and his family much of the time from 1843 until 1867.

Word of Kit's death quickly spread. Newspapers from New York to California printed obituaries, for he had been nationally famous for more than twenty years. Today Carson's name is fixed upon—among other places—a mountain in Washington State, a highway and a National Forest in New Mexico and Colorado, a mountain pass in the Sierra Nevada, a military post in Colorado, and the state capital of Nevada. Statues and paintings of him adorn numerous western city parks, museums, and public buildings. A commemorative granite obelisk in front of a federal courthouse in Santa Fe bears the terse inscription: "He led the way."

Given the adulation tendered Carson during his lifetime and for several decades following his death, it may seem surprising that the old mountaineer's reputation has sharply declined over the past twenty-five or thirty years. (Actually, Carson's reputation has been in dispute for decades. In 1926 his admirer Blanche C. Grant felt obliged to defend him against criticism for his role in the Navajo Campaign. Lucius Beebe and Charles Clegg, in a popular 1955 book titled *The American West,* labeled Carson "a notable hater of Indians," insisting that he "regularly" murdered an "Indian or two before breakfast.")

The man once hailed as a heroic explorer and "friend of the Indians" is now more likely to be denounced as a "Hitleresque" genocidal killer of Native Americans. How are we to account for so dramatic a reinterpretation—amounting to a reversal—of Carson's "meaning" in American history? It is partly because, until the early twentieth century, biographers and writers used his life story as a vehicle for inculcating "American" moral and ideological principles. With passing time and changing perceptions, however, many "icons" of American history and legend have been discarded. Others—like Carson, or George Armstrong Custer—have been turned inside out to symbolize Euro-American bigotry and U.S. government repression. If Carson once symbolized positive aspects of America's "great westward movement," he now epitomizes its negative aspects: the theft of Native Americans' lands and usurpation of their sovereignty, the immoral American takeover of New Mexico, and so on.

Modern Americans in a pluralistic society have reason to deplore the use of historical characters as "hand-maidens of civics" meant to promote homogenous "American" ideals based upon a "superior" Anglo-European cultural model. Switching "positive" pasteboard icons into "negative" ones may reflect progressive social change, but it is bad history. Many people who damn the "Indian-hating" Carson seem unaware that, in the main, the available evidence belies the charges leveled against him. Close examination of these impassioned indictments reveals what historians call "presentism," the urge to interpret the past in modern terms, to impose modern ethics and sensitivities on past events and characters. Present-minded analysis is fundamentally antihistorical, for it refuses to deal with the past as it was. Measuring the past with an anachronistic "yardstick" encourages careless reasoning, and it ignores the contextual framework without which the past becomes incomprehensible.

Whatever may have been his faults or his merits, Carson was just one of many "Americans" who became "New Mexicans" in the early nineteenth century. A few hundred such men played a disproportionately important role in shaping the future of the Far West and what was formerly the Spanish-Mexican Northwest—for better or worse. Summarizing the early-nineteenth-century historical backdrop for the United States and New Mexico, and the rise of the Santa Fe trade, will shed light on why Anglo-Americans came to New Mexico. Likewise, a reasonably objective, "de-symbolized" sketch of Carson's life may encourage a more realistic appraisal of his place in New Mexico history, while reference to the "mythic" Carson may help explain why his legacy has been such a bitterly contested issue in recent years.

In the early 1820s many American men looked westward for economic opportunity. A wrenching depression gripped the nation after the Panic of

FIGURE 7.1. Kit Carson, wearing suit and tie. Courtesy Taos Historic Museums.

1819, plunging banks into ruin and forcing many mortgage foreclosures in rural areas such as Missouri, which achieved statehood in 1821. After a decade of stagnation following the War of 1812, however, the "Indian Trade" began to boom in 1822, and St. Louis boomed with it. To Missourians, the term "Indian Trade" meant a combination of fur hunting and trade with

Native Americans. From a Euro-American perspective, the "Indian Trade" had been the primary "frontier" economic endeavor for centuries, and it offered real possibilities for success in hard times. The fur and Indian trades helped make St. Louis the West's leading city.

Between 1822 and 1826 William H. Ashley and Andrew Henry's "enterprising young men" harvested thousands of beavers in Rocky Mountain streams, and their spectacular success lured other "expectant capitalists" into the Far West. Among the "Ashley men" were Jedediah S. Smith, Thomas Fitzpatrick, William Sublette, and James Clyman. Business was their first priority, but some of them made noteworthy contributions to Americans' understanding of western geography, and they acquired much knowledge about Indians. Some lived long enough to guide overland migrants during the 1840s and 1850s. Others, such as Étienne Provost, Old Bill Williams, Ewing Young, and William Workman, went southwest in the early 1820s to trap beavers in the "Mexican Country," despite legal hurdles and the threat of conflict with resident Indians. One "Ashley man," James Kirker, developed a spectacular and bizarre career as a scalp hunter and counterterrorist employed by several Mexican provinces to fight Indians during the late 1830s and early 1840s.

Like the fur trade, the Santa Fe trade was critical to St. Louis's economic health and the Southwest's future. After 1800, Americans became increasingly interested in trade with New Mexico, a land believed to possess valuable silver mines and other assets, but most early efforts failed. Spanish authorities jailed some of these adventurers; others had goods, furs, and gear confiscated. The Santa Fe trade was legalized when Mexico won independence in 1821. Jettisoning Spain's long-standing policy prohibiting foreigners from trading with New Spain, the Mexican republic welcomed American traders. Ironically, the shift reflected Mexican assumptions that the *norteamericanos* and the Republic of Mexico were "sister republics"— natural allies sharing a common ideology—and that the United States would be a good neighbor. A less happy future was in store for Mexico, but it resulted from internal weaknesses as well as external forces.

The desire for trade with Santa Fe inspired some Americans to collect information about southwestern geography, and it piqued "official" American interest in New Mexico. Lieutenant Zebulon Montgomery Pike's expedition to New Mexico in 1806–7 included a few shadowy men whose interest in commerce may have been a disguise for their interest in separating New Mexico from Spain. Pike, the first man to describe the southern plains as a "Sahara," collected much useful data. Unfortunately, when the "Lost Pathfinder" blundered into Spanish country he was arrested, and the subsequent story of his expedition became so mired in duplicity and intrigue that it has baffled scholars ever since.

When Lieutenant Stephen H. Long toured the Rockies and southern plains in 1820, his guide and interpreter was Joseph Bijou, a French Canadian who had already spent some time in New Mexico. In 1817 Spanish soldiers arrested a party of St. Louis traders—Bijou among them—on Greenhorn Creek, in Colorado, and conducted them to Santa Fe. (At the time, Spain and the United States disputed each other's boundary lines for the Louisiana Purchase. The 1819 Adams-Onís Treaty temporarily settled the question.) Spanish authorities confiscated goods and furs worth about $30,000, and the "Chouteau-DeMun party" languished in jail for two months before being released to make their way home. Bijou surely told Long's men about his New Mexico troubles, and of the possibilities for trade.

Official interest continued to grow as commerce-minded Americans, building on Pike and Long's romantic terminology, began to envision Santa Fe as an exotic port of call at the far edge of a prairie grass sea. In 1825 Congress appropriated $25,000 to mark and survey the road to Santa Fe and to purchase the cooperation of Indian nations living between the Missouri and Arkansas Rivers. By 1829 the United States was providing military escorts to help protect the traders' annual caravans, a practice that continued intermittently until the Mexican-American War broke out. Commerce, however, was not the only interest of the Americans.

A powerful popular spirit was afoot in the United States, soon to be named "Manifest Destiny." By the early 1820s American politicians, writers, and citizens began to cloak nationalistic foreign policy goals with an evangelical luster. The Americans imagined themselves as providentially chosen to undertake a special "mission" of global historical significance. This deeply rooted idea in American history can be traced to the 1630s, when the Puritan leader John Winthrop articulated his expectations for the Massachusetts Bay Colony. The Puritans' "New Eden" in North America never materialized, but a compelling secularized restatement of that vision gradually emerged. By the 1830s Americans considered themselves the logical, righteous claimants of North America, and perhaps the entire hemisphere, based upon their presumed moral, intellectual, and racial superiority. Meanwhile, as Americans pondered the West's future, the nation's economic, political, and military structures grew more coherent and more powerful.

Financial institutions such as the Bank of the United States were designed to impose order on unregulated, wildly fluctuating currency that spawned runaway inflation. Manufactories flourished in the urbanizing Northeast, churning out a dazzling array of goods in quantities scarcely imaginable just a few years earlier. Congress passed protective tariffs to nurture the nation's industries and shelter the "infant" American industrial complex from aggressive foreign competition. As American foreign policy matured, it grew more assertive. President James Monroe's annual message to Congress in 1823 included a warning to Europe that the Western Hemisphere was no longer open to colonization and that the United States would view such activity as "dangerous to our peace and safety." The "Monroe Doctrine" symbolized the burgeoning power of the United States and its growing interest in acquiring Latin American or Pacific colonies, lest other nations take the initiative.

Early-nineteenth-century New Mexico bore little resemblance to its expansive, sometimes arrogant neighbor. Since its founding in 1598, New Mexico had endured slow population growth, stunted economic development, and unstable relations between Hispanic settlers and their various Native American neighbors. By 1800, in geopolitical terms, New Mexico was an isolated and vulnerable place marker, imperial Spain's northernmost outpost in interior North America. New Mexico's population in 1830 was roughly forty thousand, of which one-half were *indios* of varying tribal affiliations. Mexico's population totaled about 6.2 million, whereas that of the United States had reached nearly 13 million and was rapidly increasing.

New Mexico lay very far from Mexico City, the wellspring of political power. Routinely neglected, it was left largely to its own devices in managing Indian-Hispanic conflicts or other matters. Even the best colonial governors, such as Juan Bautista de Anza in the 1780s, found it difficult to provide adequate defense and effective government. The rise of the Republic of Mexico brought scant relief to New Mexico's beleaguered population. Indeed, bloody rebellions erupted in several territories during 1837, when General Antonio López de Santa Anna attempted to centralize political and military control and boost revenues by levying taxes on outlying provinces that formerly enjoyed low tax rates and considerable local autonomy. Alienation from the capital and heartland of Mexico eroded the bonds linking New and Old Mexico and would help facilitate an American takeover in 1846.

A chief characteristic of the province was its lack of steel, iron, glass, textiles, and other manufactured goods. One historian recently wrote that "extreme misery, danger, and poverty" marked life in New Mexico prior to the American conquest, and "compared to life in Europe or the eastern United States, conditions in New Mexico were medieval." Few people in the province were in a position to make such a comparison, but one nineteenth-century New Mexican, Rafael Chacón, recalled that the populace "lived very simply and contentedly." Perhaps Chacón's lens was a bit rosy, for he belonged to the small *rico* class. Most New Mexicans worked modest landholdings, often within community or private land grants established under viceregal or, later, republican authority. Subsistence farming and ranching were general, though some people specialized in crafts such as woodworking, weaving, blacksmithing, and leather tanning. Prior to the Mexican Revolution, trade was restricted to a small coterie of privileged insiders with connections to Mexico City, eighteen hundred miles distant. These merchants charged exorbitant prices and preferred to sell expensive, low-bulk luxury items to the affluent rather than to ship less costly—and more bulky—goods for sale to the general public.

Spain's once fabulous colonial empire crumbled in the late eighteenth century, a period that also saw Spanish support for the American Revolutionary War and the onset of the Napoleonic Wars. Beset by many challenges, Spain was incapable of ameliorating New Mexico's woes after about 1780. As economic conditions and relationships with Native Americans deteriorated, the populace's insecurity and the province's instability increased. Mexican independence brought no relief from Ute, Apache, Comanche, and Navajo raids. In 1845, echoing several of his predecessors, Governor Manuel Armijo opined, "The war with the Navajos is slowly consuming us." Continuous political, social, and financial chaos in Mexico after 1821 meant that distant regions such as New Mexico could expect little aid from the central government.

The Santa Fe trade would significantly alter economic, social, and political conditions in the Republic of Mexico's most northerly province. After William Becknell's round-trips from Arrow Rock, Missouri, to Santa Fe in 1821 and 1822, the "Road to Santa Fe" stayed open. Josiah Gregg, a Santa Fe trader from 1831 to 1840, became the trail's first historian. In his 1844 classic, *Commerce of the Prairies,* Gregg tabulated yearly estimates of the trade. In 1822 about $15,000 in goods went to Santa Fe, mostly inexpensive mass-produced printed and plain textiles. Three years later, the trade had grown to about $65,000. By 1830 roughly $120,000 in goods went to New Mexico, of which $20,000 in merchandise was forwarded south to Chihuahua and Mexico City markets. Despite ups and downs, the trade continued to grow. By 1843 some $450,000 worth of goods went over the trail, two-thirds of which was marketed south of El Paso del Norte. After 1831 about half the goods brought down the Santa Fe Trail were slated for sale farther south in Mexico.

Most participants in the first years of the Santa Fe trade were individual males (though a few female investors were involved) who bought their own goods, transported them to New Mexico, and kept whatever profits

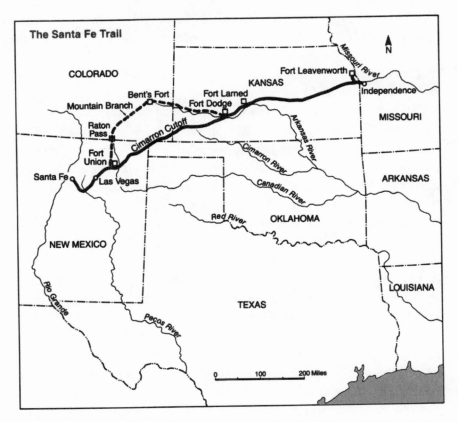

FIGURE 7.2. The Santa Fe Trail. From Calvin A. Roberts and Susan A. Roberts, *A History of New Mexico*, rev. ed. (Albuquerque: University of New Mexico Press, 1988), p. 163.

they accrued. Traders often dabbled in the Indian and fur trades as well. As time passed, investment capital increased, while the proportion of "proprietors" decreased and the number of "hired men" grew. Profitability changed over time, too. In 1821 William Becknell realized a spectacular profit of nearly 800 percent, but markets eventually became saturated and profit margins declined. Profits ranged generally between 20 percent and 40 percent, though some traders lost money because of oversupply of goods, poor timing and bad management, equipment and livestock problems, and occasional Indian raids.

Anglo-Americans only briefly constituted a majority of Santa Fe traders. During the 1830s there were many more Hispanos than Anglo-Americans, though most Hispanic traders handled small amounts of capital and goods. By 1840 numerous Hispano merchants "ventured east to New York, Baltimore, Philadelphia, and Pittsburgh, where they invested sizable assets." The Santa Fe trade succeeded because imports from the United States sold more cheaply than merchandise brought from Durango, Chihuahua, or elsewhere in Mexico, even after Mexican authorities assessed hefty duties on Americans' imported goods.

Effective trade regulation proved difficult for a variety of reasons. Bribery and corruption were commonplace, and more than a few New Mexican officials ignored laws in exchange for cold cash. Perennially unstable political conditions in Mexico enfeebled all efforts to control the trade, and one historian characterized New Mexican customs collection practices as "scandalously inefficient." American traders were equally eager to dodge the payment of duties. During the mid-1830s, Governor Manuel Armijo set a $500 fee for each wagon no matter what it carried. Armijo was apparently trying to simplify a complex customs collections system, but angry Americans resented his "arbitrary" impost. They clamored for restoration of the former ad valorem system, but they also devised a method to beat the tariff. By stuffing two or three tons of goods into very large wagons built at St. Louis or other towns, the gringos avoided paying about half the duties. Smuggling had always been part of life in colonial British and Spanish America, and it was widespread among New Mexicans and Americans. Profits from the contraband trade offered New Mexicans a way out of the debt-peonage that was common among the impoverished majority, but Americans smuggled mainly in order to maximize profits.

In purely economic terms, the Santa Fe trade offered more to New Mexico than to the United States. It boosted many New Mexicans' standard of living and brought new elements of technology, fashion, and the like to that isolated land. By the late 1830s New Mexicans could buy ready-made clothing from the eastern United States and even Europe, and such rarities as window glass, books, tools, and fancy items became readily available. It is fair to assert that substantial effects of the industrial revolution first appeared in New Mexico as a result of the Santa Fe trade. Some wealthy New Mexicans who correctly interpreted the social and political implications of the growing trade elected to send their sons east to acquire an "American" education and learn the ways of the gringos. One rico sent his son off to school at St. Louis in 1841 with the advice that "the heretics are going to over-run all this country. Go and learn their language and come back prepared to defend your people."

Overland trade with Mexico via the Santa Fe Trail accounted for only a small fraction of the United States' foreign trade; it did not even constitute a great percentage of the American trade with Mexico. On the other hand, it certainly boosted the economies of western states such as Missouri and Arkansas. Missouri banks, especially, benefited from the influx of Mexican silver pesos. After the Panic of 1837 led to a major depression in the early 1840s, many Missouri banks remained solvent while wildcat banks elsewhere went bust by the dozens. Likewise, the famous "Missouri mule" of the 1830s and 1840s originated in Mexico, not in the United States. Thousands of jacks and jennets made the trek from Santa Fe to be sold in Missouri markets. The Mexican trade also generated capital that was used to fuel other business ventures in Missouri and nearby states.

Many American fur trappers came to New Mexico over the Santa Fe Trail. Competition in the fur-rich Upper Missouri region, where a few large companies attempted to form monopolies or cartels to enrich themselves and hamstring competitors, was an important "push factor" in this process. Charles Bent and Ceran St. Vrain, having failed to crack the Upper Missouri trade, came to New Mexico in 1828 to trap furs and trade with Indians and Mexicans. By 1834 Bent, St. Vrain & Company—comprising four Bent brothers, Ceran St. Vrain, and his younger brother, Marcellin—hired New Mexican adobe experts to build Bent's Fort on the north bank of the Arkansas River, the boundary between Mexico and the United States. After they negotiated their own 1839 cartel-style agreement with the powerful St. Louis–based Pierre Chouteau, Jr., & Company, Bent, St. Vrain & Company

FIGURE 7.3. Santa Fe Trail wagon train coming into Santa Fe, New Mexico, ca.
1830s. Photo courtesy Museum of New Mexico, neg. no. 139983.

dominated the southern plains Indian bison-robe trade, and they also maintained profitable retail and wholesale stores at Santa Fe and Taos.

Between 1826 and 1830 American trappers scoured New Mexico, and several made forays to California to trap beavers and sea otters, trade or steal horses and mules, and explore the country. Ewing Young, a Tennessean who arrived in New Mexico in 1822, is the first man known to have trapped Arizona streams. In 1826 he secured a trapping license from New Mexico's Governor Antonio Narbona but the next year ran afoul of the new governor, Manuel Armijo, who jailed him and confiscated hundreds of beaver pelts. Two years later Young dodged further trouble by telling Mexican authorities he was headed for the United States, but once safely away he turned about and again trapped in Arizona. Mexican law required American trapping parties to hire some New Mexicans, but this did not prevent the illicit activities that aroused Mexican suspicions.

Most southwestern streams had been thoroughly trapped by 1830, but some mountain men remained in New Mexico. Taos was their usual residence because of its distance from probing officials at Santa Fe and its proximity to preferred mountain haunts. Exact numbers of expatriate mountain men are unknown, but at least 120 *extranjeros* (foreigners) are known to have either married or cohabited with New Mexican and Native American women during the Mexican era. An 1839 census listed thirty-four foreigners living in New Mexico. In 1840, seven out of twenty-three Americans living at Taos had become Mexican citizens. Some embraced Catholicism (formally at least) and married New Mexican or Native American women. Among them were Charles Bent, Lucien Maxwell, and Kit Carson. A number of French Canadian and Louisiana men also wound up in New Mexico, a transition perhaps made easier because they were already nominal or practicing Catholics. Only three American women are known to have traveled to New Mexico on the old trail prior to 1850: Mary Donoho, who would operate a hotel in Santa Fe; Susan Shelby Magoffin, the wife of a well-known trader; and Marion Sloan Russell, who came to New Mexico as a child in 1849.

Involvement in the Santa Fe Trade and the fur trade placed Americans and Mexicans in close proximity and helped shape their attitudes about each other. But each group embraced cultural biases that predated Mexican Independence and the opening of the Santa Fe Trail. Most Americans practiced some form of Protestantism, whereas the vast majority of New Mexicans were Catholics. Centuries of interfaith strife and bloody warfare among European Christians had bred hatred and persistent stereotypes. Americans, whose religious views generally sprang from Anglican England, Presbyterian Scotland, or Puritan New England, viewed Catholics as "mere tools" of a "foreign power," meaning the Pope. According to this reasoning, Catholics could not be trusted to think or vote for themselves, which violated the United States' democratic-republican principles. Americans' antipathy toward Spain, and Mexico, stemmed also from *la leyenda negra*, the "Black Legend," a propagandistic diatribe developed by sixteenth-century Protestants. Drawing on Bartolomé de las Casas's critique of the Spanish Conquest published in 1542, *Brevísima relación de la destrucción de las Indias,* the "Legend" cast Spaniards as ruthless and bloody-handed tyrants, in supposed contrast to the more benign practices of French, Dutch, or British conquerors and colonizers. The "Black Legend" had a long life; it continued to inform Americans' anti-Hispano attitudes until, and beyond, the Spanish-American War of 1898.

Catholics thought Protestants wrongheaded at best and dangerously apostate at worst. As well, seven centuries of the Iberian *reconquista* left Spanish Catholics with a deeply ingrained sense of their unique role in preserving and defending the Roman church. New Mexicans living on a raw frontier at the "rim of Christendom" had battled nature and man since 1600 to maintain and propagate their faith. Ironically, New Mexicans lived so far from diocesan headquarters in Durango that they received only about five visits from a bishop between 1600 and 1846. Despite general illiteracy, a shortage of priests, and numerous unsanctified marriages within a populace unable to afford priests' fees, their faith remained strong, and so did their suspicion of outsiders. New Mexicans had good reasons to mistrust the motives of some "American" traders and travelers.

Among the most threatening outsiders by 1840 were the *tejanos,* recent rebels against Mexico already famous for bluster and grandiose aspirations. In 1828 a Mexican artillery officer, José María Sánchez, described Anglo-American tejanos as "lazy people of vicious character." Technically, of course, "Texans" were not "Americans," but many New Mexicans correctly understood that in actuality few distinctions marked the two and that the United States would likely annex Texas in the near future. Tensions escalated from 1841 to 1843, when tejano filibusters twice attempted, and twice failed, to invade New Mexico. An American soldier, Lieutenant Phillip St. George Cooke, chased the Texan "border ruffians" away from New Mexico in 1843 but did not dispel New Mexicans' fears that Americans and Texans—gringos all—operated in concert.

Josiah Gregg's writing expressed some biases of *los americanos.* He considered New Mexico's backwardness a legacy of Spanish and papal policy intended to "keep every avenue of knowledge closed . . . lest the lights of civil and religious liberty should reach them from their neighbors of the North." Rural, impoverished New Mexico had no schools, but universities existed elsewhere in New Spain before the revolution, and Spain outspent the United States in funding Indian education programs. And despite the persistence of New Spain's traditional system of racially determined *castas* (castes), most people living in the Mexican possessions found social acceptance and at least some measure of legal protection. This was not so in the United States' exclusionary society, where most blacks were slaves, free blacks were shunned, and Indians were accepted neither as citizens nor neighbors.

Gregg criticized New Mexicans' literacy rates, medical practices, behavior, and general morality. He thought the architecture "clumsy," especially the "poverty-stricken and shabby-looking houses of public worship," yet he found the dwellings "extremely comfortable inside." Gregg also discerned admirable characteristics among New Mexicans—they were generous, valiant, polite, and hardworking. Like other Americans, Gregg was ambivalent in judging New Mexico's residents. New Mexican women particularly elicited ambiguous comments from American men, who found them at once alluring and repellent, immoral and saintly, decadent and upstanding. New Mexican women wore more revealing garments and were perhaps more outgoing than their Anglo-American sisters; they also puffed corn-husk *cigarillos,* rouged their cheeks with *alegría* (a cosmetic derived from a plant called red coxcomb), and sipped *aguardiente* (distilled liquor) at *fandangos* (dances), all of which added to Americans' confusion over what to make of them.

One bigoted Anglo-American "mountaineer," Rufus Sage, declared upon meeting a party of New Mexican traders that "some of them were as black as veritable negroes, and needed only the curly hair, thick lips, and flattened nose, to define the genuine Congo in appearance. A more miserable looking gang of filthy half-naked, ragamuffins, I never before witnessed." Numerous "Mexicans" or "Spaniards," mostly from New Mexico, built and worked at fur posts from the Yellowstone to the Arkansas and were considered excellent horse breakers, mule packers, and herdsmen. Even Sage admitted that Mexicans who worked at trading posts "prove quite useful as horse-guards, and also in taking care of cattle and doing the drudgery connected with these establishments." Employment at trading posts offered New Mexicans a rare opportunity to earn cash if they managed to avoid overspending on goods at inflated trade-counter prices.

Burdened though they were with the baggage of ethnic stereotyping, some Mexicans, Americans, and Native Americans still discovered sufficient common ground for creating long-term associations of friendship, marriage, and commerce. Kit Carson's marriage to Josefa Jaramillo, like that of William Bent to two Cheyenne women, was based on genuine affection and must have required some degree of cultural accommodation.

Historians, unfortunately, have discovered almost no evidence that reveals what Hispanic and Native American women may have thought about interethnic marriages. But we do know that the multiethnic and multi-lingual fur traders' society, which was more liberal minded than most Americans would tolerate, reflected two centuries of interethnic social and economic interaction. Success in the trade required that relations be reasonably amicable.

Kit Carson was in most respects a typical product of the American "frontier." He was born in Kentucky on Christmas Eve, 1809, into a poor family that moved west several times. Kit never attended school regularly, but his formal education ended in 1824 when a falling tree killed his father, forcing the youngster to choose a trade. Kit apprenticed himself to a Franklin, Missouri, saddler named David Workman but found the work stultifying. Many fur hunters passed through the shop, however, and Kit developed an irrepressible urge to become a trapper, too. His older half brothers Moses and Andrew were already in the business, and Andrew joined George Champlain Sibley's government-funded Santa Fe Trail survey in 1825. In the same year, his master's brother, William Workman, took the trail to Santa Fe. After one "distasteful" year in the saddlery shop, Kit ran off in 1826, and David Workman published a now famous reward in the *Missouri Intelligencer* offering *one penny* for the return of his wayward apprentice.

On his first western trip Carson traveled with William and Charles Bent. Within a few years, he developed a lasting and warm relationship with them and their partner, Ceran St. Vrain. In the meantime, Kit continued to Santa Fe, where he stayed briefly, then spent the winter of 1826–27 at Taos. Employed as a cook by an old friend of his father named Mathew Kincaid, Kit soaked up information about beaver trapping and began to learn Spanish. About this time, Carson first met Padre Antonio José Martínez, the Taos priest who later became adamantly anti-American. By 1828 Carson had mastered the Spanish language and made a trip to Chihuahua as an interpreter for the Missouri merchant "Colonel" Phillip Trammell. At Chihuahua, Carson met Robert McKnight, who had been arrested by Spanish authorities in 1812 for attempting to trade at Santa Fe and spent nine years under "house arrest" in Mexico. Eventually becoming a Mexican citizen, McKnight grew wealthy operating a copper mine at Santa Rita in southern New Mexico. Carson worked at the mine for a few months, then joined a trapping expedition led by Ewing Young. Under Young's expert tutelage, Carson honed the survival skills for which he was later famous. Young's men trapped westward from New Mexico through Arizona and in 1829 reached Mission San Gabriel in California. While there, Carson and eleven other trappers volunteered to assist in recovering mission Indians who had run off. Carson and his cohorts trailed the escapees and attacked the village where they hid, killing "a great number of men" before returning the runaways to the mission.

For the next several years, Kit was a "free trapper," hunting on his own hook, selling furs to the highest bidder, and reveling in the excitement of mountain life. In 1835, at the annual trappers' rendezvous at Green River, Carson got into a scrape with a blustering French Canadian called "Shunar" (likely a corruption of Chouinard). This camp bully had already beaten several men and promised to thrash any American he met. Carson snatched a pistol, jumped on his horse, and rode out to confront "Shunar." The two mounted men fired at the same instant: "Shunar's" ball grazed Carson's head, while Kit's pistol ball shattered the Frenchman's arm. Receiving wide circulation in a book published in 1840 by Samuel Parker, an Oregon-bound missionary, the encounter became an oft-told tale that boosted Carson's reputation for reckless bravery and high-mindedness.

Kit's dealings with Native Americans ran the gamut from fighting to friendship to marriage. In 1835 Carson wed a young Arapaho woman named Waa-nibe ("Singing Grass"), whom he called "Alice." Two children resulted from this marriage. Adaline, born about 1837, survived to adulthood, but another daughter, born in 1840, lived for only about three years. When Alice died around 1841, allegedly at Bent's Fort, Kit temporarily placed his daughter Adaline with an unidentified Native woman and briefly held a job as hunter for the fort. One tradition has it that Carson then married a Cheyenne woman "of bad disposition," though Carson family members firmly deny that the marriage took place. At any rate, Carson's marriage to one or more Indian women according to the "custom of the country" was standard fur trade practice. Some of these marriages were brief, lustful, or abusive, but others lasted a lifetime. Carson may have found it difficult to acknowledge his liaisons with Native American women. He mentioned no "marriages" to Indian women in his autobiography and avoided discussing them with female family members, though he apparently did with male relatives. There is also a tradition that Carson briefly cohabited with a New Mexican woman named Antonina Luna, formerly the consort of the famous mulatto trapper Jim Beckwourth.

Kit Carson officially wed fifteen-year-old María Josefa Jaramillo at Taos on February 6, 1843; the marriage certificate bore Padre Antonio José Martínez's signature. When Carson was baptized a Catholic on January 18, 1842, he was still employed as a hunter for Bent's Fort but probably had already begun to court Josefa. Her parents, Francisco Jaramillo and Apolonia Vigil, were members of prominent New Mexican families of the Rio Arriba region. Josefa was born and resided for some time at Santa Cruz de la Cañada and later came into ownership of land near Fort Lyon as a result of her connection to Donaciano Vigil, one of the heirs of the gigantic Vigil–St. Vrain land grant of 1843. Kit and Josefa had eight children: Charles (1849–51), William (1852–89), Teresina (1855–1916), Christopher (1858–1929), Charles (1861–1938), Rebecca (1864–85), Estefana (1866–99), and Josephine (1868–92). Also with the family at Taos was a daughter from Kit's earlier marriage to Waa-nibe, but the child died in 1843 after falling into a boiling kettle of soap. In spring of 1842, while visiting relatives in Missouri, Kit had left his daughter Adaline with a sister to be cared for and educated. She eventually returned to live in New Mexico, then moved to California. Unlike Kit, his "brother-in-law" Charles Bent never actually married María Ignacia Jaramillo and apparently had not legally acknowledged his children before he was killed in 1847 during the Taos Rebellion.

Carson's national fame did not originate with his trapping career. He might well have remained simply another obscure mountain man had it not been for Lieutenant John Charles Frémont, the self-promoting "Pathfinder," who produced the first "road atlas" for western emigrants in the mid-1840s. Indeed, but for sheer happenstance, a mountain man named Andrew Drips would have guided Frémont on his adventures. In 1842 Frémont sought out Drips on a steamer bound for the Upper Missouri and offered him the job. Drips was unavailable, for he had just been hired by the government to stifle the illegal liquor trade at fur trading posts between the Missouri and Platte Rivers, but Carson happened to be aboard the same vessel. Having recently visited St. Louis to see relatives and grown "tired of settlements," Kit decided to take an Upper Missouri trip. His acceptance of Frémont's offer inaugurated a long association with Frémont and his wife, Jessie, the daughter of Senator Thomas Hart Benton, a powerful political ally and the greatest western "booster" of his time.

Kit Carson guided Frémont on three of his four expeditions, participated in the American takeover of California, and carried war dispatches back east

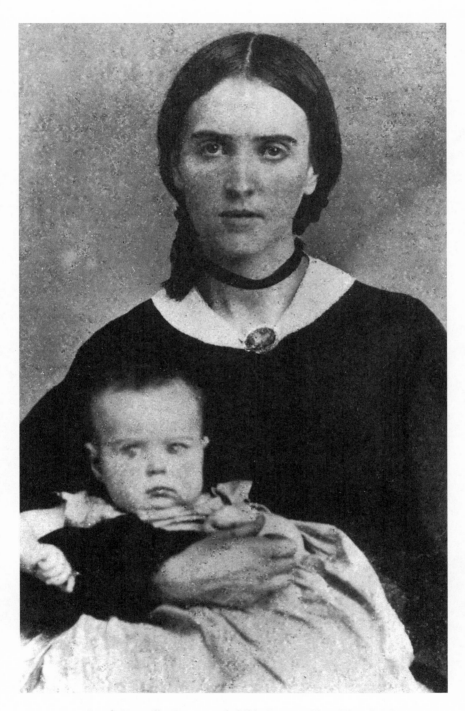

FIGURE 7.4. Josefa Jaramillo Carson and child. Courtesy Taos Historic Museums.

three times. In 1848 Kit brought Washington, D.C., some of the first reliable information regarding the California gold strike. When Jessie Benton Frémont edited her husband's journals for publication, she gave Carson a prominent role that launched his national celebrity. Carson and Frémont endured many hardships together, saved each other's lives more than once, and developed an abiding mutual loyalty. The two men deeply admired, even loved, each other. Carson's allegiance to Frémont probably sharpened his sense of duty, and he usually found it impossible to ignore other military officers' appeals to that obligation later in his life.

Carson's travels with Frémont provide examples illustrating good and bad qualities of character. In April 1843, during the second expedition, the party encountered two Mexicans, a man and a boy, about one hundred miles east of El Pueblo de Los Angeles. Indians had ambushed the party of four men and two women driving a horse herd, forcing the two to abandon their companions as they tried to save the livestock. Leaving the herd at a spring, the Mexicans searched for help and stumbled into Frémont's camp. Kit Carson and Alexander Godey volunteered to help Andreas Fuentes recover his lost horses and search for survivors. Fuentes's jaded horse soon gave out, but Carson and Godey continued the pursuit, found the horse thieves, killed two of them, and returned with some of the stolen stock but no survivors. Two scalps dangled from Godey's gun when the two rode into camp. In Frémont's view, Carson and Godey had heroically risked their lives not for personal gain, but simply to "punish the robbers of the desert, and to avenge the wrongs of Mexicans who they did not know." Frémont's bilious and hypercritical German cartographer, Charles Preuss, saw the event in a different light. Carson and Godey, Preuss wrote, had "shot the Indians [while] creeping up on them from behind," like cowards, and he was disgusted that they had taken the dead men's "entire scalps" instead of "only a piece . . . as large as a dollar" as the "more noble Indian" would.

In the spring of 1846 the men of Frémont's third expedition were encamped at Peter Lawson's ranch on the Sacramento River, not far from Mount Shasta, waiting for war to break out with Mexico. Early in April, Carson and most of Frémont's men joined American "settlers" in a preemptive strike against a large Indian encampment that they believed was preparing to attack them. Carson described the fight that left more than 175 Indians dead as a "perfect butchery" and thought the "chastisement" would prevent the Indians from "attacking the settlements." Even Harvey

L. Carter, a sympathetic Carson biographer, concluded it was "doubtful that such a preventive expedition was justified."

In May 1846, Carson and the others were bivouacked in northern California when Lieutenant Archibald Gillespie, U.S. Marines, arrived with news that the war with Mexico had begun and orders for Frémont to return south. The "Pathfinder" read dispatches until past midnight, then rolled into his blankets by the fire. A while later Klamath Indians crept into camp, killed two men with axes, and were about to finish off the rest when Carson awoke and alerted the camp to danger. In the melee that followed, one more of Frémont's men—a Delaware Indian named Crane—died. The attackers were repulsed, but the Klamaths and Frémont's party continued skirmishing for several days.

Another incident that might have tarnished Carson's reputation occurred in July 1846 when he participated in the killing of three Mexican Californians whom Frémont said were spies. Lieutenant Gillespie later claimed the three were murdered in cold blood, but Frémont retorted that it was a retaliatory action because Mexicans had killed two of his men, adding that "mainly Delawares" had done the deed. Edward M. Kern, an artist with the expedition, believed the killings resulted because the murder of the two Americans had "produced an order [from Frémont] to take no more prisoners." Modern-day defenders of Carson have argued that Frémont's small company was in a dangerously exposed situation and had already lost men, so wartime exigencies justified the killings. Still, the event reflects little in the way of compassion or high-mindedness.

It is certainly true that Kit Carson killed Indians, possibly as many as twenty-five or more. Much of his repute as an "Indian killer" resulted from the many outrageous fabrications of his adventures appearing in dozens of dime novels during and after his life. These tales helped create the mythic Carson, and that myth has crept into historical studies of the man, too. But it is also quite true that violence was part and parcel of Indian life on the plains and in the mountains. Bitter intertribal animosity and bloodshed were common, fueled by traditional hatreds, horse thefts, kidnappings and murders, territorial squabbling, and competition for economic resources such as game or access to fur traders. American trappers had to be prepared for violence if they were to survive in that environment, and like other frontier-dwelling Americans, they were not noted for their pacific temperaments. Throughout the Rocky Mountain fur trade era (roughly 1820 to 1850) hundreds of Indians as well as Euro-Americans met violent deaths. The close-knit trappers' fraternity, ignoring that they were basically illegal intruders in "Indian country," harbored intense loathing for any Indians whom they considered responsible for killing their comrades.

In Native warfare, the killing of a member of one tribe called for retribution against any member of the offending nation. This applied to "Americans," too. If a tribe lost someone at the hands of a trapper, then any trapper was fair game, even if he had no connection to the previous offense. Most Native American nations embraced this rule, and American mountain men adopted it, to some degree, because survival demanded it. Trappers rarely murdered Indians for entertainment or to "exterminate" them, unlike American miners in gold rush California, who routinely killed Indians simply to be rid of them.

Carson's violent behavior toward Indians was based on the principle of "retributive justice," which resembles the ancient Babylonian Code of Hammurabi that required "an eye for an eye." In practice, this meant that any injury done by an Indian to a white man must be revenged, lest Indians find that killing a white man brought no reprisal. Much violence between trappers and Indians resulted from the theft of horses, pelts, or trade goods, all of which the trappers deemed vital to their survival and economic success.

Trappers in the Southwest frequently clashed with Natives. Jedediah S. Smith, a famous trapper and explorer, lost more than a dozen men in a fight with Mohaves while attempting to cross the Colorado River on his way to California in 1827 and was himself killed by Comanches while en route to Santa Fe in 1831. American trappers who followed Smith's trail to the Spanish missions—as Carson did in 1829—kept a close eye out for Mohaves and Apaches and were liable to kill those they encountered. Ethnic hostility was sadly characteristic among most nineteenth-century southwestern residents.

Besides trapping and scouting, Kit found other things to do. In 1853 Carson, John Hatcher, and Lucien Maxwell drove several thousand sheep over the Old Spanish Trail for sale to the multitude of gold miners in California. Hispanic New Mexicans had first moved sheep to California back in 1828, but the Americans jumped at the opportunity to make profits out of the west coast's meat shortage. From 1854 to 1861 Carson also served as an Indian agent in New Mexico for the Cheyenne, Arapaho, Ute, Apache, and Navajo nations and earned a reputation for fair dealing.

When the Civil War came to New Mexico, he resigned to command the First New Mexican Volunteer Regiment, which helped repel General Henry H. Sibley's Texan-Confederate invasion. His regiment performed well during the February 1862 battle at Valverde near Fort Craig. In October he led an expedition against Mescalero Apaches, who had taken advantage of the Civil War to step up their raids on New Mexican settlements. After a brief and successful campaign, the army forcibly moved the Mescaleros to a new home at the Bosque Redondo in eastern New Mexico.

Navajo raids had likewise increased. General E. R. S. Canby decided to undertake a campaign against the Navajos late in 1861 in the belief that "there is now no choice between their absolute extermination or their removal and colonization" far from their ancestral homeland west of the Rio Grande. Canby was soon transferred back east, leaving his successor, General James H. Carleton, to put the plan in motion. General Carleton led his "California Column" into New Mexico too late to help defeat Sibley's Confederates, but his new orders called for commencing the Navajo Campaign. Carson, who had no role in planning the campaign, would be ordered to lead soldiers to the Navajo country, force their surrender, and take them, too, to the experimental "reservation" at the Bosque Redondo on the edge of the buffalo plains.

Most modern critics who label Kit Carson an "Indian killer" focus almost exclusively on his role in the army's campaign in 1864 against the Navajos. Unhappily, the Navajo nation posed a serious security threat to many New Mexico inhabitants—Natives and non-Natives alike. Canby's plan, reflecting the army's response to demands for action from New Mexico citizens, aimed to remedy a long-standing problem: the practically ceaseless rounds of raid and counterraid that had disrupted life in the province for more than a century. Hundreds of Hispanic settlers and Pueblo Indians, as well as Navajos, had been killed, injured, or captured over the decades since the end of the Spanish regime and through the Mexican era.

Carson was reluctant to undertake this operation. Josefa was pregnant again, though Kit had only rarely seen her or their children during the previous two years. Past his fifty-fifth birthday, Carson could no longer overlook the ill effects of his 1860 accident. He repeatedly submitted his resignation only to be talked out of doing so, for he was still under army authority after the failed Confederate invasion, and he felt compelled to

The Civil War in New Mexico, 1861–1862

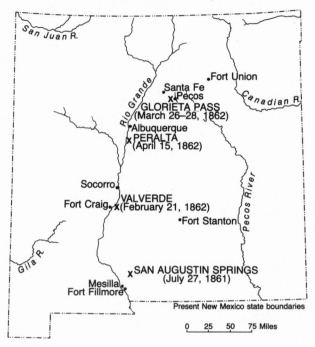

FIGURE 7.5. The Civil War in New Mexico. From Calvin A. Roberts and Susan A. Roberts, *New Mexico* (Albuquerque: University of New Mexico Press), p. 122.

serve. Most other officers saw him as uniquely qualified for the task, though he probably would have preferred an easier job with the army, for he was thinking of retirement.

Obviously, Carson did not capture thousands of "hostile" Navajos by himself. Success and, more importantly in some respects, the historical legacy of the campaign would depend upon the forgotten officers and enlisted men who carried it out. The sad truth is that most of the men in Carson's command were no advertisement for military excellence. A rough lot overall, more than a few were alcoholics, some were bigots, some were embezzlers, a few were murderers, and the Californians generally got on badly with Kit's New Mexicans. By the campaign's end, the army had cashiered almost half of the participating officers. One lieutenant was thrown out after being caught drunk and in bed with an enlisted man; another was discharged after being found drunk and in bed with a woman "of bad character."

Kit Carson's involvement effectively began in July 1863, when he led about 340 soldiers from Los Lunas to Fort Wingate and the Navajo country. His Ute scouts found Navajos, killing some and capturing others, whom they refused to give up for removal to the Bosque. Disciplinary problems with soldiers and officers included insubordination, drunken scuffles, and the killing of Navajos. In January 1864 Carson led his troops out of Fort Canby to search for "hostiles" in the reputed Navajo "stronghold" at Canyon de Chelly, a mysterious place rarely visited by non-Natives. In the following weeks, according to official reports, twenty-three Navajos were "killed" (none by Carson), while 234 were "captured" or "surrendered."

Carson's role in the Navajo Campaign was a limited one. He did not originate the plan, and although he did not fully approve of it, he performed what he saw as his duty. Neither Carson nor any of his subordinate officers destroyed the Navajo peach orchards, though he basically approved of the army's "scorched earth" policy. The fruit trees were cut down by Captain John Thompson months later, in July–August 1864, by which time Carson had been reassigned as a supervisor at the Bosque Redondo.

Navajo casualties mounted rapidly, however, as more and more surrendered at Fort Canby and then waited at Fort Wingate for relocation hundreds of miles away at the Bosque Redondo. Under guard, several large contingents of Navajo prisoners made their way east past Albuquerque and on to Fort Sumner. Among one group numbering about twenty-five hundred at Fort Canby, almost 130 died before leaving in March 1864, and another two hundred perished from exposure or were killed by vengeance-seeking New Mexicans while en route.

Isolation, despair, and death stalked the penned-up Navajos at the Bosque Redondo. A major contributing factor was that the army had grossly underestimated the total number of Navajos, and it failed to furnish sufficient rations for those incarcerated. The army supposed there were no more than about five thousand Navajos, so when eight thousand surrendered (out of nearly twelve thousand), the army simply called off further campaigning. Several thousand Navajos remained in the Canyon de Chelly to face starvation under fearful winter conditions. Department of Interior officials, legally empowered to oversee Indian affairs, refused to fund supplies for the reservation "experiment" because they thought it unwise for the army to house traditional enemies, Navajos and Mescalero Apaches, at the Bosque Redondo. Consequently, the army purchased food and supplies, but never in sufficient quantities. Crops failed, the water was polluted, and a government program designed to transform Navajos into "American-style" farmers did not succeed. Carson had nothing to do with these problems, nor did he play a prominent role in the "Long Walk." He was ordered to go to the Bosque to help out but served only intermittently, quitting in disgust by September 1864.

Perhaps Carson's reactions to another infamous military campaign of 1864 can shed light on whether he merits consideration as a genocidal killer. In November of that year a contingent of Colorado volunteers accompanied "Colonel" John M. Chivington on a search-and-destroy mission against Black Kettle's Cheyenne camp at Sand Creek. Black Kettle had never made war on the United States. In front of his lodge fluttered an American flag and a white flag, which he expected would prevent an attack. Young warriors over whom he had no control, however, had recently killed white settlers on the Colorado plains, and the summer of 1864 saw many skirmishes between Indians and whites. Chivington's raiders devastated the camp, killing and horribly mutilating men, women, and children. Just before Christmas, the soldiers returned to Denver, where they displayed dozens of grisly trophies to admiring crowds.

Chivington, likely influenced by reading dime novels about Carson, boasted that he had "eclipsed . . . Carson, and posterity will speak of me as the great Indian fighter." Carson expressed only contempt for "that dog Chivington," as he labeled the former Methodist preacher more than once, and he offered a congressional investigating committee damning testimony regarding the Sand Creek attack. Carson was no "Indian hater," but he embraced a prevailing "American" notion that predicted the disappearance of the Native people. He once said, "I've seen as much of 'em as any white man livin', and I can't help but pity 'em. They'll all soon be gone, anyhow."

Among modern Carson scholars, Harvey L. Carter devoted the most care to defining his man's character. Carter concluded that Kit Carson did not develop "in any marked degree, the characteristic of leadership" until he became a soldier in 1861. By then his self-confidence was at a high level, and his reputation offered a credible source of authority. Like practically all mountain men, Kit was highly individualistic, but he was neither overly aggressive nor ambitious. By contrast, his friends Charles and William Bent, Lucien B. Maxwell, and Ceran St. Vrain all ardently pursued financial and political success. Carson also lacked the flamboyant "personality" that made his fellow trappers John L. Hatcher and Joe Meek so memorable. On the other hand, he was impetuous and sometimes showed poor judgment in risk taking, especially as a young man. Almost all contemporaries who wrote about him portrayed him as a decent man: honest, steadfast, and unassuming.

Kit Carson's friends knew that his inability to read or write caused him considerable embarrassment. Barely able to scrawl his name, he had to request others to read and write his letters. After the Civil War he briefly commanded a few forts but was hampered by illiteracy and inadequate bookkeeping skills. Carson had no head for business, and he had to answer more than once to charges of financial mismanagement, though he was never found guilty. Like many trappers, Kit's speech strongly reflected his backwoods upbringing: the use of *bar* for *bear,* *whar* for *where,* *fit* for *fought,* and the like persisted throughout his life. One Taos associate, Tom Tobin, recalled that Kit "never swore more'n was necessary." Kit's illiteracy required dependence on his memory, which contemporaries said was remarkably good. This faculty helped him learn Spanish, develop a working vocabulary in several Indian languages, and master the sign language of Plains Indians.

The "real" Carson was in essence an illiterate backwoodsman who possessed a special knack for survival in tough circumstances, an average man caught up in extraordinary events. What made him famous was a combination of the sincere admiration of friends who publicized his exploits and an early version of the "media blitz" in the form of inexpensive, sensationalized dime novels. In actuality, there are two Kit Carsons, one historical, the other a media creation, and these incompatible realities diverged. As a result of the many portrayals of Carson in books, movies, and television, by the late twentieth century the iconic Carson became more important in the public's imagination than the real one.

Kit Carson and men like him, despite limited education, biases, and human failings, exerted real influence over the destiny of New Mexico. Some of them, undoubtedly, had little idea that they were key pawns in a geopolitical contest of continental dimensions. A few traders, however, definitely aspired to power in New Mexico. Such a man was Charles Bent, who married a Hispanic woman, spent almost twenty years in New Mexico making money and building political support, and was named the first American territorial governor, only to be killed a few months later in the Taos Rebellion of 1847.

Charles Bent and Padre Martínez's well-documented mutual hatred produced several acts of violence in Taos, mainly perpetrated by their respective supporters, which exacerbated political and interethnic tensions in New Mexico before the war began in 1846 and resulted in major administrative changes in the territory after Bent's death. Perhaps, even, their relationship played a significant role in engendering a negative tone for "American" public opinion on New Mexico that helps account for its sixty-five years of territorial limbo. From a historical viewpoint, these two men had a far more direct impact on New Mexico's future than Kit Carson did. But relatively few people outside of New Mexico have ever heard of Martínez or Bent, whereas Carson achieved world renown. This notoriety, over which the real Kit Carson had no control and in which he showed little interest, eventually coalesced into a pseudohistorical icon of great symbolic resonance. Carson's name conjures up images in many Americans' minds—irrespective of whether those images correspond with historical reality or not. More than any historical aspect of Carson's life, it is the powerful resonance of his mythic life that explains why he has been recruited many times over the years to symbolize positive or negative aspects of our national character.

ESSAY ON SOURCES

Readers interested in Kit Carson may want to begin by consulting his autobiography, *Kit Carson's Own Story of His Life,* Blanche C. Grant, ed. (Taos: Kit Carson Memorial Foundation, 1926). The first biography to be published was DeWitt C. Peters, *The Life and Adventures of Kit Carson, the Nestor of the Rocky Mountains* (New York: Clark & Meeker, 1858). Reprinted several times, it contains a good deal of romanticized nonsense. Several later Carson biographies offer more credible details and reasoned analysis. Harvey Lewis Carter's *Dear Old Kit: The Historical Kit Carson* (Norman: University of Oklahoma Press, 1968) provides solid annotations for Carson's autobiography and includes a useful reappraisal of the man. Less reliable is M. Morgan Estergreen's *Kit Carson: A Portrait in Courage* (Norman: University of Oklahoma Press, 1962), which includes demonstrably false information about Carson as well as other errors. A highly positive appraisal, and generally reliable data, appears in George Brewerton's *Overland with Kit Carson: A Narrative of the Old Spanish Trail in '48* (New York: Coward-McCann, 1930; Lincoln: University of Nebraska Press, 1993).

The first Carson biography to include documents related to the Navajo Campaign was Edwin Legrand Sabin's *Kit Carson Days, 1809–1868: Adventures in the Path of Empire*, 2 vols. (New York: Press of the Pioneers, 1935; Lincoln: University of Nebraska Press, 1995, with an introduction by Marc Simmons). Very useful in some respects, it also includes many fabrications by a charlatan named Oliver Wiggins Perry. Lawrence Kelly's *Navajo Roundup: Selected Correspondence of Kit Carson's Campaign Against the Navajo, 1863–1865* (Boulder, Colo.: Pruett Publishing Company, 1970) presents dozens of annotated documents relative to the campaign and offers a persuasive defense of Carson's limited role in the roundup. Kelly's interpretation stands in marked contrast to Clifford Trafzer's *The Kit Carson Campaign: The Last Great Navajo War* (Norman: University of Oklahoma Press, 1982), which casts Carson as a major player. R. C. Gordon-McCutchan's collection of essays, *Kit Carson: Indian Fighter or Indian Killer?* (Niwot: University of Colorado Press, 1996), presents articles on the mythic and the real Carson and offers a basically positive assessment. Carson's role in Frémont's expeditions is ably digested and analyzed in Mary Lee Spence and Donald Jackson, eds., *The Expeditions of John Charles Frémont*, vols. 1 and 2 (Urbana: University of Illinois Press, 1970, 1973). For more recent work, see David Roberts, *A Newer World: Kit Carson, John C. Frémont, and the Claiming of the American West* (New York: Simon & Schuster, 2000), and Thomas W. Dunlay, *Kit Carson and the Indians* (Lincoln: University of Nebraska Press, 2000).

David J. Weber provides solid background on New Mexico during Carson's time in two narrative works: *The Mexican Frontier, 1821–1846: The American Southwest Under Mexico* (Albuquerque: University of New Mexico Press, 1982), and *The Taos Trappers: The Fur Trade in the Far Southwest, 1540–1846* (Norman: University of Oklahoma Press, 1971). For U.S.-Mexican attitudes and relationships, see David J. Weber, ed., *New Spain's Far Northern Frontier: Essays on Spain in the American West, 1540–1821* (Albuquerque: University of New Mexico Press, 1979), especially Weber's article, "'Scarce More Than Apes': Historical Roots of Anglo-American Stereotypes of Mexicans." The same author presents a selection of useful documents in David J. Weber, ed., *Foreigners in Their Native Land: Historical Roots of the Mexican Americans* (Albuquerque: University of New Mexico Press, 1973). Among many books and articles by Marc Simmons, see *Coronado's Land: Essays on Daily Life in Colonial New Mexico* (Albuquerque: University of New Mexico Press, 1996); *Murder on the Santa*

Fe Trail: An International Incident, 1843 (El Paso: Texas Western Press, 1984); and The Old Trail to Santa Fe: Collected Essays (Albuquerque: University of New Mexico Press, 1996).

For women on the trail, see Stella N. Drumm, ed., Down the Santa Fe Trail and into Mexico: The Diary of Susan Shelby Magoffin (New Haven, Conn.: Yale University Press, 1927; Lincoln: University of Nebraska Press, 1985); Marion Meyer, Mary Donoho: New First Lady of the Santa Fe Trail (Santa Fe: Ancient City Press, 1991); and Marion Sloan Russell, Land of Enchantment: Memoirs of Marion Russell Along the Santa Fe Trail, As Dictated to Mrs. Hal Russell (Evanston, Ill.: Branding Iron Press, 1954; Albuquerque: University of New Mexico Press, 1981). An excellent summary of interethnic marriages can be found in Rebecca McDowell Craver, The Impact of Intimacy: Mexican-Anglo Intermarriage in New Mexico, 1821–1846, Southwestern Studies Monograph No. 66 (El Paso: Texas Western Press, 1982).

A standard, reliable treatment of the Santa Fe Trail and its extension into Mexico via the Camino Real is Max L. Moorhead, New Mexico's Royal Road: Trade and Travel on the Chihuahua Trail (Norman: University of Oklahoma Press, 1958). More recent work appears in David N. Wetzel, ed., The Santa Fe Trail: New Perspectives, Essays in Colorado History No. 6 (Denver: Colorado Historical Society, 1987), and Susan Calafate Boyle's Comerciantes, Arrieros, y Peones: The Hispanos and the Santa Fe Trade (Santa Fe: Department of Interior, National Park Service, 1994), which offers much new research on the role of Hispanos in the trade. New research on the Camino Real and its relationship to the Santa Fe trade is presented in Gabrielle G. Palmer, comp., and June-el Piper and LouAnn Jacobson, eds., El Camino Real de Tierra Adentro, Cultural Resources Series No. 11 (Santa Fe: Bureau of Land Management, 1993), and June-el Piper, ed., El Camino Real de Tierra Adentro, vol. 2, Cultural Resources Series No. 13 (Santa Fe: Bureau of Land Management, 1999).

8

Billy the Kid, Susan McSween, Thomas Catron, and the Modernization of New Mexico, 1865–1912

KATHLEEN P. CHAMBERLAIN

In February 1878 two Lincoln County, New Mexico, merchant/cattlemen groups declared war on each other when John Tunstall and Alexander A. McSween challenged Lawrence G. Murphy and James J. Dolan's economic stranglehold on the area. During the first six months of 1878, men on both sides ambushed, assassinated, and generally tried to blast each other to the devil. In July they met head-on in the tiny town of Lincoln. A dozen men perished in the five-day shoot-out—including McSween—and a few weeks later a garbled *Philadelphia Times* article reminded readers that the New Mexico territory was a violent place, ill prepared for statehood.

A young bucktoothed cowboy named William Bonney or Billy the Kid emerged from the fiery July battle as leader of the fragmented Tunstall-McSween faction and for three years led a cattle-rustling spree across New Mexico and Texas. *The New York Times* reported the chaos, and by the time Sheriff Pat Garrett tracked down and killed the Kid on July 14, 1881, journals and dime novels across America had described New Mexico's barbaric customs in graphic detail. The five-day battle left Susan McSween a widow, and to survive economically, she took control of her husband's estate and purchased a ranch that earned her the title "Cattle Queen of New Mexico." The Lincoln County War cost territorial attorney Thomas Benton Catron his job, but he soft-landed with a mortgage to the Murphy-Dolan property in one hand and control of New Mexico's political machinery in the other.

Yet the Lincoln County War is part of a much larger story. Between 1865 and 1912, New Mexico transformed its feudal economy and corrupt political structure and modernized its backward educational system to achieve statehood. After 1880 the pace of change intensified. That February the railroad reached Santa Fe. A decade later irrigation projects turned the Pecos and San Juan River valleys into farm country. Miners opened gold, silver, and coal operations, and ranchers created lucrative cattle and sheep industries. Whereas in 1865 only four small newspapers operated in the territory, by 1900 New Mexico boasted sixty-three, five of them dailies. Two banks existed in 1878; more than fifty were chartered by 1900. Finally, the population increased from 119,000 in 1880 to 195,000 in 1900. Still, until 1910 Congress continued to turn thumbs down to statehood in large part because the Lincoln County War image dominated. Embarrassed New Mexicans realized they must overcome both the anarchistic outlawry that the conflict symbolized and the corruption that the territorial system encouraged.

The Lincoln County War also brought together Billy the Kid, Susan McSween, and Thomas B. Catron—albeit briefly—and their lives mirror the transformation from isolation to modernization, from lawlessness to respectability that took place in the territory after 1880. Billy exemplifies the old outlaw order, when men found it expedient to take the law into their own hands. Susan capitalized on dramatic economic advances and turned personal tragedy into wealth. Her emergence as Cattle Queen suggests that women played a more dynamic role in this modernization process than previously thought. Certainly nobody wanted statehood more than Catron, but his own business dealings and Old Guard politics blocked modernization and reform. Together this trio provides a series of windows into turbulent New Mexico, modernization, and the path toward statehood in 1912.

Thomas Catron was the first of the three to lay eyes on New Mexico, in 1866. What he saw was scattered sleepy villages and subsistence farmers overwhelmingly of Spanish heritage. Santa Fe bustled with merchants, government workers, and ne'er-do-wells. But Utes and Navajos to the west and Mescalero Apaches in southern New Mexico had terrorized the outlying settlements for decades. Just three years before Catron arrived, James Carleton, commander of the Military Department of New Mexico, sent hundreds of soldiers into Navajo and Apache country and mercilessly pursued them into submission. In 1864 he impounded the tribes together at the Bosque Redondo. On this harsh and barren eastern plain, Apaches and

Navajos were exposed to caustic winds and icy snowstorms, starvation, and occasional Comanche raids. In 1868 both tribes were resettled on a portion of their traditional homelands, creating a safer territory for whites and making the U.S. government the primary market and only source of ready cash. Fort Stanton, established in 1855 on the Rio Bonito, had primary responsibility for the Mescaleros, whereas Fort Wingate oversaw Navajo operations in the west. Fort Union, situated in northeastern New Mexico near Las Vegas, served as the primary distribution point for many of the goods intended for these and other forts across the region.

With Native Americans forcibly removed, New Mexicans fanned out over the land. Some took sheep herds into the San Juan Basin or north into the lush Sangre de Cristo ranges and discovered ready markets among the military forts and Indian reservations. Other families migrated south. By 1868 about four hundred Hispanos and fifty Anglos herded sheep, goats, and cattle and raised corn, beans, and chilies along the Bonito, Ruidoso, and Hondo Rivers. These farmers encountered Texans seeking rich pastures and cheap lands; one was John S. Chisum, who with brothers James and Pitzer amassed vast amounts of rangeland and herds beginning in 1867. For a time Chisum was probably the largest cattle producer in the United States.

Still, politics remained relatively local, at least outside Santa Fe. The old Spanish system of *alcaldes* who served as mayors, justices of the peace, probate judges, and sometimes militia leaders still operated. Executive, legislative, and judicial branches of government were unknown, as were free elections and trial by jury. However, territorial machinery was assembled, and with it came federal subsidies for offices, military posts, Indian service, mail routes, and even internal improvements such as roads or bridges. Congress used territorial offices as political plums, which virtually guaranteed inept and unresponsive government and provided every opportunity for corrupt men to milk the territory of land and other resources. Worse, the machine invited federal employees to conspire with locals for personal gain.

Land was the most lucrative resource. Before 1846 Spanish and Mexican administrations had awarded land grants to individuals and to communities for settlement. Even with community grants, citizens usually received small personal grants along a riverbed or an irrigation ditch, with the remainder of the land designated for common grazing. Land was unsurveyed. Boundaries were determined by rivers or streams and sometimes even less exact landmarks such as rocks, trees, or seasonal water holes. Then, too, owners might lease portions of the grants, and in most cases these agreements were verbal and vague. In one instance, Santa Clara Pueblo allowed a farmer sufficient land to plant a "hat full of corn" and the use of "several days" worth of water. Anglos recoiled in horror at such undefined boundaries—and at community holdings in general—and the imposition of an American legal system opened the way for fraud and corruption.

Congress established the Office of Surveyor General in 1854 to sift through and affirm land grant titles, but the Civil War prevented completion of the task. When speculators and homesteaders arrived after 1866, land grant tangles proved lucrative for lawyers such as Catron, who gladly accepted land in payment from cash-poor residents. The losers were native New Mexicans, most of whom spoke little English and discovered too late the consequences of American laws.

Yet during the territorial period, which lasted from the end of the Mexican-American War in 1848 until 1912, Hispanos managed to retain much of their culture despite Anglo intrusion. Baptist, Presbyterian, and Methodist missionaries tried but could not undermine Catholic domination. Bishop Jean B. Lamy arrived in 1851, made significant reforms to the clergy, and supervised the construction of forty-five new churches. Lamy also pioneered parochial schools for his parishioners, thereby strengthening Roman Catholic influence even further and delaying attempts to initiate a public school system throughout most of the nineteenth century.

Nevertheless, newcomers to New Mexico watched the rest of America explode with opportunity and wanted their share. After the Civil War ended, for example, railroads sped across the continent; New Mexicans eagerly sought connections. Miners flocked west in search of mineral resources, and although New Mexico lagged behind, gold strikes in Elizabethtown in 1866 and in White Oaks in 1879 turned these communities into boom towns. Silver lured miners to Kingston in 1887 and to Mogollon two years later. Behind individual miners came corporations seeking copper, lead, zinc, and coal. Mining, like the military, also encouraged merchants, millers, farmers, ranchers, laundry owners, even prostitutes to establish businesses.

Elsewhere, Europeans by the hundreds of thousands arrived in America in the decades after the Civil War, seeking rags-to-riches success and furnishing cheap labor. Businesses in the East and Midwest boomed during this period; the size of industries mushroomed. In 1865 annual production of goods in the United States was $2 billion; by 1900 it was $13 billion. But despite mass expansion, ownership fell into the hands of a few. Andrew

Carnegie, for instance, battled for control of steel while John D. Rockefeller monopolized oil exploration, pipelines, and refining; J. P. Morgan was the uncrowned king of banking. In the West, eastern and European land speculators bought up grazing lands and mining property, and some of these investors eyed territorial New Mexico.

Elevated government spending and enormous economic growth produced corrupt political machines such as William Marcy Tweed's infamous Tammany Hall, which controlled New York City offices. Ideologically, businessmen and politicians alike justified their actions with a formula that equated a good Protestant upbringing, determination, and hard work with success. For New Mexicans this "gospel of wealth" excused the exploitation of the region's large Indian and Mexican American populations. Moreover, naturalist Charles Darwin's theories of evolution and survival of the fittest not only explained success and failure to the satisfaction of nineteenth-century minds but championed laissez-faire capitalism, unscrupulous politics, and environmental exploitation and encouraged the formation of powerful political and economic rings.

New Mexico after the Civil War was a microcosm of the United States. Nobody in the territory was more successful at capitalizing on such Gilded Age excesses than Thomas B. Catron. Born October 6, 1840, in Lexington, Missouri, Thomas was a blunt, no-nonsense young man. First he attended the University of Missouri and graduated in 1860. Then, when the war broke out, he had quite a decision to make—fight or flee. His college roommate Stephen Elkins chose the latter and headed for New Mexico. For Thomas, however, the decision was more difficult. His father was a staunch Democrat and southern sympathizer. So, after much soul-searching Catron joined the Confederate cause and enlisted in the army. On May 10, 1865, he was mustered out of the service. Missouri held little attraction for a Democrat whose Confederate involvement barred him from practicing law.

Elkins sent letters lauding opportunity in New Mexico for young men of ability, and Thomas reacted. He arrived in Santa Fe on July 27, 1866, with two wagons of flour, which he sold for $10,000. As his wagons jostled down the Santa Fe Trail, he read a Spanish grammar book. Catron's biographer Victor Westphall claims that his subject's personality defies clear analysis but calls Thomas a mental giant, reserved, and hardworking. One colleague called him jolly, kindhearted, and genial. Yet Thomas also had a dark side, which manifested itself in a ruthless quest for power and a biting sarcasm used to upbraid rivals. Single-minded and direct almost to a fault, once

FIGURE 8.1. Thomas Benton Catron. Exact date of photo is unknown, but it was apparently taken when Catron was U.S. attorney, so about 1872. Photo by Edwin L. Brand. Courtesy Museum of New Mexico, neg. no. 56041.

Catron reached New Mexico, he immediately made important contacts and in December 1866 was named district attorney for the Third Judicial District in La Mesilla. In an ironic juxtaposition, he was not admitted to the bar until the following year.

By 1868 Catron was a member of the territorial legislature and in January 1869 became territorial attorney general. His meteoric rise continued with appointment as U.S. attorney in 1872. A photo taken about this time reveals a tidy, light-haired young man with a neatly trimmed handlebar mustache and a determined gaze. Most of all, Catron wanted wealth, and land was the place to begin. With Elkins he became involved in the Mora Land Grant, which had been awarded to seventy-six Mexican citizens on September 28, 1835. Northeast of Santa Fe, the region had flourished with the arrival of American troops in 1846: the Santa Fe Trail passed directly through the grant, and farmers found themselves in an excellent position to supply newcomers. Fort Union was built within its confines in 1852, and farmers on the Mora Grant provided fruits, vegetables, grains, and wool. Elkins and Catron got involved in 1869 when they represented a resident owner in a criminal case. As payment, they accepted a deed to part of the client's "undivided interest," meaning that title to the land was held jointly by all grantees. Consequently nobody could obtain title to a specific portion without first acquiring the entire grant.

In November 1870 Catron, Elkins, and others, including New Mexico surveyor general T. Rush Spencer, devised a plan to purchase the Mora Grant from its original grantees and their heirs. There is some evidence that in order to do so, Catron falsely promised grantees that if they deeded their property to him "temporarily," he would secure title under U.S. law and deed the land back to them. Although some owners were persuaded, the plan overall failed when Spencer died suddenly and a power struggle ensued between the rest. By 1895, however, Catron had managed to amass two hundred forty thousand acres of the Mora Grant, which he eventually turned over to his son in 1909.

During his lifetime Thomas obtained an interest in at least thirty-four grants, making him the largest landowner in the United States. But it was the famed Beaubien-Miranda or Maxwell Land Grant that earned him the enmity of New Mexicans and created the Santa Fe Ring. Like those Gilded Age robber barons back east, Catron concluded that to ensure success he needed lawyers, judges, politicians, and a friendly territorial press to back him up. From this grew the Santa Fe Ring, a loose confederation of lawyers, politicians, and businessmen determined to run the territory. As author Joel Jacobsen so aptly put it in *Such Men as Billy the Kid*, the Santa Fe Ring was an informal confederation of men whose goals were to swap favors and tell no tales. It differed from other rings in the United States primarily in its medium of choice—land.

The Maxwell Land Grant was a kingly domain originally granted to Charles Hipolyte Trotier, Sieur de Beaubien, a French Canadian who became known as Carlos Beaubien, and Guadalupe Miranda, a Mexican citizen. When Beaubien died in 1864, his enterprising son-in-law Lucien B. Maxwell bought out the in-laws and purchased Miranda's share as well. Maxwell constructed an imposing house at Cimarron and raised cattle and grain for the army. By 1867, however, Maxwell decided to sell and asked for a survey to determine the exact boundaries and size of the grant. Congress in 1860 had confirmed the grant in keeping with Mexico's Colonization Law of 1824, which limited an individual grant to about ninety-seven thousand acres. Maxwell's grant was thus determined to be ninety-seven thousand acres.

Four groups sought to purchase the grant from Maxwell; one of these included Colorado businessman Jerome Chaffee and native New Mexican Miguel A. Otero. In 1869 Maxwell's legal adviser—Catron—persuaded him to sell the grant to Chaffee's group for $650,000. The Maxwell Land Grant and Railway Company was established to handle the deed, and its president was none other than Catron's law partner, Stephen Elkins. The deal was concluded in April 1870, at which time Maxwell established the First National Bank of Santa Fe with part of the proceeds to handle the company's securities. Catron, Elkins, and several of their partners became the bank's directors and officials.

But Catron, for one, had larger plans. The Maxwell Land Grant and Railroad Company hired W. W. Griffin, U.S. deputy surveyor, to resurvey the land. This survey put the acreage at 2 million acres, suddenly multiplying the grant by more than ten. At the same time Otero, vice president of the Atchison, Topeka and Santa Fe Railroad, investigated the possibility of expanding the line south. Without awaiting confirmation of the second survey, Catron and the others sold out to an English company for $1.3 million.

Disaster threatened in 1871 when Secretary of the Interior Columbus Delano reissued the original decision, stating that the Maxwell Land Grant measured only ninety-seven thousand acres. The English investors consequently demanded their money back. At this time Elkins successfully ran for territorial delegate from New Mexico, and Chaffee was elected Colorado delegate, hoping to use their influence to stop Delano, achieve statehood, and settle land claims once and for all. Catron insisted on a third survey and hired J. T. Elkins—Stephen's brother—who not surprisingly determined the grant was 1.7 million acres. This final survey was affirmed, and on May 19, 1879, title was granted. But the British deal collapsed; the British claim was sold for taxes and repurchased by none other than Catron.

This long and arduous road to grant ownership made Thomas realize how badly he needed support from officials, attorneys, bankers, and the press. Thus the Santa Fe Ring took shape. At its core, of course, were Republicans Catron and Elkins but also Democrats such as Henry L. Waldo, and so the ring was generally nonpartisan and sought political advantage, not party accolades. The ring embraced whoever was the current surveyor general, county probate judges, federal judges, and the *Santa Fe New Mexican,* which until 1894 served as its mouthpiece. Territorial governors either joined or were too short-lived and weak to matter. Over time important ranchers, mine owners, merchants, and bankers became members and to some extent spawned smaller rings. Catron used the network to purchase silver mines and ranches. The American Valley Company was his largest ranch investment, but it was the Carrizozo Ranch that involved Thomas in the Lincoln County War.

Historian Howard R. Lamar accurately claims that the Santa Fe Ring was pragmatic enough to embrace anyone of use. One of these marginal players was Lawrence G. Murphy, who mustered out of the army at Fort Stanton in 1864 and with partner Emil Fritz opened a brewery and a store at the fort, calling their operation L. G. Murphy and Company. The War Department licensed them to operate as official Indian traders, which put them in a position to sell inferior goods and inflate the numbers of Indian recipients for which they received payment. The only mercantile around, Murphy sold to farmers at high prices and to newcomers at usury-level credit. Worse, the firm sold land that it did not own. If victims later resisted, Murphy simply attached goods and land; if they left the region, the firm repossessed and resold. By April 1869 Murphy hired another former soldier and an Irish immigrant like himself, twenty-year-old James J. Dolan, who eventually became a partner. In 1872 the firm was expelled from Fort Stanton after a violent confrontation between Dolan and an officer and reestablished in nearby Lincoln. The new two-story building— dubbed "The House"—dominated the village physically and financially.

The territorial legislature created Lincoln County in 1869 and made Lincoln its county seat. Murphy ruled the county's Democratic Party, and his friendship with army acquaintance and territorial attorney general William L. Rynerson drew him at least marginally into the Santa Fe Ring. Another tie was the Masons: Catron, Rynerson, Murphy, Dolan, and William Brady, Lincoln County sheriff, helped organize the first Grand Lodge in New Mexico.

Murphy's challenge came in the form of twenty-three-year-old Englishman John H. Tunstall, who in 1872 had sailed to America seeking land and investments to secure his family's fortune back home. Tunstall wrote to his father in London that he planned to "grab" as much land as he could. Moreover, he wanted his own ring. His ally was attorney Alexander A. McSween, who with his wife, Susan, also longed for a piece of the American dream.

Susan was always vague in regard to her husband. In fact, his life before 1873 remains a complete mystery. She told writers he was an ordained Presbyterian minister, but that possibility has not been verified. Furthermore, Susan was equally as elusive about her own life, calling herself Susan Homer when she was born Susanna Ellen Hummer on December 30, 1845, in rural Adams County, Pennsylvania, twelve miles from Gettysburg. Family tradition says that Sue ran away from home and a strict Church of the Brethren upbringing in 1863, but no documentary evidence supports this or pinpoints her whereabouts until an announcement in the *Eureka* (Kansas) *Herald* proclaimed a marriage to "Judge McSween" on August 23, 1873. In September 1874 the couple abandoned a house that Alex also used as an office and headed for New Mexico. A chance encounter with Miguel A. Otero steered the McSweens to Lincoln, where they arrived in March 1875.

Susan was described by one of the few Anglo women in Lincoln as a "very nice looking woman," although preoccupied with wardrobe, makeup, and hair. Indeed, even photographs taken in her later years show a well-dressed, elaborately coiffured woman. She vainly shaved years off her age by the time she reached her thirties and well into old age was reported to dye her hair. Unlike Anglo women, the largely Hispanic population considered Susan aloof and unfriendly. Tunstall's observations offer still another dimension; he said her shrewd business mind and ability to discuss investment opportunity in Lincoln was "about as good as any man could have done." However, Susan took a backseat as her husband rented a law office, joined the Republican Party, and petitioned Philadelphia for a

Presbyterian minister. Alex also worked for The House as bill collector and over the course of one year collected $30,000. What McSween thought about Murphy's business tactics is not known. But the relationship fell apart after Fritz died in June 1874, leaving a $10,000 insurance policy.

McSween agreed to collect the sum and went to New York City in October 1876 to sort out the complications. He eventually obtained $7,148.49 after fees were paid to lawyers and bankers. Of that, his own fees and expenses amounted to about $4,000. Instead of relinquishing the remaining $3,000 to the estate administrators—Charles Fritz, Emil's brother and allegedly an alcoholic who was indebted to Murphy, and Charles's sister Emilie Scholand—McSween deposited the money in his personal East St. Louis bank account, claiming that to do otherwise was to turn the money directly over to Murphy and Dolan.

Ironically, en route to New York, McSween met Tunstall in Santa Fe and encouraged the young man to consider Lincoln. As Alex headed east, Tunstall traveled south, well warned against the Murphy-Dolan "welcome wagon" but determined to establish his own store and to challenge the Irishmen over lucrative government corn and cattle contracts. On February 8, 1877, Tunstall purchased land on the Rio Feliz; that summer he opened a store in Lincoln in direct competition with The House.

Murphy and Dolan retaliated. They persuaded Fritz's heirs to charge McSween with embezzlement. At Christmas, Alex was arrested as he and Susan headed to St. Louis on business. Sue went on alone, apparently convinced all was well. When she returned in March, however, Alex had appeared before Catron associate Judge Warren Bristol, who permitted District Attorney William L. Rynerson, another Ring member, to harshly interrogate him. Bristol deferred the case until the April grand jury and ordered Sheriff William Brady to attach sufficient McSween property to pay the $8,000 bail. Convinced that the two were partners, Brady drew little distinction between McSween's and Tunstall's belongings. He gleefully took possession of the mercantile and inventory, then sent a posse to attach the Englishman's cattle.

Susan heard the horrifying news that on February 18 at about 5:30 P.M., a posse led by Brady deputy Billy Mathews had encountered Tunstall and six of his hired men on a lonely trail outside of Lincoln and shot him down in cold blood. Outnumbered and too far away to assist, Tunstall's companions fled. One of these was eighteen-year-old William Antrim, sometimes called Kid Antrim but by this time signing his name as William H.

FIGURE 8.2. Susan McSween, probably taken at the time of her marriage in 1873. Courtesy of University of Arizona Library, Special Collections.

Bonney. Susan discovered that immediately after Tunstall's murder, men siding with her husband and calling themselves Regulators began to clash with men allied to Murphy and Dolan.

Since the Santa Fe Ring controlled most of the courts and officials and because Murphy had strong military connections, the Regulators believed they could obtain no justice. Their position was made worse by Catron's direct involvement: Murphy and Dolan had found themselves so cash poor by January 1878 that they mortgaged land, inventory, and the Carrizozo ranch, east of Lincoln, for $25,000. Catron's brother-in-law Edgar Walz acted as manager, and now the Ring had a stake in Lincoln County.

During the spring court term the grand jury indicted several Murphy-Dolan men, including known rustlers and gunmen Jessie Evans, Tom Hill, and William Baker for Tunstall's murder, and cleared McSween of embezzlement. Tensions rose. Dolan dissolved The House on May 1; Murphy left Lincoln and died in October apparently of alcohol-related illnesses. Meanwhile Alex hid out in surrounding hills while indictments piled up against him and the others. Susan remained in Lincoln but, fearing for her life, encouraged Regulators to sleep at her house, later resulting in accusations of sexual impropriety.

On July 14 Alex returned to Lincoln with about forty Regulators determined to fight it out to the bitter end. Murphy-Dolan men followed, and both sides positioned themselves in houses, the former Tunstall store, the *torreón* watch tower, and the Wortley Hotel. McSween, Susan, her sister Elizabeth Shield, Elizabeth's five children, and about a dozen men, including Billy, barricaded themselves in the sprawling nine-room McSween home. For four days both factions tried to exterminate the other. Murphy-Dolan men waved arrest warrants for nearly every McSween man while, fearful of falling into their hands, Regulators hoarded food and water, burrowed portholes into the adobe, barricaded windows with flour sacks, and resisted. One of them expressed disdain of the Santa Fe Ring in a letter to Walz: "Steel [sic] from the poorest or richest American or Mexican and the full measure of the injury you do, shall be visited upon the property of Mr. Catron."

Residents dodged bullets and sent word to Colonel N. A. M. Dudley, the pompous commanding officer at Fort Stanton, while gunfire intensified. Not until the fifth day—July 19—after somebody shot at a Fort Stanton private delivering a note did Dudley order one company of cavalry to saddle up. One company of infantry—for a total of about thirty-five men—

joined the march, dragging with them a brass howitzer, Gatling gun, and two thousand rounds of ammunition.

Their arrival gave Dolan allies the advantage. Susan reported that as the column passed by, enemies across the street unfurled a black flag, the sign given by Santa Anna at the Alamo, signifying no quarter. The McSween men hunkered down inside the house. That afternoon Dolan men managed to pile lumber against an outside wall and light a fire. Terrified, Susan later told researchers how she crawled on hands and knees to Dudley's camp and demanded assistance. Unless Alex surrendered, the army could offer no help, Dudley was said to have snapped at her.

The house burned slowly. Occupants scurried from room to room, allegedly dragging Sue's prized parlor piano with them. Walter Noble Burns's 1926 *Saga of Billy the Kid* described Susan playing "rousing airs" to inspire the men, but she angrily dismissed the notion, finding the idea insulting. She did note that Alex grew more and more despondent, while Billy became animated. Billy finally ordered the women and children to leave, and when soldier volunteers evacuated the family next door, a reluctant Sue kissed her husband good-bye for the last time. Thus Susan did not see the "big killing," as the final shoot-out was called.

It is at this point that Billy, the individual most closely associated with the Lincoln County War, emerged as leader. Prior to July 1878 Billy had participated simply as one of the Regulators. Afterward he became one of the best-known characters in New Mexico history. Twentieth-century researchers have sifted through documents, firsthand reports, even hearsay, to piece together Antrim's life. Hundreds of books, journal articles, and films exist covering Billy's life during and after 1878. The Kid's early years, however, remain a mystery. Born Henry McCarty, he probably breathed his first in New York City, but Tunstall biographer and historian of the Lincoln County War Frederick Nolan says that Billy's birthplace is as likely Ohio, Illinois, Kansas, Indiana, or New Mexico. Similarly, although Billy's birth date is said to be November 23, 1859, nobody has absolutely verified this fact, either. In 1880 the Kid told a census taker that he was twenty-five years old and hailed from Missouri. Again, no direct evidence has surfaced to support or refute this assertion, but for the most part, historians have discarded Billy's claim.

It is documented, however, that his mother, Catherine McCarty, married William H. Antrim in Santa Fe in 1873, with Henry and his brother, Joseph, witnessing the ceremony. The Antrims moved to Silver City, where, sadly,

Catherine died of tuberculosis on September 16, 1874. Antrim was reportedly not a bad stepfather, just a hardworking and absent one. In need of a heavier hand, Henry got into mischief, then ran away. He ended up in Arizona, where he shot a blacksmith named Frank Cahill. After two years in Arizona, young Henry rode back to New Mexico, this time to Lincoln County. He may have worked briefly for John Chisum. In September 1877 legend says he rode with a group of brash cattle thieves called The Boys, which included Jessie Evans, Tom Hill, and William Baker, Tunstall's alleged killers. Billy was not arrested with gang members that October, but instead found honest work with Tunstall and was with him that fateful February afternoon. Billy was one of several McSween men who ambushed Sheriff Brady and his deputy on April 1, 1878, but was the only one who ever stood trial for this killing.

On July 19, as the McSween house burned, Billy drew up a desperate plan. He and four others would run decoy. "Wait until dark," he told them, "then run like hell for the Tunstall store next door." With any luck at all, McSween would then lead his group straight back to the steep incline between the house and the Rio Bonito, down the bank, and across the river to the hills beyond. It was a risky plan, Billy admitted, but given their predicament, it was all they had.

After the July sun sank behind the Capitan Mountains, Billy's group sprinted from the burning house and zigzagged across the backyard. One was killed, but the rest escaped. Unfortunately the gunfire immobilized McSween, and he waited ten, maybe fifteen minutes. Smoke engulfed the building, and flames lapped at the darkness. Opponents closed in. McSween shouted his surrender, then suddenly changed his mind. Pinned down by guns and illuminated by the flames, McSween and four others died, two were badly wounded, and, unbelievably, two escaped unharmed. One, maybe two, lay dead inside the house.

Following the big killing, Billy regrouped the Regulators and eluded Dolan men, soldiers, and the law. When newly appointed governor Lew Wallace issued a proclamation of general amnesty in November 1878, Billy, like most others, remained on the run; just because the governor was willing to forgive did not mean Billy's enemies were. Still, when Dolan and others were accused of murder three months later, Wallace needed an informant and arranged to meet Billy secretly in Lincoln on March 15, 1879. With the authority to exempt Billy from all prosecution and to protect him, Wallace persuaded a tired young man to turn state's evidence. Sick of fighting, Billy put his life into Wallace's hands.

FIGURE 8.3. William H. Bonney, alias Billy the Kid, ca. 1879. Photo courtesy
Museum of New Mexico, neg. no. 30769.

As per the agreement, Billy submitted to a fake arrest and went in handcuffs to La Mesilla to testify. Billy discovered, however, that neither Judge Bristol nor District Attorney Rynerson intended to honor the agreement. Even Billy's capable attorney, Ira Leonard, sent word to Wallace that Rynerson was pressing forward with charges. Busy writing *Ben Hur*, Wallace ignored Leonard's plea while Billy's trial for killing Brady was scheduled for July 1879. In May he testified at a military court of inquiry, then on June 17 slipped out of his shackles and walked out of jail for Fort Sumner, friends, and sweethearts.

Little is known about the blue-eyed, baby-faced former Regulator after the escape, but he did assemble a new gang, which stole horses from the Mescaleros and rustled Chisum cattle. In January 1880 Billy killed Joe Grant, a local rowdy, in a Fort Sumner saloon. Although Billy later told a newspaper reporter that his goal in life was to settle down, buy a ranch, and marry, by November 1880 time was running out. Chisum and another Pecos-area rancher, Joseph C. Lea, persuaded Pat Garrett, a onetime friend of the Kid, to run for sheriff of Lincoln County and chase down Billy and his gang. Garrett won and set about his task with relish. Thus with Garrett, federal marshals, and Texas cattle detectives hot on his heels, the wily outlaw trekked from one hiding place to another through the coldest December on record and waist-high snow. Holed up at an isolated cattle forage station called Stinking Springs, Billy awoke to an icy, gray Christmas morning with Garrett's posse surrounding him. After a brief standoff, Billy surrendered.

The newly arrived Atchison, Topeka and Santa Fe Railroad rapidly transported Billy from Las Vegas to Santa Fe and from there to Mesilla. He stood trial, was convicted, and was sentenced to hang on May 13, 1881. Returned to Lincoln to await execution, the Kid cheated the hangman on April 28 when one deputy went to lunch and the other let down his defenses momentarily. Garrett was out of town, making arrangements to build the scaffold. After shooting both guards, Billy fled.

Billy rode right back to his old stomping grounds in Fort Sumner. Two months later he emerged from hiding long enough to visit a sweetheart. He did not know when he stepped onto Pete Maxwell's porch that night to cut himself a slab of beef that Garrett was inside. Hatless, shoeless, and unnerved by two unknown men on the porch, Billy slipped into Maxwell's dark bedroom, asking "*¿Quién es?*" or, "Who is it?" No answer. A split second later Garrett's bullet tore into the Kid's chest, and within minutes Billy lay dead. Native New Mexicans and sweethearts mourned the outlaw's passing, but most saw the end of his so-called reign of terror as the start of a new age for New Mexico. In one sense, they were correct. The Lincoln County War was anathema to pro-statehood forces, and its violent aftermath only reinforced the notion that New Mexico was indeed a wild, lawless place, not ready to join the Union. There is little doubt that Billy represented what many considered the very worst of the territory's raw frontier era. Clearly his brand of outlawry threatened the economic stability of southeastern New Mexico, especially businessmen like Chisum, Lea, and even James Dolan, who after the war struggled to recuperate his losses and to attain respectability. However, it seems unlikely that Billy and his ragtag band could have held back the forces of change for long, and so it is possible that Billy simply remained an embarrassing symbol of an episode many wanted to put behind them.

The economic face of New Mexico was already changing by the time Billy breathed his last. Where individual merchants and government money once dominated, new markets opened. As the railroad arrived, towns such as Raton, Gallup, and Las Cruces sprang up and others, such as Albuquerque, boomed. Property values in New Mexico skyrocketed from $41 million in 1880 to $231 million a decade later. The number of cattle alone went from about three hundred fifty thousand in 1880 to 1.6 million in 1890. In Lincoln County, the population increased by 39 percent between 1870 and 1880; by 1890 it rose another 180 percent. According to historian Darlis Miller, as businesses multiplied throughout the county overall, so too did establishments owned and operated by women. Like men, women also amassed farm and grazing lands under the Homestead, Timber Culture, and Desert Land Acts.

Susan McSween was one of many who capitalized on this massive economic growth. However, after the big killing, she found little justice. Almost immediately following Alexander's death, Susan visited Justice Department investigator Frank Warner Angel in Las Vegas, who had come to Lincoln in spring 1878 seeking affidavits in regard to territorial corruption. Susan provided plenty of information about Murphy-Dolan, Colonel Dudley, and other officials. Governor Samuel B. Axtell was subsequently replaced as one result of Angel's investigation, and with the handwriting on the wall, Catron resigned. Although it is doubtful that Susan's evidence caused Axtell's removal, certainly data previously compiled by Alexander and turned over to Angel resulted in the termination of Mescalero Indian agent Frederick C. Godfroy, a House cohort, who had helped the firm defraud the federal government and Indians.

Still, McSween received little legal redress for herself. Through attorney Huston I. Chapman and with Governor Wallace's help, Susan accused Dudley of her husband's death. Her accusations generated a May 2, 1879, military court of inquiry, which earned Dudley nothing more than an official reprimand. Nor did civilian courts offer much. On December 6 a jury took two minutes to acquit Dudley of arson, and the verdict brought raucous applause from Bristol's court. Susan's satisfaction was knowing her legal pursuits cost Dudley thousands of dollars of his own money. But the vindictive colonel lashed back; he collected affidavits that labeled Sue an "immoral and lewd" woman, a common means of putting a Victorian-era female "in her place," especially an attractive and vulnerable widow.

Economically Susan did better, lending credence to John Tunstall's assessment of her as a cunning businesswoman. She took control of Alex's estate and that of Richard Brewer, a farmer who died owing McSween money. Charging Brewer's IOU 2 percent per month interest, Sue persuaded his aging parents in Wisconsin to sign over the property and valuable corn contracts that went with it. After the administrator of Tunstall's estate left town, Susan was named administratrix. She recovered two hundred head of his cattle and rented out the store for $40 per month. In 1883 Charles Fritz obtained a judgment against the McSween estate for the $3,300 in outstanding insurance money, and Sue turned over the Tunstall store and several years of rent in payment. Here another mystery remains unsolved: What happened to the nearly $7,000 allegedly collected by Alexander McSween in early 1878 and deposited in St. Louis? Hopefully future research will find the answer. For the most part, however, the widow McSween lined her pockets well. A former Tunstall employee expressed the general feeling throughout Lincoln: "Mrs. McSween is not going to pay any creditor except herself." Another said that whom Susan could not get along with, she paid off. Nolan called her ambitious with a desire for wealth and few scruples over how she achieved it.

On June 20, 1880, Susan married George B. Barber, who read law in Leonard's law office. Barber was admitted to the New Mexico bar in October 1882. Susan McSween took her estate into the marriage. By this time she had also bought several widely scattered properties. In November 1879, for example, she entered a widow's claim for 160 acres of South Spring property near the Chisum ranch under the Timber Culture Act.

She filed for another 320 acres under the Desert Land Act and purchased 160 additional acres of homestead land.

The Barbers as a couple purchased a ranch in 1883 at Three Rivers, about twenty miles north of Tularosa in the shadow of Sierra Blanca, and built a stone house on their land. Susan used the Tunstall cattle to start her herd, but some believe Chisum also contributed a gift of cattle for "services rendered." Rumors that she and Chisum had been lovers circulated but remain unsupported. During their marriage George and Susan maintained separate brands. Perhaps that is to be expected since they also appear to have kept separate abodes. Susan controlled the ranch, while George operated law offices in Lincoln. Because she operated during New Mexico's cattle boom, Susan commanded top dollar for beef, and her property attracted investors. In 1887 she sold one-half interest in her property to two Milwaukee investors and took over as general manager, calling the new partnership the Three Rivers Land and Cattle Company. In 1888 Susan claimed improvements on yet another four hundred acres patented under the Desert Land Act, including a dam across the river and an irrigation ditch.

In 1891 the Three Rivers Ranch was valued at $49,000 and boasted more than five thousand head of cattle. In 1891 Susan also filed for divorce from George, claiming he had abandoned her; the divorce was final on October 6, 1891. Sue continued to run the ranch. Newspapers reported that she made her cowboys wash, comb their hair, and take off their hats in the house. Darlis Miller notes that Susan McSween Barber conformed to the stereotype of the "woman as civilizer," but in the capacity of employer. It is noteworthy that some of Susan's eastern relatives suggested she was stingy, lending strength to previous allegations.

In July 1902 Susan sold the bulk of her property to Monroe Harper for $32,000; in 1917 the rest went to Albert Bacon Fall, one of Catron's political rivals and of Teapot Dome fame. Afterward Susan speculated in town lots in Tularosa and White Oaks, where gold discoveries in 1879 had once caused rapid growth. By 1893 gold mines closed and the railroad bypassed White Oaks, turning Corona and Carrizozo into prosperous trading centers instead. For some reason, Susan McSween Barber built a small house and retired in White Oaks, perhaps hoping the town would come back. When oil-seeking geologists arrived in the early twentieth century, Susan—ever the entrepreneur—tried in vain to interest them in her holdings. By this time developers James J. Hagerman and Charles B. Eddy had succeeded in turning the former Chisum property into a massive irrigation project that lured farmers to the Pecos Valley about fifty miles east of Lincoln. The population of that region tripled between 1900 and 1910.

Susan Hummer McSween Barber's career spanned more than two decades of radical change and steady growth in nineteenth-century New Mexico. Involved in the notorious Lincoln County War, she never looked back. She cared little for Billy and the other Regulators, who had once slept at her home to protect her. Instead she blamed these men for Alexander's death and moved forward. Susan took full advantage of New Mexico's economic growth and participated in male-dominated activities, albeit without abandoning accepted female roles.

In some ways Susan and Thomas Catron were much alike: they shared a belief in economic progress but always put personal goals first. In his case, when forward-looking politicians attempted to institute a public school system in the 1880s, Catron, eager to keep his taxes low, fought the measure, even though without public schools New Mexico could not hope for statehood. In December 1890 Republicans drafted a proposed state constitution that finally approved a public school bill but, at Catron's insistence, outlawed property taxes over 1 percent.

Catron's economic interests ran counter to the welfare of New Mexico in other ways as well. In 1891 Congress established the Court of Private Land Claims to settle land grants. Too often grants still fell into the hands of large landowners or attorneys. Catron was again a big winner when by 1903 the court approved nearly all of his massive holdings. In the case of the Maxwell Land Grant, the Court of Private Land Claims upheld the nearly 2-million-acre survey.

At the same time, although Catron's political star was fading to some extent by 1890, it was not yet out. The Republican Party divided as newcomers vied for control. Third-party movements during the 1890s ushered in a reform spirit, but less in New Mexico than elsewhere. In 1892 arguments ignited a series of politically motivated murders. That summer assassins killed former Democratic Santa Fe County sheriff Francisco Chávez. Five men—two of them brothers named Borrego—were tried in 1895, with Catron serving as their defense attorney. The thirty-eight-day trial was vicious and revealed vast political corruption and secret deals. The Borrego trial, as it was nicknamed, ended with a guilty verdict for the men and a contempt citation and temporary disbarment for Catron. The *Santa Fe New Mexican,* which had previously championed the Santa Fe

Ring, came under Democratic Party control in 1894 and castigated Catron regularly.

Still, when Catron chose to put his concerns aside and gaze out of his window upon Santa Fe, he would have seen a very Spanish-looking town. Its central rectangular plaza and narrow, meandering streets recalled New Mexico's past. But he also saw changes creeping in. Anglo culture was encroaching. If Catron looked down Palace Avenue, for instance, he would have seen large American-style mansions and, farther down, St. Vincent's Hospital, begun by Archbishop Lamy but now a bustling three-story building. Historian Paul Horgan notes in *The Centuries of Santa Fe* that as myriad white Americans arrived in the last decade of the nineteenth and early years of the twentieth century, they were captivated by New Mexico's unique blend of ancient Pueblo-style architecture and romantic Spanish design. But as Americans came in ever larger numbers, they altered what had attracted them.

Whether he approved or not, Catron saw other changes as well, changes that finally set New Mexico on the path to statehood. In 1898 Congress called for volunteers to fight in the Spanish-American War. New Mexicans enthusiastically answered the call. But it was Governor Miguel A. Otero, Jr., not Catron, who promised the 340 New Mexico "cowboys" to Theodore Roosevelt's Rough Rider cavalry unit. Otero, the first Hispano governor since 1846 and an avid proponent of statehood, eagerly sought opportunities for Mexican Americans to prove their loyalty to the United States. In part, the ploy worked. As vice president in 1900, Roosevelt remembered the New Mexico Rough Riders and promised statehood. The problem was, when he became president in 1901, he failed to expedite an enabling act, and therefore, again, New Mexicans had to wait. It was President William Howard Taft who finally signed the proclamation making New Mexico the forty-seventh state.

By 1910 Catron and the Old Guard Republicans had regained sufficient control of the party to dominate the statehood convention. As a result, the constitution safeguarded their special interests, particularly low land taxes. The new constitution also avoided reforms like women's suffrage, direct election of senators, and initiative, referendum, and recall that many other states had already enacted and that would spawn amendments to the U.S. Constitution in just a few years. New Mexico could have written a progressive, forward-looking document but failed to do so because of the authority that right-wing Republicans such as Catron and Fall wielded.

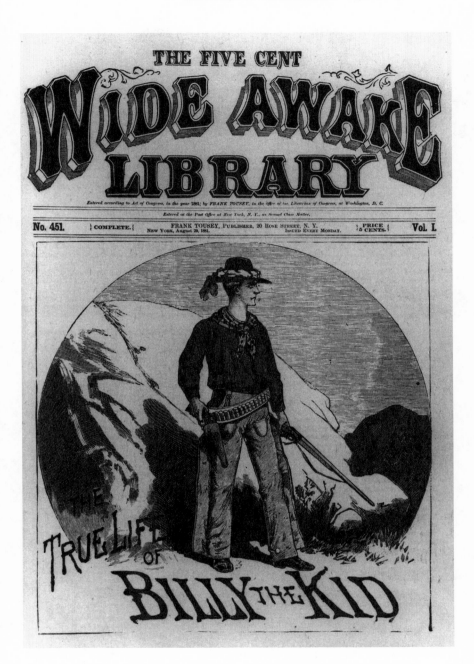

FIGURE 8.4. Front cover, *Wide Awake Library,* "The True Life of Billy the Kid,"
August 29, 1881. Written a month after Billy's death, such sensational-
ism was harbinger of things to come. Photo courtesy Museum of New
Mexico, neg. no. 92018.

Nevertheless, New Mexicans approved the constitution on January 19, 1911. They had simply waited too long to do otherwise.

On November 7, 1911, New Mexicans elected their first state officials. Democrats won the governor and lieutenant governor slots, but Republicans controlled both houses of the legislature. This meant that not only would Republicans chose New Mexico's first U.S. senators, but that the party would undoubtedly select members of the Old Guard. Sure enough, Catron was appointed U.S. senator on March 11, 1912; the other was Albert B. Fall. As senator, Catron's most notable moves were opposition to President Woodrow Wilson's tariff-reducing Underwood-Simmons Act and support for U.S. military intervention into Mexico to protect American investments. He also favored entry into World War I. In 1916 party politics went against Catron, and he lost his senate seat. Catron retired to New Mexico to attend to his lands and law practice, although by this time his sons largely controlled both. Catron's health declined after 1917. He died in May 21, 1921, of cirrhosis of the liver and bronchitis.

Catron's was a mixed legacy. He was a talented lawyer and usually an advocate of statehood. His extensive library—one of the largest in the Southwest—was donated to the New Mexico Historical Society after his death. Even so, Catron does not truly represent the forces of modernization in New Mexico. His own interests often dominated to the detriment of the territory; although future research may one day prove otherwise, there appears no instance of Catron putting his own quest for economic and political power aside for New Mexico's greater good. Although Catron frequently gave lip service to statehood, he also backed measures—such as the move to thwart public schools—that virtually guaranteed a continuation of New Mexico's territorial period. Just as Billy the Kid represents New Mexico's raw frontier, Catron is forever associated with the corrupt Santa Fe Ring and feudal conditions it struggled to preserve. As U.S. senator, Catron remained a member of the reactionary Republican Old Guard.

It is noteworthy that Catron and McSween retired at about the same time. But Susan continued to entertain writers at her home in White Oaks with tales of pioneer New Mexico. Journalist Emerson Hough first interviewed her in preparation for his 1907 book *The Story of the Outlaw*. She later spoke with writer Walter Noble Burns, collector J. Evetts Haley, and professor/researcher Maurice Garland Fulton, with whom she also carried on a lengthy correspondence. Susan lived to see Billy's story immortalized in a 1930 film titled *Billy the Kid*, starring Johnny Mack Brown. Overall, she

FIGURE 8.5. Delegates to the New Mexico state constitutional convention, Santa Fe, New Mexico, 1910. Photo by William R. Walton. Courtesy Museum of New Mexico, neg. no. 8119.

resented the Kid's popularity, which tended to diminish the roles played by her husband, John Tunstall, and even Chisum, but ironically, her tales of Old Lincoln helped perpetuate his myth. Few interviewers sought personal information about Susan, but when they asked, it appears that she frequently lied to them about her background. She was similarly elusive concerning Alexander, suggesting there were details to hide or she knew little about her first husband. Susan Hummer McSween Barber died on January 3, 1931, in White Oaks, of influenza.

By 1931 tourists were stopping at Billy's grave in Fort Sumner and eating lunch at the Wortley Hotel in Lincoln. America's fascination with Billy and New Mexico's lawless past—of which Lincoln County remained a symbol—mushroomed even as New Deal funds after 1932 strengthened the Democratic Party and swept away the last remnants of the Santa Fe Ring. In fact, New Mexico had barely achieved statehood before citizens began nostalgically recalling its wild past.

Through Billy the Kid, Susan McSween, and Thomas Catron we can explore New Mexico's rocky trail to modernization and statehood to see how the territory differed from other sections of the United States and how it simply reflected the economic and political growth occurring elsewhere. Susan's success reveals growing opportunity available to nineteenth-century western women. Thomas's ability to use the legal system to amass land and political power mirrors the corruption that characterized America's Gilded Age. Although his Santa Fe Ring was unique because it focused on land and helped itself to the enormous Spanish and Mexican land grants, it was also a mere shadow of larger, much more lucrative rings that dominated late-nineteenth-century America. Billy's brief life epitomizes the chaotic frontier period. His story also exposes an antimodernization response that began soon after his death, accelerated after 1900, and manifested itself in the nostalgic search for a romantic Old West that had never existed. Ironically, Susan and others helped to create Billy's legend even as they tried to put the frontier behind. Hence the three played significant roles in this dynamic period of New Mexico history and in the backlash against modernization, which resulted in New Mexico's foremost legend.

Essay on Sources

Of these three historical figures, only Billy the Kid boasts a massive historiography. No less than 250 books and hundreds of journal articles have been written about Billy and the Lincoln County War. Some of the most current books include Frederick Nolan, *The West of Billy the Kid* (Norman: University of Oklahoma Press, 1998), and Nolan, *The Lincoln County War: A Documentary History* (Norman: University of Oklahoma Press, 1992); Joel Jacobsen, *Such Men as Billy the Kid: The Lincoln County War Reconsidered* (Lincoln: University of Nebraska Press, 1994); and Robert M. Utley, *Billy the Kid: A Short and Violent Life* (Lincoln: University of Nebraska Press, 1989). The first semischolarly study was Maurice G. Fulton's *History of the Lincoln County War*, Robert N. Mullin, ed. (Tucson: University of Arizona Press, 1968, 1992), which is based in part on information from Susan McSween but lacks footnotes and a bibliography. The inaccurate basis for most Kid legends comes from Pat F. Garrett, *The Authentic Life of Billy, the Kid, the Noted Desperado of the Southwest . . .* (1882, 1954; Norman: University of Oklahoma Press, 1988, 2000). A useful bibliography is Kathleen Chamberlain, comp., *Billy the Kid and the Lincoln County War: A Bibliography* (Albuquerque: Center for the American West, 1997).

The best sources on Thomas B. Catron are the 325 boxes of personal papers, land records, titles, and territorial and senatorship papers housed at the Center for Southwest Research, University of New Mexico. The only biography is Victor Westphall, *Thomas Benton Catron and His Era* (Tucson: University of Arizona Press, 1973), which unfortunately glosses over Catron's flaws. Other accounts include William A. Keleher, *The Maxwell Land Grant: A New Mexico Item* (Albuquerque: University of New Mexico Press, 1942, 1984), Mary Elizabeth Sluga, *The Political Life of Thomas Benton Catron, 1896–1921* (Albuquerque: University of New Mexico Press, 1941), and Vioalle C. Hefferan, "Thomas B. Catron" (master's thesis, University of New Mexico, 1940).

Similarly, little has been written about Susan McSween Barber. Aside from Darlis A. Miller, "The Women of Lincoln County," in *New Mexico Women: Intercultural Perspectives*, Joan M. Jensen and Darlis A. Miller, eds. (Albuquerque: University of New Mexico Press, 1986), studies of McSween are found only in larger works on the Lincoln County War. For a well-rounded examination of women in New Mexico, Cheryl J. Foote, *Women of the New Mexico Frontier, 1846–1912* (Niwot: University Press of Colorado, 1990), is useful.

Nineteenth-century New Mexico political and economic history needs additional research, but at long last Howard Roberts Lamar's seminal work *The Far Southwest, 1846–1912: A Territorial History*, rev. ed. (1966; Albuquerque: University of New Mexico Press, 2000), has been updated. Jack E. Holmes's *Politics in New Mexico* (Albuquerque: University of New Mexico Press, 1967) is, however, nearly forty years old. So is Porter A. Stratton, *The Territorial Press of New Mexico, 1834–1912* (Albuquerque: University of New Mexico Press, 1969), which offers a thorough look at the role of journalism in territorial New Mexico, and Robert W. Larson, *New Mexico's Quest for Statehood, 1846–1912* (Albuquerque: University of New Mexico Press, 1968), traces the painstaking—and painful at times—road to statehood. A new study on Albert B. Fall by David H. Stratton, *Tempest Over Teapot Dome: The Story of Albert B. Fall* (Norman: University of Oklahoma Press, 1998), is an excellent biographical sketch of Catron's fellow senator and the man who purchased some of Barber's property; this book also details the political and economic turmoil of the post–Civil War era.

9

Mabel Dodge Luhan and New Mexico's Anglo Arts Community

LOIS PALKEN RUDNICK

In December 1917 Mabel Sterne traveled by train to New Mexico from New York. Salon hostess, art patron, writer for radical and popular journals, she was an internationally celebrated model of the "New Woman," sexually emancipated and free to do and be as she pleased. Sterne had already lived four lives: Mabel Ganson, born and raised the only child of upper-class Victorians in Buffalo, New York (1879–1904); Mrs. Edwin Dodge, the padrona of a magnificent Italian villa in Florence (1905–12); Mabel Dodge, the queen of New York's Greenwich Village bohemia (1912–15); and Mabel Sterne, the hostess of a country estate in Croton-on-Hudson, New York (1915–17).

In the fourth and final volume of *Intimate Memories,* the sixteen-hundred-page autobiography that Luhan published serially during the 1930s, she tells us of her arrival in Santa Fe: "My life broke in two right then, and I entered into the second half, a new world, that replaced all the ways I had known with others, more strange and terrible and sweet than any I had ever been able to imagine." Within the first year of her stay, Sterne moved to Taos, sent her husband Maurice back east, and began an affair with Taos Pueblo Indian Antonio Lujan, who became her fourth and final husband in 1923, their marriage lasting until her death in 1962.

Luhan had spent much of her adult life trying to create a world in which she could be "at home." In the early 1920s, a Chicago newspaper reporter claimed she was "the most peculiar common denominator that

FIGURE 9.1. Mabel Dodge Luhan and Tony Lujan (1920s?), Mary Austin Collection.
This item is reproduced by permission of The Huntington Library, San
Marino, California.

society, literature, art and radical revolutionaries ever found in New York
and Europe." Luhan was indeed a "common denominator," whose life con-
nects many of the important themes discussed in this chapter, particularly
as they relate to New Mexico's becoming an important center for the arts
in the twentieth century.

Luhan's search began in childhood. In those years, she was schooled in
charm and groomed to marry, like most women of her class. Starved emo-
tionally and intellectually at home and in school, she yearned for a life of
poetry and beauty. After the accidental hunting death of her first husband
and the birth of her only child, John Evans, Mabel was sent to Europe to

end a scandalous affair she was having with a prominent and married Buffalo doctor. In Paris she married Edwin Dodge, an architect from Boston. When they moved to Florence in 1905, Mabel determined to make a new life that would express her artistic impulses. She devoted the next eight years to realizing her dream of bringing back the Renaissance. The magnificent villa she and her husband reconstructed, the clothes she wore, the attitude she applied to her daily life—all were materials for her living theater. So too were the many artists and writers she collected to grace her home and share her table.

By 1912 Mabel found herself tired of living among the dead ghosts of the European past. She returned to America and settled on the edge of Greenwich Village, where for the next three years she presided as hostess of another salon, this one devoted not to preserving the "best" of European civilization but to blasting all kinds of traditions. Her apartment at 23 Fifth Avenue became a gathering spot where the "movers and shakers" of the pre–World War I era engaged in a free exchange of ideas on art, politics, and society that included discussions of free love, sexual equality, modern art, psychoanalysis, and the struggles of the working class. Mabel became a symbol of the spirit of her times, supporting, writing, and speaking about the various causes that promised to liberate her and her fellow men and women from the spiritual and psychological bondage of the past.

What was it that led this sophisticated woman of the world, who had immersed herself in the cosmopolitan heart of European and American cultures, to find in rural New Mexico not only her heart's desire but the key to redeeming Anglo-American civilization? To answer this intriguing and complex question, we need to look at the movement of artists and writers to New Mexico that began as a trickle in the late nineteenth and early twentieth centuries and increased to a steady stream in the era between World War I and World War II. For Mabel Luhan's embrace of New Mexico's indigenous cultures was part of a much larger migration of Anglo writers and artists to the state, a migration she encouraged and that her life's story illuminates.

In the first decade of the twentieth century, New Mexicans had to fight to enter the union because their predominantly Hispano and Indian populations gave them a presumably un-American ethnic cast. By the 1920s the postwar influx to New Mexico of some three hundred Anglo artists, writers, and social visionaries was well under way, the most famous of whom claimed that the two indigenous groups legitimized New Mexico as *the* most "American" state within the nation.

THE CREATION OF "THE LAND OF ENCHANTMENT"

New Mexico has been subject to various kinds of utopian fevers ever since the mid-nineteenth century, when the land and climate began to be promoted for a variety of uses, including the improvement of mental and bodily health. In the late nineteenth century the romantic lure of New Mexico as a remote outpost of the American frontier, with its dramatic landscapes and "exotic" Indians and Hispanos, provided local color for readers avidly interested in the little-known regions of America. This interest in the New Mexico was stimulated by a number of factors: government-sponsored geographic surveys of the area, archaeologists' reports of prehistoric sites in the Southwest, photographs and romantic paintings of southwestern scenes, and articles in national magazines, such as those published by Charles Lummis, whose *The Land of Poco Tiempo* (1893) evoked New Mexico as a timeless and peaceful land, inhabited by poor but contented natives.

Both the Santa Fe Railroad, which came to New Mexico in 1880, and its affiliate, the Fred Harvey hotel and restaurant chain, relied on the works of artists to lure tourists to these new destinations. They commissioned and purchased paintings from the growing Santa Fe and Taos art colonies and then gave their images national distribution in calendars, railroad stations, restaurants, and advertising campaigns. Thus began a long tradition in New Mexico that tied artists and writers directly to the invention of New Mexico as "the land of enchantment" and to the tourist economy, which by the 1930s would become the economic backbone of the state.

At the time that Mabel Sterne arrived in Taos, in January 1918, there was already a flourishing art colony that banded together in 1915 as the Taos Society of Artists (TSA). These artists, who relied on the patronage of wealthy collectors throughout the country to sell their work, achieved national exposure through traveling exhibitions, as well as through the Santa Fe Railroad and Harvey Company displays. In fact, Luhan was inspired to come to New Mexico at least in part because of the paintings of Taos Indians that she saw in the TSA's 1917 tour, when it came to New York City. The now legendary founding of the first Anglo arts community in Taos, by Bert Phillips and Ernest Blumenschein, laid claim to a myth of New Mexico that had elements in common with Luhan and her circle, even though their tastes in art differed considerably.

Phillips and Blumenschein had started out on a sketching trip in 1898 from Denver and lost one of their wagon wheels twenty miles north of Taos. Impressed with the people and surrounding beauty, Blumenschein decided to settle there, later joined by Phillips, Joseph Sharp, Oscar Berninghaus, Irving Couse, Walter Ufer, and Victor Higgins. The Taos artists worked within the grand manner of European landscape and figure painting, but they were also seeking fresh visions for their art and wanted to contribute to developing an American canon in painting. However, their romantic landscapes and often sentimentalized Hispanic farmers and Indians earned them the scorn of the modern artists who arrived in the post–World War I era.

The Taos artists benefited, as did the artists who were settling in Santa Fe, from the close relationship that developed between the new state government and the business and arts communities. In 1912 New Mexico was suffering from a thirty-year economic decline and looking for new ways to attract people who would spend money and boost the economy. The economic growth of the state was seen as tied to the tourist industry, which the city fathers of Santa Fe recognized could be furthered by turning Santa Fe into "the City Different." The desire to distinguish the state capital by identifying it with native forms of architecture and an alluring arts community created an atmosphere in which New Mexico's business and political elites were very hospitable to artists and writers, even those whose work was not to their taste.

In 1909 the entrepreneurial anthropologist Edgar Hewett turned the Palace of the Governors in Santa Fe into a historical museum and headquarters for the School of American Archeology. His plan was to unite art, science, and history under one roof, which he did with the completion of the Museum of New Mexico (1917). The Museum of New Mexico was unusual in offering exhibition space and studios free to artists and also serving as a commercial outlet for their art. Studio space was made available not just for Anglo artists but for Native American painters as well, for Hewett was an ardent booster of Indians as inherently artistic, claiming that their culture "towers above anything Caucasian." He encouraged such self-taught Pueblo artists as Crescencio Martinez and Awa Tsireh, who would become important influences on a growing school of Pueblo painters.

Artists were also aided by local banks and hotels (such as La Fonda, in Santa Fe) that displayed their works; by local newspapers, such as the *Santa Fe New Mexican* and *The Taos News*, which publicized their activities; by magazines, such as the Museum of New Mexico's *El Palacio*, which devoted space to reviews and commentaries on the art colonies; and by a variety of tourist-oriented bulletins that made artist studios and artist sitings a central part of the local scene. Annual group shows coincided with the Santa Fe Fiesta, which Hewett helped bring back to life in 1919 as a celebration of the Spanish reconquest and a vehicle for selling art and local crafts.

The Southwest was the first region in the United States to promote its own indigenous style of architecture. What became known as the Santa Fe–Pueblo style was part of a national and international reaction against urban-industrial civilization and cultural standardization. The search for an architectural image that represented the newly formed state of New Mexico culminated in the "revival" (invention) of a regional architecture that blended traditional Pueblo and Spanish types of housing: clustered and irregular massings with setback stories, sloping walls and rounded corners, projecting roof beams, and portals. The "civic symbolism" of this new architecture promoted the Spanish as the founders of the Southwest's civilization.

THE MODERN ERA AND THE NEW YORK AVANT-GARDE

Like their predecessors, many of the artists and writers who came to New Mexico after World War I were searching for the "real" America among cultures that had been ignored, rejected, or despised by the mainstream. What distinguished the postwar "moderns" from earlier Anglo migrants to New Mexico was that many of them were positioned at the center of national debates about the nature of American civilization and the kind of democracy the United States should be. Some of them were also on the cutting edge of new ideas and forms in the arts that radically altered the ways in which their fellow Americans were intended to see and experience the world around them.

In the pre–World War I era, the most broad-minded progressive thinkers and reformers argued that the continued social and political health of the nation was dependent on the cultural and economic benefits provided by immigrants and peoples of color. They were helping the United States become a model of multicultural democracy, an emblem to the world of how to end the centuries-long battles among nationalities and religions that had marked most of human history.

For the cultural radicals in Mabel Dodge's Greenwich Village circle, a number of whom followed her to New Mexico, art was intended to transform both human personality and society. These "modernists," as they have come to be called, broke with a number of traditions that had been part of the art world for five hundred years: they asserted the importance of the artist's personal vision in the creation of art, often shattering traditional uses of perspective, color, and form in order to destroy the illusion that art imitated an already known reality (one that typically served the social and economic values of wealthy patrons). Their art often celebrated groups that traditional conservatives wanted to exclude from the very idea of civilization: "primitive" or premodern societies that seemed better able to integrate the unconscious and conscious forces within human creativity, and the spiritual and material worlds, in their art and everyday life.

The entrance of the United States into World War I in 1917 had a profoundly negative impact on many in the New York vanguard of modernists. Wartime hysteria, censorship, and repression were directed at anyone who spoke out against the government or who was less than "100 percent [Anglo] American." The migrants who moved to or visited New Mexico during this era were not, however, rejecting modern ideas and modern art. What they rejected was the possibility that the urban landscape could provide the conditions necessary to their personal, artistic, and social visions. The city was the home of "machine" civilization, a turbulent reminder of the power of the nation-state to steamroll its populations into conformity and reduce human life to rubble in its capacity to make war. It was also the home of the uprooted immigrants and blacks that some of them came to associate with the chaos of the urban centers they inhabited.

Santa Fe and Taos were neither the first nor the only colonies established by early-twentieth-century artists who were searching for a sense of place that would nourish their work and their lives, in such communities as Provincetown, Massachusetts, and Carmel, California. It is no accident that Andrew Dasburg, who worked and taught at the Woodstock, New York, art colony in the 1910s and 1920s, became a leader of the modernist movement in New Mexico, nor that Luhan, Dasburg, and others who visited Santa Fe and Taos had been part of the Provincetown artist and writer colonies as well. Those who joined art colonies typically shared a dislike of machine-made and mass-produced goods and favored high-quality craftsmanship and individualized designs. Some art colonists, including many who came to Santa Fe and Taos, had a further mission to cultivate an environment that would encourage positive humanizing influences.

Two important factors distinguish the modern artist and writer colonies established in Santa Fe around Alice Corbin Henderson and Mary Austin and in Taos around Mabel Luhan: powerful women took leadership roles in creating and sustaining them, and they did not view themselves as segregated retreats from the surrounding world. Their agendas were ambitious and outward looking as they sought a national audience for their alternative models of community and culture and as they became actively involved, for good and ill, in the cultural and economic politics of their communities.

THE MODERNISTS COME TO NEW MEXICO

What was it that convinced Luhan and her more visionary peers that New Mexico was the place that would help them to heal themselves *and* "save" humanity?

Art historians tell us that after the destructiveness of World War I, many American artists turned to the "sacred world" of prehistoric nature for inspiration. Northern New Mexico had some of the best that was available of that commodity. The insistence of its dramatic geography and climate put humans in their place at the same time that it challenged them to find the creative resources to match its power. For the mostly citified Anglo migrants who came there, New Mexico offered the traditional western myth in a new form. Instead of the lone cowboy or pioneer going off into the wilderness to prove himself a man by wielding his gun or pitting himself against an unforgiving land on the fringe of civilization, artists pitted their paintbrushes, pens, and cameras against a landscape so overwhelming in its grandeur that it could have easily eclipsed personal vision and individual creativity. (Indeed, some artists fled New Mexico just because of that fear.) At the same time, the land beckoned them with the promise that they would find a connection there to something larger than themselves.

If northern New Mexico was particularly attractive to women writers, artists, and anthropologists such as Alice Corbin Henderson, Mabel Luhan, Mary Austin, Willa Cather, Georgia O'Keeffe, and Elsie Clews Parsons, it was because no one had mastered its vast, spacious, and thinly populated expanse of desert, mesa, and mountains. Indeed, that it could not be mastered was attractive to their sense of themselves as women who were seeking to make their own imprint on American culture and as environmentalists who believed that their fellow Americans needed to learn how to engage in nondestructive relationships with the land.

For both the male and female Anglo seekers who came to New Mexico, its greatest attraction was the relationship of Native peoples to their land

and the cultural practices that were generated from that relationship. Both Pueblo and Hispano communities were based in subsistence economies that depended on agriculture, pastoralism, and hunting and that took relatively little from the land other than what was needed to feed and clothe themselves. Native American and Hispano arts and crafts were central to their daily lives—to work, play, and religious expression—and were created for beauty as well as use, whereas art in the Anglo world was segregated in museums and theaters. Modern Anglo artists were attracted to the abstract and stylized patterns of Pueblo pottery and rituals and to the simplified and expressive forms of Hispano wood carving. But most impressive to them were the cultural beliefs that art could be *effective* as well as *affective:* that ceremonial dances and *santos* did more than appeal to people's emotions; they influenced them psychologically and spiritually.

The modern artists and writers who arrived in Santa Fe and Taos after World War I benefited from the already established identities of these cities as meccas for arts and tourism, but they also contributed greatly to the growth of both these sectors. (Santa Fe's claim today that it is the third-largest art market in the country, after New York City and Los Angeles, has its origins in this period.) The newcomers also exerted a disproportionate influence on cultural and civic affairs because of their national connections to centers of social and political power and their privileged social and economic positions within the small and predominantly impoverished populations of these communities.

In northern New Mexico the modernists could reconstruct their vision of themselves and their roles in the formation of American culture on a relatively uncontested terrain. Their exaggerated insistence that Native Americans and Hispanos produced the only original art in the United States, and thus should serve as the foundation for an emerging national culture, can partly be explained by these facts. Their avoidance of the increasing poverty, wage labor, and labor unrest that marked the New Mexican economy in the 1920s, and even more in the 1930s, can partly be explained by their investment in what they believed were the more "authentic" premodern traditions of these cultures. Whether they were seeking to create a more vital American art or to counter the various social and economic blights of the modern world, they focused on those elements of the Pueblos and Hispanos that most satisfied their own needs and concerns.

Unlike the Anglo artists who preceded them, the modern artists rarely painted portraits of the "natives," and when they did, they were typically not romanticized. Native cultures were referenced chiefly by their ceremonies and religious objects, landscapes were organized through their expressive and structural powers rather than realistically, and the built environment (particularly adobe forms) and its surrounding nature were represented as connected to each other. In their poetry, essays, and fiction, Anglo writers emphasized the organicism of Pueblo and Hispanic cultures, sometimes displaying remarkable sensitivity to their ways of life and sometimes relying on racial or class stereotypes that reveal their outsider status.

THE SANTA FE AND TAOS ART COLONIES

Tuberculosis brought poet Alice Corbin Henderson from Chicago to Santa Fe's Sunmount Sanitorium in 1916. Henderson wasted no time in writing poems that connected the physical and spiritual healthfulness of the landscape. She described the land in her first book of New Mexico poetry, *Red Earth* (1920), as ancient, peaceful, religious, and of human scale as opposed to the strident, aggressive, gigantic, and accumulative city: "Here is the desert of silence,/Blinking and blind in the sun—/An old, old woman who mumbles her beads/And crumbles to stone."

The writers Henderson invited to New Mexico shared her desire to make poetry a central experience in the lives of their fellow Americans, as Indian song and ritual were for Native Americans and Spanish ballads and oral folk traditions were for Hispanos. She made her home a center for committed regionalist poets, including Carl Sandburg, Witter Bynner, Harriet Monroe, and Vachel Lindsay, and carried out her interest in communal ideals by establishing what we now call a poetry collective: fellow poets met once a month to read their work and get much-needed response. Henderson's writers' circle also included native New Mexicans, such as Erna and Harvey Fergusson, who were born and lived in Albuquerque and wrote fictional and nonfictional accounts of New Mexico history.

Through her husband, architect and painter William Penhallow Henderson, she was also connected to the artists of Santa Fe. Among the most notable were those who had made reputations for themselves in New York City: painters such as Robert Henri and John Sloan, members of the "Ashcan School," which got its name because of their interest in painting realistic scenes of contemporary city life, as well as artists more engaged in modernist styles, such as B. J. O. Nordfeldt and Raymond Jonson. The

Hendersons worked and socialized with architect John Gaw Meem, who was involved in the reconstruction of Santa Fe Plaza, and Mary Wheelwright, a patron and collector of Navajo art who was responsible for the Navajo Ceremonial Arts Museum. Two other members of the colony, Gustave Baumann and Will Shuster, created a new "tradition" for Santa Fe in 1926 when they fabricated the towering puppet "Zozobra" ("the gloomy one"), whose burning still signals the opening of Spanish Fiesta.

Mabel Dodge Luhan came to New Mexico shortly after marrying her third husband, Maurice Sterne, a painter with whom she had been living in rural Croton-on-Hudson, New York. She had sent him to Santa Fe to find new ideas for his art. (She said that she married him in the hope that he would turn from painting to sculpture.) From there he wrote her, on November 30, 1917, the letter that would change the course of her life: "Dearest Girl—Do you want an object in life? Save the Indians, their art-culture—reveal it to the world!"

Among the Pueblo Indians of Taos, Mabel discovered a culture that offered everything she had lacked in her childhood, failed to re-create in Florence, and could not find in Greenwich Village. They seemed a model of permanence and stability, a six-hundred-year-old community where individual, social, artistic, and religious values were fully connected. The Pueblos' lack of interest in material wealth, their devotion to communal values, their healthy respect for human limitations and for the natural environment seemed a sane counterpoint to the frantic white civilization she saw as heading for self-annihilation.

At the end of her first summer in Taos, Maurice Sterne returned to the East, and Mabel began to live with Antonio Lujan, a native of Taos Pueblo. (She presumably changed the Spanish *jota* to *h* because her Anglo friends couldn't pronounce it correctly.) That same summer Mabel began to build her Taos home, which eventually included a three-story, twenty-two-room Big House, surrounded by a twelve-hundred-foot gatehouse and several other guest houses, on twelve acres of land contiguous to Taos Pueblo.

Luhan intended to make her home in Taos the center of what she called a "new world plan" that would turn the United States away from its urban-industrialist bias, its individualist and materialist values, and its European-focused vision of culture. Through her marriage to Tony, she hoped to become "a bridge between cultures," an interracial model of how the Anglo and Indian cultures could be blended to produce a superior American civilization. Together they would attract the nation's (and Europe's) great writers, artists, and activists to Taos, where they would discover the social and cultural benefits to be gained from native communities.

In Taos, Mabel found her voice as a writer, in good part because of her relationship with Tony Lujan, which gave her the rationale and support she needed to write her many books and articles that highlighted the power and beauty of New Mexico's physical and cultural landscapes. Luhan had much to do with creating the image of Tony as a Native American seer and sage. Never in her published work did she talk about the serious difficulties their relationship created because of their very different needs and temperaments, nor the controversy their marriage caused at the pueblo because Tony divorced his Indian wife and violated tribal law by marrying a white woman. Tony gained wealth and power as a result of his marriage to Mabel, and he later earned the respect of many at the pueblo for his work with Anglo reformers who helped the Pueblos organize to protect their lands and culture.

When Mabel wrote her memoirs, she presented herself as the symbol

FIGURE 9.2. Laura Gilpin, *Residence, Mabel Dodge Luhan, Taos,* ca. 1935. © 1981 Laura Gilpin Collection, Amon Carter Museum, Forth Worth, Texas, bequest of the artist.

of the decline and fall of Anglo-American civilization and Tony and the Pueblo Indians as the vehicle for rebirth offered by the Indian Southwest. In her last volume, *Edge of Taos Desert*, she highlighted how "the purity and freshness" of the New Mexican landscape cleansed her of the waste and sickness of white civilization while providing a powerful stimulus to her imagination: "There was no disturbance in the scene, nothing to complicate the forms, no trees or houses, or any detail to confuse one. It was like a simple phrase in music or a single line of poetry, essential and reduced to the barest meaning."

Luhan "put Taos on the map," as one of her art critic friends insisted some years later. She appealed to the artistic, emotional, and spiritual needs of her modernist friends, who responded to the spirit of place for much the same reasons that she did. She brought modern art to Taos, beginning with her telegram to artist Andrew Dasburg two weeks after she arrived there. In 1920, when he first began spending his winters in Taos, Dasburg wrote Mabel about the way Taos fulfilled his spiritual hunger, articulating the feelings of many others who were to come over the next two decades: "Taos has the quality of a place in which . . . to find God. In Taos one could create the condition, the form of discipline, that is like the tuning of an instrument of harmony." Dasburg spent most of his time in Santa Fe in the 1920s, settling in Taos in the 1930s. His presence attracted numerous modern artists who became important figures in the art colony, including Ward Lockwood, Cady Wells, and Louis Ribak.

During the 1920s and 1930s, many who came to the Luhan house were at a critical point in their lives, physically, psychologically, or vocationally. For them the house functioned as a kind of life crisis center: breaking down and healing, making—and sometimes unmaking—love affairs and marriages. Because several visitors often stayed with the Luhans simultaneously, the opportunities for cross-fertilization and feuding were very rich, as attested to by the many portraits of the Luhans and their guests that appeared in paintings, photographs, and fiction. In remarking that Mabel Luhan had "talons for talent," Ansel Adams humorously summed up the double-edged climate that produced much creativity and conflict there over the years.

The work these visitors and residents produced helped to make northern New Mexico an important site in the development of modern American literature, painting, and photography. Although most stayed for brief periods (a few weeks or months), the quality and quantity of the

FIGURE 9.3. Andrew Dasburg, *New Mexican Village* (also known as *Taos Houses*), 1926. Oil on canvas, 24 x 30 inches. Museum of New Mexico. Photo courtesy Museum of New Mexico.

work they produced was astonishing. Many who came to the Luhan house also spent time in Santa Fe, as well as in Mexico, an indication of the important border crossings that took place during the 1920s and 1930s in the exchange of new ideas about art and its relationship to society. Mexico's indigenous heritage had also produced profound and complex symbols that suggested a western hemispheric lineage for American art independent of European traditions.

The English writer D. H. Lawrence spoke of New Mexico as "the greatest outside experience" on his life and lauded the Indians' religion. For them, Lawrence stated, there was "no division in Spirit and Matter, God and non-God." The landscape—and Mabel—figure in many of his novels and short stories of the 1920s (which are set in Mexico as well as New Mexico). When Lawrence arrived in Taos, in November 1922, he hoped to found a utopian colony there, where men and women would learn to live simply, in harmony with one another and with the land. Disturbed by Mabel Luhan's desire to have him write *her* gospel of the new Eden *she* discovered, he moved up to a ranch she gave him in the mountains north of Taos and continued to write from there.

Two other visitors, painters Marsden Hartley and Maynard Dixon, hoped to create a national culture that was rooted in regional and ethnic cultures. In 1919 Hartley wrote of Native American art: "The redman is the one truly indigenous religionist and esthete of America. He knows every form of animal and vegetable life adhering to our earth, and has made for himself a series of striking pageantries in the form of stirring dances to celebrate them, and his relation to them." Twelve years later, Dixon wrote about the best-known work from his Taos period, *Earth Knower:* "He is a sage, calm Indian who stands against his own background of mountains, from which he draws his health, wealth, religion and pattern of living."

Visiting Taos for the first time in 1929, painter Georgia O'Keeffe found the vision that would inspire her art for the rest of her life and bring her acclaim as America's best-known and most admired woman artist. There she learned to paint her world as though she were "the first . . . looking at it." Looking back, in her seventies, on her 1931 painting *Cow's Skull: Red, White, and Blue,* she wrote that when she first came to New Mexico, all the men back east were proclaiming they were going to write the Great American Novel or Poem or Play. But most of them wished they were in Europe. It was up to her to create "the Great American Thing"—and she did, indeed, create the signature landscape that most Americans imagine when they think of New Mexico.

Ansel Adams's Taos experience helped turn him toward becoming one of the most popular American photographers of the West in the twentieth century. A professional concert pianist who practiced photography as an avocation, Adams's sense of himself as a professional photographer solidified in Taos, as can be seen in his first great photography book, *Taos Pueblo* (1930), on which he collaborated with Mary Austin.

Looking for alternatives to both American capitalism and Russian communism, reformers Mary Austin and John Collier searched for alternative models of community in the village socialism that they associated with Pueblo (and for Austin, Hispano) culture. Mary Austin was already a prominent writer, essayist, and Indian rights activist when she first visited Taos in 1919. In a 1925 article she published in a national magazine (the year she built her home in Santa Fe), she argued that Americans who were seeking a healthier social order would discover in the indigenous communities of the Southwest egalitarian values that "would fill the self-constituted prophets of all Utopias with unmixed satisfaction." In 1922 Collier, a social activist who had worked to preserve the traditions of immigrant communities in New York, wrote that Taos Pueblo offered a model of a working community that could teach the rest of America how to live. His commitment to Indian affairs, which began in Taos, led him eventually to an appointment as commissioner of Indian affairs in 1933, under Franklin Roosevelt's administration.

Writers Jean Toomer and Frank Waters scoured the world's myths and religions, searching for what psychologist Carl Jung called the "reconciling symbol" that would bring inner peace and promote social harmony. Jean Toomer, a noted African American writer, discovered in Taos fertile ground for his desire to blend the numerous ethnic and racial groups in the United States into one American race, a concept he rendered most powerfully in his poem "Blue Meridian"(1936). Frank Waters, already an accomplished western novelist when he first visited Taos in 1937, spent

FIGURE 9.4. Georgia O'Keeffe, *Taos Pueblo,* 1929. Oil on canvas, 24 x 40 inches. Eiteljorg Museum of American Indians and Western Art, Indianapolis, Indiana. Photo by Robert Wallace.

much of his life's work after moving to Taos pursuing the similarities between Southwest Indian and Eastern religions in an attempt to promote an environmentalist faith built on the correspondences between humans' inner psyche and the outer world. He began his most admired Taos novel, *The Man Who Killed the Deer* (1940), while he was a guest of the Luhans.

THE IMPACT OF THE ANGLO ARTS COMMUNITY

The powerful and positive influence of New Mexico's physical and cultural landscapes on the myriad of Anglo artists and writers who visited and moved to Santa Fe and Taos in the 1920s and 1930s is unquestionable. More complicated is the question of their impact on the Native American and Hispano communities of northern New Mexico.

Many Anglo artists and writers worked hard to promote attitudes toward Indians and Hispanos that were neither racist nor assimilationist at a time when the majority of Americans barely acknowledged their existence, let alone their contributions to American civilization. They did this most effectively when they portrayed the vitality, beauty, and significance of Pueblo and Hispano forms of cultural expression as important contributions to the making of a democratic society. They collected, preserved, and encouraged Hispano and Indian folk arts, some of which had fallen into decline for a variety of reasons. These included the transformation from a subsistence to a cash economy that began in the 1920s, the commercialization of traditional handicrafts for tourist consumption, and attempts by the federal government and religious agencies to destroy the Pueblos' traditional cultures.

Artists and writers from both communities worked in many beneficial ways to protect the cultures of Hispanos and Pueblo Indians. Alice Henderson helped to form the New Mexico Association on Indian Affairs (1922), which fought for Pueblo land rights and religious freedom. She collected Hispano religious songs and wrote a still respected book on the controversial sect of Penitentes, *Brothers of Light* (1937). Mary Austin and Mabel Luhan, along with John Sloan and others, worked with the Indian Arts Fund (1925) to promote Indian arts and handicrafts and educate the public about them. Austin also helped to organize the Spanish Colonial Arts Society (1925), dedicated to preserving the best specimens of folk art, supporting the work of Hispano artisans, and conserving colonial-era buildings (including the Santuario de Chimayó, which the society purchased and saved from demolition).

Throughout the years that Mabel Luhan lived in Taos, she invested time, energy, and money in the town, including the donation of one of her homes, La Posta, as the first hospital to serve the predominantly Hispano community. She also aided the Pueblos with matters of health care and schooling, as well as bringing their culture to national attention. Alongside the Pueblo Indians, John Collier, and many artist, anthropologist, and writer friends, she worked on publicity materials for one of the few successful battles to protect Indian rights in the 1920s: the defeat of the Bursum Bill in 1923, which would have deprived the Pueblos of sixty thousand acres of mostly valuable irrigated land. Their success helped lay the groundwork for Collier's "Indian New Deal" legislation in 1934, which recognized Indian civil rights and instituted practices to conserve their lands and economy through cooperative enterprises and industrial assistance programs sponsored by the federal government.

As a result of the advocacy and interest of such community leaders as Edgar Hewitt, John Sloan, and Dorothy Dunn, numerous Indian artists received training, promotion, and help with traveling exhibitions and sales, leading to the creation of an extraordinary body of paintings of daily tribal and ceremonial life that is one of the great treasures of New Mexico's art heritage. Artists such as Pablita Velarde, Pop Chalee, Harrison Begay, and Allan Houser established prominent careers as a result of their training in the Santa Fe Indian School (founded in 1932). The stimulation of new markets and national recognition for Hispano and Indian arts and crafts was beneficial to individual artists and, to some extent, to the economies of their communities.

But it is also true that the Anglo arts colonies of Santa Fe and Taos helped increase the value (and cost) of the land they loved by their extraordinary testimonies in paint and literature to its power, beauty, and healing properties. Moreover, although few of them were wealthy, they benefited from living among Hispano and Indian populations on whom they could rely for cheap labor as models, servants, cooks, and maids. Some Anglo artists made money from the sale of cultural artifacts whose value they had helped to increase by their promotion of them. Andrew Dasburg, who opened up the Santa Fe Trading Post in 1926, with Mabel Luhan's son, was one of the first to buy Hispano santos, furniture, and Indian blankets cheaply and sell them more dearly, earning more from the income of his store than from his art.

When the Great Depression brought a collapse of the art market nationally and locally, many Anglo artists lost savings and commissions and were reduced to barter. The depression also brought the collapse of the pastoral subsistence economy in New Mexico. By 1935, 60 to 70 percent of northern New Mexicans were on relief. In fact, the New Deal relief programs instituted under Franklin Roosevelt's presidency employed half the adult citizens of New Mexico. A variety of federal arts programs, inspired by Harry Hopkins's pragmatic statement that "artists have to eat like other people," became crucial to the lives of more than two hundred New Mexican artists, craftspeople, arts teachers, and folklore collectors between 1933 and 1943. These included Anglo artists who were not members of the Santa Fe and Taos colonies, such as the noted painter Peter Hurd, who was born in Roswell and whose stark realist paintings have come to symbolize the landscape of southern New Mexico.

New Deal programs were run by and particularly benefited Anglo artists and writers. Yet they also supported Native American painters and Hispano arts and crafts: painting, embroidery, weaving, metalwork, and wood carving, including the work of the brilliant Taos expressionist Patrocino Barela. A recent survey of the state has located sixty-five murals and frescoes, 657 paintings and prints, and forty-three carvings and crafts items that were brought "to the people" by federal arts projects, most of them in places where artists had rarely been employed or had their works shown: schools, hospitals, courthouses, and libraries all benefited from these government-sponsored projects.

In constructing their literary and artistic landscapes, the Anglos had always tended to ignore the other "landscapes" that existed in New Mexico, particularly those that bore the scars of mining and forestry, as well as of racism and poverty. This oversight was even more striking during the Great Depression, when labor strikes and labor activism, often inspired by radical alliances that crossed the Mexico–New Mexico border, threatened the state's growing commitment to tourism as the center of its economic recovery. Anglo artists and writers, whose work focused mainly on the preindustrial agricultural and cultural practices of Hispanos and Indians, fed the image of the state as an escape from the turmoil of the rest of the country at the same time that they encouraged the creation of "authentic" (traditional) native crafts that served their own romantic needs.

The Santa Fe and Taos art colonies may not have created what one folklorist has called the "Disneyfication" of the Southwest—the commercialization of native arts and the tourist and real estate industries that have increasingly made northern New Mexico a playground for wealthy Anglos who control the economy. But they certainly contributed to these developments when they portrayed it as a pristine land untouched by industry or modern times. In creating an art and literature that rarely referenced the daily social and economic realities of Hispanos and Native Americans, they helped mask the interethnic, racial, and class strife that has been a persistent reality of the region.

MABEL DODGE LUHAN'S LEGACY

Luhan was in the forefront of promoting the romantic myth of northern New Mexico as a place of communal harmony. Whether she did more harm than good in making her home in Taos and bringing "the great souls" there to celebrate it remains a subject for ongoing debate. Her home was created with the intention of altering human consciousness and human relationships through art and culture; yet it evolved into a rather lavish hacienda with many of the "civilized" comforts and human ailments of the world it wanted to reform.

Although she never achieved her utopian goals, Luhan can certainly take credit for helping to make Taos "a fabulous honeycomb, irresistible and nourishing" to artists, writers, and social activists, as she wrote in her later years. For most who came, the Luhan estate was a physical and spiritual oasis. Visitors took what they needed from Mabel, Tony, and the surrounding environment and moved on. Whether establishing themselves permanently in northern New Mexico or returning to the East or West Coast, they typically left Taos with their social ideals, their art, and themselves reenergized. Mabel Dodge Luhan's legacy to the cultural history of New Mexico is rich, problematic, and fascinating—like the woman herself.

ESSAY ON SOURCES

Over the past twenty years, several excellent studies of the Anglo arts community, and its relationship with New Mexico's indigenous communities, have been written from a number of different perspectives. Three early studies of the history and development of northern New Mexico as a mecca for Anglo spiritual seekers, writers, and artists are Marta Weigle and Kyle Fiore, *Santa Fe and Taos: The Writer's Era, 1916–1941* (Santa Fe: Ancient City

Press, 1982); Stephen Fox, "Healing, Imagination, and New Mexico," *New Mexico Historical Review* 58, no. 3 (July 1983): 213–37; and Lois Rudnick, "Re-Naming the Land: Anglo Expatriate Women in New Mexico," *The Desert Is No Lady: Southwestern Landscapes in Women's Writing and Art*, Vera Norwood and Jan Monk, eds. (New Haven, Conn.: Yale University Press, 1987; reprinted by the University of Arizona Press, 1997).

Two important histories of the Anglo artist colonies of northern New Mexico are Sharyn Rohlfsen Udall, *Modernist Painting in New Mexico, 1913–1935* (Albuquerque: University of New Mexico Press, 1984), and Charles Eldridge, Julie Schimmel, and William Truettner, *Art in New Mexico, 1900–1945: Paths to Taos and Santa Fe* (Washington, D.C.: National Museum of American Art, 1986). For the impact of Mexican culture on New Mexican (and American) art and culture in this period, see Helen Delpar, *The Enormous Vogue of All Things Mexican: Cultural Relations Between the United States and Mexico, 1920–1935* (Tuscaloosa: University of Alabama Press, 1992).

For a collection of lively essays that examine the commercial and tourist contexts of New Mexican art in the early twentieth century, see Marta Weigle and Barbara Babcock, eds., *The Great Southwest of the Fred Harvey Company and the Santa Fe Railway* (Phoenix: Heard Museum, 1996). The major cultural history of Santa Fe's construction as a tourist and arts mecca in the twentieth century is Chris Wilson's *The Myth of Santa Fe: Creating a Modern Regional Tradition* (Albuquerque: University of New Mexico Press, 1997).

Mabel Dodge Luhan's most important writings are *Winter in Taos* (New York: Harcourt, Brace and Company, 1935; republished by Las Palomas de Taos in 1982, with a foreword by Frank Waters), and *Intimate Memories: The Autobiography of Mabel Dodge Luhan*, Lois Rudnick, ed. (Albuquerque: University of New Mexico Press, 1999; an abridged edition of Luhan's four-volume memoir published in the 1930s). For biographies of Mabel Dodge Luhan and her home in Taos, see Lois Rudnick, *Mabel Dodge Luhan: New Woman, New Worlds* (Albuquerque: University of New Mexico Press, 1984), and Rudnick, *Utopian Vistas: The Mabel Dodge Luhan House and the American Counterculture* (Albuquerque: University of New Mexico Press, 1996).

Two illuminating studies of early-twentieth-century relationships between Anglo patrons and teachers and New Mexico's Native American artists are Bruce Bernstein and W. Jackson Rushing, *Modern by Tradition:*

American Indian Painting in the Studio Style (Santa Fe: Museum of New Mexico Press, 1995), and J. J. Brody, *Pueblo Indian Painting: Tradition and Modernism in New Mexico, 1900–1930* (Santa Fe: School of American Research Press, 1997). For a critical examination of the Anglo art colony's treatment of Hispanos in Taos, see Sylvia Rodriguez, "Art, Tourism, and Race Relations: Toward a Sociology of the Art Colony," *Journal of Anthropological Research* 45, no. 1 (spring 1989): 79–97.

For a survey of New Deal arts projects in New Mexico during the Great Depression, see Kathryn Flynn, ed., *Treasures on New Mexico Trails: Discover New Deal Art and Architecture* (Santa Fe: Sunstone Press, 1996). See also Sarah Deutsch's complex study of Anglo artists, patrons, and government agents and their sometimes adverse impact on the economy and cultural production of Hispanos in New Mexico during the Great Depression in "Depression, Government, and Regional Community," *No Separate Refuge: Culture, Class, and Gender on an Anglo-Hispanic Frontier in the American Southwest, 1880–1940* (New York: Oxford University Press, 1987), and Curtis Marez, "The Artist Colony and the Penal Colony: Marijuana Crimes and the Policing of Chicano Labor in 1930s New Mexico," presented at the "New Modernisms" Conference, Modernist Studies Association, State College, Pa., October 1999.

10

Dennis Chavez and the Making of Modern New Mexico

MARÍA E. MONTOYA

On May 20, 1935, Dennis Chavez entered the U.S. Senate chamber to take his oath as senator of the United States. New Mexico governor Clyde Tingley had recently appointed Chavez to take the place of Senator Bronson Cutting after the latter's untimely death. As Vice President John Vance Garner called Chavez to the front of the chamber to administer the oath, Senator Charles L. McNary of Oregon suggested the absence of a quorum. McNary's question must have confused Chavez, since the Senate chamber looked full to him. Nevertheless, the vice president asked the clerk to call the roll. As the clerk called each senator's name, he stood and answered. However, as six of the senators answered, they stood and turned their backs as Chavez walked down the aisle toward the front of the chamber. Then they left the chamber in protest.

Why did the senators do this? Did they resent Chavez because he had been appointed to take the place of their beloved colleague Bronson Cutting? Chavez had run against Cutting for the Senate and lost in a close election. Chavez then launched a complaint against Cutting for voter fraud. Unfortunately, Cutting died in a plane crash as he returned to New Mexico to answer those charges. Although Cutting was a Republican, he had been a progressive who strongly supported Roosevelt's New Deal. Many senators, including those who had walked out of the chamber, felt that Roosevelt and the Senate had not sufficiently supported Cutting and had let the proceedings drag on. Now Chavez had unjustly profited from the tragedy. Or did the senators who turned their backs to Chavez resent having a Mexican American, someone who many of them thought below their station, in their elite midst?

Curiously, whether this snubbing of Senator Chavez on the first day of what was to become his illustrious Senate career occurred remains unclear. There is no discussion of the incident in the official records of the Senate and only a brief mention in Chavez's personal papers. Nevertheless, historical myth and legend have perpetuated the story about the painful induction of Dennis Chavez into the most prestigious club in the United States. Veracity aside, this story remains a telling moment about how New Mexicans have perceived themselves in relation to the rest of the United States. Statehood and all its privileges aside, Chavez's induction has been seen as emblematic of how poorly New Mexicans, particularly Mexican American and Native American citizens, had been treated by the federal government and eastern lawmakers. New Mexico's low status in Washington, however, would end as Chavez came to wield immense power within the Senate during his career.

The Senate's snubbing of Chavez in the midst of the New Deal can be read in two ways. First, in the eyes of many lawmakers, Chavez epitomized the political corruption that plagued several western states. For many eastern critics, Chavez's questioning of the election results, and implicitly the democratic process, illustrated that New Mexicans were incapable of nonpartisan self-government. This negative, and somewhat racist, view of New Mexicans had pervaded American political rhetoric since 1848 and the Mexican-American War, when senators such as John Calhoun wondered how New Mexicans with their "mongrel" heritage and "debased" political system could thrive in the American republic. Anti–New Mexican rhetoric ebbed and flowed throughout the territorial period (1850–1912) as New Mexican legislators tried to gain statehood and the rights of citizenship for their people. The U.S. Senate probably did not view Dennis Chavez, a young Mexican American from a poor family, as an appropriate replacement for the older, dashing, and patrician Bronson Cutting. Chavez represented a kind of populism and ethnic politics that the Senate liked to believe it was above.

Second, the senate's treatment of Chavez can be read as illustrative of the overt hostility and racism of the nation toward Mexican Americans in the 1930s. Chavez came to the Senate just as state and local governments in the American Southwest were engaged in some of their most discriminatory behavior against Mexican nationals and Mexican American citizens in U.S.

history. City and state governments all across the Southwest, with the help of the federal government, deported Mexican nationals and Mexican American citizens. How many people were "repatriated" is unknown, but probably more than a half million people were torn from their jobs, homes, and families and shipped across the border to an alien place. Newspapers

FIGURE 10.1. Senator Dennis Chavez in his office. Center for Southwest Research, General Library, University of New Mexico, neg. no. 000-394-0004.

and public officials from Los Angeles to Denver to Albuquerque denounced the "hordes" of Mexicans who crossed the border and pushed American citizens out of work just at the moment that the nation faced its most devastating economic crisis—the Great Depression.

Ironically, until the early 1930s American businesses such as the mining and logging industries, agricultural interests, and the railroads had welcomed Mexican laborers because these men provided a readily available and relatively cheap labor force. The female immigrants, moreover, gave wealthy American families across the Southwest a reliable supply of domestic workers—cooks, nannies, home nurses, maids, and laundresses. After the stock crash and the onset of the Great Depression, however, Mexicans and Mexican Americans were no longer welcomed. Government officials and vocal citizens feared that people of Mexican heritage would overcrowd relief agencies and prohibit "deserving"—read white— Americans from receiving government aid.

Within this historical context of discriminatory political rhetoric and repatriation, Dennis Chavez constantly reshaped his ethnic identity, but not his political agenda, as he struggled for power within the Senate. He was consciously aware of the political and public role he played, not only for himself within the world of the Washington beltway and New Mexico's *patrón* politics, but also for his constituents, most of whom still suffered as second-class U.S. citizens in terms of employment, voting, and education. Acknowledging the low status of most Mexican Americans in the middle of the twentieth century, Chavez was quoted as saying, "If they [Mexican Americans] go to war, they're Americans; if they run for office, they're Spanish Americans; but if they're looking for a job, they're damned Mexicans." Chavez astutely observed that the racialization of Mexican Americans depended on the political climate as well as the class status of Mexican Americans within American society. Chavez knew that money and higher class status allowed more opportunity for racial minorities, and he worked hard to equal the playing field for all New Mexicans, regardless of social or economic status. During his illustrious career, Chavez attended the most elegant of state dinners in Washington, D.C., yet despite his prestigious social position, he always remembered what it was like to grow up poor and hungry for success. It was for the people who came from similarly disadvantaged backgrounds that Chavez worked the hardest during his career, which spanned from the New Deal to the cold war.

Senator Dennis Chavez was born Dionisio Chavez on April 8, 1888, in a small community just outside of Albuquerque, New Mexico, in Valencia County. He was the eldest son of a farming couple, David Chavez and Paz Sanchez Chavez, who eventually raised eight children. Seven years after Dennis was born, the Chavez family moved to Albuquerque to find better employment opportunities for the family and to allow the children to attend school. Because the family was in such dire economic circumstances, however, Dennis had to drop out of school after the eighth grade and worked as a grocery delivery boy. He worked long days that began at 6 A.M. Thirteen-year-old Chavez earned $2.75 a week, which he added to his family's income.

Dennis Chavez, however, never gave up on the idea of educating himself. He had an intense interest in biography and history, and many of his neighbors commented on the long hours he spent in the public library, reading voraciously. His interest in history perhaps encouraged him to think about politics long before he could vote. Moreover, his father was a stalwart in Hispano Republican politics, and although Dennis Chavez disagreed politically with his father and eventually joined the Democratic Party, he admired and mimicked his father's political activism. There was also a much more practical side to Chavez's desire to attain an education. When not working or reading history, Chavez attended night school and studied land surveying. His extra studying paid off; in 1905 Chavez went to work for the Albuquerque city engineering department. In his new position, he earned five times more than he had as a grocery deliverer.

After changing jobs and earning financial stability, Chavez found his place in the city. First he married Imelda Espinosa in 1911. Then he began to take an active role in New Mexico politics, particularly in the struggle to secure statehood in 1912. Four years later he entered his first political campaign but lost his bid for county clerk. In that same election year, however, he also acted as the Spanish interpreter for Andreius A. Jones, a successful Democratic candidate for the U.S. Senate. Jones rewarded Chavez by giving him a job as a clerk in his Washington, D.C., office. While clerking, Chavez was accepted into Georgetown University law studies by special examination because he did not have a high school diploma. After three years of night law school, he earned his Bachelor of Law (LL.B.) degree in 1920 at the age of thirty-two.

Chavez and Imelda returned to Albuquerque, where he established a law practice and restarted his political career. He quickly won a seat in the state House of Representatives and constantly campaigned for Democratic candidates across the state. In 1930 he easily won a seat in the U.S. House of Representatives as part of the New Deal landslide that swept the nation. After that success, he was consistently associated with Franklin D. Roosevelt and his policies. In 1934 Chavez felt confident enough to take on the popular Bronson Cutting for his U.S. Senate seat. Chavez lost that race, but the Democratic governor, Clyde Tingley, then Chavez's strong supporter, intervened and appointed Chavez to the empty seat left after Cutting's unfortunate death.

Although Dennis Chavez had already established a successful political career prior to his appointment as senator, he cut his political teeth on President Franklin D. Roosevelt's New Deal. Moreover, he was largely responsible for New Mexico's political shift in the 1930s, when the state became a stronghold for the Democrats. During the New Deal and World War II, New Mexico moved away from the Republican Party, with which it had been closely aligned during the first part of the twentieth century, and sought the largesse of the federal government through the Democrats. The major reason for this shift was that for the first time in the state's history the federal government, because of New Deal programs, began to pay close attention to local problems and met the needs of the state's people. New Mexicans' benefits from these New Deal programs resulted from Chavez's power in the Senate and his ability to bring federal government patronage to his constituents.

Ironically, New Mexicans did not immediately feel the effects of the depression or the dust bowl as both swept across the nation. At the end of the 1920s, while most of the United States was basking in the economic boom of the Roaring Twenties, New Mexico was one of the poorest states in the nation. It had one of the country's highest unemployment and illiteracy rates. In addition, New Mexico had relatively little industry, with the exception of extractive industries such as coal mining, and no large-scale agriculture on which to base an expanding economy. Instead New Mexico languished in a colonial state, with entrepreneurs shipping the region's raw materials to the east. Furthermore, much of the state's land and property was controlled by the federal government or eastern and European investors. Since U.S. occupation and conquest in 1848, New Mexicans had slowly been losing their land base to Anglos and other outsiders. Politically, while politicians such as Senator Bronson Cutting had been successful in bringing federal dollars to the state, others, such as Senator

Albert Fall, associated with the Teapot Dome scandal, had brought little but disrepute to the state. Consequently New Mexico had never mustered a powerful congressional delegation in Washington, D.C., that could work together to benefit the state. All this changed in the 1930s, when Chavez came to dominate the state's Democratic Party and gained power in the Senate. His well-oiled political machine backed by the largesse of the New Deal created opportunity for New Mexico's citizens.

The New Deal spawned a myriad of national programs. Among the most popular and well known, the Agricultural Adjustment Act and the Taylor Grazing Act benefited the state tremendously. There were, however, two other sets of programs that more clearly addressed the most troubling problems facing the majority of New Mexicans at the height of the depression: inadequate job training, unemployment, and hunger. First, the federal government, through programs such as the Work Projects Administration

FIGURE 10.2. Agricultural Adjustment Administration agent talking to Spanish-
speaking New Mexican. Center for Southwest Research, General
Library, University of New Mexico, neg. no. 990-036-0089.

(WPA), attempted to revive the culture and arts of New Mexico's Hispano and Pueblo Indian populations. Second, through programs such as the Civilian Conservation Corps (CCC) and the National Youth Administration (NYA), the New Deal trained New Mexico's youth to participate more fully in the industrial and market economy slowly emerging in New Mexico. Although Senator Chavez supported all programs that brought money and aid to the state, he was particularly interested in measures that retrained New Mexicans to move away from their agriculturally based lifestyles to become better educated workers.

One of the most enduring legacies of the New Deal for New Mexicans was the impact of the WPA and the Public Works Administration (PWA) in the state. Many of New Mexico's public buildings, from the capitol in Santa Fe to the University of New Mexico to the Colfax County Courthouse, benefited from the fine craftsmanship and artwork of professional artists and burgeoning artisans. Moreover, potters and weavers from the Rio Grande Pueblos, as well as Hispano *santeros* and weavers, were paid to rediscover and work in their historic arts and crafts. Artists such as Pablita Velarde recalled the important role that the WPA played in helping them to practice their art during the lean years of the depression. Since New Mexico already had a national reputation in the art world, because of patrons such as Mabel Dodge Luhan, the state was an ideal place for the WPA to experiment with aiding artists and reviving traditional arts and crafts. Reformers such as Mary Austin, who had gained notoriety because of her book *The Land of Little Rain,* saw Hispanos and Pueblo Indians as people who stood outside the modern world. She and others who urged this revival of traditional arts and crafts thought that Hispanos and Indians could provide a model for the rest of American society of how to live a simpler life more in harmony with nature. Perhaps Austin and others saw what capitalism had wrought in the form of the depression and the dust bowl, and they wanted Americans to return to their preindustrial origins. Because this view was an oversimplified and romantic vision of the state's residents, relief agents saw the Pueblos and Hispano villages as vestiges of a premodern, preindustrial utopia that needed to be preserved.

Out of this attitude came programs that paid Indians to make pottery, weave blankets, carve and paint kachinas, and copy their oral histories and traditions in written form. But the WPA and other agencies were not interested in preserving the arts and crafts that Indians already created in their day-to-day lives. Agents thought modernity had corrupted these communities, and they wanted Indians to return to their traditional methods of production. For instance, agents pointed out that the Navajos used synthetic material instead of wool and commercially produced dyes rather than traditional dyes made from indigenous plants. Navajos had adopted these changes because they were modern, more convenient, and they thought produced a finer product. In the case of the Navajo blanket weavers, WPA agents had to reteach Navajos how to engage in their traditional craft. They helped the Navajos to remember and relearn to spin the wool for rugs and to create the native dyes that made Navajo rugs so distinctive. Ironically, federal WPA agents and national reformers who took an interest in this revival, and not Navajos artisans, became the arbiters of what was authentically and traditionally Native.

Implicit in much of the work of the WPA was the desire to create a premodern culture that would attract tourists to the region. In this respect, the WPA reformers were following on the heels of writers and artists such as D. H. Lawrence and Georgia O'Keeffe, who had already brought the region to America's attention as a place of sublime beauty and ancient cultures. Regional boosters such as Mabel Dodge Luhan, the ostentatious New Yorker turned Taos patron of the arts, and John Collier, Roosevelt's head of the Bureau of Indian Affairs, extolled the virtues of Native American and Hispano culture, which they saw as a more moral way to face the emptiness of modern industrial society. The New Deal, in attempting to preserve these cultures in an idealized form that probably had never existed, tried to stop time in New Mexico in a pre-1848, preconquest era when Pueblos and Hispanos lived free from Anglo imposition and modernity. The problem with these programs, however, was that although they preserved oral histories, culture, and art, they did so at a cost. New Mexicans were more often encouraged to look to the past to find the solution to the economic problems the Great Depression caused rather than directed to look forward to find their place in the modern industrial world that stood just outside their reach.

Even though Senator Chavez supported these programs and worked to secure their funding, he did not see this first set of programs as directly addressing New Mexico's most pressing economic needs. Instead he used his influence to bring a second set of programs to the state, best exemplified by the CCC and the NYA, both of which took different views of how New Mexicans should face the hardships brought on by the depression. These programs trained young men in the industrial and vocational arts so that they could find wage work outside the agricultural sector. The NYA, created

FIGURE 10.3. Pie Town, New Mexico. Farm Security Administration photo. Center
for Southwest Research, General Library, University of New Mexico,
neg. no. 990-036-0136.

under the WPA, was a particularly favorite project of Senator Chavez, and he
worked to keep it well funded. The program took a two-pronged approach
to dealing with New Mexico's youth. The student aid program provided a
small stipend of $6 to high school and college students to encourage them
to stay in school and not join the workforce, which provided few opportunities. In return, the students performed clerical work, library duties, and, in
some cases, research for school staff, teachers, and professors. The second
program addressed the problem of unemployment among those young
people who simply could not afford to stay enrolled in school. The NYA paid
them $17 a month, and they worked primarily in the area of public works,
providing upkeep of public facilities, beautification of parks, and construction of playgrounds, swimming pools, and other recreational facilities. These
young people also served as recreational leaders and worked in hospitals,
schools, and libraries.

In New Mexico, the NYA pumped more than $1 million into the

economy during the program's first three years of existence. About one-fourth of the funding went to students enrolled in school, the rest to students seeking employment. By the time the program ended, more than three thousand New Mexican students had been helped by the program. Chavez, through his constituents, realized the benefits of this program. Whenever the program was threatened, he worked to maintain the funding levels that had made it such a success. For example, in 1937, when Congress discussed decreasing the program's budget, E. H. Wells, president of the New Mexico School of Mines, complained directly to Chavez, who immediately went to work to ensure that funding was not cut to the NYA. Even after World War II began and there was talk of phasing out the program, Chavez worked to preserve the program by changing the NYA's mission. After 1941 it trained young people to work in the defense industry to meet the labor shortage resulting from the military buildup and the simultaneous departure of young men to the war.

The CCC was similarly situated to provide job training and an introduction to industrial life for the nation's young men. Unlike the NYA, however, this program targeted men over the age of eighteen: young men who were beyond high school age but not college bound. The CCC addressed two of the major problems facing the nation at the height of the depression. First, the program tried to diminish the problem of massive unemployment and the consequent mobility of jobless young men who roamed the country, riding on railcars and looking for work. These down-on-their-luck men came to be exemplified by the hobo: the dirty young man, the bindle stiff with his worldly possessions tied to a pole. The CCC also tried to alleviate the environmental destruction that faced the nation as the result of the dust bowl. Nationwide, thousands of young men went to work planting trees, creating trails and roads, fighting fires, and improving the nation's national parks. In New Mexico, the CCC carried out a number of ambitious projects, including the creation of all the buildings and roads at Bandelier National Monument. The program also ran a separate set of programs within the pueblos, which were administered by the CCC in conjunction with the Bureau of Indian Affairs (BIA), employing only Native men. In exchange for the labor they provided on these projects, the men and their families were paid $25 a month (quite a large sum during the depression). Five dollars went to the recruit, and the other $20 went directly home to his family. This cash infusion into the New Mexican economy provided an essential component for the recovery of the state.

The CCC, aside from simply putting cash into the economy, also left a long-term legacy to the state's inhabitants when preparing its young men to face the rigors of a wartime economy. The Department of War oversaw the supplying and assembling of the CCC camps, and so a military model was stylized to establish the hundreds of camps across the nation. Men applied and were inducted into the camps, where the young recruits spent the first couple of weeks in a "boot camp" environment that helped them adjust to the rigors of camp life. The men rose at 6 A.M., showered and shaved, made their bunks, and cleaned up before reporting for reveille at 7 A.M. After breakfast, men were sent to the agency they worked for—the National Park Service, the National Forest Service, or the Bureau of Reclamation, just to name a few—to complete their work for the day. In the evening, after they had eaten, the men had free time, although they were encouraged to improve themselves through working on their high school diplomas, acquiring a trade, learning to read English, or undertaking other kinds of personal improvement. The time that these men spent in the CCC prepared them to enter the rapidly changing world that resulted from World War II. Many graduates from the CCC went directly into military service or used their new skills as carpenters, mechanics, welders, and heavy machine operators to work in the military-industrial complex developing in New Mexico, Colorado, California, and in other parts of the American West.

The depression marked a turning point for New Mexico. During the 1930s, the federal government came to have a pervasive influence over the state's inhabitants and their economic development. The power of the federal government could be seen across the state, with Bureau of Reclamation, WPA, or CCC projects springing up in most communities. Senator Chavez, in his position as chair of the Senate Public Works Committee, had a tremendous amount of influence and power to bring these New Deal programs to New Mexico. Chavez, along with the rest of New Mexico's delegation to Congress, worked closely with Harry Hopkins to ensure that New Mexicans benefited significantly from the New Deal. This increasing presence of the federal government during the depression, however, was just the beginning.

The years surrounding World War II, from 1940 to 1945, marked the expansion of the federal government in the state and began a legacy of military presence that still exists today. World War II profoundly changed New Mexicans and their worldview for two reasons. First, the war, with its

European and Pacific fronts and the growing war industries in western cities such as Los Angeles, Oakland, Denver, and Phoenix, lured thousands of New Mexicans away from the state. Second, New Mexicans fought World War II right in their own backyards when Los Alamos, the Trinity site, and other military installations across the state became an integral part of the war effort.

New Mexicans possessed a long and illustrious history of participating in U.S. wars against foreign enemies. New Mexicans at Glorieta Pass had defended the Union against Confederate forces during the Civil War. In 1898 New Mexicans marked themselves with their valiant fighting efforts in the Spanish-American War, particularly with the participation of men such as Solomon Luna in Theodore Roosevelt's Rough Riders, which gained national fame for their supposed role in taking San Juan Hill and liberating Cuba from Spain. During the Spanish-American War, New Mexicans wanted to demonstrate their patriotism and loyalty to the United States and to show that they no longer had sympathy with the country that first ruled the region. New Mexicans again revealed their patriotism and nationalism by fulfilling their obligations during World War I. World War II, however, would see the largest ever participation of New Mexicans in the war effort. Virtually every family in the state was touched by the war in one capacity or another when fathers, mothers, sons, and daughters went off to the military or to work in defense jobs that would help the United States defeat the Axis powers of Germany, Italy, and Japan.

New Mexican men left their homes to fight on both the Pacific and European war fronts. New Mexicans such as Joe Martínez from Española were among the first Americans to see the atrocities of the Nazi concentration camps and to liberate Jews and others persecuted by Hitler and the Nazis. Mexican Americans in general, and New Mexicans in particular, stood out among U.S. soldiers. In fact, Mexican Americans earned more Congressional Medals of Honor per capita than any other ethnic group, including Anglos, during the war. But perhaps New Mexicans' greatest sacrifice for their nation came at the battles of Bataan and Corregidor in the Philippine Islands during the early months of the war.

New Mexican National Guard units—the 200th and 515th Coast Artillery Regiments—were federalized, sent to Fort Bliss to train, and then sent to the Philippine Islands prior to the bombing of Pearl Harbor to help defend the Filipinos from Japanese imperial ambitions. Because of these men's knowledge of Spanish, the U.S. Army thought they would help create crucial alliances with the Filipino defense forces. With the destruction of the U.S. fleet on December 7, 1941, at Pearl Harbor, however, the U.S. forces on the Philippine Islands were one of the few major fighting forces left in the Pacific. Consequently the Japanese military next focused on the islands as they sought to take control of the Pacific theater away from the United States. Despite the departure of their commander, General Douglas MacArthur, just before the islands fell to the Japanese, the U.S. forces struggled to hold them in some of the most intense fighting up to that point in the war. Nevertheless, by April 1942 the Japanese had taken over the Philippines, and all of the Filipino and U.S. troops, including a corps of army and navy nurses, were taken prisoner and held in Manila. For their valor, the 200th received three presidential unit citations and one Filipino presidential unit citation. They were one of the most highly decorated single units during World War II.

Yet despite their bravery and intense fighting, the U.S. units were forced to surrender because of overwhelming Japanese forces and no backup support from the U.S. Navy. In Manila and Corregidor, where the surrender had occurred, the women and many of the Filipinos were held until their liberation almost eighteen months later. The Japanese sent over twenty-seven thousand U.S. and thousands of Filipino soldiers over one hundred miles to a prisoner-of-war camp on the northern part of the island on what became known as the Bataan Death March. The march occurred in the heat of the summer and without adequate supplies provided by the Japanese. U.S. servicemen and their Filipino allies alike suffered from malaria, yellow fever, dysentery, dehydration, and starvation when their Japanese captors forced them to move north. These deprivations, combined with the brutality of the Japanese army, who killed men who lagged behind or those who were too sick to proceed, made the Bataan Death March and the POW camp at the end of the march one of the most horrific experiences of World War II. Less than half of the U.S. forces taken prisoner would survive to the end of the war and be liberated.

As word leaked about the treatment of U.S. soldiers and their bravery in the face of such brutality, anti-Japanese sentiment in the United States erupted, focusing on the Japanese army and the Japanese people in general. Just as news stories and newsreels were telling the story of Bataan, the U.S. War Department was in the process of rounding up Americans of Japanese descent and placing them in internment camps across the intermountain West. For many Americans, the Bataan Death March came to symbolize the

brutality of the Japanese and the experience of America's minority populations during the war. After the war, Mexican Americans wrote *corridos* to
tell their story about the march and the war. Later, authors such as Leslie
Marmon Silko, through her characters in *Ceremony*, used the incidents in
the Pacific to highlight the horror that the war brought to New Mexico's
Native and mixed-blood population. New Mexicans' participation in
World War II connected thousands of residents to the rest of the world as
people saw new places and witnessed atrocities that no one should have to
endure. These experiences profoundly changed New Mexicans as they
began to see their connections to the larger, outside, and modern world
that surrounded them and that would soon be on their doorstep.

New Mexicans not only contributed to the war effort through their participation in the armed forces, but thousands of the state's inhabitants left
their rural homes to work in the war industries springing up across the
American West. Never in the history of New Mexico had there been such an
out-migration. These young men and women left their homes to find new
jobs and careers and make new lives in other western cities, creating what
historian Sarah Deutsch called "regional communities." As a result of these
migratory patterns, New Mexicans established outposts of the region's culture in cities as far away as Seattle, Washington, and Oakland, California,
where these migrants would establish their own ethnic enclaves and "New
Mexico" clubs, where they would gather to catch up on family news from
home and eat the New Mexican food on which they had grown up.

The war effort at home depended on these migrants and others such
as African Americans and women, traditionally excluded from the nation's
workforce, to help the nation prepare for war. First, the government itself
hired many people to build the infrastructure of the nation, such as the
building of dams that would supply the energy and economic base to build
up the military war machine. The completion of Grand Coulee Dam and
other huge projects created the energy needed by the burgeoning alu-
minum, aircraft, and shipbuilding industries to complete the orders generated by the United States and its allies. Second, private businesses such
as Kaiser, Bechtel, Boeing, and General Electric, spurred back into business
as a result of the wartime economy, hired hundreds of thousands of people to meet the war demands. This new demand for labor could not be met
by local men and women, so employers looked to places such as New
Mexico, which did not have its own industrial base, to fill these labor
shortages. This out-migration of New Mexicans to Colorado, Arizona,

Utah, and California began a migratory pattern that continued through-out the twentieth century, when New Mexicans left their rural homes and economy to make their lives in the urban centers of the American West.

Moreover, these migration patterns began to alter gender roles among men and women. Prior to World War II, New Mexicans had lived relatively isolated ways of life. Most families depended on some form of agriculture, either ranching or farming, to make their living. Relatively speaking, New Mexico was more a rural than an urban space and economy, and as a result, the gender roles in families were fairly well prescribed. Women maintained the home and gardens surrounding the house and traded small animals, such as goats or chickens. Men were responsible for the exterior spaces of the household: the herding of sheep and cattle or the larger-scale farming that produced grains and other market products. Men, whether Native, Hispano, or Anglo, would be expected to conduct most, if not all, commercial business that occurred outside of the house-hold economy. When times were economically tough, as they had been in the 1920s and early 1930s, men left their homes to work at jobs that took them away from the home. They worked at coal mining, sheepherding, and growing sugar beets in Utah, Colorado, and even more far-flung west-ern locations. Women had stayed at home in their villages and towns and maintained the family culture, economy, and society so integral to New Mexicans during the first half of the twentieth century.

The labor shortage of World War II, however, began to unravel these established gender relationships. Unlike the New Deal, which had catego-rized jobs according to gender—women worked as seamstresses, cooks, or secretaries, whereas men worked as manual laborers—the World War II buildup forced Americans to set aside their gendered ideas about labor. Because of the labor shortage created by men heading off to war, women for the first time went to work in jobs that had traditionally been open only to men, such as welder, plumber, and laborer. There was also an increased demand for women to work outside the home in jobs that had traditionally been held by women, such as receptionist, cleric, nurse, and schoolteacher. Consequently married women and young women went to work, whereas prior to World War II they would have been expected to stay home and maintain the household economy. The opportunities opened by the war, as well as the expectation that everyone had to con-tribute to the war effort, allowed many New Mexican women to leave the confines of their home for the first time.

In some cases, New Mexicans did not need to look far from their homes to work in the wartime economy. During the war, New Mexico saw its economy expand rapidly when the federal government situated a number of important military installations within the state. This military buildup reflected the growing power of Senator Chavez, who worked to make sure that New Mexico became a primary beneficiary of the federal dollars pouring into the American West to win the war. Perhaps the most influential of all the new facilities was one of the components of the Manhattan Project, which took over the Los Alamos Boys School on the Pajarito Plateau, northwest of Santa Fe. The siting of Los Alamos National Laboratory in northern New Mexico dramatically transformed the region and left a lasting legacy with which New Mexicans still deal.

When Robert Oppenheimer and General Leslie Groves were searching for the perfect location at which to assemble the nuclear device that they hoped would end the war, they wanted an isolated place safe from spies and loose-tongued employees who could leak critical information. The lonely plateau proved to be the perfect site because few people lived there, and the plateau had only one access road, which could easily be guarded. On this site, the U.S. military created one of the most isolated and secretive places on earth. Most people who came to work at Los Alamos were uncertain why they had been called there or what they were trying to accomplish precisely. When scientists and military personnel were assigned to the Manhattan Project in New Mexico, they were told only to report to an address or a post office box in Santa Fe, New Mexico. After they had been processed, they were driven undercover to the site and put to work. Only the most senior personnel could bring their families or leave Los Alamos, and everyone had their movements, mail, and phone calls monitored regardless of their status within the project. The few local people who worked "up on the hill" or who heard the strange sounds or saw the fireworks that emanated from Los Alamos could only guess what was so secret. But with the guidance of a few brilliant scientists and under the tight control of the military, hundreds of men and women worked around the clock to create the first nuclear bomb, which was tested at the Trinity site, near Alamogordo, New Mexico, in July 1945. Because of the secretive work done at Los Alamos and at other locations of the Manhattan Project, World War II ended in August 1945 when the Japanese government surrendered after the nuclear bombs fell on Hiroshima and Nagasaki.

Ironically, Senator Chavez had been reluctant about the U.S. entry into

World War II. He consistently counseled President Roosevelt to remain neutral. Chavez even voted against the first Lend-Lease Bill in March 1941, which provided aid to the Allies fighting Hitler. By October 1941, however, he had changed his position and solidly backed Roosevelt's support of the Allied forces in Europe. Moreover, after the bombing of Pearl Harbor, Chavez became a supporter of U.S. entry into the fighting, and through his work on the Defense Appropriations Committee, he worked to prepare Americans to win the war. In foreign policy, Senator Chavez was integral to the success of the Good Neighbor Policy, which sought to create closer ties between the United States and nations to the south, especially Mexico. Roosevelt and other advocates of the policy hoped that by creating better relationships, Mexico would become a strong ally against the Axis powers. Americans still remembered the Zimmerman Telegraph incident from World War I, when Germany had supposedly proposed an alliance with Mexico, which if successful would return the territory lost during the Mexican-American War to Mexico. Chavez, with his command of Spanish and his interest in the Caribbean and Latin America, became an important player in Roosevelt's foreign policy initiative. His position as an American statesman and a diplomat was a role that he would play throughout the rest of his political career in expanding this idea of good neighborliness. Chavez worked to improve relations with Mexico and pushed for the creation of the Pan American Highway, which sought to link the Americas through a modern highway system.

Today Los Alamos National Laboratory is just the most famous imprint that the federal government left on the New Mexican landscape as a result of World War II and its aftermath. During World War II and the ensuing cold war, Senator Dennis Chavez came to wield immense power within the U.S. Senate. Through his influence he brought many federal facilities—White Sands Missile Range, Sandia National Laboratories, and Kirtland Air Force Base—and consequently opportunities and jobs to New Mexico. Chavez combined his deep loyalty and patriotism to the United States with his desire to bring prosperity and modernity to New Mexico. In 1960, when Senator Chavez served as chair of the Senate Defense Appropriations Committee, President Dwight D. Eisenhower recommended one of the largest ever peacetime budgets for military preparedness. Chavez, however, recommended a budget that added $1 billion more to the Eisenhower budget, saying, "There can be no price tag on freedom," revealing his commitment to fighting the cold war. His desire to

FIGURE 10.4. Dennis Chavez and an American serviceman. Center for
    Southwest Research, General Library, University of New Mexico,
    neg. no. 000-394-0591.

fund the cold war at such an intense level, however, also revealed Chavez's
political pragmatism since he sought to funnel much of that spending to
his own state's constituents. New Mexico's residents were one of the great
beneficiaries of this increased federal spending during the cold war years,
when thousands of New Mexicans went to work for the federal government in a myriad of jobs brought to the state by Chavez's deft political skill
in the Senate.

This increased federal spending had two profound influences on New
Mexico's economy and political position nationwide. First, the cold war
and New Mexico's ability to attract federal contracts made it extremely
dependent on the U.S. federal government. For every dollar that New
Mexicans pay in federal income taxes, they receive almost $4 in direct fed-
eral benefits in federal paychecks and appropriations to the state's facilities.

Although New Mexicans have entered the modern world of high-tech enterprise, they have continued to depend on the federal government to provide those jobs and contracts. During the nineteenth century, New Mexico maintained a colonial relationship with the rest of the United States because of its dependence on eastern and foreign investment. Still, New Mexico in many ways remained in that same colonial stance throughout the late twentieth century. Since the New Deal and World War II, the state has continued to depend on the largesse of the federal government and expenditures associated with the cold war buildup of the military-industrial complex.

Second, the cold war era brought increased opportunity for many New Mexicans, particularly for Mexican Americans and Native Americans. Because of the increased federal presence in contracts, as well as in civil rights protection and fair employment practices, many New Mexicans began to reap the benefits of industrialism and wage work. The prevalence of the federal government allowed for thousands of New Mexicans to work their way into America's middle class. These federal jobs provided wages and benefits that allowed New Mexicans to complete high school, go to college or vocational school, own homes, and begin to take their share of the American dream. Senator Dennis Chavez seemed to understand that civil rights and fair-employment-practices legislation had to go hand in hand with federal appropriations for the military-industrial complex if New Mexicans were to benefit. Throughout the latter part of his career, Chavez pushed for civil rights protection for African, Native, and Mexican Americans. He also drafted the Fair Employment Practice legislation that sought to protect American workers from job discrimination, which, regrettably, did not pass when he first introduced it into the Senate. Unfortunately, Senator Chavez would not live to see the sweeping civil rights legislation and fair employment legislation the Lyndon Johnson administration passed as part of its Great Society programs. Nevertheless, it is important to remember that Chavez pioneered the push for fair employment and civil rights in the 1940s, long before his colleagues in the Senate came around to accepting the legislation.

Senator Chavez died in 1962 after a long struggle against cancer. At his death he was the fourth-highest-ranking senator in the U.S. Senate. He had come a long way in his career since his first date in the Senate chamber in 1935, when many questioned his ability and right to be a U.S. senator. Chavez had lived to prove them all wrong and alleviate any doubt about his capabilities as a legislator and political leader. Throughout his career, Chavez transformed New Mexican politics and the state's economy. Through his influence, New Mexico left the fold of the Republican Party and became a Democratic stronghold that lasted well into the 1960s. Just as Chavez had supported Roosevelt's New Deal, he also chaired the Viva Kennedy campaign in New Mexico and voiced his support for President Kennedy's and Johnson's visions of America. But Chavez's most enduring legacy in New Mexico was that he helped usher its economy and people into the modern world of the twentieth century. Whether through New Deal programs such as the WPA or the NYA or through later military buildup, Chavez always made sure that New Mexico received a generous share of federal appropriations. Chavez worked consistently to ensure that New Mexicans were well trained, fairly employed, and had access to the best jobs and opportunities available to Americans during the middle part of the twentieth century.

ESSAY ON SOURCES

For a general discussion of western politics and the context in which Dennis Chavez came to power, see Peter F. Galderisi, Michael S. Lyons, Randy T. Simmons, and John G. Francis, eds., *The Politics of Realignment: Party Change in the Mountain West* (Boulder, Colo.: Westview Press, 1987); Richard Lowitt, ed., *Politics in the Postwar American West* (Norman: University of Oklahoma Press, 1995); Gerald D. Nash, *The American West in the Twentieth Century: A Short History of an Urban Oasis* (Englewood Cliffs, N.J.: Prentice-Hall, 1973); Nash, *The Federal Landscape: An Economic History of the Twentieth-Century West* (Tucson: University of Arizona Press, 1999); Nash and Richard W. Etulain, eds., *The Twentieth-Century West: Historical Interpretations* (Albuquerque: University of New Mexico Press, 1989); Etulain and Michael P. Malone, *The American West: A Twentieth-Century History* (Lincoln: University of Nebraska Press, 1989); and Peter Wiley and Robert Gottlieb, *Empires in the Sun: The Rise of the New American West* (New York: Putnam, 1982). Richard White's *"It's Your Misfortune and None of My Own"* (Norman: University of Oklahoma Press, 1991) provides the most thorough discussion of western politics and its relationship to the federal government.

Unfortunately, there is no comprehensive biography of Dennis Chavez or a monograph that adequately covers this era of New Mexico's history.

However, for an outline of Chavez's life and career, see Tom Popejoy, "Dennis Chavez," *Hall of Fame Essays* (Albuquerque: Historical Society of New Mexico, 1963). Juan Gómez-Quiñones, *Roots of Chicano Politics, 1600–1940* (Albuquerque: University of New Mexico Press, 1994), includes a brief paragraph on Chavez's career. A longer discussion of Chavez appears in his *Chicano Politics: Reality and Promise, 1940–1990* (Albuquerque: University of New Mexico Press, 1990), where he looks at Chavez's participation on the Good Neighbor commission, his support for the Fair Employment Practice Commission, his work with the CIAA (Committee on Inter-American Affairs), and his role as cochair of the Viva Kennedy campaign in New Mexico. Jack Ellsworth Holmes, *Politics in New Mexico* (Albuquerque: University of New Mexico Press, 1967), provides a general discussion of New Mexico's political scene by examining the history of political parties and Hispanic political acculturation in New Mexico from 1900 to 1965. Maurilio Vigil's *Hispanics in Congress: A Historical and Political Survey* (Lanham, Md.: University Press of America, 1996) includes a two-page assessment of Chavez's contributions to Hispanic leadership in politics. See also the short essay by Maurilio Vigil and Roy Lujan, "Parallels in the Career of Two Hispanic U.S. Senators," *Journal of Ethnic Studies* 13 (winter 1986), which compares the careers of Dennis Chavez and Joseph Montoya. By far the most comprehensive look at Chavez and his political career is the dissertation by Joe Roy Lujan, "Dennis Chavez and the Roosevelt Era, 1933–1945" (Ph.D. dissertation, University of New Mexico, 1987). Lujan examines Chavez's support and work with New Deal legislation, including the Civilian Conservation Corps, the Federal Emergency Relief Administration, and the Civil Works Administration. For a view of the Good Neighbor Policy in Chavez's own words, see Alonso Perales, ed., *Are We Good Neighbors?* (San Antonio, Tex.: Artes Graficas, 1948).

On the depression and the New Deal in the American West and New Mexico, the best place to start is Suzanne Forrest, *The Preservation of the Village: New Mexico's Hispanics and the New Deal* (Albuquerque: University of New Mexico Press, 1989). Her book studies the impact of the New Deal on Hispano arts and craft revival in New Mexico and Chavez's role in supporting WPA programs in the state. Those interested in the PWA and Chavez's role in that organization should see William Reeves, "PWA and Competition Administration in the New Deal," *Journal of American History* 60 (September 1973): 357–72. See also María E. Montoya, "The Roots of Ethnic and Economic Division in Northern New Mexico: The Case Study of the Civilian Conservation Corps," *Western Historical Quarterly* 26 (spring 1995): 14–34. One of the most important books for understanding the first half of the twentieth century in New Mexico is Sarah Deutsch, *No Separate Refuge: Culture, Class, and Gender on the Anglo-Hispanic Frontier in the American Southwest, 1880–1940* (New York: Oxford University Press, 1987). Finally, for the most comprehensive look at the New Deal in the larger context of the American West, see Richard Lowitt, *New Deal in the West* (Bloomington: Indiana University Press, 1984).

In regard to World War II, the cold war, and their effects on the American West and New Mexico in general, see Gerald D. Nash, *The American West Transformed: The Impact of the Second World War* (Bloomington: Indiana University Press, 1985). For New Mexicans' contributions specifically, see Gerald W. Thomas, Monroe L. Billington, and Roger D. Walker, eds., who produced a fine collection of essays and primary documents called *Victory in World War II: The New Mexico Story* (Las Cruces, N.Mex.: Rio Grande Historical Society, New Mexico State University, 1994). On the cold war, see the collected essays in Kevin Fernlund, ed., *The Cold War West* (Albuquerque: University of New Mexico Press, 1998). The most detailed look at Chavez's role in pushing for fair employment practices is Tobias Duran, "Social Reform Politics in New Mexico: The Fair Employment Practice Act of 1949" (unpublished manuscript, 1974). For a detailed examination of the FEPC's dealings with Mexican/Chicano workers during World War II and a brief mention of Chavez's work assisting in the investigation of complaints, see Cletus Daniel, *Chicano Workers and the Politics of Fairness: The FEPC in the Southwest, 1941–1945* (Austin: University of Texas Press, 1991).

11

"The Inalienable Right to Govern Ourselves"

Wendell Chino and the Struggle for Indian Self-Determination in Modern New Mexico

MYLA VICENTI CARPIO AND PETER IVERSON

In the summer of 1996, the U.S. attorney for New Mexico attempted to shut down the slot machines at the Mescalero Apaches' new casino, Casino Apache. John Kelly believed he had to take such action because the New Mexico legislature had refused to ratify recent compacts signed between the Mescaleros and Governor Gary Johnson. Without a compact, the casino became illegal, and under these circumstances Kelly concluded he had no alternative but to try to close Casino Apache.

By 1996 the Indian communities had achieved considerable progress in their efforts to take charge of their lives and lands. This headway defied what many observers had predicted when the century began—that Indian reservations would be disbanded and their occupants would scatter. However, the Native peoples of New Mexico proved far more resilient than these onlookers could have imagined. The leadership of the tribes made a significant difference in this ongoing struggle. At Mescalero, Wendell Chino served as its leader for nearly fifty years. Even though he was not in good health, he would not let Kelly's action go unchallenged.

"This is a fight the Mescalero people did not ask for," Chino said. "We have sought for over two hundred years to regain the pride and independence we once had, and we will not let one man destroy all that we have attempted to build up." Indeed, the Mescalero leader saw this battle as part of a larger campaign: "I will not make any concessions. . . . If we give too much in the area of gaming, I'm afraid we'll find it difficult to hold the trenches as far as tribal sovereignty goes, water rights, criminal jurisdiction. They'll want us to concede all those areas to them." He shook his fist and added: "If the state thinks it can lead us around by the nose, the fight hasn't started yet."

In the spring of 1997 the state legislature of New Mexico finally approved the compact. Chino expressed quiet satisfaction. "It's been a long battle," he noted, "but I think we as tribal leaders are happy with the outcome of the legislative process."

Unlike these events in 1996 and 1997, the first years of the twentieth century yielded little for the Mescalero Apaches and other Indian communities in New Mexico to be optimistic about their future. The Mescalero reservation in southeastern New Mexico included only a small portion of the land the Mescaleros claimed as their country. At least they had a land base, unlike Geronimo's Chiricahuas, who had been shipped out of the Southwest—at first to the Southeast and eventually to Fort Sill, Oklahoma. Yet even though a reservation had been created, few expected it to exist for many years. Non-Indians resented any land being set aside for Native use. They kept knocking on the Mescalero door, demanding access or seeking control of Apache acreage. By 1923, the year of Wendell Chino's birth, community members had already weathered a series of assaults on their presence. Thanks primarily to Chino's later leadership, the Mescalero Apache Tribe moved from being a presence to becoming a power. For countless New Mexicans, he was the Mescalero Apache Tribe. Chino embodied and emboldened his community. He always reflected the determination of the residents of Mescalero to remain and to prosper. At the time of his death from heart failure on November 5, 1998, he had served as president of the Mescalero Apache Tribe for seventeen consecutive, two-year terms. Well before that day, it had become difficult to imagine either Mescalero or New Mexico without him.

In 1873 an executive order created a reservation for the Mescalero Apaches in southeastern New Mexico. The reservation system reflected the two prevailing, and ultimately conflicting, American impulses toward peoples of color in the American West: segregation and assimilation. Regardless of the language in the treaties and agreements, reservations were perceived as temporary institutions—necessary evils required to isolate Indians long enough so that their values, behavior, and appearance more resembled that of Euro-Americans. In the long run this experiment proved counterproductive. In time the reservation became home, became

FIGURE 11.1. Wendell Chino, Mescalero Apache leader (1924–98). Courtesy Jicarilla Apache tribal chieftain.

an island on which cultural continuity and change could be maneuvered. That happier outcome could not be anticipated in the late nineteenth century, however, for the Mescaleros exercised no sense of self-determination. They were prisoners on their own land, seemingly unable to protect themselves against the imposition of Christianity, schooling, and disease.

As the American frontier began to close and farming, ranching, and mining lands became less available, the federal government faced unrelenting pressure to reduce Indian landholdings. In response federal officials came up with a series of unfortunate schemes that were applied to many of the newly established reservations. In the Northern Plains, particularly, the ax of allotment splintered Native land bases. New Mexico reservations were largely spared allotment, but Mescalero shared the fate of Fort Belknap and Fort Peck of Montana and Wind River in Wyoming in having other people(s) placed within its boundaries. Just for good measure, they tended to be people with whom the original reservation residents had not always enjoyed the best of relations.

At Mescalero this meant a steady procession of unwilling and unlikely tenants—all of them Apaches. The Jicarillas came, and left, first. After several attempts had been made to find a home for them, including two abrogated executive order reservations, the Jicarillas were forced to the Mescalero Apache reservation in August 1883. The Mescaleros were willing to accept the Jicarillas on their reservation, but by November 1886 most of the Jicarillas managed to escape its confines and resume residence where they belonged, in northern New Mexico. A generation later, in 1903, thirty-seven Lipan Apaches arrived—and remained—at Mescalero. Ten years subsequent to the advent of the Lipans, a portion of the Chiricahuas, a total of 271, moved in from Fort Sill in 1913. They too remained.

Boundaries not only marked the reservation but characterized the relations between and among these different bands. Especially during the first decades of the twentieth century the three groups were determined to exercise, to the extent they could, a degree of autonomy and separation. At first a degree of separate residence could be maintained, but in time the limited Lipan population and the larger but still minority Chiricahua population could not keep entirely apart from the Mescaleros. Although band affiliation and heritage remained important, even in those first uncertain years some of the people from the three bands recognized common bonds. A person from one band married a person from another; their children would grow up with an awareness of combined heritage and a shared determination never to be moved again. Memories persisted of lands that had been lost, yet out of this despair also eventually emerged a growing sense of identification with this place the white people called a reservation, with this one place their children would know as their home.

In telling the stories of Indian communities during the final two or three decades of the nineteenth and the first two or three decades of the twentieth centuries, historians customarily fashion a chronicle that emphasizes victimization. Such a rendition is easy to fathom and hard to avoid, for the people of Mescalero, like other Native communities, suffered considerably in this transitional age. All that was inflicted upon them forms a part of this narrative, too. But to speak only of deprivation and decline is to omit another vital component of the full history of Mescalero because during this period the foundation for the future was constructed.

Whether they attempted to wrest control over Mescalero lands, language, or souls, newcomers to Apache country shared a common belief that Apache culture possessed little, if anything, that should be preserved. American farmers, ranchers, miners, teachers, and missionaries all reached a similar conclusion: the people of Mescalero would be better off doing things the way Americans did. They needed to adopt American farming and ranching practices, to make available their mineral resources, to send their children to school, and to become Christians. To these newcomers any degree of Apache recalcitrance or resistance could only stem from ignorance. And the changes needed to start taking place right away. As a commissioner of Indian affairs memorably phrased it, it was time to make Indians feel at home in America.

In retrospect the purveyors of new ways appear stunningly heavy-handed, but they mirrored the prevailing perspectives of the era, at a time when most Americans had few doubts about the superiority of national institutions. In this environment, the Indian agent played a pivotal role in brokering the way change would take place. Change was inevitable, but agents could help broker that change. Agents varied tremendously in character and kind. Some were devoted to the communities they administered and attempted to ease the transition to a different time. Others provided only an unswerving devotion to themselves and to the gospel of individualism, economic development, and religious conversion.

At Mescalero, W. H. H. Llewellyn and V. E. Stottler exemplified the range of personal qualities and personal agendas an agent might bring to his assignment. Llewellyn came in 1881 and stayed until 1884. He established a local school so that Mescalero parents would not have to send their children far away and so that tribal members could gain employment. He brought in cattle to begin a tribal herd. The agent even praised traditional Apache religion, contending that "their religion bears as good fruit as that of others." V. E. Stottler, who arrived in 1895, never reached such a conclusion. Even in an age noteworthy for ardent assimilationism, Stottler stood out. He jailed grandmothers and denied supplies to parents if their children did not attend school. He ordered all men to cut their hair, persecuted those who practiced the old religion, and required men to work on digging ditches and constructing fences. Few Mescaleros expressed disappointment when his residence on their reservation came to an end in 1898.

Since Stottler despised all indigenous Apache institutions, he tried to replace the authority of the old leaders of the bands with more attention to individualism. Although the traditional leaders' influence persisted, part of the cultural baggage of the Fort Sill Chiricahuas consisted of a business committee to consider matters of general import. By the 1930s the chairman of the business committee, Solon Sombrero, could say: "The tribal business committee acts as a chief of the tribe. We have done away with the chief and we use the business committee form on account we have more educated Indians than uneducated and they are to transact tribal business. . . ." The composition of the business committee at Mescalero paralleled its counterpart on other reservations at this time. It gave more weight and opportunity to the opinions of younger men who had access to more formal education.

In turn, those who had gained more schooling were not always devout assimilationists; they often tried to use the linguistic skills and knowledge they had acquired about the outside world for more conservative cultural purposes. These men were cultural brokers who mediated, negotiated, and held the line where they could against the destruction of traditional Apache values. While men maneuvered in the world of tribal politics, Mescalero women quietly labored to keep families together. Even in a new era, they reasoned, the old values of reciprocity and generosity did not have to disappear.

In the late 1940s and 1950s the harsh winds of assimilation would blow again across Apache country, but the "Indian New Deal" of Commissioner of Indian Affairs John Collier offered a temporary respite from many of the excesses of imposed cultural change. Although Collier was far more inclined toward cultural pluralism than his predecessors, he too demonstrated his capacity for imposing new ideas and institutions. The Indian Reorganization Act of 1934 encouraged individual Indian communities to establish new forms of tribal government based upon concepts of majority rule and freely chosen leadership rather than any form of traditional or inherited forms of authority.

On some reservations—the Navajo in particular—Collier earned enmity for his intrusion into local affairs. Livestock reduction on the Navajo reservation struck at the heart of Diné culture. The Tohono O'odham of southern Arizona also were devastated by imposed forms of soil conservation and drastic cuts in the number of stock they could have graze on reservation lands. At Mescalero, however, the bureau supported the successful campaign waged by the tribe to curtail leasing of their lands to outside cattle interests and to use that acreage for their own herds. Many Mescalero students switched from boarding schools to local day schools. The bureau schools now presented a positive image of Apache culture and even encouraged the employment of the Apache language in instruction.

Because the Mescaleros voted to adopt the Indian Reorganization Act, they gained access to federal funds that enabled the people to build new homes and barns and to generate a far more productive farming and ranching industry. In fact, the Mescalero income from their cattle industry went from $18,000 in 1935 to $101,000 just two years later; during the same two-year period, the value of feed raised at Mescalero multiplied by eight, from $5,000 to $40,000. Through the leadership of business committee presidents Asa Daklugie (1938), Sam Kenoi (1939–40), Homer Yahnozha (1941), Eric Tortilla (1942), and Solon Sombrero (1943–44), the Mescaleros obtained $328,000 from this fund by 1944, reportedly the most gained by any tribal government. Although rapid turnover characterized the leadership of the business committee, the chief justices of their court system served long terms and through the length of their tenure seemed to gain the independence necessary to make tough but fair decisions regardless of local pressures.

The war years ended the swing of the bureau pendulum toward reform. When the war ended, the bureau and Congress began to take a more conservative stance in regard to Indian country. In some ways the goals of many Indian communities and the new order in Washington, D.C., overlapped. Native men and women wanted more independence from bureau control; congressional representatives were talking about "liberating" Indians from federal supervision. Once again the Mescalero situation resembled that of countless other Native communities. Many Mescalero men and smaller numbers of Mescalero women had served in the armed forces or worked in off-reservation wartime industries. With so many males absent, more than a few women had assumed new responsibilities in the reservation workforce. Whether they had left Mescalero or remained at home, Mescalero men and women would not be satisfied with limited economic opportunities and second-class citizenship. They began to push for a stronger local economy and equal rights as New Mexicans. By 1948, working in alliance with Indians from other reservations in the state, they had won the right to vote in New Mexico elections regardless of where they resided.

As part of its effort to move toward wiping the federal slate clean in regard to Indian affairs, the federal government established the Indian Claims Commission in 1944. The process took far longer than anyone had imagined or hoped, but eventually in 1967 the Mescalero treasury gained $8.5 million in compensation from the federal government for the myriad ways the Mescaleros had been shortchanged in the lands they had relinquished. This sum was hardly insignificant, but in some ways the process yielded another result of equal importance. To pursue their claims, tribes had to be represented by legal counsel. In most instances, this attorney constituted their first formal legal representation. On one reservation after another, newly employed attorneys began to be involved in other reservation matters and quickly gained positions of power within tribal communities.

In 1947 the Mescalero Apaches hired attorney James Curry to represent them. Curry served as the attorney for the National Congress of American Indians and enjoyed the confidence of individuals such as NCAI stalwart Ruth Muskrat Bronson (Cherokee). He was just the kind of lawyer that newly appointed Commissioner of Indian Affairs Dillon Myer detested because of his abrasive criticism of the bureau and his ability to galvanize tribal opposition to bureau policies. Myer not only did not get along well with Curry, he also clashed with Mescalero business committee president Rufus Sago, a firm supporter of the attorney. The commissioner was also displeased with John Crow (Cherokee), the head Bureau of Indian Affairs official at Mescalero (now termed a superintendent rather than an agent), a holdover from the Collier era who did not enjoy universal support from the tribal community.

In the autumn of 1949 simmering disagreements boiled over into major controversy. The maelstrom at Mescalero damaged all the combatants. According to historian Kenneth Philp, "Younger people and veterans who favored more self-determination favored Sago, while more conservative Apaches and those interested in a claims settlement looked to the federal government for guidance." Although Sago gained reelection, he did not have the support of all other business committee members. He and two others on the committee resigned in May 1950 following their conviction in the reservation border town of Tularosa for drunk and disorderly conduct. Those who replaced this trio sided with the superintendent. By February 1951 Myer had dispatched Crow to the Colorado River reservation and had browbeaten the business committee into formally declaring that Curry should no longer represent the Mescaleros. Although Myer had gotten his way in the fracas, he could no longer pretend to be above the battle and a champion of Native self-determination. His credibility and thus the remainder of his administration was irreparably damaged.

Myer's commissionership marked the beginning of the so-called termination era, during which the federal government attempted to terminate its trust responsibilities with Indian communities. This movement brought an end to reservations such as the Menominee in Wisconsin and the Klamath in Oregon. The state of New Mexico did not call for Mescalero's termination, but it did attempt to assume greater authority. In 1948 Mescalero representatives had made the long journey to Washington, D.C., to testify against Montana representative Wesley D'Ewart's bill that gave the states jurisdiction over crimes committed by or against Indians on reservations and permitted state police to enter reservations in the name of law enforcement. So the shock waves of the period swept as surely over this community as any other.

At Mescalero and elsewhere in New Mexico, the talk turned to how to combat termination. Mescalero had to find a way to assert its own right of self-governance and to demonstrate its own capacity to look after itself. This capacity included economic development in order to permit younger members of the tribe to remain at home rather than be pushed into relocating to Albuquerque or another metropolitan center. New avenues of economic opportunity had to be explored.

Wendell Chino's emergence as a leader in the 1950s and his ability to remain president at Mescalero for virtually half a century must be understood in this context. The fifth of eleven children, Chino was born a year before Congress had bestowed citizenship on all American Indians. He was half Mescalero and half Chiricahua in his heritage. That combination worked to his advantage, for it allowed him to learn from the people of both bands and eventually to call upon them to transcend old divisions. Chino grew up in a Christian family, yet also learned respect for traditional ways and the struggles of the past to establish and preserve a homeland. He learned as a young man that his people had to make their way in a rapidly changing society.

Chino was raised in the Christian Reformed Church, the first Christian

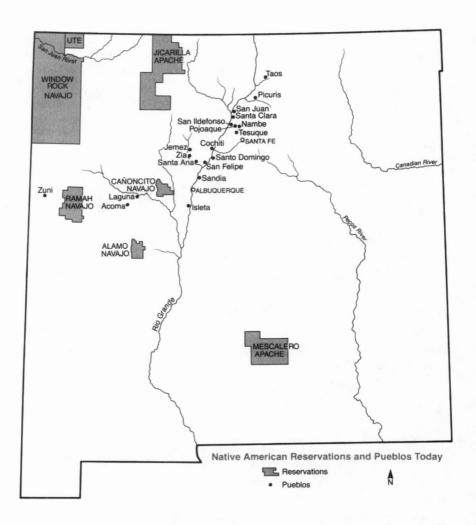

FIGURE 11.2. Native American reservations and pueblos. From Calvin A. Roberts and Susan A. Roberts, *A History of New Mexico* (Albuquerque: University of New Mexico Press, 1988), p. 36.

denomination established at Mescalero. He attended the church's Western Theological Seminary in Michigan and became an ordained minister. From the beginning of his political career, therefore, he possessed two extremely useful attributes: he knew how to speak to an individual or a group, and he was circumspect in his personal behavior. Only thirty years of age when he assumed leadership of the business committee, he offered new leadership, buoyed by a youthful optimism. His training at seminary had taught him that a minister must lead his congregation rather than poll it about how to proceed. The Reverend Chino brought that sense about leadership to his political responsibilities.

The people at Mescalero were tired of infighting and weary of federal and state interference in their own affairs. Although they had made some headway in the expansion of their economy, they had some distance still to travel. The community needed a person strong and articulate enough to take on Washington and Santa Fe as well as Tularosa and Roswell. It wanted an individual freed from any personal difficulties that would embarrass the tribe and limit one's ability to lead. It desired a person who knew where Mescalero had been but who also had a vision of what it could become. It found all of that in the person of Wendell Chino.

Except for a four-year period out of office, Chino served as the elected leader of Mescalero from 1953 until his death in 1998. This tenure not only was unprecedented at Mescalero, it is highly unusual in Indian country. The demands upon the head of any Native community are enormous, and almost by definition any leader cannot please all of the people even most of the time. For his part, Chino always downplayed his electoral success. "I just offer my name as a candidate," he once observed, "and if they want me, they vote for me and if they don't want me they vote me out." Although he remained the central force in Mescalero tribal politics for decades, he also recognized the obligation to participate in organizations that addressed the aspirations and needs of all American Indians. Among the many associations in which he played leadership roles, the National Congress of American Indians was perhaps the most important. Chino served for a term as its president and continued to take an active interest in its capacity to address common concerns.

Chino's personal qualities and life experience permitted him to stay the course in his home community. The recent political past at Mescalero joined with the growing economic instabilities of the cattle and timber industries in the 1950s to create a demand for strong leadership. In an interview conducted in 1989, he observed, "Too many tribal leaders want consensus because they're afraid to exercise real leadership." Even though he attracted criticism as well as praise over the course of an extraordinarily long political career, he was not deterred from his own vision of Mescalero well-being. His fierce pride and self-confidence combined with the abilities and resources of the Mescalero people yielded impressive long-term results.

FIGURE 11.3. Wendell Chino ". . . and the Mescaleros make money." Courtesy
Mescalero Apache Tribe.

When Chino first entered the political arena, the old business committee still functioned. But by the early 1960s many Mescaleros wanted a revised tribal government operating under a new constitution. On December 11, 1964, by a vote of 190 to 103, the people approved a new constitution formally declaring the tribe "the Mescalero Apache Tribe." Under the new constitution, the business committee became an eight-member tribal council elected at large. Recalling past difficulties, the community opted for two-year rather than four-year terms for all elected tribal officials, including the head official, now called the president. In 1965 Chino was elected president under the terms of the new constitution and remained in office until his death.

Perhaps the foremost challenge that confronted Chino when he became a tribal leader was building a viable economy. In the 1950s, many observers thought of reservations as economic dead ends. This perspective prompted the creation of the relocation program, which brought thousands of Indians to urban centers in search of better jobs and a more secure future. However, the Reverend Chino did not believe in that gospel. Instead he recognized that relocation did not offer a panacea. Although some Indians realized economic success in the city, many more struggled not only economically but socially and culturally. As did other Indian communities in New Mexico, Mescalero had to find new ways to keep its young at home. Chino reasoned that the platitudes of self-determination had their place, but ultimately that rhetoric had to be backed by a viable economy.

Chino liked to say that the Navajos made rugs, the Pueblos made pots, and the Mescaleros made money. He also realized that the most significant economic component at Mescalero was the land itself. With modern transportation now available, tourists could be enticed from Bernalillo and Santa Fe Counties in New Mexico and from population centers in nearby Texas. New Mexicans might groan about being far from God and near to Texas, but Chino understood that even Texans had the right to seek higher ground, and if they were going to come to New Mexico, they might as well come to Mescalero. But for that to happen, the tribe needed better roads and better facilities for tourists. As a result the Mescaleros joined other Indian communities in working to develop a transportation network and appropriate accommodations to attract and serve this vital source of income. The Navajos, for example, took advantage of the Navajo-Hopi Long Rehabilitation Act, passed in 1950, to transform its road system and to further develop tribal parks and campgrounds.

Along with Fred Pellman, who also served as president of the business committee for brief periods in the 1950s and 1960s, Chino worked to create Apache Summit. This development offered a place to stay (a twelve-unit motel), a place to eat (a restaurant and picnic area), and still another place to spend money (a crafts and curio shop). The Mescaleros had to borrow $200,000 to construct Apache Summit, but that loan turned out to be a modest investment in comparison to subsequent ventures. In 1962, with Chino back as president, the Mescaleros borrowed $1.5 million from the federal government to buy a ski operation from non-Indians. Ski Apache, situated on Sierra Blanca, not far from Ruidoso, became a steady moneymaker for the tribe. Its reputation only improved over the years. In 1989 a *New York Times* headline read: "Sierra Blanca Peak Lures Skiers to God's Country: Apaches Turn Tribal Lands into Top Resort."

"Our people are on the move," Wendell Chino emphasized. He added: "We are developing our people and lands so that we and our children can participate wholly in the full American way. We want to improve the social, political, economic, and educational development of our people while at the same time preserving tribal autonomy." A trout hatchery of the Bureau of Sport Fisheries and Wildlife began operation in 1966, attracting still more tourists. Next the Mescaleros embarked upon their most ambitious endeavor: a major destination resort that became known as the Inn of the Mountain Gods. The project included a fine hotel, a golf course, and two man-made lakes. When the state engineer of New Mexico balked at the Apaches pumping water from one part of the reservation to another to fill the lakes, Chino took the matter to court, arguing, "This is the aboriginal home of the Mescalero Apaches. This is Apache water." A federal court concurred. The Inn of the Mountain Gods brought in a lot of money to Mescalero, but as important, it created new employment. Tribal members constituted a majority of the employees, who eventually numbered more than 350.

Chino had other ideas for further diversification of the Mescalero economy. For example, he wanted to reintroduce elk at Mescalero and take greater advantage of the fish and game on the reservation. As a result, the tribe developed a comprehensive plan for the management of its fish and wildlife resources, including tribal ordinances that permitted hunting and fishing for tribal and nontribal members. But the state of New Mexico wanted to apply its own hunting and fishing laws to nonmembers on Mescalero. In fact, state laws often conflicted with and were more restrictive than tribal regulations. When New Mexico enforced its regulations by arresting non-Indian hunters for illegal possession of game killed on the reservation, Chino called the action a direct threat to Mescalero Apache sovereignty. The Mescaleros filed suit against the state and won another victory in court in 1983.

Chino was always willing to consider new alternatives for continuing economic development. In the 1990s that willingness encouraged him to support Mescalero becoming a place to store nuclear waste. This emotional and complicated issue created a firestorm of disagreement within Mescalero and brought Mescalero into the unwelcome glare of adverse national publicity. Chino had grown accustomed to exercising authority without significant opposition. In this instance it got him in trouble.

In 1982 the federal government passed the Nuclear Waste Policy Act to deal with the growing stockpiles of radioactive waste from commercial nuclear power plants. The negotiator for the U.S. Office of Nuclear Waste, David Leroy, promised any community willing to accept a nuclear waste facility a sizable financial incentive. The office provided planning grants of $100,000 to tribes willing to consider the possibility, followed by $200,000 for those who chose to pursue the idea to a second stage, labeled Phase IIa. Four Indian communities applied for the subsequent $2.8 million that accompanied Phase IIb. After one tribe dropped out, three tribes remained under consideration: the Paiute-Shoshones of Nevada, the Skull Valley Goshutes of Utah, and the Mescalero Apaches.

Chino discounted the emotional rhetoric of environmentalists about the storage facility, labeling the project as another business opportunity. He and the Mescalero Apache tribal council considered the project "a twenty-first-century industry with the attendant complement of high-tech, high-wage jobs not often available to Indian tribes." They called the initiative "in the best interest of tribal people, utilizing the best technological knowledge and expertise in the nuclear waste field."

Many at Mescalero disagreed, however, and by a 490 to 362 vote on January 31, 1995, defeated the plan. Undaunted, backers of Chino gathered signatures by petition to permit a reconsideration of the issue. After weeks of intense lobbying by environmentalists and supporters of the facility, the proposal passed by a vote of 593 to 372. Critics charged that tribal members had been promised "dividends" of $2,000 if the proposal passed. Tribal officials vigorously denied the allegation. Opponents of the development ultimately emerged victorious after discussions with the Northern States

Power Company of Minnesota could not result in an agreement and Congress halted the IIb feasibility grants. A facility would not be constructed at Mescalero. Chino may have been disappointed with the outcome, but in retrospect he should have been relieved. He had made a major miscalculation and had suffered a short-term embarrassment rather than a long-term disaster.

The matter of economic development continued to occupy center stage in the final decades of the twentieth century.

The years of the Ronald Reagan administration were noteworthy for severe cutbacks in federal support and assistance. Programs such as the Concentrated Employment Training Act were abolished. Indian Health Service facilities languished. Chino had recognized the danger signals from the beginning of Reagan's first term. Speaking at a conference sponsored by the National Tribal Chairmen's Association—yet another organization in which he played an active role—Chino stated in May 1981: "I would like to share with you this morning the Reagan administration attitude toward the forgotten American Indian tribes. Just about every group of American society has appeared at the White House except the Indians. No one," he emphasized, "has better credentials than our Indian tribes." Chino and other Indian leaders in the region attempted to counter the impact of Reaganomics by seeking new forms of revenue. They therefore fought to open and maintain casinos. Indian gaming emerged as one of the major questions facing New Mexicans during this decade. Chino was never far from the center of this battle.

In New Mexico in 1984 Acoma Pueblo initiated bingo as a way of raising the necessary sums. Other Indian nations across America began to see in gambling a way of bringing in significant infusions of money, although certain tribes, such as the Navajos and Hopis, eventually decided not to tap this source. These two Indian nations may have balked at the possible negative social and cultural consequences of gaming, but many other Native communities believed that regardless of their misgivings, they had to take advantage of this opportunity. The 1987 U.S. Supreme Court decision of *California v. Cabazon Band of Mission Indians* opened the door to legalized Indian gaming. The court determined that since California did not altogether prohibit gambling, it could not prohibit gambling on Indian lands.

In the following year Congress passed the Indian Gaming Regulatory Act, which divides Indian gaming into three classes. Class I included social games with little if any financial investment involved. Class II encompassed bingo and comparable games. Class III constituted casino gaming. The tribes could regulate Class I and, with the National Indian Gaming Commission, Class II. However, Class III gaming had to be approved by the state in which the tribe was situated. It required the negotiation of a compact between the tribe and the state.

Five years after the passage of the Indian Gaming Regulatory Act, eight New Mexico Indian communities, including Mescalero as well as seven pueblos—Acoma, Isleta, Pojoaque, San Juan, Sandia, Santa Ana, and Taos—had chosen to expand beyond bingo to slot machines and card games. The Inn of the Mountain Gods had a new neighbor: a casino. But New Mexico governors Garrey Carruthers and Bruce King did not sign compacts with the tribes, despite tribal efforts to bring about such agreements. In 1994 state voters elected a Republican businessman from Albuquerque, Gary Johnson, who had received support during his campaign from Indian communities. Johnson quickly signed compacts with the tribes, but unhappy state legislators took the matter to the state supreme court, which not surprisingly ruled in favor of the state. Given the opportunity to reach agreement through new compacts, the New Mexico legislature failed to act. As the New Mexico tribal governments waited, the U.S. Supreme Court decision in March 1996 in regard to the Seminole nation in Florida determined that an Indian community could not sue the state for refusing to negotiate a compact. By the summer of 1996, the inevitable confrontation finally occurred.

In this debate opponents always had to confront Chino's steadfast commitment to Indian sovereignty. He always fought for the right of communities such as Mescalero to make decisions and chart their futures. Chino knew that this process never stopped and that Indian people always had to be vigilant in defense of hard-earned victories. In poor health, he traveled nevertheless to Washington, D.C., to testify against Senator Slade Gorton's proposed "American Indian Equal Justice Act." Chino criticized the bill for denying equality or justice for Indian nations. Gorton's legislation allowed, Chino added, for state and federal courts to "decide to what extent tribal governments are allowed to assert sovereign immunity." In response, Chino asserted, Indian sovereignty "has nothing to do with rights or powers given to us by the United States. We possessed this very sovereignty long before the United States was even thought of." "We must not lose sight of what our sovereignty means," he declared before the U.S. Senate Committee on Indian Affairs on May 6, 1998, five months before his death. "Our sovereignty means the inalienable right to govern ourselves." The declaration, it turned out, constituted a final, emphatic reiteration.

Wendell Chino had the considerable satisfaction in his final years of observing the kind of economic and political progress his community and other Native American nations in New Mexico had achieved. Chino understood that Indians must remember the past and act in the present to create a better future. He knew that at the start of the twenty-first century, there would no longer be any doubts about the continuing presence of the Mescalero Apache Tribe or the other Indian communities of New Mexico.

Writing in *New Mexico Magazine* in August 1999, Steve Larese analyzed the contemporary Native economy in the state. In "Awakening the Giant: Tribal Governments See Business as a Means to Preserve Way of Life," Larese emphasized how Indian communities now were "attracting private businesses that until a few years ago wouldn't dream of entering into deals with tribal governments." Phil Tsosie of Isleta Pueblo commented, "We're a force to be reckoned with now, and some people don't like it." Santa Clara, San Juan, and Santa Ana were among the pueblos following Mescalero's lead in building destination resorts. "We're waking up," said Judy Tafoya of Santa Clara Pueblo, "and flexing muscles we never knew we had. And no one knows what we're capable of."

In September 1999 the *Albuquerque Journal* published a feature story about individuals and families who "helped make New Mexico what it is today." The newspaper remarked that "the 1900s have seen New Mexico grow from an out-of-the-way U.S. territory to a state known for science, sports, literature and the arts as well as for its unique cultural mix and brand of politics." Pete Domenici, Manuel Lujan, Georgia O'Keeffe, Tony Hillerman, and J. Robert Oppenheimer were included on the list. So too were two noteworthy American Indians: San Ildefonso potter Maria Martinez and a short man "with a booming voice" who, the *Journal* declared, had "used his position as the Mescalero Apache's longest standing president as a bully pulpit for the sovereign status of Indian tribes." "Before Wendell Chino," the newspaper concluded, "there were skillful and brave Indian leaders, great chiefs and tireless warriors." In the modern era, however, Chino had "set the standard." As had his compatriots in this impressive contingent, Chino left "a legacy that helped define the state."

Wendell Chino once observed, "As American Indians we have been grossly wronged, hurt, and abused, but we cannot linger in the past. For too long," he added, "other people have been telling us what is good for us. Let us make America believe that the American Indian is the final arbiter of his own future."

ESSAY ON SOURCES

The Mescalero Apaches in general and Wendell Chino in particular have received relatively little attention from historians. The standard history of the tribe remains C. L. Sonnichsen, *The Mescalero Apaches* (Norman: University of Oklahoma Press, 1958), although this study pays little attention to the twentieth century. A brief overview with useful material on the more recent past is Henry Dobyns, *The Mescalero Apache People* (Phoenix: Indian Tribal Series, 1973), which should be supplemented by Stephen Trimble's useful journalistic synthesis, *The People: Indians of the American Southwest* (Santa Fe: School of American Research Press, 1993).

Anthropologist Morris Opler was a pioneering student of Apache life in the Southwest, and his article "Mescalero Apache," published in Alfonso Ortiz, ed., *Handbook of North American Indians,* vol. 10 (Washington, D.C.: Smithsonian Institution, 1983), 419–39, furnishes a helpful introduction. Eve Ball of Ruidoso includes in *Indeh: An Apache Odyssey* (Provo, Utah: Brigham Young University Press, 1980) oral histories of the Chiricahuas as prisoners of war and of the first years of the Mescalero Apache reservation. For additional information on that period and on the Chiricahuas at Fort Sill, see John Turcheneske, *The Chiricahua Apache Prisoners of War: Fort Sill, 1894–1914* (Niwot: University Press of Colorado, 1997). Kenneth Philp considers the transitional years of the late 1940s and early 1950s at Mescalero and other reservations in "From Federal Paternalism to Full Independence," a chapter in *Termination Revisited: American Indians on the Trail to Self-Determination, 1933–1953* (Lincoln: University of Nebraska Press, 1999), 89–107. Thomas Cowger also discusses this era in *The National Congress of American Indians: The Founding Years* (Lincoln: University of Nebraska Press, 1999). For coverage of Chino's career and more recent developments at Mescalero, see, for example, Judy Gaines, "Modern-Day Warrior Champions Dignity for Mescalero Apaches," *New Mexico Magazine* 67, no. 8 (August 1989): 67–76; Daniel Gibson, "Sierra Blanca Peak Lures Skiers to God's Country: Apaches Turn Tribal Lands into Top Resort," *New York Times* (March 26, 1989), 8E; Randal D. Hanson, "Indian Burial Grounds for Nuclear Waste," *International Monitor* (September 1995), 2–9; Tony Davis,

"Flip-Flop on Storing Nuclear Waste Shakes Up Tribe; *High Country News* (May 29, 1995); Tina Griego, "The Tribes. The State. The Making of a Deal," *Albuquerque Journal* (a four-part series published in the autumn of 1997); Steve Larese, "Awakening the Giant: Tribal Governments See Business as Means to Preserve Way of Life," *New Mexico Magazine* 77, no. 8 (August 1999): 49–57; profiles of Wendell Chino and other New Mexicans, *Albuquerque Journal*, September 19, 1999.

The classic text on the Indians of the Southwest is Edward H. Spicer, *Cycles of Conquest: The Impact of Spain, Mexico, and the United States on the Indians of the Southwest, 1533–1960* (Tucson: University of Arizona Press, 1961). Volumes 9 and 10 of the *Handbook of North American Indians* (Washington, D.C.: Smithsonian Institution, 1979, 1983) offer valuable analyses of different Native communities in the region. In addition to Trimble's book, a few other helpful volumes that pay significant attention to the twentieth century are Keith H. Basso, *Wisdom Sits in Places: Landscape and Language Among the Western Apache* (Albuquerque: University of New Mexico Press, 1996); E. Richard Hart, ed., *Zuni and the Courts: A Struggle for Sovereign Land Rights* (Lawrence: University Press of Kansas, 1995); Peter Iverson, *The Navajo Nation* (Albuquerque: University of New Mexico Press, 1983); Alfonso Ortiz, *The Tewa World: Space, Time, Being, and Becoming in a Pueblo Society* (Chicago: University of Chicago Press, 1969); and Veronica E. Velarde Tiller, *The Jicarilla Apache Tribe: A History, 1846–1970*, rev. ed. (Lincoln: University of Nebraska Press, 1992).

12

Tony Hillerman and the Turn-of-the-Century American Southwest

FERENC M. SZASZ

"The Land of Enchantment." New Mexico's motto greets us from over a million license plates. Yet in spite of the hyperbole, most people agree with the concept. New Mexico *is* different. The Anglo-Hispanic-Native cultures, the mountains, the endless plains, the sky, the deserts, the canyons, the isolation, and the infrequent rain combine to mark the state out as *tierra encantada*. Add the continual presence of the past and one has all the makings of a genuine land of wonder.

No writer has captured this mood better than Albuquerque novelist Tony Hillerman. At the dawn of the twenty-first century, Hillerman has become one of the nation's most highly regarded mystery writers. His novels have been translated into twenty foreign languages, and director Robert Redford has produced a film version of *The Dark Wind*. Hillerman's fictional Navajo Tribal Police detectives, Joe Leaphorn and Jim Chee, have become real people to countless readers. The Farmington Public Library, where Chee checked out books, once issued a library card in his name and mailed it to Hillerman. Just as nineteenth-century visitors to America carried their James Fenimore Cooper or travelers to Scotland their Sir Walter Scott, so modern visitors to the Southwest arrive with copies of Hillerman stuffed in their suitcases, hoping to catch a glimpse of the legendary Leaphorn or Chee. For millions of travelers—both foreign and American—the Southwest has become "Hillerman Country."

What, then, is the vision of New Mexico and the Southwest that Tony

Hillerman presents to his readers? The answer is as complex as some of his plots. Hillerman is well versed in southwestern history and anthropology, but his books are neither history texts nor primers in anthropology or archaeology. His years as a reporter in Santa Fe have acquainted him with the region's social problems: unemployment, poverty, alcohol and drug abuse, and high crime rates, but his novels aren't sociology textbooks either. Rather, Tony Hillerman's mysteries embody three important themes of turn-of-the-century New Mexican life: the endless jousting among the region's ethnic groups; background settings that reflect contemporary local concerns, such as "pot hunting," Native American sovereignty, hantavirus, and the omnipresence of the federal government; and the central role of the landscape in shaping the contours of life.

Most of all, however, Hillerman's best-selling mysteries provide what he has termed "entertainments," fast-paced adventure tales that interweave murder, astute detective work, the land, and (most importantly) the Navajo view of the world. Perhaps the most admired mystery novelist of our time, Hillerman's vision of the Southwest has spread around the globe.

New Mexico, 1960–2000

The Southwest that Hillerman describes is awash with change. Of course, major change has been an integral part of the region ever since the Spanish *entrada* of the 1540s, but what has characterized New Mexican life from the 1960s forward has been the *pace* of change. During the last forty years New Mexicans have wrestled with a host of problems created by the uneasy interactions among the "historic triad" of Anglo-Hispanic-Native relations, as well as the ever encroaching surge of "mainstream" culture. Although ethnic relationships have long been recognized as the central pivot of New Mexican history, the 1960s revival of ethnic consciousness has focused national attention on these issues. Labor activist César Chávez drew on the theme of Christian nonviolence to secure bargaining rights for the United Farm Workers who labored in California's "factories in the fields," and Rodolfo "Corky" Gonzales helped form civil rights groups in both Texas and Colorado to highlight Chicano political power. But New Mexican ethnic politics have seldom displayed the harsh edges of either California or Texas. From territorial times forward, Hispanic politicians have wielded enormous weight in Santa Fe. Thus the postwar careers of Governors Jerry Apodaca (1975–78), Toney Anaya (1983–86), U.S. Senators

FIGURE 12.1. Tony Hillerman in the early 1960s, when he served as editor of the
Santa Fe New Mexican. Center for Southwest Research, General
Library, University of New Mexico, neg. no. 000-501-0001.

Dennis Chavez and Joseph Montoya, as well as UN Ambassador and later
Energy Secretary Bill Richardson, simply continued an older, more established Hispanic political tradition in New Mexico.

Simultaneously a series of dramatic incidents produced a rising tide of
national interest in Native American life. In 1968 a band of angry young
Natives met in Minneapolis to found the American Indian Movement
(AIM). Soon Indian militants occupied the old prison at Alcatraz in San
Francisco Bay and took over the offices of the Bureau of Indian Affairs in
Washington. In a related incident, a young University of New Mexico
Navajo student died in a 1968 Gallup shoot-out with the local police.

Although the militants often grabbed the headlines, far more profound
changes in Native life occurred behind the scenes with the passage of Indian
Self-Determination legislation. In 1966 the Navajo tribe began its Rough
Rock Demonstration School, the first all-Indian-controlled schooling of the

twentieth century. A decade later the Rio Grande Pueblos assumed operation of the Santa Fe Indian School. Simultaneously state Native groups began to take control of many aspects of the Indian Health Service. From the late 1960s on, the message emerged loud and clear: in spite of tribal differences, there existed a distinct "Native way of looking at things."

No event better symbolized this position than the federal government's return of Blue Lake, plus fifty thousand acres of surrounding land, to the pueblo of Taos in 1970. The Blue Lake story had deep roots. In 1906 President Theodore Roosevelt created the Carson National Forest in northern New Mexico, largely from Indian lands, and opened the Blue Lake region to general recreational activities. Pueblo spokesmen protested in vain that the lake was sacred to the Taos people, for they had held traditional ceremonies there for centuries. The federal Indian Claims Commission once offered Taos a cash payment for the region, but the tribal elders refused. Pointing to the discarded beer cans and environmental damage, Pueblo leaders insisted that the land be returned to tribal control.

In the mid-1960s the chief Taos cacique joined with others to visit Oklahoma Democratic senator Fred Harris in Washington. In broken English, they convinced Harris that the land was, indeed, central to their religion. Working through his Comanche wife, LaDonna, Harris secured cooperation from the Richard Nixon White House. The main opposition came from ailing New Mexican senator Clinton P. Anderson, but Harris successfully debated him on the Senate floor, and the bill passed with ease. President Nixon signed the act in December 1970, remarking that although it was the Christmas season, the bill represented not a "gift" to Taos Pueblo but long overdue justice.

When the jubilant Taos contingent landed at the Albuquerque airport, they met hundreds of well-wishers, including Governor David Cargo. "God has given us this land back," the chief cacique told the crowd. "The spiritual things that we said about our land are true. . . . We are going to use it like we said, the religious way." This federal return of Native land for religious reasons—the first of its kind—marked a growing awareness of Native American spirituality.

In addition, many southwestern tribes drew on this atmosphere to reassert their special treaty relationship—their sovereignty—with the federal government, often juxtaposed against their relationship with the various states. Selling cartons of cigarettes at low cost marked one aspect of this movement, but by the mid-1990s many New Mexico tribes had moved into the field of gambling casinos. By the year 2001 groups such as Pojoaque, Isleta, and Jicarilla all boasted gaming establishments, the most elaborate of which were the beautiful Inn of the Mountain Gods on the Mescalero reservation and the luxury resorts at Santa Ana and Sandia. Although promises of "Las Vegas–style entertainment" seldom panned out, the casinos employed hundreds of workers (largely Natives) and attracted countless tourists. But the casinos also drew the ire of local merchants, and the question of "fair payment" of taxes became a constant source of irritation with the legislature in Santa Fe. The issue of Indian sovereignty, however, had become firmly embedded in the New Mexican cultural map.

THE DILEMMAS OF GROWTH

From midcentury forward, New Mexico grew at an unprecedented pace. From 1960 to 1980 the population rose by almost 40 percent. State population statistics told a relentless tale:

1950	681,187
1960	951,023
1970	1,017,055
1980	1,303,393
1990	1,515,069
2000	1,819,046

Moreover, this growth proved decidedly uneven. Albuquerque, Las Cruces, and Santa Fe all mushroomed, while Grants, the eastern plains, and many northern Hispanic villages either stagnated or declined. By 2000 the population of the Albuquerque region approached half a million people. Lacking a shared public life, the city became, in the words of journalist V. B. Price, "a city of islands. . . . People hole up here, they don't communicate, there's no common denominator, no sense of civic identity that all can share."

Albuquerque also housed the state's flagship university, the University of New Mexico, which by 2000 enrolled over twenty-three thousand students from all over the world and boasted world-class programs in anthropology and Western history. By 2000 the physics department had a Nobel laureate on its staff.

In-migration by northerners seeking a Sun Belt climate produced tremendous change in the Ruidoso and Deming regions, and the social unrest of the 1960s and 1970s enticed more than fifty alternative communities to the state. During the 1980s Santa Fe achieved fame as "America's Salzburg," and "Santa Fe style" began to be recognized in the capitals of Europe. As wealthy retirees moved to the "City Different," however, they began to edge poorer Hispanic residents out of their homes. Native Santa Feans watched in dismay as their beloved plaza transformed itself into a sea of shops designed solely for the tourist trade.

THE NUCLEAR WEST

Part of this rapid growth had direct links to New Mexico's long-term connection with the nuclear West. The creation of the secret city of Los Alamos in 1943 and the detonation of the world's first atomic weapon at the Trinity site in July 1945 forever placed New Mexico at the center of the postwar atomic world. The 1950s–early 1960s uranium boom in the Grants region, the growth of White Sands Missile Range, plus the rise of Kirtland Air Force Base and Sandia Corporation (formed from Z division of Los Alamos in 1948) helped keep it there.

Much of the funding for nuclear New Mexico may be credited to Clinton P. Anderson. As a bulwark of the Joint Committee on Atomic Energy, Anderson funneled millions of federal dollars into various New Mexico cold war projects. In 1961 Anderson estimated that two-fifths of all federal spending in the state was somehow atomic related. The recent opening of the Waste Isolation Pilot Project (WIPP) near Carlsbad as a burial ground for low-level nuclear waste reflects this continual involvement. Some WIPP advocates argued that since New Mexico began the atomic age at Los Alamos and the Trinity site, it was only fitting that the state should serve as a repository for nuclear waste products as well.

These cold war projects were all highly technical, and the number of engineers, scientists, and technicians in New Mexico rose steadily from 1950 on. From the early 1960s forward, Albuquerque and Los Alamos have vied with each other as to which city contained more Ph.D.'s per capita.

The arrival of these well-educated, moderately affluent immigrants enlivened the state on a number of cultural fronts. Their interest helped fuel New Mexico's long-standing art and photography worlds, so that by 2000 Old Town in Albuquerque claimed about twenty-five art galleries and Santa Fe more than two hundred. The artwork of Santa Claran Pablita

FIGURE 12.2. Trinity Site, New Mexico. The first atomic bomb was exploded from this tower at White Sands Missile Range, 1945. Photo courtesy Museum of New Mexico, neg. no. 147362.

Velarde, Navajo R. C. Gorman, San Patricio's Peter Hurd and Henriette Wyeth, and Abiquiu's Georgia O'Keeffe began to command stellar prices.

Yet there was a dark side to this growth as well. The steady demands on water resources have long-term planners very concerned. The sparse population, great distances, and lack of industry all mean a low tax base, and salaries for New Mexico public school teachers rank forty-fifth out of the fifty states. Public transportation is sparse and erratic. Many needed social services are underfunded. Local ethnic politics—including issues such as Indian gaming or the proposal to honor colonizer Juan de Oñate with a public monument—produce endless controversy.

The state's social problems are equally bewildering. The teenage birthrate is among the highest in the nation. A recent Department of Agriculture report concluded that New Mexico led the country in percentage of households (15.1 percent) that were threatened with hunger. In 1999 the state's unemployment rate was fifth highest in the nation. The poverty and isolation of several northern counties have spawned a black tar heroin epidemic so severe that the local Penitentes marched in protest against it on Easter Sunday, 1998. Alcohol abuse, especially in the border towns of Gallup and Farmington, remains a constant worry. When a brown bear attacked a Philmont Ranch Boy Scout camper in 1986, a Santa Fe spokesman viewed the incident as a metaphor for the state's growth dilemmas: "Everybody is running out of room."

Given the complexity of the recent period of New Mexican history, one could not expect that any writer could touch every base. Indeed, Hillerman's fiction rarely treats issues such as population pressures, urban sprawl, or potential water shortages. His characters might visit Albuquerque or Santa Fe, but they seldom journey to the eastern parts of the state. No Hillerman tale is based in Portales, Clayton, or Hobbs.

Still, a number of recent New Mexican themes, both good and bad, have found their way into Tony Hillerman's fiction: the nuclear world and the cold war, Southwestern anthropology and Western history, Indian gaming, the absence of community, alternative lifestyles, alcohol abuse, hantavirus, Indian education, and (especially) the Navajo worldview on these matters. Taken together, Hillerman's novels provide a virtual primer on the last four decades of life in the American Southwest.

Anthony G. Hillerman was born on May 27, 1925, in the hamlet of Sacred Heart, Oklahoma. His German immigrant father farmed and ran the local general store, while his American-born mother managed the household and raised Margaret, Barney, and Tony. Their nearby neighbors were Potawatomie, Blackfeet, and Seminole Indians, all small farmers and all equally devastated by the dust bowl of the 1930s. Young Tony grew up poor, very conscious of social class. He learned early what it meant to be an "outsider": "Our Seminole and Potawatomie Indian neighbors were part of us, fellow barbarians teamed against them, the town-boy Greeks [of nearby Konawa, Oklahoma]."

This outsider role increased with his early education. The local schools proved so poor that his mother convinced the Sisters of Mercy, who ran a nearby boarding school for Potawatomie girls, to allow the Hillerman brothers to attend. "The nuns forgave us for not being Potawatomie," he later remarked of his eight-year stay there, "but they never forgave us for not being girls."

The Hillerman family also shared in another aspect of "outsider" status: they were Roman Catholics in a sea of Oklahoma evangelical Protestantism. Hillerman has remained strong in his faith, saying grace before meals and seldom missing Sunday Mass. Catholic schools and priests often appear in his fiction. "I'm a religious fellow," he told a reporter in 1996. "I believe we were created by a God who loves us and tries to teach us how to live."

This deep-rooted faith has allowed Hillerman to empathize with Native American spirituality. He once termed his retelling of a traditional Zuni tale, *The Boy Who Made Dragonfly,* as the tribal equivalent of a bible story—that is, a story intended to teach both "the history and morality of a people." Similarly he has shown great admiration for the Navajo concept of *hózhǫ*—harmony, wholeness—that lies at the heart of tribal spiritual life. Indeed, a decided moral/spiritual dimension runs through all of Hillerman's mysteries. He once observed that his books are as much about love as they are about crime.

After Sacred Heart, Hillerman attended high school in nearby Konawa. Meanwhile his father had died, his mother sold the farm, and his older brother, Barney, had enlisted to fight against the Nazis. After an awkward semester as a chemistry major at Oklahoma State University in Stillwater, Tony enlisted, too. He was shipped to France and after two years of combat was severely wounded. Either a grenade or a mine—he still does not know which—left him with a shattered leg and temporary blindness. Of his original company of 212, only eight survived.

Released from the army in early 1945, Hillerman took a temporary job hauling oil equipment to the Navajo reservation in northwest New Mexico. There he saw a group of mounted Indian veterans, decked in silver, on their way to a healing ceremony, The Enemy Way, which was designed to reintegrate them back into Navajo society. Hillerman asked if he could watch and thus saw his first Navajo ceremonial. Since he too was a veteran, The Enemy Way left a deep impression on him.

Meanwhile a reporter for the Oklahoma City *Daily Oklahoman* had read some of his letters to his mother and asked to see him when he returned home. She urged him to become a reporter, a profession he had never dreamed of. So, drawing on the GI Bill, Hillerman entered the University of Oklahoma in Norman to major in journalism. When he graduated in 1948, he married Marie E. Unzner, a Phi Beta Kappa in microbiology who spoke five languages. She has remained his most perceptive critic and a lifelong rock of support.

After graduation Hillerman took a job as a police reporter in Borger, Texas, a rough-and-tumble oil town that provided him with plenty of copy. In 1950 he switched to political reporter for United Press International in

Oklahoma City and two years later was posted to Santa Fe. In 1954 he became editor of the influential *Santa Fe New Mexican,* where he remained for nine years. By then he and Marie had become parents of five children.

During his stint in Santa Fe, Hillerman became a prominent local figure. He presided over a fine daily paper with wit and élan. His friends suspected that on slow news days he wasn't beyond penning a fictitious letter to the editor from "Mrs. Pinkus of Dallas," urging Santa Feans to tear down their "dull brown buildings" and build more parking lots for tourists. This tactic invariably brought forth howls of protest in subsequent issues.

By all accounts, Hillerman had reached the top of his profession, but somehow he remained unsatisfied. He knew he could write descriptive prose, but he wanted to write fiction. So, at Marie's urging, he resigned his post in 1963 and moved to Albuquerque to enroll in the M.A. program in English at the University of New Mexico. He also served as part-time assistant to President Tom Popejoy and to his successor, William "Bud" Davis.

At UNM, Hillerman immersed himself in English literature, taking classes from such legendary teachers as Katherine Simons, Edith Buchanan, and Morris Friedman. He received his M.A. in 1964. As soon as he completed his M.A., Hillerman switched hats. From graduate student in English (1963), he became associate professor (1964) and then professor and head of the Journalism Department (1966), which ranks as one of the most rapid rises in UNM history. In the course of his twenty-three years at UNM, Hillerman trained scores of students, including many of the key reporters for several New Mexican newspapers. In 1967 he also began working on his first novel, tentatively titled *Enemy Way.* He finished it two years later.

Hillerman first sent the manuscript of *Enemy Way* to his then literary agent, Ann Elmo, but she didn't like it. Neither did her colleagues. If you insist on rewriting it, Elmo advised, take out all that Indian stuff.

Hillerman remained unconvinced. He then asked famed mysteries editor Joan Kahn, at Harper & Row, if she would resolve the dispute. Kahn agreed and after reading the manuscript gave him the opposite advice. If he would use "more of the Indian stuff and Leaphorn," plus write a new last chapter, she promised that Harper & Row would publish it. In the revision Hillerman augmented the role of then minor character Joe Leaphorn, and the now legendary Navajo detective was born. The book appeared in 1970 under the revised title *The Blessing Way.*

The Blessing Way met with modest success. It sold more than three thousand copies and was nominated for the Edgar Allan Poe award given by the Mystery Writers of America. Local reviewers, however, were ecstatic. As one noted, the author "has opened a Pandora's box for himself, for no one who reads this book is going to permit him to forget that we want more." Equally important, it proved to Hillerman that he could write fiction. His second mystery, *The Fly on the Wall,* came out the next year. This non-Indian thriller drew from his experiences as a political reporter and editor in Santa Fe and pivoted on the question of journalistic ethics. Although *The Fly on the Wall* was well received in journalistic cultures, it never became the "great American novel" that he had hoped for. Still, like *Blessing Way, The Fly on the Wall* again proved to Hillerman that he could write successful crime fiction, and over the next two decades he published a new mystery novel almost every other year.

After *The Fly on the Wall,* Hillerman returned to the Native American world. Joe Leaphorn solved murders in *Dance Hall of the Dead* (1973) and *Listening Woman* (1978). *Dance Hall* won the Edgar Allan Poe award for the best mystery of the year, and Hillerman's fan club steadily increased. By now, however, he felt restricted by the character of the middle-aged, somewhat cynical Leaphorn and introduced another, younger Navajo policeman, Jim Chee. Like Leaphorn, who had majored in anthropology at Arizona State in Tempe, Chee had been an anthropology major at the University of New Mexico. Ironically, the younger Chee was far more traditional than Leaphorn. He was in training to become a *hataalíí,* a Navajo medicine man.

Chee starred in three novels of his own: *People of Darkness* (1980), *The Dark Wind* (1982), and *The Ghostway* (1984). After this, Hillerman wrote three more mysteries where the two worked together, often in a strained manner: *Skinwalkers* (1986), *A Thief of Time* (1988), and *Talking God* (1989).

The adventures of these Navajo Tribal Police detectives were praised by the national press. The *Library Journal* termed *The Blessing Way* "a mystery with literary value," whereas *The New Yorker* called *Dance Hall of the Dead* "high entertainment." The *Los Angeles Times* termed his work "unique in American crime fiction." Before long, critics began to compare his later works to his earlier ones. As *The Atlantic* said of *Talking God:* "If Mr. Hillerman's latest mystery is less exciting than his best, blame the setting. Washington is a dreary place compared with New Mexico."

Indeed, the New Mexico dimension forms the central background for almost all of his tales. *People of Darkness,* for example, deals with the rise and fall of uranium mining in the Grants area. The archeological riches of the area—and the theft thereof—lie at the heart of *A Thief of Time*. Regional concern over the repatriation of Native American human remains and artifacts forms the pivot of *Talking God*. New Mexico's battles with the bubonic plague and hantavirus drive the plot in *The First Eagle*. *Hunting Badger* (1999) draws most heavily from the recent history of the region. Here Hillerman uses the actual 1998 murder of a Four Corners policeman by a group of survivalists as the backdrop to his (fictional) raid on the Ute-run casino in southern Colorado, a case that forces Chee and Leaphorn to familiarize themselves with Ute culture in order to solve the crime.

In spite of all of his success, Hillerman wore his fame lightly. He continued for years to live in his modest home in the Northeast Heights and to relish his weekly Tuesday night poker game with his cronies. His telephone number remained listed in the Albuquerque directory until 1990. Then one morning he received twenty-one calls, mostly from strangers. The final straw came with a query from a Michigan man who planned to visit the Navajo reservation and wanted a recommendation for a good garage in case his vehicle broke down. That afternoon the Hillermans requested an unlisted telephone number.

By the late 1980s Hillerman had acquired an international audience. Harper & Row sales representatives sought him out for autographs, and the company sent him on exhausting, multicity book-signing tours. The Book-of-the-Month Club and the Quality Paperback Book Club each featured a compilation called *The Joe Leaphorn Mysteries* (1989). Every novel sold better than the last. *Coyote Waits* (1990) had an initial print run of 160,000; that of *Sacred Clowns* (1993) was 400,000.

Critics compared him with Arthur Conan Doyle and Agatha Christie. Imitators—the sincerest form of flattery—began to flood the market with adventures of Hispanic detectives, a Ute detective, an Albuquerque female detective, and so forth. By introducing readers to the Navajo worldview and inviting them to solve crimes by a leap of the imagination, Hillerman in essence created the genre of southwestern ethnic mystery fiction.

Contemporary New Mexicans may be justly proud of their stable of fine writers. Just a partial list would include Rudolfo A. Anaya, *Bless Me, Ultima* (1972), and *Alburquerque* (1992); Leslie Marmon Silko, *Ceremony* (1977), *Storyteller* (1981), and *Garden in the Dunes* (1999); Frank Waters, *The Man Who Killed the Deer* (1942); John Nichols, *The Milagro Beanfield War* (1974); Richard Bradford, *Red Sky at Morning* (1969); Simon Ortiz, *From Sand*

FIGURE 12.3. A reflective Hillerman in the early 1990s. Photo by Cynthia Farah. Center for Southwest Research, neg. no. 986-008-0020. Used by permission.

Creek (1981); and Norman Zollinger, *Corey Lane* (1981) and *Passage to Quivera* (1989).

Talented though these writers are, Hillerman has been able to reach a far larger audience. Unlike the others, Hillerman's fiction is available in virtually every regional National Park or National Monument, on all major U.S. airport newsstand shelves, and in most large British bookstores. Why has Hillerman been able to spread his vision of the Southwest so widely? The answer, in part, lies with his choice of genre: the mystery novel.

THE MYSTERY GENRE

The mystery genre has remained a staple of the reading public for over a century. In the 1990s about 20 percent of all books sold in Britain and the United States were mysteries. In the hands of master wordsmiths, good mystery novels thrill rather than threaten their readers. Mystery writing is especially popular among the educated: students, academics, and the middle class in general. Perhaps these readers relish mysteries because they can easily identify with the hero/detective. Few middle-class readers can identify with (say) tramps, pirates, talk show hosts, or billionaire tycoons. But they can all try to sort out the evidence laid before them. Thus each mystery engages the author and reader in a cat-and-mouse game of wits.

Sherlock Holmes remains the archetypal intellectual craftsman, for he finds patterns where others see only chaos. Holmes was based on Dr. Joseph Bell, Doyle's instructor at Edinburgh University Medical School. Bell proved a real-life master of deduction, as Doyle's favorite anecdote attests. On one occasion after a patient approached Bell with a problem, Bell surveyed him closely and then said:

"Well, my man, you served in the army."
"Aye, sir."
"Not long discharged?"
"No, sir."
"A Highland Regiment?"
"Aye, sir."
"A non-com. officer?"
"Aye, sir."
"Stationed at Barbados?"
"Aye, sir."

Bell then turned to his medical students and explained his reasoning. The man was respectful but had not removed his hat. They don't do this in the army, but had he been long discharged, he would have learned civilian ways. He was obviously Scottish and had a distinct air of authority. He had elephantiasis, which is found in the West Indies.

Sherlock Holmes imitated Bell at every turn. When he first met Dr. Watson, he correctly deduced that Watson had recently returned from Afghanistan. In "Silver Blaze," a short story that treats a missing prize stallion and a dead jockey, one finds the following:

> "Is there any point to which you would wish to draw my attention?" [asked Inspector Ross.]
> "To the curious incident of the dog in the night-time."
> "The dog did nothing in the night-time."
> "That was the curious incident," remarked Sherlock Holmes.

Like Holmes, Tribal policemen Leaphorn and Chee find patterns where others see only chaos. And they usually resolve the puzzles by reasoning in a Navajo way. In *Listening Woman,* for example, Leaphorn reviews a tape-recorded interview that the FBI made with the blind character Margaret Cigaret. She begins to talk about a cave containing several sand paintings, but the FBI agent cuts her off. Leaphorn later seeks out Margaret Cigaret, for he realizes that there should have been only one sand painting in the cave.

> "I listened to the tape recording of you talking to the white policeman," Leaphorn said. "But I noticed, my mother, that the white man didn't really let you tell about it. He interrupted you. . . . I came to find you because I thought that if we would talk about it, you could tell me what the white man was too impatient to hear. . . ."
> "What the white man was too impatient to hear was all about what was making the one who was killed sick," Mrs. Cigaret said.
> "I would like to hear that when there is time for you to tell me, my mother."
> Mrs. Cigaret frowned. "The white man didn't think it had anything to do with the killing."
> "I am not a white man," Leaphorn said. (94–95)

Similarly, in *Skinwalkers,* Leaphorn asks Chee if he thought the killer was a Navajo. Chee says yes. Can he prove it?

> "Funny. I knew he was Navajo. But I didn't think about why," Chee said. He counted on his fingers. "He didn't step over the body, which could have just happened that way. The arroyo, he took care not to walk where the water had run. And on the way back to the road, a snake had been across there, and when he crossed its path, he shuffled his feet." Chee paused. "Or do white men do that, too?" (63–64)

The central pivot of Hillerman's books rests on the uneasy intersection between the world view of the Navajos and that of mainstream society. Leaphorn and Chee spend a great deal of time trying to understand the ways of the *bilagaána* (white people), especially their greed and their willingness to kill one another. In *The Ghostway,* Hosteen Joe witnesses a murder in front of the Shiprock Economy Wash-O-Mat. "'The driver was Navajo,' he thought, 'but this was white man's business'" (3).

Some of the dilemmas are metaphysical: traditional Navajos have no concept of revenge. The idea of an "eye for an eye" is totally foreign to them. They also have a decided aversion to entering a building where someone has died, even going so far as to destroy a hogan where a death occurred. A person of wealth is feared rather than revered; he might have used witchcraft to gain his possessions. The ultimate goal of life is the prosperity of the tribe, not the individual. In the Navajo Emergence myth, the Holy People gave a name to evil: they termed it "the way to make money."

A less metaphysical but more practical aspect of the Navajo/mainstream interaction involves the question of police jurisdiction. The legal forces of the Southwest—federal, state, and tribal—overlap in a byzantine fashion. This overlap is especially noticeable in the Checkerboard area of northwest New Mexico, where surveyors are often called in to determine whether the infraction happened on Navajo or state land. This is no small matter. One statutory rape case occurred in an automobile that straddled the New Mexico–Navajo reservation line, and investigators had to determine whether the criminal act occurred in the front seat or backseat. (The maximum penalty in New Mexico for such a crime is life in prison; the tribal penal code sets the Navajo maximum at six months hard labor and a $500 fine.) Thus the fictional Leaphorn and Chee are often at odds with the FBI and the Arizona or New Mexico State Police in similar matters. For most readers, this is foreign land.

Although Hillerman's tales focus chiefly on the Navajo, he is well aware that New Mexico contains twenty-two different Indian tribes. In *Dance Hall of the Dead*, Leaphorn (who had a Zuni college roommate) acknowledges that many Zuni look down on the Navajo. *Sacred Clowns* centers on a ceremony at the fictional "Tano Pueblo." *The Dark Wind* treads cautiously around the still volatile Hopi-Navajo land dispute. Hopi leaders' objections to Hillerman's depiction of their ceremonies probably accounts for the fact that the film version of *The Dark Wind* was released only in Europe and on videocassette. As Hillerman is well aware, the Southwest presents no single "Indian" point of view.

Hillerman treats the similar divisions within the Hispanic and Anglo-American communities largely in terms of social class. His rascals often come from privileged backgrounds. Randall Elliot in *The Thief of Time* and Harold Breedlove in *Fallen Man* both were born with silver spoons in their mouths. There is no question where Hillerman's sympathies lie in these depictions. Thus the vast gaps in New Mexico's social landscape find echoes in Hillerman's fiction.

In the immediate post–World War II years, Albuquerque writer Erna Fergusson argued that the cultural diversity of New Mexico should serve as a model for the recently created United Nations. She pointed with pride to the cultural harmony of New Mexico and how each group had "selectively borrowed" from the others in the realms of technology (pickup trucks), holidays (Thanksgiving, July Fourth, Cinco de Mayo), and foods (corn, beans, squash, chile, soft drinks). Out of necessity, Fergusson suggested, the cultures of the Southwest had learned to tolerate one another.

Hillerman is less didactic, but he is much in her camp. Unlike Fergusson, he never preaches. He is primarily a storyteller. Still, it is a dull reader who finishes one of his novels without a greater sense of appreciation for the complicated cultural interactions of the American Southwest.

Hillerman's mysteries all end well. Leaphorn and/or Chee always solve the crime. Justice, often a Native American justice, prevails. In various interviews Hillerman has stated that one of his purposes in writing has been to present the Navajos and other Indians as "good, normal and solid human beings." All the Native peoples in his books have a right to the tree of life.

This ecumenical theme may be seen in Hillerman's concentration on the Navajo concept of hózhǫ, or harmony with one's surroundings.

Navajos who fall out of harmony need ceremonies, such as The Nightway, The Enemy Way, or The Blessing Way, to restore them to wholeness. In *Talking God,* the seriously ill Agnes Tso requests a *Yeibichai* ceremony. The Yeibichai will not cure her—she is dying of liver cancer—but it will help her come to terms with her condition. Both ritual and myth are needed. As the singer in The Nightway ceremony says:

> In the house made of dawn
> in the house made of sunset light
> in the house made of rain cloud
> with beauty before me, I walk
> with beauty behind me, I walk
> with beauty all around me, I walk . . .

In a larger sense, Hillerman's books provide the same sense of harmony for their readers. Leaphorn and Chee are always successful. The disharmony caused by evil is resolved. When readers finish the books, they too have been restored to a sense of hózhǫ.

Finally, Tony Hillerman's writings reflect an almost poetic sense of the southwestern landscape. Here one must turn to his nonfiction as well as his fiction. Over the years, he learned his state history and geography well. In 1974 Fodor Guides asked him to write the section on New Mexico, and he crisscrossed the state doing research. His essays on Folsom Man, the Rio Grande, Chaco Canyon, the sky, and clouds reflect his appreciation of the harsh beauty of the New Mexican landscape.

Many of his descriptions treat the wonder of his surroundings. The cliffs at Canyon de Chelly remind him "of how little space I occupy; the pictographs of how little time." As he has often noted, the New Mexico climate and land are so demanding that humankind has seldom been in control of events. Once he described the Southwest as "a landscape not designed for human occupancy." In *The Spell of New Mexico,* he explores several New Mexican landmarks:

> I could list a dozen such [magic] places—the lava flow that stretches south from Interstate 40 east of Grants; the Bosque del Apache on winter mornings when the snow geese are flying and the sky is full of the sound of birds; the ruined, eroded one-time grazing country

that stretches south of Shiprock; the cold ridge on which the village of Truchas is built; and the eastern plains, which inspired in Conrad Richter the concept of his classic *The Sea of Grass.* I have never yet made that long, monotonous drive through the great vacancy between Albuquerque and Roswell without finding my head filling with ideas crying to be written (3).

His fictional descriptions of nature evoke similar reactions. In *Listening Woman,* he needed a reason for Joe Leaphorn to abandon his vehicle. He decided to do it with an elaborate description of a sudden thunderstorm that took up two pages. A Boston reviewer, who had obviously never visited the Southwest, complained that Hillerman had wasted too much space in describing the storm. But all New Mexicans can recognize the accuracy of his portrayal of a spring cloudburst:

> There was sound now—the muted approaching roar of billions of particles of ice and water striking stone. The first huge drop struck the roof of Leaphorn's carryall. Plong! Plong-plong! A torrent of rain and water dimmed the landscape for a moment, the droplets reflecting the sun like a rhinestone curtain, and then the light was drowned. Leaphorn sat, engulfed in sound. He glanced at his watch, and waited, enjoying this storm as he enjoyed all things right and natural (135).

This sense of the power of nature and the importance of place forms an integral part of all of Hillerman's books. One could almost say that the sky, clouds, hard rains, canyons, and deserts are as much protagonists in his fiction as are Leaphorn and Chee.

CONCLUSION

In sixteen novels, numerous works of nonfiction, plus an autobiography recently published, Tony Hillerman has tried to capture the elusive spirit of modern New Mexico. From pot hunters to cold war scientists, from researchers on the trail of hantavirus to casino robberies, Hillerman has laced his mysteries with scores of New Mexican themes. But the heart of his fiction always involves the celebration of the Navajo way of looking at the world.

This message has reached out to countless households. One Chicago

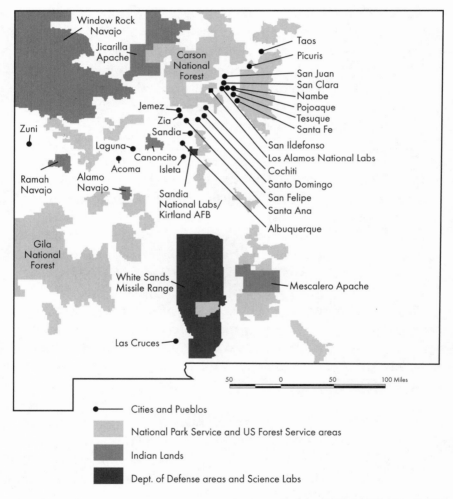

Window Rock
Navajo
Jicarilla
Apache
Carson
National
Forest
Taos
Picuris
San Juan
San Clara
Nambe
Pojoaque
Tesuque
Santa Fe
Jemez
Zia
Sandia
Zuni
Laguna
Canoncito
Acoma Isleta
Ramah
Navajo
Alamo
Navajo
Sandia
National Labs/
Kirtland AFB
San Ildefonso
Los Alamos National Labs
Cochiti
Santo Domingo
San Felipe
Santa Ana
Albuquerque
Gila
National
Forest
White Sands
Missile Range
Mescalero Apache
Las Cruces

50   0   50   100 Miles

● — Cities and Pueblos

National Park Service and US Forest Service areas

Indian Lands

Dept. of Defense areas and Science Labs

Data Courtesy of RGIS, University of New Mexico
Some borders have been realigned for presentation purposes.

FIGURE 12.4. New Mexico in 1990. Data courtesy RGIS, University of New Mexico.
Map layout by Brian Freels-Stendel.

woman described the impact thus: she was leafing through a recent issue of the *Chicago Tribune* when she spotted an article detailing an argument between the state of Wisconsin and one of its Native groups. She read the article through in its entirety, she told reporter Jim Belshaw, only because she knew Hillerman's works and realized that there was an Indian way of viewing the world. A young Anglo-American couple from the Pacific Northwest who currently reside in Albuquerque sign their letters home "Jeff and Kate Chee."

The popularity of Hillerman's fiction has meshed nicely with New Mexico's number-one industry: tourism. Although tourism has held first place ever since the late 1930s, from the 1970s forward "the selling of New Mexico"—from the Gallup Inter-tribal Indian Ceremonial to the widespread ski industry to the celebration of Santa Fe—has increased tremendously. Recent estimates suggest that tourism employs more than sixty thousand New Mexicans and that visitors spend millions of dollars annually.

Hillerman has played no small role in the tourist upsurge. In 1988 a regional map company produced a full-color "Tony Hillerman's Indian Country Map and Guide." During the 1990s a Santa Fe tour company packaged special excursions that took visitors to the actual locations where the fictional Navajo detectives solved their mysteries. Jim Belshaw has suggested that Hillerman's novels have probably enticed more people to New Mexico than any other single source.

Tony Hillerman has been remarkably successful. From an Oklahoma country lad, he has become one of the nation's most respected mystery novelists. In spite of the accolades, he has repeatedly said that he derives his greatest satisfaction from Indian responses to his books. In 1973 Zuni High School students asked him to deliver their graduation address. An instructor at the Navajo Community College wrote that his books had enticed her students to read extensively—many for the first time. Once when he asked a young Navajo if he had ever read his novels, the boy replied, "Mr. Hillerman, I've got to either read your books or drop out of school." On another occasion, Hillerman was discussing contemporary Native American fiction with a Navajo librarian in Arizona. "We read other contemporary Indian authors, such as Leslie Marmon Silko and James Welch," she said, "and we recognize ourselves. But their tales are often so sad. In your fiction we read of Leaphorn and Chee and say, 'Yes, this is us. But now we win.'"

Victory. Justice. Evil overcome. The triumph of faith, reason, and the "Navajo way." Harmony. Wholeness. Hózhǫ. All set against the complex cultures and overpowering landscape of the American Southwest. By melding these ingredients in a mystery format, Tony Hillerman provides a genuine sense of enchantment for millions of readers, all across the globe.

ESSAY ON SOURCES

I would like to thank Maria Szasz for her research assistance in the preparation of this essay.

The historical literature on post-1960s New Mexico is sparse, especially when compared to the richness of earlier periods. One should probably begin with Richard W. Etulain, Jon Hunner, and Jacqueline Etulain Partch, comps., *The American West in the Twentieth Century: A Bibliography* (Norman: University of Oklahoma Press, 1994). Appropriate sections may be found in Calvin A. Roberts and Susan A. Roberts, *A History of New Mexico,* rev. ed. (Albuquerque: University of New Mexico Press, 1991), Dan Murphy, *New Mexico: The Distant Land* (Northridge, Calif.: Windsor, 1985), and Rubén Sálaz Márquez, *New Mexico: A Brief Multi-History* (Albuquerque: Cosmic House, 1999), but there is no comprehensive overview. See, however, the essays in Richard W. Etulain, ed., *Contemporary New Mexico, 1940–1990* (Albuquerque: University of New Mexico Press, 1994), and in Judith Boyce DeMark, ed., *Essays in Twentieth-Century New Mexico History* (Albuquerque: University of New Mexico Press, 1994). The religious dimension is discussed in Ferenc Morton Szasz and Richard W. Etulain, eds., *Religion in Modern New Mexico* (Albuquerque: University of New Mexico Press, 1997).

Respected journalist V. B. Price has penned the story of Albuquerque in *A City at the End of the World* (Albuquerque: University of New Mexico Press, 1992), and Chris Wilson has done the same for Santa Fe in *The Myth of Santa Fe: The Creation of a Modern Regional Tradition* (Albuquerque: University of New Mexico Press, 1996). The Museum of New Mexico has compiled a study that in part touches on the modern period in *Artists of 20th-Century New Mexico: The Museum of Fine Arts Collection* (Santa Fe: Museum of Fine Arts: Museum of New Mexico Press, 1992).

There are a number of books on more specific aspects of the state's history. Fern Lyon and Jacob Evans have edited a fine collection of primary documents in *Los Alamos: The First Forty Years* (Los Alamos: Los Alamos Historical Society, 1984), and R. C. Cordon-McCutchan has written a definitive account in *Taos Indians and the Battle for Blue Lake* (Santa Fe: Red Crane Books, 1991). Although somewhat dated, Peter Nabokov, *Tijerina and the Courthouse Raid* (Berkeley, Calif.: Ramparts Press, 1970), is still valuable. *Albuquerque Journal* reporter Toby Smith has explored the popularity of the Roswell phenomenon in *Little Gray Men: Roswell and the Rise of a Popular Culture* (Albuquerque: University of New Mexico Press, 2000).

One can derive a surprising amount of material from Jerry L. Williams, ed., *New Mexico in Maps,* 2d ed. (Albuquerque: University of New Mexico Press, 1986), and from the *Albuquerque Journal*'s "New Mexico at the Millennium" special issue (September 19, 1999). Probably the best source for this time period lies in the colorful pages of *New Mexico Magazine.*

Any study of Tony Hillerman should begin with his own works, both nonfiction and fiction. His major nonfiction books include *The Boy Who Made Dragonfly: A Zuni Myth* (Albuquerque: University of New Mexico Press, 1972); *The Great Taos Bank Robbery* (Albuquerque: University of New Mexico Press, 1973); *Rio Grande* (Portland: Charles H. Belding, 1975); *The Spell of New Mexico* (Albuquerque: University of New Mexico Press, 1976); *New Mexico* (Albuquerque: University of New Mexico Press, 1980); *Indian Country* (Flagstaff, Ariz.: Northland Press, 1987); and *Hillerman Country: A Journey Through the Southwest with Tony Hillerman,* photographs by Barney Hillerman, text by Tony Hillerman (New York: HarperCollins, 1991).

The heart of his oeuvre, of course, rests with his mysteries. In order of publication, they are *The Blessing Way* (1970), *The Fly on the Wall* (1971), *Dance Hall of the Dead* (1973), *Listening Woman* (1978), *People of Darkness* (1980), *The Dark Wind* (1982), *The Ghostway* (1984), *Skinwalkers* (1986), *A Thief of Time* (1988), *Talking God* (1989), *The Joe Leaphorn Mysteries* (omnibus—1989), *Coyote Waits* (1990), *Finding Moon* (1995), *The Fallen Man* (1996), *The First Eagle* (1998), and *Hunting Badger* (1999). His publisher is Harper & Row/HarperCollins.

Thanks to the efforts of UNM librarian Louis A. Hieb, Hillerman has donated the drafts of his manuscripts and his correspondence to the Center for Southwest Research, Zimmerman Library, the University of New Mexico. Hieb has also compiled the definitive bibliographies of Hillerman's works. For complete listings up to the time of publication, one should consult Louis A. Hieb, *Tony Hillerman: From Blessing Way to Talking God, A Bibliography* (Tucson: Press of the Gigantic Hound, 1990), and Louis A. Hieb, *Collecting Tony Hillerman* (Santa Fe: Vinegar Tom Press, 1992).

Over the years Hillerman has written several quasi-autobiographical essays, and a number of writers have interviewed him. One can derive a good deal from his frank and forthright comments about his boyhood and working methods. The best of these are Rosemary Herbert, "Tony Hillerman," in *The Fatal Art of Entertainment: Interviews with Mystery Writers* (New York: G. K. Hall, 1990); Sue Bernell and Michaela Karni, "Tony Hillerman," in *This Is About Vision: Interviews with Southwestern Writers*, William Balassi, John F. Crawford, and Annie O. Eysturoy, eds. (Albuquerque: University of New Mexico Press, 1990), 42–51; Hillerman, "I Am Carrying Jim Chee's Library Card," *Book Talk: New Mexico Book League* 16 (July 1987): 1–3; Dale H. Ross and Charles L. P. Silet, "Interview with Tony Hillerman," *Clues: A Journal of Detection* 10 (fall/winter 1989): 119–35; Catherine Breslin, "Tony Hillerman," *Publishers Weekly* 233 (June 10, 1988): 57–58; Hillerman, "Mystery, Country Boys, and the Big Reservation," in *Colloquium on Crime*, Robin Winks, ed. (New York: Scribner, 1986), 127–47; Patricia Holt, "Tony Hillerman," *Publishers Weekly* 218 (October 24, 1988): 6–7; Rob Crisell, "A Conversation with Tony Hillerman," *American Archaeology* 3 (spring 1999): 29–32; and Katharine Beebe, "High Stakes Hillerman Style," *Mirage* 13 (spring 1996): 4–7.

The two most perceptive interviews/conversations are those by Ernie Bulow and David K. Dunaway: Ernie Bulow, *Words, Weather and Wolfmen: Conversations with Tony Hillerman* (Gallup, N.Mex.: Southwesterner Books, 1989), and Tony Hillerman and Ernie Bulow, *Talking Mysteries* (Albuquerque: University of New Mexico Press, 1991). Dunaway's interview may be found in *Writing the Southwest*, David King Dunaway, ed. (New York: Penguin, 1995), 62–77.

Michael Parfit's essay, "Weaving Mysteries That Tell of Life Among the Navajos," *Smithsonian* 21 (December 1990): 92–105, marked Hillerman's entry into the mainstream national press. He has been there ever since.

So far there have been two biographies, a brief study by Fred Erisman, *Tony Hillerman* (Boise: Boise State University, Western Writers Series, 1989), and a longer one by John Sobol, *Tony Hillerman: A Public Life* (Toronto: ECW Press, 1994). Interestingly, Sobol was forced to concentrate on Hillerman's "public life" because the author declined to be interviewed for his biography.

There are two major compendiums: Martin Greenberg, ed., *The Tony*

Hillerman Companion: A Comprehensive Guide to His Life and Work (New York: HarperCollins, 1994), and John M. Reilly, *Tony Hillerman: A Critical Companion* (Westport, Conn.: Greenwood, 1996). His autobiography, *Seldom Disappointed: A Memoir* (New York: HarperCollins, 2001), has just been published.

Finally, one can travel to the Navajo Nation with *Tony Hillerman's Indian Country Map and Guide* (Mancos, Colo.: Time Traveler Maps, © 1988).

13

New Mexico History
A Bibliographical Essay

RICHARD W. ETULAIN

$\mathcal{D}$uring the past century, professional and lay scholars have produced thousands of books and essays dealing with New Mexico history. Their writings treat nearly every subject imaginable. And not surprisingly, their views of the state's history have changed considerably over time. This bibliographical essay provides a brief, very selective guide to some of these numerous sources. After commenting on important bibliographies, references works, and general overviews, this discussion moves chronologically and thematically through the New Mexico past.

BIBLIOGRAPHIES AND REFERENCE WORKS

The most useful bibliographical source on the state's history is Jon Hunner's handy guide, *A Selective Bibliography of New Mexico History* (Albuquerque: Center for the American West, University of New Mexico, 1992). A listing of more than a thousand items, Hunner's bibliography is topically organized within the major chronological periods of New Mexico history. Other bibliographies published by the UNM Center for the American West, especially those on Chicanos, Native Americans, the environment, and Billy the Kid and the Lincoln Country War, will be particularly helpful for teachers and researchers. Nor should anyone overlook back issues of the *New Mexico Historical Review* (1926–) as a prime source for titles of important essays and books published about the state. From time to time, the *Review* has issued bibliographies on specific topics, and its staff has compiled guides to several topics emphasized in the seventy-five years of the journal's existence. Finally, the sections on sources appended to each of this volume's essays also list pertinent bibliography.

Two recent reference guides are notably useful for New Mexico historians. Editor Howard R. Lamar's indispensable volume, *The New Encyclopedia of the American West*, rev. ed. (New Haven, Conn.: Yale University Press, 1998), is the best reference book of its kind on the American West. Also very helpful are the essays gathered in Clyde A. Milner II, et al., eds., *The Oxford History of the American West* (New York: Oxford University Press, 1994). We badly need reference volumes like these on New Mexico.

For those who wish to examine New Mexico history visually, three useful volumes are available. Thomas E. Chávez has prepared an attractive photographic history in *An Illustrated History of New Mexico* (Niwot: University Press of Colorado, 1992). And the two most helpful sources for New Mexico historical maps are Warren A. Beck and Ynez D. Haase, *Historical Atlas of New Mexico* (Norman: University of Oklahoma Press, 1969), and Jerry L. Williams, *New Mexico in Maps*, 2d ed. (Albuquerque: University of New Mexico Press, 1986). The Williams volume, with text by several historians and other scholars, is particularly useful.

GENERAL HISTORIES OF NEW MEXICO AND THE SOUTHWEST

Over the years, historians, journalists, and other scholars and writers have prepared dozens of general histories of New Mexico. Still noteworthy among the earliest volumes is Hubert Howe Bancroft's *History of Arizona and New Mexico, 1530–1888* (San Francisco: History Company, 1889). Even though cluttered with excessive detail, Ralph Emerson Twitchell's *The Leading Facts of New Mexico*, 5 vols. (Cedar Falls, Iowa: Torch Press, 1911–17) remains helpful. Frank Driver Reeve wrote—or gathered—much of the material that appears in his *History of New Mexico*, 3 vols. (New York: Lewis Publishing Company, 1961). Another general volume, intended primarily as a college text, is Warren A. Beck's *New Mexico: A History of Four Centuries* (Norman: University of Oklahoma Press, 1963, 1974). Two recent books are much less dated than Beck's. Marc Simmons's volume in a notable series, *New Mexico: A Bicentennial History* (New York: Norton, 1977), provides general and specialist readers with a smoothly written overview. Given Simmons's research specialties, it's not surprising that he emphasizes the pre-1900 period. Meanwhile, Susan A. Roberts, Calvin A. Roberts, and Kathy Chilton's *A History of New Mexico*, 2d rev. ed. (Albuquerque: University of New Mexico Press, 1998), remains the most widely adopted text for high school and college classes. It too stresses New Mexico history before 1900. Finally, one should also sample Rubén Sálaz Márquez's *New Mexico: A Brief Multi-History* (Albuquerque: Cosmic House, 1999). The volume is neither brief nor a "history" in the usual sense, but it is a mammoth chronology and guide to important events and people.

A handful of other volumes aid readers in seeing New Mexico in its larger southwestern context. The earliest of these is W. Eugene Hollon's lively overview of the entire region, *The Southwest: Old and New* (New York: Knopf, 1961). More workmanlike and intended primarily as a college text is Lynn I. Perrigo's *American Southwest: Its Peoples and Cultures* (New York: Holt, Rinehart and Winston, 1971). Geographer D. W. Meinig's brief, stimulating overview, *Southwest: Three Peoples in Geographical Change, 1600–1970* (New York: Oxford University Press, 1971), helps readers to visualize how historical occurrences and people made their marks on historical/geographical landscapes. David Lavender provides another inviting, smoothly written overview in *The Southwest* (New York: Harper & Row, 1980).

Several other important volumes furnish thematic overviews of important subjects in New Mexico history. Among these is Ira Clark's monumental, 830-page study *Water in New Mexico: A History of Its Management and Use* (Albuquerque: University of New Mexico Press, 1987). A much briefer but well-written book on this same subject is John O. Baxter's *Dividing New Mexico's Waters, 1700–1912* (Albuquerque: University of New Mexico Press, 1997). Another important thematic book is the collection of essays edited by Joan M. Jensen and Darlis Miller, *New Mexico Women: Intercultural Perspectives* (Albuquerque: University of New Mexico Press, 1986). Still another valuable anthology is that of David R. Maciel and Erlinda Gonzales-Berry, eds., *The Contested Homeland: A Chicano History of New Mexico* (Albuquerque: University of New Mexico Press, 2000).

INDIANS IN EARLY NEW MEXICO

Those interested in this subject should begin with two superb reference guides: volumes 8, 9, 10, and 11, as well as scattered essays in other volumes of the Smithsonian Institution's *Handbook of North American Indians*, provide scholarly and readable essays on Paleo-Indian and modern Native

American histories. Bibliographies published by the Center for the North American Indian at the Newberry Library in Chicago also furnish handy lists of publications on the major tribes of the Southwest.

Several Native American scholars have written important books about the Indians of early New Mexico. Edward P. Dozier, an anthropologist and of Pueblo ancestry, produced a general overview in *The Pueblo Indians of North America* (New York: Holt, Rinehart and Winston, 1970). Another Pueblo scholar, historian Joe S. Sando, has published extensively about his people. See his *The Pueblo Indians* (San Francisco: Indian Historian Press, 1976) and Sando, *Pueblo Nations: Eight Centuries of Pueblo Indian History*, rev. first ed. (Santa Fe: Clear Light Publishers, 1998). For the views of another Pueblo anthropologist, see the important study by Alfonso Ortiz, *The Tewa World: Space, Time, Being, and Becoming in a Pueblo Society* (Chicago: University of Chicago Press, 1969). In addition, Veronica E. Velarde Tiller has published a helpful study of her own people in *The Jicarilla Apache Tribe: A History*, rev. ed. (Lincoln: University of Nebraska Press, 1992).

Dozens of other scholars have also provided important books on the Indians of early New Mexico. Anthropologist Bertha P. Dutton summarizes her career-long research in *American Indians of the Southwest*, rev. enl. ed. (Albuquerque: University of New Mexico Press, 1983). For the Navajos, one may consult James F. Downs, *The Navajo* (New York: Holt, Rinehart and Winston, 1972), and Peter Iverson, *The Navajo Nation* (Westport, Conn.: Greenwood, 1994). For the Apache, in addition to the Tiller volume noted above, one should examine C. L. Sonnichsen's *The Mescalero Apache*, 2d ed. (Norman: University of Oklahoma Press, 1973), and Donald E. Worcester's *The Apaches: Eagles of the Southwest* (Norman: University of Oklahoma Press, 1992). The most recent overview of Apaches is Trudy Griffin-Pierce's *Native Peoples of the Southwest* (Albuquerque: University of New Mexico Press, 2000).

A number of other scholars approach this subject through studies of Indian-white contact. Among these books, two especially stand out. See anthropologist Edward H. Spicer's well-researched *Cycles of Conquest: The Impact of Spain, Mexico, and the United States on the Indians of the Southwest, 1533–1960* (Tucson: University of Arizona Press, 1970), and the equally extensive work by historian Elizabeth A. H. John, *Storms Brewed in Other Men's Worlds: The Confrontation of Indian, Spanish, and French in the Southwest, 1540–1795* (College Station: Texas A&M University Press,

1975). Two additional volumes of this kind are particularly provocative. Jack D. Forbes's *Apache, Navajo, and Spaniard* (Norman: University of Oklahoma Press, 1960, 1974), although stimulating, is also decidedly anti-Spanish. Equally provocative, and perhaps even more controversial, is Ramón Gutiérrez's *When Jesus Came, the Corn Mothers Went Away: Marriage, Sexuality, and Power in New Mexico, 1500–1846* (Stanford, Calif.: Stanford University Press, 1991).

Other volumes that deal with Indian-Spanish contacts include John L. Kessell's *Kiva, Cross and Crown: The Pecos Indians and New Mexico, 1540–1840* (Albuquerque: University of New Mexico Press, 1987). Readers should also examine Oakah L. Jones's *Pueblo Warriors and Spanish Conquest* (Norman: University of Oklahoma Press, 1966) and Carroll L. Riley's *The Kachina and the Cross: Indians and Spaniards in the Early Southwest* (Salt Lake City: University of Utah Press, 1999). For a brief collection of important essays on the Pueblo Revolt, plus insightful editorial comment and bibliographical listings, see David J. Weber, ed., *What Caused the Pueblo Revolt?* (Boston: Bedford/St. Martin's, 1999).

EARLY SPANISH HISTORY

Scholars and students interested in Spanish influences on early New Mexico must begin with David J. Weber's mammoth volume, *The Spanish Frontier in North America* (New Haven, Conn.: Yale University Press, 1992). Containing nearly six hundred pages of oversized text, this immensely useful book is balanced, clearly written, and thoroughly researched; the meaty footnotes and extensive bibliography also run to nearly two hundred pages. Weber's superb book replaces two classic volumes: Herbert Eugene Bolton's *The Spanish Borderlands: A Chronicle of Old Florida and the Southwest* (New Haven, Conn.: Yale University Press, 1921) and the less romantically written and more fact-driven synthesis by Bolton's student John Francis Bannon, *The Spanish Borderlands Frontier, 1513–1821* (New York: Holt, Rinehart and Winston, 1970). The most recent overview of the subject is Donald C. Cutter and Iris Wilson Engstrand's *Quest for Empire: Spanish Settlement in the Southwest* (Golden, Colo.: Fulcrum Publishing, 1996).

These volumes place New Mexico in the context of the larger Borderlands area. Other writers focus on Spanish influences in New Mexico. Among these is Marc Simmons's very readable biography, *The Last Conquistador: Juan de Oñate and the Settling of the Far Southwest* (Norman:

University of Oklahoma Press, 1991). Simmons also authored an earlier, still useful volume, *Spanish Government in New Mexico* (Albuquerque: University of New Mexico Press, 1968). Those who wish to savor the work of a pioneering scholar in this area should read two compact monographs by France V. Scholes, *Church and State in New Mexico, 1610–1650* (1937), and his *Troublous Times in New Mexico, 1659–1670* (1942), both published by the University of New Mexico Press.

Several other scholars discuss Spanish contacts with Native Americans. In this regard, one should see Frances Leon Swadesh's *Hispanic Americans of the Ute Frontier from Chama Valley to the San Juan Basin, 1694–1960* (Boulder: University of Colorado, Tri-ethnic Research Project, 1966), Oakah L. Jones's *Los Paisanos: Spanish Settlers on the Northern Frontier of New Spain* (Norman: University of Oklahoma Press, 1979), and Carroll L. Riley's *Rio del Norte: People of the Upper Rio Grande from the Earliest Times to the Pueblo Revolt* (Salt Lake City: University of Utah Press, 1995). A new monograph is also noteworthy: Ross Frank, *From Settler to Citizen: New Mexico Economic Development and the Creation of Vecino Society, 1750–1820* (Berkeley: University of California Press, 2000).

Still useful are two collections of essays dealing with the Borderlands. See David J. Weber's edited volume, *New Spain's Far Northern Frontier* (Albuquerque: University of New Mexico Press, 1979), and Weber's own collected essays in *Myth and the History of the Hispanic Southwest* (Albuquerque: University of New Mexico Press, 1988). Adrian Bustamante deals with a complex issues of Spanish/Indio history in his important essay "'The Matter Was Never Resolved': The *Casta* System in Colonial New Mexico, 1693–1823," *New Mexico Historical Review* 66 (April 1991): 143–64.

Finally, those wishing to examine important Spanish documents revealing much about seventeenth- and eighteenth-century New Mexico must sample the multivolume Diego de Vargas Papers, edited by John L. Kessell, Rick Hendricks, and others and published by the University of New Mexico Press. These volumes, and the impressive research on which they are based, remain models for all scholars and historical editors.

NEW MEXICO IN THE NINETEENTH CENTURY

The Mexican Period and the Mexican-American War

As he does in so many areas of New Mexico scholarship, David J. Weber provides the beginning place for the study of the Mexican period in his thorough study *The Mexican Frontier, 1821–1846: The American Southwest Under Mexico* (Albuquerque: University of New Mexico Press, 1982). The book's extensive footnotes and bibliography are a guide to the most important research on this twenty-five-year period. Janet Lecompte, *Rebellion in Rio Arriba* (Albuquerque: University of New Mexico Press, 1985), provides a brief account of an important event. For accounts of Padre Antonio José Martínez of Taos, one should consult Fray Angélico Chávez, *But Time and Chance* (Santa Fe: Sunstone Press, 1981), and E. A. Mares, et al., *Padre Martinez: New Perspectives from Taos* (Taos: Millicent Rogers Museum, 1988). Although these two volumes contain much valuable information on the important—and controversial—priest, we badly need a full-scale, thoroughly researched biography. Well-known New Mexico writer Paul Horgan provides a sympathetic biography of Padre Martínez's opponent, *Lamy of Santa Fe: His Life and Times* (New York: Farrar, Straus, Giroux, 1975). Another noteworthy biography that covers religious controversies in mid-nineteenth-century New Mexico is Lynn Bridgers's *Death's Deceiver: The Life of Joseph Machebeuf* (Albuquerque: University of New Mexico Press, 1997).

Other volumes treat the years from 1821 to 1846 as part of longer studies. Marc Simmons's *Albuquerque: A Narrative History* (Albuquerque: University of New Mexico Press, 1983) covers the subject from its beginnings into the twentieth century. A recent monograph is Deena J. González's *Refusing the Favor: Spanish-Mexican Women of Santa Fe, 1820–1880* (New York: Oxford University Press, 2000). Although these books provide important information on the Mexican period, we still need a good deal more research on this era, including a biography of Manuel Armijo, the leading Mexican figure of the period. Of the numerous accounts of the Mexican-American War, one might begin with a recent study by John S. D. Eisenhower, *So Far from God: The U.S. War with Mexico 1846–1848* (New York: Random House, 1989).

American Entry into New Mexico

For several years, Marc Simmons has published numerous essays and collections on the Santa Fe Trail. One of those collections is his *The Old Trail to Santa Fe: Collected Essays* (Albuquerque: University of New Mexico Press, 1996). For a recent, lively written account, see David Dary's *The Santa Fe Trail: Its History, Legends, and Lore* (New York: Knopf, 2000). David J. Weber's *Taos Trappers: The Fur Trade in the Far Southwest,*

1540–1846 (Norman: University of Oklahoma Press, 1971), his first book, remains *the* study on this subject.

Although the subtitle of Howard R. Lamar's *The Far Southwest, 1846–1912: A Territorial History* (1966; Albuquerque: University of New Mexico Press, 2000) suggests this indispensable volume deals with a later period, it also includes valuable information on the pre-1846 era. This notable book also deals with other southwestern territories becoming states. Robert W. Larson's *New Mexico's Quest for Statehood, 1846–1912* (Albuquerque: University of New Mexico Press, 1968), focuses on the political history of New Mexico Territory. A useful biography of New Mexico's most important political figure during this period is Victor Westphall's *Thomas Benton Catron and His Era* (Tucson: University of Arizona Press, 1973).

Still other authors provide volumes that deal with significant subjects of the second half of the nineteenth century. For an important economic history, see William J. Parish's *The Charles Ilfeld Company: A Study of the Rise and Decline of Mercantile Capitalism in New Mexico* (Cambridge, Mass.: Harvard University Press, 1961). Cheryl J. Foote treats another noteworthy subject in her clearly written *Women of the New Mexican Frontier, 1846–1912*, 2d ed. (Niwot: University Press of Colorado, 1990). In one of the most important recent books on New Mexico, William deBuys furnishes a memorable environmental history, *Enchantment and Exploitation: The Life and Hard Times of a New Mexico Mountain Range* (Albuquerque: University of New Mexico Press, 1985).

Several other studies discussing varied cultural groups deserve mention. Edwin R. Sweeney's *Mangas Coloradas: Chief of the Chiricahua Apache* (Norman: University of Oklahoma Press, 1998) is a notable biography of an important Indian leader. Also helpful is Gerald Thompson's *The Army and the Navajo* (Tucson: University of Arizona Press, 1976). On Hispanic history, see Richard L. Nostrand's *The Hispano Homeland* (Norman: University of Oklahoma Press, 1992) and Robert J. Rosenbaum's *Mexicano Resistance in the Southwest: "The Sacred Right of Self-Preservation"* (Austin: University of Texas Press, 1986). Overall, we lack sweeping overviews of Hispanic experiences during these decades. Leonard Pitt's often cited study, *The Decline of the Californios: A Social History of the Spanish-Speaking Californians, 1846–1890* (Berkeley: University of California Press, 1966), is a model for a much needed similar overview of New Mexico Hispanic history of this period. One book treating African American experiences in New Mexico also deserves mention: Monroe Lee Billington, *New Mexico's Buffalo Soldiers 1866–1900* (Niwot: University Press of Colorado, 1991).

Even though the American Civil War tangentially influenced New Mexico, several accounts have been written about the subject. Of these numerous sources, three recent monographs should be mentioned. See John Taylor, *Bloody Valverde: A Civil War Battle on the Rio Grande, February 21, 1862* (Albuquerque: University of New Mexico Press, 1995), for a stirring account of one incident. A second book also focuses on one clash: Don E. Alberts, *The Battle of Glorieta: Union Victory in the West* (College Station: Texas A&M University Press, 1998). Darlis Miller covers an important segment of the conflict in *The California Column in New Mexico* (Albuquerque: University of New Mexico Press, 1982).

A great deal has been published about two notable New Mexicans of the mid- to late nineteenth century, Kit Carson and Billy the Kid. Harvey L. Carter's *"Dear Old Kit": The Historical Christopher Carson* (Norman: University of Oklahoma Press, 1990) is the best account of that subject, but also consult Lawrence C. Kelly's *Navajo Roundup: Selected Correspondence of Kit Carson's Expedition Against the Navajo, 1863–1865* (Boulder, Colo.: Pruett, 1970) for a balanced account of Carson's controversial dealings with the Navajo. The most recent study of Carson is Tom W. Dunlay's *Kit Carson and the Indians* (Lincoln: University of Nebraska Press, 2000).

On the outlaw Billy the Kid, about whom more has probably been written than any other New Mexican, there is a useful bibliographical guide: Kathleen P. Chamberlain, ed., *Billy the Kid and the Lincoln County War* (Albuquerque: Center for the American West, University of New Mexico, 1997). Of the many books on this subject, readers should begin with two volumes by Englishman Frederick Nolan, *The Lincoln County War: A Documentary History* (Norman: University of Oklahoma Press, 1992), and *The West of Billy the Kid* (Norman: University of Oklahoma Press, 1992). The best biography, smoothly written and lively, is Robert M. Utley's *Billy the Kid: A Short and Violent Life* (Lincoln: University of Nebraska Press, 1989). Larry D. Ball treats other significant topics in his richly researched volumes *Desert Lawmen: The High Sheriffs of New Mexico and Arizona, 1846–1912* (1992) and *The United States Marshals of New Mexico and Arizona Territories, 1846–1912* (1999), both published by the University of New Mexico Press.

TWENTIETH-CENTURY NEW MEXICO

Many researchers are just beginning to discover twentieth-century New Mexico. At the beginning of a new century, the period after 1900 remains the most fertile field for new research on the state's history. Thus far we lack an overview of New Mexico in the twentieth century, but a few reference volumes, overviews of the American West, and discussions of specific topics provide jumping-off places for new research. Those interested in an extensive guide to research on the twentieth-century American West, which includes many references to New Mexico, should consult Richard W. Etulain, et al., eds., *The American West in the Twentieth Century: A Bibliography* (Norman: University of Oklahoma Press, 1994). General overviews of the West are available in Gerald D. Nash's pioneering work *The American West in the Twentieth Century: A Short History of an Urban Oasis* (Albuquerque: University of New Mexico Press, 1977) and in Michael P. Malone and Richard W. Etulain *The American West: A Twentieth-Century History* (Lincoln: University of Nebraska Press, 1989). Other, counter-interpretations of the period are Peter B. Wiley and Robert Gottlieb's *Empires in the Sun: The Rise of a New American West* (New York: Putnam, 1983), Patricia Nelson Limerick's *Legacy of Conquest: The Unbroken Past of the American West* (New York: Norton, 1987), and Richard White's *"It's Your Misfortune and None of My Own": A New History of the American West* (Norman: University of Oklahoma Press, 1991).

In addition to these overviews, readers have at hand other general topical volumes. Three collections gather essays on New Mexico and the West since 1900: Judith L. DeMark, ed., *Essays in Twentieth-Century New Mexico History* (Albuquerque: University of New Mexico Press, 1984); Richard W. Etulain, ed., *Contemporary New Mexico, 1940–1990* (Albuquerque: University of New Mexico Press, 1994); and Kevin J. Fernlund, ed., *The Cold War American West, 1945–1989* (Albuquerque: University of New Mexico, 1998). Gerald D. Nash also provides an important survey in *The Federal Landscape: An Economic History of the Twentieth-Century West* (Tucson: University of Arizona Press, 1999), with Ferenc Morton Szasz supplying an equally helpful overview in his *Religion in the Modern American West* (Tucson: University of Arizona Press, 2000). Two other books by Gerald D. Nash also merit mention: *The American West Transformed: The Impact of the Second World War* (Bloomington: Indiana University Press, 1985) and *A Brief History of the American West since 1945* (Fort Worth, Tex.: Harcourt Brace, 2000).

The paucity of scholarship on twentieth-century New Mexico is particularly evident in the fields of political and economic history. Fewer than a dozen books need be mentioned. Jack E. Holmes provides a valuable overview in *Politics in New Mexico* (Albuquerque: University of New Mexico Press, 1967), whereas Maurilio E. Vigil is both more general and focused in his two books: *New Mexico Government and Politics* (Lanham, Md.: University Press of America, 1990) and *Los Patrones: Profiles of Hispanic Political Leaders in New Mexico History* (Washington, D.C.: University Press of America, 1980). Two other scholars have contributed two of the best books on New Mexico political history by focusing on major figures: Richard Lowitt's thoroughly researched *Bronson M. Cutting: Progressive Politician* (Albuquerque: University of New Mexico Press, 1992) and David H. Stratton's invitingly written *Tempest over Teapot Dome: The Story of Albert B. Fall* (Norman: University of Oklahoma Press, 1998).

Other scholars have recently provided pioneering studies in the fields of economic and environmental history. Of these, Ferenc M. Szasz's *The Day the Sun Rose Twice: The Story of the Trinity Site Nuclear Explosion, July 16, 1945* (Albuquerque: University of New Mexico Press, 1984), is often praised by both specialist and general readers. In this regard, see also Hal Rothman, *On Rims and Ridges: The Los Alamos Area Since 1880* (Lincoln: University of Nebraska Press, 1992), and José A. Rivera, *Acequia Culture: Water, Land, and Community in the Southwest* (Albuquerque: University of New Mexico Press, 1998).

More numerous are the books dealing with minority groups in recent New Mexico. In addition to the books on Native Americans mentioned earlier, one should also consult Garrick Bailey and Roberta Glenn Bailey's *A History of the Navajos: The Reservation Years* (Santa Fe, N.Mex., and Seattle: University of Washington Press, 1986), Lawrence C. Kelly's *The Navajo Indians and Federal Indian Policy, 1900–1935* (Tucson: University of Arizona Press, 1968), Donald Parman's *The Navajos and the New Deal* (New Haven, Conn.: Yale University Press, 1976), Margaret Connell Szasz's *Education and the American Indian: The Road to Self-Determination Since 1928*, 3d ed. (Albuquerque: University of New Mexico Press, 1999), and Kathleen P. Chamberlain's, *Under Sacred Ground: A History of Navajo Oil, 1922–1982* (Albuquerque: University of New Mexico Press, 2000).

On Hispanics, one should start with an exemplary monograph, Sarah Deutsch's *No Separate Refuge: Culture, Class, and Gender on an Anglo-Hispanic Frontier in the American Southwest, 1880–1940* (New York: Oxford

University Press, 1988). A similar study is Suzanne Forrest's *The Preservation of the Village: New Mexico's Hispanics and the New Deal* (Albuquerque: University of New Mexico Press, 1998). Lynn Getz deals with another important facet of Hispanic culture in *Schools of Their Own: The Education of Hispanics in New Mexico, 1850–1940* (Albuquerque: University of New Mexico Press, 1997). On one controversial Chicano leader in New Mexico, Richard Gardner's biography is still the best source: *Grito! Reies Tijerina and the New Mexico Land Grant War of 1967* (New York: Harper & Row, 1970, 1971). Juan Gómez-Quiñones touches on several New Mexico topics in his two books: *Chicano Politics: Reality and Promise, 1940–1990* (1990), and *Roots of Chicano Politics 1600–1940* (1994), both published by the University of New Mexico Press.

A good deal has been published about the cultural history of twentieth-century New Mexico, especially on art and artists. Much less has appeared on religion and religious figures, historians, and writers. On New Mexico's best-known artist, Georgia O'Keeffe, dozens of books are available; two of the best are an interpretive study, Charles C. Eldredge, *Georgia O'Keeffe: American and Modern* (New Haven, Conn.: Yale University Press, 1993), and the most thorough biography, Roxana Robinson, *Georgia O'Keeffe: A Life* (New York: Harper & Row, 1989). On some of New Mexico's major artists, including those identified with the Taos–Santa Fe colonies, one should consult Charles C. Eldredge, et al., eds., *Art in New Mexico 1900–1945: Paths to Taos and Santa Fe* (Washington, D.C.: National Museum of American Art, 1986), and Sharyn Rohlfsen Udall, *Modernist Painting in New Mexico, 1913–1935* (Albuquerque: University of New Mexico Press, 1984). The best study of another notable cultural figure in New Mexico is that by Lois Palken Rudnick, *Mabel Dodge Luhan: New Woman, New Worlds* (Albuquerque: University of New Mexico Press, 1984).

On other cultural topics the sources are limited. On religion in New Mexico, one might begin with a collection of essays on the major religious faiths, Ferenc M. Szasz and Richard W. Etulain, eds., *Religion in Modern New Mexico* (Albuquerque: University of New Mexico Press, 1997). For leading New Mexico writers, one should consult Margarite Fernandez Olmos, *Rudolfo A. Anaya: A Critical Companion* (Westport, Conn.: Greenwood Publishers, 1999), and John M. Reilly, *Tony Hillerman: A Critical Companion* (Westport, Conn.: Greenwood Publishers, 1996). A collection of essays that treats New Mexico's extensive literary history is editor Erlinda Gonzalez-Berry's *Pasó por Aquí: Critical Essays on the New Mexico Literary*

Tradition, 1542–1988 (Albuquerque: University of New Mexico Press, 1989). Robert Gish's collection of essays, *Beyond Bounds: Cross-Cultural Essays on Anglo, American Indian, and Chicano Literature* (Albuquerque: University of New Mexico Press, 1996), suggests one way recent New Mexico literature might be treated. Unfortunately, we still lack anything of note on New Mexico historians, but lists of essays and books on most New Mexico writers are available in Richard W. Etulain and N. Jill Howard, eds., *A Bibliographical Guide to the Study of Western American Literature,* 2d ed. (Albuquerque: University of New Mexico Press, 1995). For an overview of novelists, historians, and artists in the twentieth-century West that includes commentaries on New Mexico authors and artists, see Richard W. Etulain, *Re-imagining the Modern American West: A Century of Fiction, History, and Art* (Tucson: University of Arizona Press, 1996).

Contributors

Barton H. Barbour holds a Ph.D. from the University of New Mexico and has worked as a museum curator, humanities lecturer, and university instructor. He is assistant professor of history at Boise State University. Previously he was employed as a historian with the National Park Service in Santa Fe, New Mexico. A specialist in North American fur trade history and the history of the American West, his most recent book is *Fort Union and the Upper Missouri Fur Trade* (2001). He is currently working on a biography of mountain man Jedediah Smith and a study of Fort Laramie.

Myla Vicenti Carpio (Jicarilla Apache) earned her undergraduate degree from the University of New Mexico and her Ph.D. in history at Arizona State University. She has taught at Carleton College, where she held the Anderson dissertation teaching fellowship in the 1999–2000 academic year. Ms. Carpio has presented papers at the annual conferences of the Western History Association, the American Society for Ethnohistory, and other scholarly associations. In fall 2001, she joined the American Indian Studies Department as an assistant professor at Arizona State University.

Kathleen P. Chamberlain earned her Ph.D. from the University of New Mexico and is assistant professor of U.S. history at Eastern Michigan University. She authored *Under Sacred Ground, A History of Navajo Oil, 1922–1982* (2000) and *Billy the Kid and the Lincoln County War: A Bibliography* (1997) and is currently working on biographies of Susan McSween Barber and Victorio, the Apache leader.

Richard W. Etulain is professor emeritus of history and former director of the Center for the American West at the University of New Mexico. He has authored or edited more than forty books. Among his recent publications are (editor) *Contemporary New Mexico 1940–1990* (1994); (coeditor) *Religion in Modern New Mexico* (1997); *Re-imagining the Modern American West: A Century of Fiction, History, and Art* (1996); *Telling Western Stories: From Buffalo Bill to Larry McMurtry* (1999); (coeditor) *The Hollywood West* (2001); and *César Chávez: A Brief Biography with Documents* (2002).

Deena J. González, author of *Refusing the Favor: The Spanish-Mexican Women of Santa Fe, 1820–1880* (1999), is chair of the Department of Chicano/a Studies at Loyola Marymount University in Los Angles. She is a cofounder of several Chicana feminist, academic organizations and writes on the topics of Chicana history and Chicana studies from a feminist perspective. In addition to publishing more than twenty articles in these fields, she is currently completing two other books, *A Dictionary of Latinas in the U.S.* and *Chicanas Bequeath,* a collection of nineteenth-century nuevomexicana wills in transcription and translation.

Rick Hendricks is an editor of the Vargas Project at the University of New Mexico. A historian of the Spanish colonial and early Mexican periods, he has coauthored or coedited more than a dozen books. Among his recent publications on the Spanish and Mexican Southwest are *That Disturbances Cease* (coeditor, 2000), *San Elizario: Spanish Presidio to Texas County Seat* (coauthor, 1998), *Blood on the Boulders* (coeditor, 1998), and *The Navajos in 1705: Roque Madrid's Campaign Journal* (coeditor, 1996).

Peter Iverson is Regents' Professor of History at Arizona State University. His most recent books include *"We Are Still Here": American Indians in the Twentieth Century* (1998), *Indians in American History: An Introduction* (coeditor, 1998), *Riders of the West: Portraits from Indian Rodeo* (1999), and *Major Problems in American Indian History,* 2d ed. (coeditor, 2001). Aided by fellowships from the Guggenheim Foundation and the National Endowment for the Humanities, he is completing a new history of the Navajos.

E. A. Mares is professor emeritus of English and director of the Writers' Inn at the University of New Mexico. He has also been poetry editor for the *Blue Mesa Review.* He publishes extensively as a poet, fiction writer, newspaper columnist (in Spanish), and historian. His recent publications include an on-line poetry chapbook, *In the Taverna Ononas* (2000), poetry in *Willow Street* (2000), *Frank, An International Journal of Contemporary Writing and Art* (1998), and three books of poetry. In addition, he has edited one book of essays on Padre Martínez, *Padre Martínez: New Perspectives from Taos* (1988), and he has written a dramatization based on Padre Martínez, *I Returned and Saw Under the Sun* (1989).

María E. Montoya is an associate professor at the University of Michigan in the Department of History and the Program in American Culture. Her book, *Translating Property: The Maxwell Land Grant and the Problem of Land in the American West, 1840–1900,* is forthcoming from the University of California Press.

Lois Palken Rudnick is professor of English and American Studies and director of the American Studies Program at the University of Massachusetts, Boston, where her specialties are modern American literature and cultural history, immigration history, and U.S. multiethnic literatures. She has published several studies of Mabel Dodge Luhan and the Anglo artist and writer communities of northern New Mexico.

Joe S. Sando (Jemez Pueblo) was educated in Indian and mission schools. He acquired his higher education at Eastern New Mexico and Vanderbilt University. An educator and lecturer, he has written numerous books and essays. Among his previous books are *The Pueblo Indians* (1976), *Pueblo Nations* (1998), and *Pueblo Profiles* (1998). The New Mexico Endowment for the Humanities honored him in 2000 for his lifetime contributions to the humanities.

Edwin R. Sweeney is a graduate of the University of Massachusetts (Amherst) with a degree in accounting. He has worked in the accounting profession his entire career. He is currently employed as a controller for a St. Louis–based company. His primary interest is the Chiricahua Apaches. His articles have been published by the *Journal of Arizona History, New Mexico Historical Review,* and *Wild West* magazine. He has also authored the books *Cochise: Chiricahua Apache Chief* (1991) and *Mangas Coloradas: Chief of the Chiricahua Apaches* (1998), both published by the University of Oklahoma Press.

Ferenc M. Szasz is professor of history at the University of New Mexico, where he has taught since 1967. Author/editor of over ninety articles and nine books, he concentrates chiefly on the social and intellectual history of the United States. Among his publications are *Religion in Modern New Mexico* (coedited with Richard W. Etulain, 1997), *Religion in the Modern American West* (2000), and *Scots in the North American West, 1790–1917* (2000). His best-known work is probably *The Day the Sun Rose Twice: The Story of the Trinity Site Nuclear Explosion, July 16, 1945* (1984, rpt., 1995).

Index

All place names are from New Mexico unless otherwise indicated.

Boldface numerals indicate an extended treatment of the subject.

Acoma Pueblo, 22–23, 46, 52, 56
Adams, Ansel, 232, 234
Adams-Onís Treaty, 168
African Americans, 177, 256
agriculture, 8–9, 23, 257. *See also names of individual crops*
Agriculture Adjustment Act (AAA), 248
Agustín, de Morfí, Juan 108, 124
Albuquerque, 144, 229, 246, 289, 290, 294
alcalde mayor, 36, 55
Anasazi, 10, 11, **12–17**
Angel, Frank Warner, 210
Antrim, William. *See* Billy the Kid
Antrim, William H., 206–7
Apache Canyon, Battle at, 145
Apache Indians, 17, 21, 23, 24–25, 60, 131–32, **136–43**, **146–60**, 265, 269; and Mangas Coloradas, 136–160.
See also names of individual Apache bands
archaeological research, 5, 6, 7, 8, 12
Archaic era, 7–9, 11, 12. *See also* Holocene period

Argüello, Fernando de, 59
Arizona, 12, 137, 146, 207
Armijo, Manuel, 116–19, 170, 172, 174
artists, 223–24, **225–28** (modernists), **236–39**, 290–91
arts and crafts, 228, 238, 249
Ashley, William H., 167
Atchison, Topeka and Santa Fe Railroad, 200, 209, 223
Athapascan peoples, 17, 23, 136–37, 143, 159. *See also* Apaches *and* Navajos
Austin, Mary, 226, 227, 236–37, 249
Axtell, Samuel B., 210
Ayeta, Francisco de, 60
Aztec, 12

Baca, María Magdalena, 102
Barber, George B., 211–12
Barber, Susan McSween. *See* McSween, Susan
Barbour, Barton H., 2, **163–92**, 323
Barceló, Gertrudis (Doña Tules), 123–24, 125
Basket Maker periods, 12–13, 14
baskets, 13
Basques, 54–55

Bataan Death March, 255–56

beans, 9, 21

Beaubien, Carlos, 119, 200

Becknell, William, 170, 172

Bent, Charles, 173, 175, 178, 180, 188, 189–90; and Mexican New Mexico, 119–20, 122

Bent, St. Vrain & Company, 173–74

Bent, William, 177, 178, 188

Bering Strait, 6

Bijou, Joseph, 168

Billy the Kid, 2, 193, 194, 203, 205, **206–10**, 213, 215, 216–18, 318; and the Lincoln Country War, **203–10**

biographies, 1–3

bison, 5, 6

blacks. *See* African Americans

Blessing Way, The, 294–95, 302

Blue Lake, 288

Blumenschein, Ernest, 223–24

Boggsville, Colorado Territory, 163, 164

Bonney, William. *See* Billy the Kid

Bosque Redondo, 185, 187–88, 194

Bourbon kings, 82, 87

Boy Who Made Dragonfly, The, 293

Brady, William, 203

Brewer, Richard, 211

Bristol, Warren, 203, 211

British, 200–201

Bureau of Indian Affairs (BIA), 252

Bureau of Reclamation, 253

burial rituals, 8, 11, 13, 16–17

Burns, Walter Noble, 206, 216

cabildo, 48, 66, 69

California, 144, 145, 174, 180, 182–83

California Column, 185

Camino Real, 27, 107

Canada, 6, 23

Canby, Edward R. S., 144–45, 185

Canyon de Chelly, 12, 15, 187

Carleton, James H., 145–46, 157, 185, 194

Carpio, Myla Vicenti, 3, **265–84**, 323

Carson, Adaline, 179, 180

Carson, Christopher ("Kit"), 2, 107, 163–65, 166, **178–90**, 318; and Indians, 164–65, 179, 182, **183–89**

Carson, Josefa. *See* Jaramillo, María Josefa

Carter, Harvey L., 182–83, 188

casinos. *See* gaming and casinos

castas/castes, 91, 176–77

Cather, Willa, 107, 129, 227

Catholics. *See* Roman Catholic

Catiti, Alonzo, 39, 62

Catron, Thomas, 2–3, 193, 194, **197–201**, 212–14, 215, 216–17

census records, 92, 175

Chaco Canyon, 12, 13, **14–17**

Chacón, Rafael, 170

Chamberlain, Kathleen P., 2, **193–219**, 323

Chavez, Dennis, 3, **242–47**, 250–51, **258–62**

Chávez, Fray Angélico, 120, 121

Chee, Jim (fictional character), 285, 295, 299–303

Chicanos, 107, 127, 128, 286

Chichimeca Indians, 55

Chihuahua, Mexico, 119, 132, 153, 178

Chimayó rebellion, 115–16

Chino, Wendell, 3, 265–67, **273–83**

Chiricahua Apache, 131, 132, 140, 141, 142–43, **146–54**, 156–58, 160, 268, 270; and the frontier military, 131–32, **135–43**, 154–55, **157–60**

Chisum, John S., 195, 209, 212

Chivington, John M., 145, 188

Christianity, 38, 273–75. *See also* Protestants, religious beliefs and ceremonies, *and* Roman Catholics

Cigaret, Margaret (fictional character), 299

Civil Rights legislation, 261

Civil War, the American, **143–46**, 185, 186, 196

Civilian Conservation Corps (CCC), 249, 250, 252–53

class structures and divisions, 8, 11, 16–17, 25–26, 51, 90–91, 245

Clemente, Esteban, 60

cliff dwellings, 12, 15

Clovis, 5, 6, 7

Clovis people, 5, 6, 7

Cochiti Pueblo, 80–81, 83, 86, 89–90, 92–93

Codallos y Rabal, Joachin, 80–82, 87, 89–90, 101

Cold War, 259–62

Collier, John, 234–35, 237, 250, 270–71

Colorado, 12, 163, 164, 188

Comanche Indians, 23

Confederates and Confederacy, 143–46, 185

Constitutional Convention, New Mexico. *See* New Mexico Constitutional Convention

Cooke, Phillip St. George, 176

corn, 20. *See also* maize

Coronado, Francisco Vásquez de, 25, 50

Court of Private Land Claims, 213

coyota/coyote, 39, 80, 83, 87–89, 92

Creation Stories, 1, 21–22

crops, 9, 11, 15, 20. *See also names of individual crops*

Cubero, Pedro Rodríguez, 48, 66, 69

Culture areas, **10–16**

Curry, James, 272–73

Custer, George Armstrong, 165

Cutting, Bronson, 242, 243, 247

Dance Hall of the Dead, 295, 301

Dark Wind, The (novel and film), 285, 295, 301

Dasburg, Andrew, 232, 233, 237

Delano, Columbus, 200–201

Democratic Party, 202, 213, 214, 217, 246–49, 262

demographic trends, 289

dime novels, 189, 215

Diné, 24. *See* Navajo Indians

divisions of labor, sexual. *See* sexual divisions of labor

Dodge, Mabel. *See* Luhan, Mabel Dodge

dogs, 13

Dolan, James J., 193, 201, 206–7, 210

Doña Tules. *See* Barceló, Gertrudis

Donoho, Mary, 175

Drips, Andrew, 180

droughts, 14, 17

Dudley, N. A. M., 205–6. 210–11

Durango, Mexico, 112, 176

Dust Bowl, 252

economic policies and developments, 28–29, 65

education. *See* schools and schooling

Eisenhower, Dwight D., 259

El Paso, Texas, 46–47, 62, 63

El Río Bravo del Norte, 78, 85

El Tano, Juan, 37–38

Elkins, Stephen, 197, 199–201

encomienda, 25–26, 28, 31, 46, 58, 70

Enemy Way, The, 293, 294, 302

environmental influences and controversies, 17, 83, 252, 279–80. *See also* nuclear waste

estufa (kiva), 29. *See also* Kivas

ethnic relations, 286–89

Etulain, Richard W., **5–18**, 322, 323–24

Euro-Americans, 86, 165

Europe and Europeans, 24, 25, 27, 29, 50, 63, 221–22. *See also names of individual countries*

Euskera (Basque language), 54

Fall, Albert B., 212, 214, 216, 247–48

families, 9, 54, 65, 84, 91, 98, 147, 257

farmers, 11, 20

farming and ranching, 20, 257

Fergusson, Erna, 113, 229, 301

Fly on the Wall, The, 295

Folsom, 5, 6, 7

Folsom Man, 5, 6, 7

food gatherers, 7–8

Fort Craig, 144, 185

Fort Lyon, Colorado, 163

Fort Sill, Oklahoma, 266, 268, 270

Fort Stanton, 144, 195, 201, 205

Fort Sumner, 209

Fort Union, 140, 144–45, 195

Four Corners area, 10, 14, 23
Franciscan priests, 26, 29, 37, 50, 52, 57–59
Fremont, Jessie Benton, 182
Frémont, John Charles, 180, 182–83
Fritz, Charles, 203, 211
Fritz, Emil, 201, 203
Fuentes, Andreas, 182
fur trade, 173–75, 179, 183–84

Gálvez, José de, 82
gaming and casinos, 280–81, 289
García, Alonso, 61–62
Garrett, Pat, 193, 209
gender identities, **83–86**, 257
gendered divisions of labor, 257, 271–72
genízaros, 111
Geronimo, 158
Ghostway, The, 295, 300
Gillespie, Archibald, 183
Glorieta Pass, Battle at, 145
Godey, Alexander, 182
González, Deena J., 2, **78–105**, 324
graves. *See* burial rituals
Great Depression, 238, 245, 250, 253
Greenwich Village, New York, 220, 222, 225, 230
Gregg, Josiah, 170, 176–77
Guatemala, 67

Harris, Fred, 288
Hartley, Marsden, 234
Henderson, Alice Corbin, 226, 227, 229–30, 236
Henderson, William Penhallow, 229–30
Hendricks, Rick, 2, **45–77**, 324
Hewett, Edgar, 224–25
Hidalgo, Miguel, 115
Hillerman, Tony, 3, 285–86, **292–98, 300–303**, 305–6; as a writer, 285–86, **294–98, 299–303**, 305–6.
Hillerman Country, 285
Hispanics, 134, 172, 228. *See also* Chicanos, Mexican Americans, *and* Spaniards

historians and biographers, 164–65, 178, 201, 206, 268, 322
hogans, 23
Hohokam, 10–11, 12, 13
Holmes, Sherlock (fictional character), 298–99
Holocene period, 7, 8
Holtby, David, 4
Horgan, Paul, 214
horses, 24, 25
horticulture, 8–9, 20. *See also* agriculture
"The House," 201, 203. *See also* Murphy, Lawrence G.
hózhǫ́, 293, 301–2, 306
Hunner, Jon, 310
hunters, 6–8, 9
hunting camps, 6–7, 8
Hurd, Peter, 239, 291

Indian artists, 224, 228–29
Indian Claims Commission, 272
"Indian killer" (Kit Carson), **183–88**
Indian New Deal, 270–71
Indian Reorganization Act of 1934, 270–71
Indian self-determination legislation, 280–83, 287–89
Indians, 134–36, 142, 164–65; and Kit Carson, **183–88**. *See also names of separate tribes*
Indo-Hispanics, 108, 109, 110–11, 123, 127
Inn of the Mountain Gods, 278
intermarriage, 74, 91, 147, 177–78, 180, 230, 268
irrigation. *See* water and irrigation
Isleta Pueblo, 33, 61, 62
Iverson, Peter, 3, **265–84**, 324

Japan and Japanese, 254–55
Jaramillo, María Ignacia, 164, 180
Jaramillo, María Josefa, 164, 177, 180–81
Jemez Pueblo, 59
Jicarilla Apache, 136–39, 142–43, 268
Johnson, Gary, 265, 281

Jones, Andreius A., 246

Juanotilla of Cochiti, 2, 80–81, **83–94,
97–101**, 103

kachinas, 23

Kearny, Stephen Watts, 131–32, 154, 155

Kelly, John, 265

Keresan peoples and languages, 22, 83

Kessell, John L., 314, 315

kill sites, 6–7

King Philip II of Spain. *See* Philip II, King
of Spain

Kirker, James, 153, 167

kivas, 11, 13, 14, 16, 29, 34

Klamath Indians, 183

labor systems, 16, 28, 58, 71, 257

la leyenda negra, 175–76

Lamar, Howard R., 201, 311, 317

Lamy, Jean B., 107, 120, **124–28,** 196

land grants. *See* Mexican land grants

Land of Enchantment, 285

landscapes, and artists, 227–28, 229, 233,
302–3

Las Casas, Bartolomé de, 175–76

Lawrence, D. H., 233–34, 250

Laws of the Castes, 91

Leaphorn, Joe (fictional character), 285,
294, 295, 299, 301–3

Leonard, Ira, 209, 211

limpios, 80

Lincoln, 201, 209, 217

Lincoln County, 193, 205, 209, 210, 217

Lincoln County War, 193, 194, 203, 205–6,
210, 213

Lipan Apaches, 268

literacy, 89, 100, 176, 189

literature, 321–22. *See also* Hillerman, Tony

livestock, 25, 93, 97

Llano Estacado, 29, 118

Llewellyn, W. H. H., 269

lobo, 83

Lobo Blanco, 138, 139

Long, Stephen H., 168

"Long Walk," 187–88

López de Santa Anna, Antonio, 109, 114,
169

Los Alamos, 258, 290

Los Alamos National Laboratory, 258, 259

los Indios bárbaros, 23

Luhan, Mabel Dodge, 3, 220–22, 223,
230–34, 237, 239, 250

Lujan, Antonio (Tony), 220, 230–32

Lujan Diego, Juana, 88–89, 99–100

Lummis, Charles, 223

McCarty, Catherine, 206–7

McCarty, Henry. *See* Billy the Kid

Machebeuf, Joseph P., 124–26

McKnight, Robert, 178

McSween, Alexander A., 202–3, 205–7, 210,
211

McSween, Susan, 3, 193, 194, **202–6,** 210–13,
216–18

Madrid, Spain, 53, 56, 67

Magoffin, Susan Shelby, 175

maize, 9

mammoths, 6

Mangas Coloradas, 2, 131–33, **147–50,
152–60**

Manifest Destiny, 112–13, 168

Manso, Juan, 59

Mares, E. A., 2, **106–30,** 324–25

marriages, 91, 176, 180

Martínez, Antonio José (Padre Martínez),
2, 106–8, **111–16,** **119–28,** 190

matrilineal organization, 85

Maxwell, Lucien B., 119, 164, 188

Maxwell, Pete, 209

Maxwell Land Grant, 119, 199–201

megafauna, 6

Meriwether, David, 142–43, 156

Mesa Verde, 12, 13, 15

Mescalero Apache, 136–37, 140–43, 185,
194–95, **266–82**; and Wendell Chino,
265–66, **273–82**

mestizos, 83, 87

Mexican Americans, 127, 243, 245, 254–55. *See also* Chicanos *and* Hispanics

Mexican-American War, 107, 134–35

Mexican land grants, 118–19, 195

Mexican New Mexico, 2, **106–30**

Mexico City, Mexico, 48, 53, 56, 64, 69, 169, 170

midden, 8

military installations, 258–59

Miller, Darlis, 210, 212

Mimbres, 11

mining and miners, 55, 156–57, 196

Miranda, Guadalupe, 119, 200

Missouri, 166, 173, 197

mixed race, 80, 83, 87, 90–91. *See also* intermarriages

modernism and modernization, 194, 218; in art, **225–28**

Mogollon, 10–12, 13

Monroe Doctrine, 169

Montoya, María E., 3, **242–64**, 325

Mora Land Grant, 199

Murphy, Lawrence G., 193, 201, 203, 205

Murphy House. *see* "House, The"

Museum of New Mexico, 224

Myer, Dillon, 272–73

mystery novels, 298–300

Nash, Gerald D., 319

National Youth Administration (NYA), 249, 250–52

Native American Creation Stories, 1, 22–23

Native American women, 177–78

Native Americans. *See* Indians *and names of varied tribes*

Navajo Campaign, 164, 185–88

Navajo Indians, 17, 21, 23–24, 136–37, 146, 194, 250, 270–71; and Kit Carson, **185–88**; and Tony Hillerman, 293, **300–303**, 305

New Deal, The, 237, 238, 247, **248–53**, 262

New Mexican landscape. *See* Landscapes

New Mexican women, **84–87**, 123–24, 177. *See also nuevomexicanas*

New Mexico Constitutional Convention, 214, 216

New Mexico Historical Review, 310–11

New Mexico State Legislature, 265–66

New Spain, 53, 71, 78, 176–77

New York, 220, 225–26

New York City, 203, 206, 222

Nieto, José, 37

Nixon, Richard, 288

Nolan, Frederick, 206, 211

novels and fiction. *See* Hillerman, Tony

nuclear waste, 279–80, 290

nuclear west, 279–80, 290

Nueva Galicia, Mexico, 54, 64

Nueva Vizcaya, Mexico, 64

nuevomexicanas, 80–81, **83–87**, **89–92**, 97–103

Oke Owinge. *See* San Juan Pueblo

O'Keeffe, Georgia, 234, 235, 250, 251

Oklahoma, 292–93

Old West, 218

Oñate, Cristóbal de, 53–54

Oñate, Juan de, 2, 25, 45–46, **50–57**, 71–72, 74

oral stories, 31, 32, 100. *See also* Creation Stories

Ordóñez, Isidro, 57

Otermín, Antonio de, 35, **37–40**, 61–62

Otero, Miguel A., 200, 202, 214

Pacheco y Heredia, Alonso, 59

Paleo-Indians, 5–8

Panic of 1819, 165–66

Pánuco, 53–54, 55, 56

Pecos Pueblo, 35

Penitentes, 120–21

People of Darkness, 295–96

Peralta, Pedro de, 57

Pérez, Albino, 115, 116

Philip II, King of Spain, 50, 53, 55, 63

Philippine Islands, 254–55

Phillips, Bert, 223–24

Pike, Zebulon Montgomery, 167–68

Pino, Pedro Bautista, 108

Pío, Juan, 36

Piro pueblos, 60

Pisago Cabezón, 152–53

pit houses, 9, 11, 13, 14

plants, 7–9, 11, 13. *See also* horticulture

Pleistocene Era, 6–7

Popé, 2, 19–20, **27–35**, **40–42**, 60, **61–62**

population growth. *See* demographic trends

pottery, 11

Prado Vélez de Olazábal, Beatriz Pimentel de, 67 ,69

prehistoric man, **5–18**

prehistoric woman, **5–18**

Presbyterians, 175, 196

presentism, 165

Presidio, 48

Preuss, Charles, 182

Price, Sterling W. 122, 134

priests, 114, 124–27. *See also* Franciscans

Protestants, 124, 128, 175–76, 196

Public Works Administration (PWA), 249

Pueblo Bonito, 15–17

Pueblo Indians, 10, 11, 13, **19–42**, 46, 51–52, **60–66**, 71–72, 90–91, 110–11, 230–31; and the Spanish, 19–20,

25–27, 28–29, **32–42**, 46, **57–66**, 72–75

Pueblo Revolt, 2, 19–20, 26–27, **29–41**, 42, **60–62**, 72, 74–75

pueblos (towns), 15, 81

Pueblo style (art), 225

Quivira, 46, 52, 53

racial status, 80, 90–92. *See also* ethnic relations *and* intermarriage

Rael de Aguilar, Manuela, 99–100

railroads, 194, 196, 209, 210. *See also* Atchison, Topeka and Santa Fe Railroad

rainfall, 13, 14, 15, 17

rancherías, 24–25

Reagan, Ronald, 280

Reconquest of New Mexico, The, 41–42, 48, **64–66**, 72–73

Reconquista (Spain), 26, 176

regulators, 205, 206–7, 213

religious beliefs and ceremonies, 23–24, 26, 28, 29, 41, 148, 175–76, 273–75, 302

religious freedoms, 26, 29, 30, 60, 62

repartimiento, 25–26

Republican Party, 202, 213–14, 216, 246, 247, 262

Rio Grande, 14, 45, 47, 78

Rio Grande Valley, 17

Rocky Mountain fur trade. *See* fur trade

Roman Catholic, 26, 28, 46, 62, 81–82, 91–92, 120–21, **124–28**, 175–76, 292–93

Romero, Juana, 95, 98, 99

Roosevelt, Franklin D., 238, 259

Roosevelt, Theodore, 214

Rosas, Luis de, 58–59

Rough Rider, 214

Rudnick, Lois Palken, 3, **220–41**, 325

Russell, Marion Sloan, 175

Rynerson, William L., 202, 203, 209

Sage, Rufus, 177

Sago, Rufus, 272–73

St. Louis, 166–67

St. Vrain, Ceran, 178, 188

Salazar (Oñate), Catalina de, 53–54

San Buenaventura de Cochiti Pueblo. *See* Cochiti Pueblo

San Gabriel, 52–53

San Juan Pueblo, 19, 27, 33, 51–52

San Luis Potosí, Mexico, 55

Sand Creek Massacre, 188

Sando, Joe S., 2, **19–44**, 325

Sangre de Cristo Mountains, 78

Santa Bárbara, Mexico, 51

Santa Fe, 35, 37–40, 58, 61, 64, 123–24, 214; as art center, 224–25, 226, 290

Santa Fe Ring, 199–201, 202, 205, 218

Santa Fe Trail trade, 107, 112–14, 167–68, **170–73**

Santa Lucía Springs, 134, 199
Santa Rita del Cobre, 140, 141, 149, 150, 154–55
Santo Domingo Pueblo, 57
Scheurich, Aloys, 164
schools and schooling, 112, 128, 213, 214
Scurry, William R., 145
sexual division of labor, 8, 257, 271
Shunar, 179
Siberia, 6
Sibley, Henry H. 144–45, 185
Simmons, Marc, 311–12, 314–15, 316
Sipapu, 13, 22–23, 28
Skinwalkers, 295, 300
Smith, Jedediah S., 167, 184
social hierarchies and organization, 9, 11, 14, 15–17, 23, 74, 90–91, 290–91
Sonora, Mexico, 149, 152, 153, 154, 160
Spain, 54, 67, 70, 108, 118, 170
Spaniards, 19, 20, 25–26, 35
Spanish, 17, 19, 24, 25–26, 28–33, 36–42, **45–77**, 147, 214
Spanish American War, 214, 254
Spanish Americans. *See* Chicanos, Hispanics, *and* Mexican Americans
Spanish entradas, 286
squash, 9, 21
Sterne, Mabel. *See* Luhan, Mabel Dodge
stories, 1, 100, 268–69, 301
stories, oral. *See* oral stories
Stottler, V. E., 269–70
SU ("Shoe"), 11–12
Sumner, Edwin Vose, 139–40, 155
Sweeney, Edwin R., 2, **131–62**, 317, 325
Szasz, Ferenc M., 3, **285–309**, 325

Talking God, 295, 296
Tanoan groups, 22, 30
Taos, 106–7, 112–13, 164, 220, 230–32
Taos Pueblo, 230, 235, 288
Taos Rebellion, 122–23, 180, 189
Taos Society of Artists (TSA), 223–24
Tarahumara Indians, 63

Tejanos, 176
termination of Indians, 273
Tesuque Pueblo, 32
Tet-sugeh (Tesuque), 32, 35, 36
Tewa groups, 22, 29, 35
Texas, 115, 116, 118, 140, 176, 277
Three Rivers Ranch, 212
Timber Culture Act, 210, 211
Tingley, Clyde, 242
Tiwa groups, 22
Tlalpujahua, Mexico, 69
Tohono O'odham Indians, 10, 271
Tolosa Cortés Moctezuma, Isabel de, 55
tool kits, 6, 8
Toomer, Jean, 235
tourism, 277–79, 305
Towa groups, 22
trade systems, 15, 16, 78, 112, 166–67, 172–75, 178; and the fur trade, 166–67, 173–75, 184
traders, 15, 24, 111, 167, 173–74
trappers. *See* fur trade
Treaty of Guadalupe Hidalgo, 107, 135, 140
Treviño, Juan Francisco, 32, 60, 61
Trinity Site, 290
Tules, Doña. *See* Barceló, Gertrudis
Tunstall, John, 193, 202, 203, 205, 207, 211
Tupatú, Luis, 61

U.S. Congress, 195, 196, 280–81
U.S. House of Representatives, 247
U.S. Senate, 242, 243, 247, 260
U.S. Supreme Court, 280, 281
University of New Mexico, 249, 289, 294
Ute Indians, 23, 42, 137, 138

Vargas, don Diego de, 2, 41, **46–50, 63–72**, 74–75
vecina, 88, 91
Velasco, Luis de, II, 55
Victorio, 146, 150
Vigil, Donaciano, 115–16, 180
Vigil, Juan, 88, 101

villa, 38, 65
villages, 14–17
Villanueva, Fernando de, 60
Virgin Mary, 89

Waa-nibe ("Singing Grass"), 179, 180
Wallace, Lew, 207, 208, 211
Walz, Edgar, 205
war gods, 35, 40
Washington, John Macrae, 135, 137
Washington, D.C., 245, 246, 248, 271
Waste Isolation Pilot Project (WIPP), 290
water and irrigation, 11, 15. *See also*
    droughts *and* rainfall
Waters, Frank, 235–36
Weber, David J., 314, 315–16
West, Joseph Rodman, 157, 158, 160
White Oaks, 196, 212, 216, 217
wickiups, 24
wills, 80–81, 86–87, 88–90, **98–103**

women, 14, 84–87, 177, 210, 257. *See also*
    Native American women *and* New
    Mexican women
women, Native American, 179, 271. *See also*
    Native American women
women, New Mexican, 84–87, 102–3, 177,
    180–81. *See also* New Mexican women
Works Projects Administration (WPA),
    248–51
World War I, 216, 225, 226
World War II, 252, **253–59**

Yeibichai (ceremony), 302
Young, Ewing, 167, 174–75, 178–79

Zacatecas, Mexico, 51, 53, 54, 55, 56
Zaldívar, Juan de, 52, 57
Zaldívar, Vicente de, 53
zambos, 180
Zuni, 22